Sayagyi U Ba Khin

Journal

A Collection Commemorating

the Teaching of Sayagyi U Ba Khin

Vipassana Research Publications

Vipassana Research Publications
an imprint of
Pariyatti Publishing
867 Larmon Road, Onalaska, WA 98570
www.pariyatti.org

First North American Edition: 2017

ISBN: 978-1-68172-051-7 (print)

LCCN: 2016944377

Grateful acknowledgement is made for permission to print from the following:

Copyright © *Yoga Journal* (reprinted by permission of the publisher) for "S. N. Goenka: Master of Meditation," interview conducted by Stephan Bodian (editor, *Yoga Journal*), September/October 1989, No. 88.

Maha Bodhi Journal, Vol. 80 April 1972, No. 4, for various accounts in "Sayagyi's Students Remember Him."

Thint Bana magazine (Myanmar) for report of S. N. Goenka's Nov. 1991 visit to Myanmar.

The Light of Dhamma magazine (Myanmar) for "Revolution With a View to Nibbāna" by Sayagyi U Ba Khin.

Buddha Sāsana Council Press (Myanmar) for "The Real Values of True Buddhist Meditation."

Table of Contents

The Chain of Teachers

The Venerable Webu (Vipula) Sayadaw (1896–1977)

Essays by S.N. Goenka

Interviews

Assistant Teachers

Personal Experiences

The Vipassana Research Institute

Glossary of Pāli Terms

Publisher's Foreword to the American Edition

In recent years, many people in the West have been exposed to the teachings of the Buddha through the practice of Vipassana meditation as taught by S.N. Goenka. Mr. Goenka was born in Burma (now Myanmar) where he learned this technique of meditation from Sayagyi U Ba Khin, who had in turn been taught by Saya Thetgyi. Saya Thetgyi had the fortune to learn Vipassana from the highly respected scholar and meditator monk Ledi Sayadaw.

We are grateful to the Vipassana Research Institute for allowing us to co-publish *Sayagyi U Ba Khin Journal*. It is our sincere wish that this publication will prove valuable to those interested in understanding the Buddha's teaching at a deeper level, while providing the inspiration to continue walking step by step on the path.

Introduction

Two decades have elapsed since the death of the great Burmese meditation teacher, Sayagyi U Ba Khin, whose life spanned the first seventy years of this century.

U Ba Khin was one of the outstanding figures of his time. His accomplishments, in two usually incompatible fields, were singular: he was a master meditation student and teacher as well as a government official of tireless devotion and impeccable conduct. His service to the country of Burma is noteworthy, but his example to the citizens of the world is no less remarkable; for, in a time of increasingly complex global crises, his life demonstrates a simple, powerful truth—that an individual of pure mind exerts a positive, corrective influence on society. U Ba Khin's career was that of an ideal householder, combining unwavering dedication to Dhamma (the truth, the teaching) with unwearied commitment to public service.

Before he died on 19 January 1971, U Ba Khin was able to realize one of his most cherished dreams. He saw the ancient meditation technique of Vipassana, which had been preserved in his country for over two thousand years, returned to India, its land of origin. It was returned to its birthplace by U Ba Khin's devoted student, S.N. Goenka.

When his Teacher passed away in 1971, S.N. Goenka had been conducting ten-day Vipassana courses at scattered sites in India for less than two years, and the seedling of Dhamma was very young and fragile. In the intervening years, its growth has proceeded in leaps and bounds. For the past two millennia, the sublime practice of Vipassana—the heart of the teaching of the Buddha—has been the province of only a small number of meditator monks and householders in a few Asian countries. Today, thousands of seekers have had the opportunity to receive the teaching and experience its benefits. These people come from scores of different countries, Eastern and Western, representing all religions, creeds, castes and communities.

Because of the pressing demands on his time, Sayagyi confined his teaching to a relatively small number of students who came to his meditation centre in Rangoon. Now, in 1994, there are over twenty-five international centres—nine in India, the remainder in ten other countries—where the technique of Vipassana taught by Sayagyi U Ba Khin, and carried on by his student, S.N. Goenka, is being offered.

In his teaching, S.N. Goenka has always placed primary emphasis on the actual practice of Dhamma—what is called, in the language of the Buddha, *paṭipatti*. It is only through practice that one can have the direct experience which will take one to the final goal of freedom from all suffering. In this approach, Goenkaji follows the example of his Teacher, who always insisted that Dhamma must be applied if it is to have real meaning.

Nevertheless, there is another important aspect of Dhamma: *pariyatti*—understanding at the theoretical, intellectual level. This is helpful to inspire one to undertake the actual practice of meditation, and to elucidate questions that may arise while one is practising. Unfortunately, the amount of material in English which provides a suitable theoretical foundation for a student of Vipassana, has not kept pace with the growth in the availability of the practice of Dhamma. This journal of historical and theoretical research has been compiled to respond to this need, and to shed light on various aspects of Vipassana meditation.

This collection is a tribute to Sayagyi U Ba Khin and, indeed, its contents are an outgrowth of his life's work. The book begins with a section describing the contribution of Sayagyi and the chain of Burmese Vipassana teachers before him, who continued their country's noble tradition of preserving the teaching of the Buddha. This is the first time that biographical material and discourses of these teachers has appeared in one collection in English.

The Journal includes a selection of essays by the present Teacher, S.N. Goenka. Although his primary focus in twenty-two years of teaching Vipassana has always been to offer the actual practice (in over 390 ten-day courses worldwide), Goenkaji, like his teacher, has been highly productive in other areas as well. He has given a large number of public discourses in different countries, to audiences of meditators and non-meditators alike. He has written hundreds of inspirational articles about Dhamma, the majority of them for the monthly Hindi Vipassana Newsletter (which is sent to 15,000 students in India). He has written many articles in English as well.

Goenkaji is also a prolific poet. Over his years as a student and teacher, he has spontaneously composed thousands of rhymed couplets called dohas, some of which are included here. This traditional form of inspirational poetry is derived from the ancient anuṭṭhuba chandas, the poetic form most frequently used by the Buddha. To the basic couplet form, the doha adds a rhyme at the end of each line. Many Indian spiritual teachers have used this form as a medium for their teachings. Dohas have penetrated so deeply into the Indian psyche that even illiterate villagers recite them.

The Journal goes on to feature articles by some of the many assistant teachers whom Goenkaji has appointed in recent years to meet the increased demand for Vipassana courses, as well as accounts of personal experiences by Vipassana students.

A brief but important section highlights the significant textual research work of the Vipassana Research Institute.

The Journal concludes with a description of some of the tangible fruits of the seeds sown by Sayagyi in the tiny country of Burma over two decades ago: facilities in different parts of the world where students can go to learn Vipassana.

This collection is offered primarily to inspire the practice of Dhamma, for those who have taken courses as well as those who have no experience in Vipassana meditation. It should not, however, be used as a teaching manual for the technique. Attending a ten-day course under the careful guidance of a qualified, authorized teacher is essential to properly establish oneself in the practice of Vipassana.

It is an indication of the need for this timeless teaching that Vipassana courses are much in demand, with over two hundred ten-day courses per year now being conducted. Moreover, every course is run solely on the basis of freely-offered donations. The Teacher and his assistants do not receive remuneration; they and the Dhamma workers serve on a volunteer basis. This is consistent with the tradition of pure Dhamma, a tradition adhered to by Sayagyi. Donations are accepted only from students who have completed a Vipassana course and wish to share the benefits they themselves have received by giving dāna (donation) for the students who come after them.

All of the work of Sayagyi and Goenkaji, all
the present worldwide Dhamma activity, have
only one purpose: to help people find the way
out of suffering. The technique which provided
this path was lost in India, and unknown in most
of the rest of the world, for many centuries. It
is now available once again. Sayagyi believed
in the ancient prophecy that 2,500 years after
the time of the Buddha, Dhamma would arise
anew and spread around the world. This belief
is being verified. As he used to say, "The time
clock of Vipassana has struck."

A Note on the Use of Pāli

Pāli is the language in which the Buddha taught, and in which his teachings (the Dhamma) have been preserved. As with Sanskrit and Latin, Pāli is not a contemporary spoken language, but a so-called "dead language"—a medium, nevertheless, conveying and illuminating a living tradition.

Pāli is unique in many ways. One of the meanings of the word pāli is "that which protects, or preserves." Pāli exists to preserve the words of the enlightened person, Gotama Buddha. The tradition is that, by expressing the sublime teaching which allows beings to be liberated from the rounds of suffering, Pāli protects the people; it preserves the invaluable treasure of the Buddha's own words.

Adherence to the use of the Buddha's language has been a profoundly significant part of the living tradition handed down in the Theravāda Buddhist countries, which have preserved Pāli in its oldest form.

The question arises: if the Dhamma is universal and non-sectarian, relevant to people from different nationalities and backgrounds—why are words from Pāli used in its teaching? The answer lies in the nature of language itself.

No language, no matter how rich it is, can adequately express the highly sophisticated, technical terms used by the Buddha. There are no equivalents for these concepts in other languages; words that attempt to be equivalents will only be approximations.

For example, the word "Dhamma" is a term which encompasses a wide spectrum and depth of meaning. It means the truth, the teaching, the law of nature. It also refers to the characteristics, or nature, of everything manifest in the world; hence it means "phenomenon," and "object of mind." To attempt to render such a term into an equivalent would not do justice to the depth of its meaning. The same is true of many words used by the Buddha to explain extremely subtle concepts.

Faithfulness to the Pāli words of the Buddha has therefore been a central part of the teaching of S.N. Goenka, and the lineage which he represents. Goenkaji's understanding of the language stems from a deep grounding in the practice of Vipassana. Students of his courses are familiar with his use of Pāli in the daily discourses (in which he explains the theory of the meditation technique), as well as in his practice of chanting the Buddha's words.

Dhamma teachers have different modes of expression. For Goenkaji (who is a poet and orator in his native languages of Rajasthani and Hindi), his melodic use of Pāli is a medium through which his abundant mettā (feelings of goodwill towards all beings) is conveyed. When he chants in Pāli, or his other native tongues, along with the sounds of his resonant voice come waves of compassion and loving-kindness. This provides a congenial, supportive atmosphere in which the Dhamma can be received and practised.

Goenkaji has given much time and importance in recent years to Pāli studies. The Vipassana Research Institute was established under his guidance to conduct research into both the theory (*pariyatti*) and practice (*paṭipatti*) of the Buddha's teaching. (See *Vipassana Research Institute: An Introduction*, p. 279)

The Vipassana Research Institute is pleased to publish this collection, hoping that this *pariyatti* will serve as inspiration to those wishing to practise and study the jewel of the Buddha's teaching, Vipassana. We have attempted to make Pāli words in the journal accessible to the average reader, by giving a simple English definition of each Pāli word when it first appears in a given article. A glossary of Pāli terms is provided at the back for reference.

In a work of this scope, derived from many and varied sources in different languages, errors are inevitable, for which the Institute offers its apologies and hopes that these can be corrected in subsequent editions.

May this volume assist many to find the way to peace.

Vipassana Research Institute
Dhammagiri, Igatpuri, India
May 1994

The time clock of Vipassana has now struck...

we have no doubt whatsoever about definite results accruing to those who would with open minds sincerely undergo a course of training under a competent teacher—

I mean results which will be accepted as good, concrete, vivid, personal, here-and-now; results which will keep them in good stead and in a state of well-being and happiness for the rest of their lives.

—Sayagyi U Ba Khin

Sayagyi U Ba Khin

(1899–1971)

Gratitude to Sayagyi

by S. N. Goenka

Most Revered Dhamma Teacher!
It is now ten years since you passed away, but your inspirational presence is still being felt. Awareness of Dhamma is virtually awareness of you. May the awareness of Dhamma be continuous so that your all-embracing presence prevails. This is my joyful resolve.

The feeling of your presence is so inspiring. Every moment that Dhamma awareness arises, I am reminded of your infinite compassion and my heart fills with vibrations of joy.

Again my heart fills with gratitude towards the Exalted One, the Enlightened One, the Sakya-sage Gotama who, through innumerable lives, accumulated to perfection all the virtues, thus attaining for himself the true happiness of liberation. He discovered such a beneficial technique and distributed it with compassion throughout the remaining years of his life: a teaching that became the source of well-being for numerous people, enabling them to reach the final goal of full liberation.

And my heart fills with gratitude towards those liberated saintly ones who, having obtained this wonderful technique from the Exalted One further abided by his instructions:

"Go forth, monks, on your journey! For the good of many, for the happiness of many, full of compassion for the people!" They spent their lives going from village to village, from town to town, from dwelling to dwelling, distributing this technique of self-liberation.

My heart fills with gratitude to the venerable Sona and Uttara who, having borne all the hardships of the arduous journey from India to Burma, carried this fountain of Dhamma to the golden land of Burma and thereby quenched the thirst of innumerable beings.

My heart fills with gratitude to the traditional Dhamma teachers of Burma who, through an unbroken chain of teachers to disciples, kept this teaching in its pristine purity from generation to generation, not permitting its adulteration by the use of any words, colours, forms or imagination. This path, leading from the apparent gross truth and penetrating on to the subtlest truth, leads like a royal highway to the ultimate truth. They did not digress from this path of truth by taking detours which only lead from one apparent truth to another. Instead, they continued straight on the path and preserved the teaching in its essential purity; thus we could receive it.

My heart fills with gratitude towards you, my magnanimous teacher, who most compassionately, most lovingly and affectionately bestowed upon me this invaluable Dhamma-jewel. If I had not received this Dhamma-jewel, what would my plight have been? I would have wasted this life in the pursuit of earning and hoarding wealth, and in the rat race for status. You nurtured the seed of Dhamma within me. If you had not, then I would have been content to remain bound in sectarian fetters, mistaking them for ornaments. I would have passed my life taking pride in the experiences of others rather than my own. Where would I have obtained this real and direct experience of the truth? I would have contented myself with the mental projections of imaginations. Where would I have had this *yathābhuta ñāṇadassana* (the wisdom of the direct experience of the truth as it is)? I would have wasted my life taking intellectual knowledge as true wisdom. I would have squandered this invaluable human life by performing rites, rituals and recitations, and in getting conditioned by non-experiential, sectarian philosophies. My peerless Dhamma teacher! You have made my human life truly successful and worthwhile by bestowing the gift of this unrivalled, incomparable Dhamma upon me.

Verily, unrivalled and incomparable is the practice of Dhamma. How easy! How clear! How scientific! How beneficial! Leading from bondage to freedom, from delusions and mirages to the reality, from the apparent truth to the ultimate truth—may this invaluable jewel remain in its unblemished purity!

I solemnly make these meritorious resolutions on this auspicious day, the anniversary of your demise:

May I not commit the monumental sin of adulterating the teaching. May this invaluable technique remain in its flawless purity. May its practice open the door of deathlessness and salvation for one and all. Fulfilling these resolutions is the only way to respect, honour and revere you.

Your humble Dhamma son,
S.N. Goenka, 19 January 1981

Sayagyi U Ba Khin (1899-1971)

by Vipassana Research Institute

Sayagyi U Ba Khin was born in Rangoon, the capital of Burma, on 6 March 1899. He was the younger of two children in a family of modest means living in a working class district. Burma was ruled by Britain at the time, as it was until after the Second World War. Learning English was therefore very important; in fact, job advancement depended on having a good speaking knowledge of English.

Fortunately, an elderly man from a nearby factory assisted U Ba Khin in entering the Methodist Middle School at the age of eight. He proved a gifted student. He had the ability to commit his lessons to memory, learning his English grammar book by heart from cover to cover. He was first in every class and earned a middle school scholarship. A Burmese teacher helped him gain entrance to St. Paul's Institution, where every year he was again at the head of his high school class.

In March of 1917, he passed the final high school examination, winning a gold medal as well as a college scholarship. But family pressures forced him to discontinue his formal education to start earning money.

His first job was with a Burmese newspaper called The Sun, but after some time he began working as an accounts clerk in the office of the Accountant General of Burma. Few other Burmese were employed in this office since most of the civil servants in Burma at the time were British or Indian. In 1926 he passed the Accounts Service examination, given by the provincial government of India. In 1937, when Burma was separated from India, he was appointed the first Special Office Superintendent.

It was on 1 January 1937, that Sayagyi tried meditation for the first time. A student of Saya

Thetgyi—a wealthy farmer and meditation teacher—was visiting U Ba Khin and explained Anapana meditation to him. When Sayagyi tried it, he experienced good concentration, which impressed him so much that he resolved to complete a full course. Accordingly, he applied for a ten-day leave of absence and set out for Saya Thetgyi's teaching centre.

It is a testament to U Ba Khin's determination to learn Vipassana that he left the headquarters on short notice. His desire to meditate was so strong that only one week after trying Anapana, he was on his way to Saya Thetgyi's centre at Pyawbwegyi.

The small village of Pyawbwegyi is due south of Rangoon, across the Rangoon River and miles of rice paddies. Although it is only eight miles from the city, the muddy fields before harvest time make it seem longer; travellers must cross the equivalent of a shallow sea. When U Ba Khin crossed the Rangoon River, it was low tide, and the sampan boat he hired could only take him to Phyarsu village—about half the distance—along a tributary which connected to Pyawbwegyi. Sayagyi climbed the river bank, sinking in mud up to his knees. He covered the remaining distance on foot across the fields, arriving with his legs caked in mud.

That same night, U Ba Khin and another Burmese student, who was a disciple of Ledi Sayadaw, received Anapana instructions from Saya Thetgyi. The two students advanced rapidly, and were given Vipassana the next day. Sayagyi progressed well during this first ten-day course, and continued his work during frequent visits to his teacher's centre and meetings with Saya Thetgyi whenever he came to Rangoon.

When he returned to his office, Sayagyi found an envelope on his desk. He feared that it might be a dismissal note but found, to his surprise, that it was a promotion letter. He had been chosen for the post of Special Office Superintendent in the new office of the Auditor General of Burma.

In 1941, a seemingly happenstance incident occurred which was to be important in Sayagyi's life. While on government business in upper Burma, he met by chance Webu Sayadaw, a monk who had achieved high attainments in meditation. Webu Sayadaw was impressed with U Ba Khin's proficiency in meditation, and urged him to teach. He was the first person to exhort Sayagyi to start teaching. An account of this historic meeting, and subsequent contacts between these two important figures, is described in the article "Ven. Webu Sayadaw and Sayagyi U Ba Khin" (p.89).

U Ba Khin did not begin teaching in a formal way until about a decade after he first met Webu Sayadaw. Saya Thetgyi also encouraged him to teach Vipassana. On one occasion during the Japanese occupation of Burma, Saya Thetgyi came to Rangoon and stayed with one of his students who was a government official. When his host and other students expressed a wish to see Saya Thetgyi more often, he replied, "I am like the doctor who can only see you at certain times. But U Ba Khin is like the nurse who will see you any time."

Sayagyi's government service continued for another twenty-six years. He became Accountant General on 4 January 1948, the day Burma gained independence. For the next two decades, he was employed in various capacities in the government, most of the time holding two or more posts, each equivalent to the head of a department. At one time he served as head of three separate departments simultaneously for three years and, on another occasion, head of four departments for about one year. When he was appointed as the chairman of the State Agricultural Marketing Board in 1956, the Burmese government conferred on him the title of "Thray Sithu," a high honorary title. Only the last four years of Sayagyi's life were devoted exclusively to teaching meditation. The rest of the time he combined his skill in meditation with his devotion to government service and his responsibilities to his family. Sayagyi was a married householder with five daughters and one son.

In 1950 he founded the Vipassana Association of the Accountant General's Office where lay people, mainly employees of that office, could learn Vipassana. In 1952, the International Meditation Centre (I.M.C.) was opened in Rangoon, two miles north of the famous Shwedagon pagoda. Here many Burmese and foreign students had the good fortune to receive instruction in the Dhamma from Sayagyi.

Sayagyi was active in the planning for the Sixth Buddhist Council known as *Chaṭṭha Saṅgāyana* (Sixth Recitation) which was held in 1954-56 in Rangoon. Sayagyi was a founding member in 1950 of two organizations which were later merged to become the Union of Burma Buddha Sāsana Council (U.B.S.C.), the main planning body for the Great Council. U Ba Khin served as an executive member of the U.B.S.C. and as chairman of the committee for *paṭipatti* (practice of meditation).

He also served as honorary auditor of the Council and was therefore responsible for maintaining the accounts for all *dāna* (donation) receipts and expenditures. There was an extensive building programme spread over 170 acres to provide housing, dining areas and kitchen, a hospital, library, museum, four hostels and administrative buildings. The focal point of the entire enterprise was the *Mahā Pāsāṇaguhā* (Great Cave), a massive hall where approximately five thousand monks from Burma, Sri Lanka, Thailand, India, Cambodia and Laos gathered to recite, purify, edit and publish the *Tipiṭaka* (Buddhist scriptures). The monks, working in groups, prepared the Pāli texts for publication, comparing the Burmese,

Sri Lankan Thai, and Cambodian editions and the Roman-script edition of the Pāli Text Society in London. The corrected and approved texts were recited in the Great Cave. Ten to fifteen thousand lay men and women came to listen to the recitations of the monks.

To efficiently handle the millions in donations that came for this undertaking, U Ba Khin created a system of printing receipt books on different coloured paper for different amounts of *dāna,* ranging from the humblest donation up to very large amounts. Only selected people were allowed to handle the larger contributions, and every donation was scrupulously accounted for, avoiding any hint of misappropriation.

Sayagyi remained active with the U.B.S.C. in various capacities until 1967. In this way he combined his responsibilities and talents as a layman and government official with his strong Dhamma volition to spread the teaching of Buddha. In addition to the prominent public service he gave to that cause, he continued to teach Vipassana regularly at his centre. Some of the Westerners who came to the Sixth Council were referred to Sayagyi for instruction in meditation since at that time there was no other teacher of Vipassana who was fluent in English.

Because of his highly demanding government duties, Sayagyi was only able to teach a small number of students. Many of his Burmese students were connected with his government work. Many Indian students were introduced by Goenkaji. Sayagyi's students from abroad were small in number but diverse, including leading Western Buddhists, academicians, and members of the diplomatic community in Rangoon.

From time to time, Sayagyi was invited to address foreign audiences in Burma on the subject of Dhamma. On one occasion, for example, he was asked to deliver a series of lectures at the Methodist Church in Rangoon. These lectures were published as a booklet titled "What Buddhism Is." Copies were distributed to Burmese embassies and various Buddhist organisations around the world. This booklet attracted a number of Westerners to attend courses with Sayagyi. On another occasion he delivered a lecture to a group of press representatives from Israel, who were in Burma on the occasion of the visit of Israel's prime minister, David Ben Gurion. This lecture was later published under the title "The Real Values of True Buddhist Meditation."

Sayagyi finally retired from his outstanding career in government service in 1967. From that time, until his death in 1971, he stayed at I.M.C., teaching Vipassana. Shortly before his death he thought back to all those who had helped him—the old man who had helped him start school, the Burmese teacher who helped him join St. Paul's and, among many others, one friend whom he had lost sight of over forty years earlier and now found mentioned in the local newspaper. He dictated letters addressed to this old friend and to some foreign students and disciples, including Goenkaji. On the 18th of January, Sayagyi suddenly became ill. When his newly rediscovered friend received Sayagyi's letter on the 20th, he was shocked to read Sayagyi's death announcement in the same post.

Goenkaji was in India conducting a course when news of his teacher's death reached him. He sent a telegram back to I.M.C. which contained the famous Pāli verse:

Aniccā vata saṅkhārā,
uppādavaya-dhammino.
Uppajjitvā nirujjhanti,
tesaṃ vūpasamo sukho.

Impermanent truly are compounded things,
by nature arising and passing away.
If they arise and are extinguished,
their eradication brings happiness.

One year later, in a tribute to his teacher, Goenkaji wrote: "Even after his passing away one year

ago, observing the continued success of the courses, I get more and more convinced that it is his **mettā** (loving-kindness) force which is giving me all the inspiration and strength to serve so many people...Obviously the force of Dhamma is immeasurable."

Sayagyi's aspirations are being accomplished. The Buddha's teachings, carefully preserved all these centuries, are still being practised, and are still bringing results here and now.

Dhamma eradicates suffering and gives happiness.

Who gives this happiness?

It is not the Buddha but the Dhamma, the knowledge of **anicca** within the body, which gives this happiness.

That is why you must meditate and be aware of **anicca** continually.

—*Sayagyi U Ba Khin*

Sayagyi U Ba Khin: A Shining Star of Dhamma

by S. N. Goenka

Sayagyi U Ba Khin was one of the foremost teachers of Vipassana of our time—a source of inspiration to many, including myself. One of his unique contributions was that he gave much attention to foreigners and non-Buddhists in his teaching. Sayagyi's predecessors were Saya Thetgyi and Ledi Sayadaw. The other disciples of these teachers who were teaching Vipassana in this tradition used only the Burmese language for the most part and so had only Burmese students. Sayagyi, however, spoke fluent English and was able to explain Dhamma in English in a way that Buddhists and non-Buddhists, Burmese and non-Burmese alike could grasp and appreciate.

Sayagyi's way was not the way of scholars. Every word that he spoke came from his own experience. Therefore his teachings have the life of experience within them, and this is why every word said by him was very powerful and encouraging to his students. He wrote little, and he spoke little, but still, many students were benefited by his teaching.

He was engaged in government responsibilities until the age of sixty-seven and had very little time to spare for the teaching of Dhamma. Therefore, he took a vow: "May only ripened people with very good *pāramīs* (virtues) from the past come to me to take Dhamma, and may these people later take the torch of Dhamma, and spread it 'round the world." He could not work with the masses; he was working to serve a few individuals for whom he could spare more time.

He used to recite a Pāli *gāthā* (verse):

*Iminā puññā-kammena
mā me bāla samāgamo;
satam samāgamo hotu
yāva nibbāna pattiyā.*

By virtue of this meritorious action
may I not come into contact with the ignorant
May I encounter only wise, saintly people
until I attain nibbāna.

One time when he came to my home, I was chanting and at the end recited this *gāthā*. Sayagyi smilingly admonished me, saying, "This *gāthā* is not for you! You are to give seeds of Dhamma to a very large number of people. If you take this vow, how will Dhamma spread? This vow is for me because I have little time, and I am just on the border of 2,500 years after Buddha when Dhamma has to start spreading. You are getting Dhamma at the time when the new era has started. So you have to work vigorously. You have to spread the seeds of Dhamma to large numbers of people. So don't recite this!" Of course I bowed to him and to his wishes.

Besides being an ideal government executive with outstanding ability and integrity, he was a very human teacher of the noble path. He taught with immeasurable love and compassion in spite of his insistence on strict discipline. He gave equally compassionate attention to the ex-president of Burma and a peasant, to a judge of the Supreme Court and a criminal.

Such was U Ba Khin, a jewel amongst men. Such was my noble teacher who taught me the art of a sane life.

He has chosen me to plant seeds of Dhamma around the world. Comparing my capacity with his, I feel very humble. And this makes me all the more confident that it is Dhamma that is working—not simply some individual. I have been chosen by my teacher as a vehicle for the Dhamma. And by helping to carry out his mission, I receive the benefits of developing my own *parāmīs*. With this understanding, I continue to work. And in the same way, you of the next generation have the responsibility—the wonderful opportunity—of carrying on the work.

It is his mission. It is Dhamma's work. He will keep on shining as a brilliant star in the galaxy of teachers from Buddha to the present and into the future.

Sayagyi was looking forward to the second *sāsana* (era of the Buddha's teaching), when the Dhamma would help people throughout the world. May his wishes be fulfilled.

May more and more suffering people around the world come into contact with Dhamma, especially now, when throughout the world there is so much misery, so much conflict, so many tensions. May more and more people come into contact with Vipassana.

Reminiscences

by S. N. Goenka

In War-time, as in Peace-time, a Man of Integrity

During the month of February, 1942, the invading Japanese Imperial Army had occupied Rangoon and were advancing towards Mandalay in central Burma. The Japanese Air Force started an aerial bombardment of the city, in which the railway station was destroyed.

At this time Sayagyi was stationed in Mandalay as Accounts Officer of the railways, with responsibility for whatever funds were kept in cash. After the bombardment was over, he went to the ruined station, searched through the debris, and found still intact the iron safe in which the cash was kept. Having the key with him, he opened the safe and removed the cash contents—a substantial sum of money.

Now what to do with this money? U Ba Khin was at a loss. The British authorities had already fled in retreat from the fast-approaching Japanese. Mandalay at that moment was a "no man's land" between the two armies—a city without any government. It would have been very easy for Sayagyi to take the money for himself, without anyone's being the wiser. After all, what right did the defeated, fleeing British colonial government have to this money? It could be construed as a patriotic action to deprive them of it. At the same time, Sayagyi had great need

of money at that time, since his young daughter was seriously ill, and his expenses were therefore unusually heavy, severely taxing his means.

U Ba Khin, however, could not even conceive of misappropriating government funds for his own use. It was his duty, he decided, to hand over the cash to his superior officers even though they were fleeing from the country.

From Mandalay, the British had fled helter-skelter, in every direction. The railways officers had retreated first to Maymyo, in hopes of making their way from there to Nationalist China and thence by plane to India. Sayagyi did not know whether he would be able to catch up with them in their flight. Nevertheless, he had to make the attempt. He hired a jeep taxi and made the three-hour journey to Maymyo.

On his arrival, he found that the British were still in that city. He sought out his superior officer and handed over the cash to him, breathing a sigh of relief at having been able to discharge his duty.

Only then did Sayagyi ask, "And now, sir, may I receive my salary for this month, and my travelling expenses to here?"

This was U Ba Khin, a man of perfect integrity, of unbreakable *sīla* (morality), of Dhamma.

Dhamma Transforms a Government Department

By introducing the practice of Vipassana meditation to the officers and staff of the Burmese Accountant General's office, Sayagyi U Ba Khin had brought about remarkable improve-

ments in that government department. The then Prime Minister, U Nu, was an honest man and wished the entire administration of the country to be similarly freed from corruption and inefficiency. At that time, one of the most important government offices, the State Agricultural Marketing Board, was in poor shape. This organization was responsible for purchasing paddy (a type of rice)—as well as other produce—from the farmers, and arranging for milling the rice and exporting the bulk of it.

In colonial times, the entire rice export business had been in the hands of British and Indian traders. After Burma's independence, the Board had taken over this function. Most of its officers and staff had little prior experience. Although the margin of profit in the trade was huge, somehow the Board suffered a chronic deficit. There was no proper system of accounting; inefficiency and corruption were rampant. The Board officials, in collusion with the rice millers and foreign buyers, were embezzling huge amounts of money from the state. Additionally, great losses occurred due to poor storage practices and inefficient loading and transport.

The Prime Minister set up a committee of inquiry headed by Sayagyi to thoroughly investigate the affairs of the Board. The report of this committee unflinchingly exposed the entire net of corruption and inefficiency. Determined to take strong action—even though it meant overriding the opposition of traders and some of the politicians of his own party who were involved in the corruption—the Prime Minister requested Sayagyi to take the post of Deputy Chairman of the Board. U Ba Khin, however, was hesitant to undertake the responsibility of reforming the Board unless he could have clear authority to undertake any necessary measures. Understanding the problem, the Prime Minister instead appointed Sayagyi to chairmanship of the Marketing Board, a cabinet-level position normally held by the Minister of Commerce. It was generally known that this position afforded great political leverage—and now it was being given to an honest civil servant!

When the intended appointment was announced, the officers of the department became nervous that the man who had exposed their malpractices and inefficiencies was now to become their superior. They declared that they would go on strike if the appointment was confirmed. The Prime Minister replied that he would not reconsider, since he knew that only U Ba Khin could undertake the job. In retaliation, the officers carried out their threat. So it was that Sayagyi took up his appointment in an office where the executive staff was striking while the clerical and blue collar workers continued to work as usual.

Sayagyi remained firm despite the unreasonable demands of the strikers. He continued the work of administration with just the clerical staff. After several weeks, the strikers, realizing that Sayagyi was not going to submit to their pressure, capitulated unconditionally and returned to their posts.

Having established his authority, Sayagyi now began, with great love and compassion, to change the entire atmosphere of the Board and its workings. Many of the officers actually joined courses of Vipassana under his guidance. In the two years that Sayagyi held the Chairmanship, the Board attained record levels in export and profit; efficiency in minimizing losses reached an all-time high.

It was common practice for the officers and even the Chairman of the Marketing Board to amass fortunes in various illegal ways during their terms of office. But U Ba Khin could never indulge in such practices. To forestall attempts to influence him, he refused to meet any traders or millers except on official business, and that too only in his office and not his residence.

On one occasion, a certain trader had submitted to the Board a tender for the supply of a huge quantity of gunny bags. According to the usual custom, he was prepared to supplement his tender with a private "contribution" to an important Board member. Wanting to assure his success, he decided to approach the Chairman himself. He arrived at Sayagyi's house, carrying with him a substantial sum of money as an offer. During the course of their conversation, when the first hint of bribery arose, Sayagyi was visibly shocked and did not hide his contempt for such proceedings. Caught in the act, the businessman hastened to emphasize that the money was not for Sayagyi himself but rather for his meditation centre. Making it clear that the meditation centre never accepted donations from non-meditators, Sayagyi ordered him out of the house, and told him he should be thankful that the police were not called into this.

As a matter of fact, already that very day the tender of this man, the lowest one submitted, had been accepted by the Board; but this decision had not yet been announced to the trader. Since all official requirements for this transaction had already been met, a bribe could be harmlessly accepted with no need to interfere with the interests of the state. In such circumstances, it would be commonplace for an official to just accept the gratuity "in the flow of the tide" (as such a situation was popularly referred to). Sayagyi might have easily accrued these material benefits, but doing so would have been totally against the moral integrity, *sīla*, of such a Dhamma person.

In fact, to thoroughly discourage any attempt to influence him, Sayagyi let it be known that he would not accept even small personal gifts, despite the common practice of such exchanges. Once on his birthday, a subordinate left a gift at Sayagyi's house when he was not at home: a silk *longyi* (article of clothing). Next day, Sayagyi brought the present to the office. At the end of the working day, he called a staff meeting. To the mortification of the staff member who had left it for him, Sayagyi berated him publicly for so blatantly disregarding his explicit orders. He then put the *longyi* up for auction, and gave the proceeds to the staff welfare fund. On another occasion, he took similar action on being given a basket of fruit, so careful was he not to allow anyone to try to influence him by bribes whether large or small.

Such was U Ba Khin—a man of principles so strong that nothing could cause him to waver. His determination to establish an example of how an honest official works brought him up against many of the practices common at the time in the administration. Yet for him the perfection of *sīla* and his commitment to Dhamma were surpassed by no other consideration.

Soft as a Rose Petal, Hard as a Diamond

A saintly person, who is full of love and compassion, has a heart that is soft, like the petal of a rose. But when it comes to his duty, he becomes hard like a diamond. Both of these qualities manifested in Sayagyi's life from time to time. A few of the many incidents illustrating this are included here.

On 4 January, 1948, Burma became independent. Unfortunately, the newly-formed national government had to face an immediate crisis. Throughout the country, followers of different ideologies were challenging the government. The insurgents had no scarcity of arms and ammunition, because during the Second World War not only the Japanese, but the Allies also had freely distributed arms and ammunition to attract the Burmese youth towards their fold.

The rebels started fighting on so many fronts that it became impossible for the newly-formed national army to handle the crisis. The situation threatened the ability of the new government to peacefully administer the country. Soon the insurgents gained the upper hand, and were masters of the situation. They had different causes and slogans: some were communists, some socialists, some provincial secessionist groups. A chaotic situation prevailed throughout Burma, as the different groups with their different causes each occupied and ruled a different territory.

> There are very few people who are free from fear or favour, or who have a love which is paternal, yet detached.

A time came when the federal government of Burma was in fact only the government of the city of Rangoon. Soon even this nucleus of control was imperilled when one group of rebels started knocking at the door of Rangoon itself. The insurgents occupied a village ten to twelve miles from the city. There was no rule of law anywhere in the country; the continued existence of the federal government was hanging in the balance. If the government of Rangoon fell, then the existence of the Union of Burma would also disintegrate, as the whole country became divided up into competing factions.

The government was distressed, the army was distressed—but what could be done? There seemed to be no hope of a way out.

Sayagyi was deeply devoted to his country, and wished peace, harmony and prosperity for Burma, but what could he do? His strength was only Dhamma strength. So, at times he would go to the residence of the Prime Minister and give *mettā* (meditation of goodwill and compassion for all). At other times in his own home, he would generate deep *mettā* for the security of his country.

In a situation such as this, his heart was very soft, like the petal of a rose. But it became, on occasion, hard as a diamond. It so happened that during the same crisis, the government appealed to a neighbouring country for assistance. This friendly country agreed to come to Burma's aid in this emergency. But whatever items were to be given had to be transported by air. The government of Burma did not have adequate air transport. The airplanes required for the purpose would have to be procured outside the country. To succeed in this plan, the government made a hurried decision which did not fall within the framework of the country's laws.

At that time U Ba Khin was the Accountant General, and he declared the decision to be illegal. The government was now in a dilemma. The Prime Minister knew very well that Sayagyi was a man of principle, that he would not compromise where principles were concerned. (Sayagyi always asserted: "I get my pay for one purpose only: to see that not a single penny of government funds should be used in a way which is contrary to the law. I am paid for this!")

The Prime Minister had great respect for Sayagyi's integrity, his adherence to duty. But the situation was very delicate. He therefore called Sayagyi for a private discussion, and told him: "We have to bring these provisions, and we must make an expenditure for the air transportation. Now, tell us how to do this in a legal way."

Sayagyi found a suitable solution, and the government followed his advice to save itself from using a wrong means for a right action.

The situation of national crisis continued, but one after another the rebels were overpowered by the national army. In most of the country except the remote mountainous areas, the rebels were defeated. The government then started giving more importance to social programmes for the improvement of the country. Thanks to the diligence of the Bhikkhu Saṅgha in bringing reading and writing to the villages throughout Burma, there was never a problem of illiteracy in the country, except for a few hill tribes. Though there was a high rate of basic literacy, higher education was lacking in Burma.

The Prime Minister undertook to address this situation. In a large public gathering, he announced a scheme to implement adult education throughout the country. He authorized a large sum of money for this purpose to be given immediately to the ministry concerned.

Sayagyi was fully sympathetic to the virtues of the plan, but he determined that the amount specified did not fit into any section of the national budget. He therefore objected. The Prime Minister was placed in a very embarrassing situation, but U Ba Khin's objection was valid: according to law, the announced amount could not be directed to its proposed purpose.

Sayagyi's determination was accepted, but the announcement had already been made, and something had to be done. So the Prime Minister sought another solution. He called the officers of the Rangoon Racing Club and requested their cooperation in helping to implement the adult education programme. He suggested that they sponsor a special horse race with high entry fees; whatever money earned would be given as a donation to the noble cause. Who could refuse the Prime Minister's request? The Racing Club agreed,

and all went according to plan. The Racing Club earned a huge amount from the special race.

Once again, a large public meeting was organized, and with great pomp and ceremony, a cheque containing a large amount was presented to the Prime Minister by the officials of the Racing Club. The Prime Minister, in turn, handed the cheque over to the minister concerned.

After this event, however, the case came before Sayagyi, and again he raised objections. The Prime Minister was nonplussed. It was, after all, a question of his prestige. Why was Sayagyi now stopping the payment of the cheque?—this is not the government's money; what right has he got to stop it? But Sayagyi pointed out that the income of the race course included a tax for the government. If the government tax was taken out, the rest could go towards supporting the adult education programme. The Prime Minister was speechless, but he smiled and accepted U Ba Khin's decision.

> Having passed through the corridors of power, which were rampant with corruption, where fortunes were often easily amassed, here was a singular man of modest means who died with the wealth of his integrity fully intact.

Just as Sayagyi was fearless in disposing his official responsibilities, so he was free from favouritism. The following incident is one amongst many incidents illustrating this trait.

In the Accountant General's department, one of the junior clerks was also one of Sayagyi's Vipassana students. This man was very humble, always willing to lend a helping hand. He was always very happy to serve Sayagyi, and Sayagyi had great paternal love for him. Even paternal love, however, could not become an obstacle to Sayagyi in his fulfilling his appointed duty.

It happened that at the end of the year it was time for staff promotions. The name at the top of the list prepared by the staff was the name of this junior assistant. He was next in line for rightful promotion because he had the greatest seniority in the department. If Sayagyi had wanted, he could easily have recommended this promotion, but he did not do so. For him, promotion should not depend only on seniority. It should also take into consideration one's ability to work efficiently. The assistant, who had many other good qualities, was unfortunately lacking in this area. Sayagyi called

Teacher of a Non-sectarian Path

One of the things which kept attracting me closer and closer to my teacher was his non-sectarian interpretation of Dhamma. The teaching of Buddha is so universal that people from different sects and communities can follow it and experience its benefits. I never found Sayagyi interested in converting people to the formal, organized Buddhist religion. Of course he himself was Buddhist by birth, and proud to be so. But for him the essence of Buddhism was Dhamma, and a true Buddhist was one who practised Dhamma. He was interested in helping people to establish themselves in Dhamma—that is, in *sīla* (morality), *samādhi* (concentration) and *paññā* (wisdom); to show people how to convert themselves from misery to happiness. If someone who had undergone this conversion from impurity to purity then wished to call himself a Buddhist, Sayagyi was pleased; but the important point was the change which had come in the person's life, not merely the change in the name he called himself.

Sayagyi would even admonish enthusiasts who were eager to convert others to Buddhism,

him and lovingly explained that if he was able to pass a certain accountancy examination, he would get the promotion. The disciple accepted the advice of his teacher, and it took him two years to study and pass the examination. It was only then that Sayagyi granted the promotion.

As with fearlessness, lack of favour was one of Sayagyi's rare qualities. There are very few people who are free from fear or favour, or who have a love which is paternal, yet detached.

Soft as a rose petal, hard as a diamond. I feel fortunate to have learned Dhamma from such a teacher. I pay my respects, remembering these shining qualities of his.

saying to them, "The only way to convert people is to become established oneself in Dhamma—in *sīla, samādhi, paññā*—and to help others similarly to get established. When you yourselves are not established in *sīla, samādhi, paññā,* what is the sense in your trying to convert others? You may call yourselves Buddhists but unless you practise *sīla, samādhi, paññā,* to me you are not Buddhists. But if someone practises *sīla, samādhi, paññā,* then even though he may not call himself a Buddhist, nevertheless he is a true follower of the teachings of the Buddha, whatever he may label himself."

One incident, illustrating this non-sectarian attitude, occurred when a staunch Christian came to take a course under Sayagyi. While the opening formalities were being explained, this man became frightened that he was being asked to convert from Christianity to Buddhism; and out of this groundless fear, he refused to take refuge in Buddha. "I can take refuge in Jesus Christ, but not in Buddha," he said. "Very well," replied Sayagyi smilingly, "Take refuge in Jesus Christ—but with the understanding that you are actually taking refuge in the qualities of Christ, in order to develop these very qualities in yourself." In this way the person began to work; and by the end of the course he realized that his initial objection had been unnecessary, that his fears of conversion had been without cause.

In the Midst of Power, a Man of Virtue and Simplicity

In Burma of Sayagyi's day, certain high government posts ensured comfort for the remainder of an appointee's life—not particularly due to the level of salary, but rather to the pervasive practice of padding all transactions with bribery. No one came out of these offices as a poor person. Sayagyi, however, entered his retirement with meagre life savings and no home of his own for his family, since they had lived in government housing all his career. Even though he had worked in as many as four government departments simultaneously, he had accepted only one salary—and, of course, avoided all illegal gains.

Wanting to build a house for his children, he asked me to help him arrange for the construction. As work on the house proceeded, we found that 10,000 rupees were lacking for completion. Where was Sayagyi to get this money? He would, of course, not ask for it. Since such a sum was so easy for me to give, I suggested this to him. But he refused, insisting that any money from a student is *dāna* (donation) and therefore to be put to proper Dhamma uses. Trying a different angle, I offered to lend him the money, thinking that later I could just tell him to disregard payment. He accepted my offer, and the house was completed.

However, each and every month thereafter, when his pension cheque arrived, he took not one paisa (penny) of it, but immediately passed the whole thing to me. This was so painful for me to accept. These 10,000 rupees meant so little to me, and here each month I had to receive my teacher's only income. Eventually 5,000 rupees remained to be paid.

During this time, my aunt (who had adopted me as her son and who had been a longtime student of Sayagyi's) was dying. She had made great progress in her seven years of meditation with Sayagyi, and he was quite fond of her. Now, it is a custom in the Eastern countries not only to care for one's parents during their lifetime, but also to remember them by making contributions in their name after death. So as I passed the last days with my adoptive mother, I asked her to tell me where she wished to give this *dāna*. She said, "Wherever you want," and I named several hospitals, organizations, and so on. "And where else would you like to donate?" I asked. When she said that she wanted 5,000 rupees to go to Sayagyi himself, I was delighted. Here was the chance to be relieved of this terrible position of having to receive money from my teacher. Surely, I thought, Sayagyi would accept the *dāna* as a last wish of a devoted dying student and then be able to use it for repayment of the loan.

As it happened, a few days later Sayagyi was present at the time of her death; he knew that she had died peacefully and consciously, with awareness of *anicca* (impermanence) at the top of her head. He went around the centre telling everyone how her final minutes were filled with *paññā*, with *anicca.* When I informed him of her volition to give him the 5,000 rupees he was delighted. "Look," he said, "she has given these 5,000 rupees as *dāna*"—and he began distributing it to this Dhamma cause and that Dhamma cause! I was so surprised to see my hopes ended.

Each month thereafter, as I received my teacher's pension cheque until, at last, the final payment, I was reminded of the high principles of this person who was such an example of moral rectitude in public office.

My Teacher's Boundless *Mettā*

Sayagyi was the epitome of compassion and loving-kindness. Although deeply engrossed in official duties, he was full of enthusiasm for giving Dhamma service to the maximum number of people. He taught Dhamma to any person who approached him, even if it caused him much inconvenience. Sometimes he would hold a course for even one or two students, and would exert as much effort for them as for a larger number. His mind remained suffused in love for every student. They seemed like sons and daughters to him. Only three days before he passed away, he completed a course. And until the day before his demise, he was still teaching Dhamma.

Sayagyi had a strong belief that Vipassana would arise once again 2,500 years after the time of Buddha, and would, spread around the world.

He had immense love and compassion for all creatures. All creatures at his centre, even snakes and scorpions, were affected by his boundless *mettā* (loving-kindness). Every particle of the centre radiated with his love. He tended the trees and plants there with great compassion. It was because of his strong *mettā*

Having passed through the corridors of power, which were rampant with corruption, where fortunes were often easily amassed, here was a singular man of modest means who died with the wealth of his integrity fully intact.

that the fruits growing in that sacred piece of land came to have an exceptional sweetness and flavour. The flowers also had a distinctive hue and fragrance.

One year something unusual happened in Burma. A situation bordering on famine developed. This was a shock for a country like Burma, which had always produced an abundant harvest. Food production was diminished and the government had to introduce rice rationing. The people were deeply affected by this. At that time Sayagyi's compassion for his afflicted countrymen knew no bounds. Not only from his lips, but from every pore of his body seemed to resound the sentiment: "May the people be prosperous, may the ruler be virtuous!"

Sometime later a famine also occurred in India, continuing for two years. Sayagyi's compassion was enlivened once again. In one corner of his centre he had arranged to have erected a model of the lofty peaks of the Himalayas. He was very fond of this reminder. He would meditate beside it every day, sending his goodwill to India with the wishes: "I cannot recall how many times I was born in India and remained in that snow-clad region for such a long time, developing my meditation. Today the people of that country are in distress. May peace and tranquillity come to them. May all abide in Dhamma!"

He Wished to Return the Dhamma to India

Sayagyi had a strong belief in the prophecy that the Vipassana-Dhamma would arise once again 2,500 years after the time of Buddha, that it would appear again in India, and would spread from there around the world. He often used to say, "The time clock of Vipassana has struck! Now it will go forth from Burma and spread afar." He himself was very eager to undertake the task of spreading Dhamma—that is, to come to India and start giving courses here, and then to travel to other countries in order to serve suffering people throughout the world. He often used to say, "Burma owes a great debt to India which must be repaid; from there has come the jewel of the Dhamma. Today this jewel has been lost in India and is sorely needed. A large number of people in India with good *pāramīs* (virtues) from the past would willingly accept the jewel of Vipassana." But despite his eagerness to go to teach Dhamma in India, he was unable to do so, since at that time it was extremely difficult for a Burmese citizen to get a passport for foreign travel.

During this period, an invitation came from Mahāthera Nandeshwar, head of the Maha Bodhi Society in Madras, inviting Sayagyi and his assistants to come to India and give a few Vipassana courses. This seemed to Sayagyi to be his hoped-for opportunity to go abroad for Dhamma service. Accordingly, he applied to the Burmese authorities for a passport.

The minister in charge was faced with a dilemma. The government policy was to issue passports to its citizens for only a limited number of reasons: if someone was planning to leave Burma and not return, or going to take up employment abroad; or, in case of extreme illness, if someone had to leave for medical treatment. Therefore he sent word through a high government official (who was also a disciple of Sayagyi) advising that, to satisfy government requirements Sayagyi should state one of these reasons. Further, it was advised that Sayagyi obtain a *pro forma* letter offering him such employment or else claiming that he needed medical care.

All this was merely to satisfy government formalities. Had he complied, Sayagyi would have been able to realize his long-standing dream of repaying Burma's debt to India and helping miserable people around the world. But my teacher could never compromise his *sīla* in such a way. He adamantly refused the proposal, saying that he could not teach Dhamma from a base which was false. He preferred to give up his much-cherished dream, rather than to abandon the fundamental principles by which he lived—the principles of Dhamma.

The Statue of Buddha

The traditional pagoda in Burma is a solid structure, used by devotees for paying respect and making offerings. But Sayagyi had no use for such a structure at his centre. His idea was to build a hollow pagoda, with cells inside built for meditation. In spite of some objections from traditional Buddhists, he had this done. He also felt no use for a statue of Buddha in the pagoda, as the meditators were not supposed to use the shape or form of Buddha as their object of meditation. The technique he taught was universal—observing the respiration and body sensations. Hence, for two years he ran the centre without a statue. But it was against the conventional practice to have a pagoda without a statue of Buddha, and opposition started mounting from traditional Buddhists, including some of his own companions in the Accountant General's office. Finally, he agreed to establish a Buddha-*rūpa* (statue of the Buddha) in one of the eight cells of the pagoda. However, the teaching was always kept universal. When any-one paid respect to the Buddha statue, he was asked to remember the qualities of Buddha for inspiration and to remember the Dhamma of *anicca, dukkha* (unsatisfactoriness) and *anattā* (egolessness) while doing so. Dhamma always remained the main object of his teachings.

His Loving-kindness Supports Me

For a number of years Sayagyi was training me to undertake the great responsibility of a Dhamma Teacher, but I remained unaware of his true intention. I assumed that he requested my assistance merely as an interpreter to help with Indian students who might not clearly understand the meditation instructions given in Burmese. In fact, however, my teacher was preparing me for future responsibilities.

As part of this preparation, I accompanied him to Mandalay and Maymyo in Upper Burma, to give courses at temporary sites outside an established, sanctified meditation centre. In the future, for the courses in India, where there were no centres for Vipassana, such temporary sites would have to be used: schools, *dharāmsālas* (rest houses), hotels, hostels and so forth—places without any Dhamma vibrations. Thus in this tour to Upper Burma, I was being given a preview of what I should soon have to face and deal with.

During these courses, Sayagyi suddenly asked me to give discourses to the Indian students in Hindi. This again was part of my training for the future task. Though well accustomed to giving public speeches, I felt rather hesitant to speak on Dhamma, especially in the presence of my teacher. Nevertheless, I did as requested.

Some time after this teaching tour to Upper Burma, a course started at the meditation centre in Rangoon, in which three young Indian students were participating. When Anapana was to be given, I went into the central room from which Dhamma was taught, and found my teacher lying down. To my surprise, he told me to give the Triple Refuge, Five Precepts, and Anapana to these students. And to encourage me and allay my feelings of nervousness, he said that I should not worry, as he would be present at the time. Despite my initial hesitation, I performed the duty assigned to me and my teacher was very pleased.

On the fourth day it was time for the giving of Vipassana, but to my great surprise, Sayagyi went to his room and told me to go ahead without him, as he could not be present. I felt quite nervous about giving Vipassana without the presence of my teacher. But again he encouraged me, saying that although he would not be there, his *mettā* would be present to help me and protect me. Strengthened and encouraged by his words, I gave Vipassana independently for the first time to these three students.

In the middle of the giving of Vipassana, suddenly one of the students started shaking violently. I was shocked to the depths for a few moments, and my first thought was to call for help from my teacher. But to do so would totally disrupt the atmosphere of giving Vipassana. I was in a quandary until I remembered the words of Sayagyi, his smiling face full of *mettā*, and the presence of Dhamma all around me. I understood that there was no need to call for his help; it was with me all the time. With the support of *mettā*, my mind became tranquil and composed; and in a few minutes the student calmed down. The first course in which I gave Vipassana proved successful.

Since then, whenever I give Dhamma to anyone, I feel the presence of my Dhamma father and his *mettā* vibrations, and I feel that I am just a humble representative of him, assisting to spread Dhamma to suffering beings everywhere, in fulfilment of his very wishes.

Do You Share Your Merits

The practice of Vipassana should not become a mechanical process, a rite or a ritual. One has to apply it in day-to-day life, keeping a balanced mind amidst all the vicissitudes. This was always strongly emphasized by my teacher and hence had a very strong impact on my mind.

When all my business concerns were suddenly nationalized and my industrial establishments were taken over by the Burmese government, Vipassana was of great help to me in maintaining equanimity. My teacher was pleased to see this.

One day he asked whether I was regularly sharing my merits with others after meditation. I replied in the affirmative. Then he asked me with whom I shared my merits. I replied that I shared them with my elders, and then with all those who have been responsible for helping to strengthen me in Dhamma directly or indirectly—including the ministers of Trade and Industry and the officials in the government, and all the others. He was extremely pleased to hear this.

I explained by saying, "I am very intimate with some of the members of the Cabinet, and through them I am fully convinced that the government has not nationalized the trade and industry with malice towards anyone. They have done so as a policy which they feel will be good and beneficial for the whole nation. Hence, I too have no malice towards them. On the contrary, I am extremely grateful to them because they have relieved me from all the responsibilities of my trade and industries which kept me so busy all the time. Now I can devote most of my time to practising *pariyatti* (theoretical study) and *paṭipatti* (practice) Dhamma which would otherwise have been impossible for me." My teacher said, "*Sādhu, sādhu, sādhu* (well said, well said)," and encouraged me to continue to share my merits with them, which I continue to do even today.

Sayagyi U Ba Khin

Remembering Sayagyi

The following comments are condensed from recollections of students of U Ba Khin.

On a little knoll, two hundred yards off Inya Myaing Road in one of the fashionable residential areas of Rangoon, stands a small stupa built in 1952 under the auspices of the Vipassana Association of the Office of the Accountant General, Burma. The president and guide of the association was Sayagyi U Ba Khin, from its inception until 19 January 1971, when he passed away. The golden stupa, named Dhamma Yaung Chi Zedi (the light of Dhamma pagoda), standing on the top of the knoll in the centre of the surrounding meditation cells, has served

as the headquarters of the International Meditation Centre (I.M.C.), and became a beacon of light for wayfarers in search of peace and Truth.

The story of this pagoda and I.M.C. is the story of the selfless devotion on the part of Sayagyi U Ba Khin to the cause of Buddha-Dhamma. His understanding of Dhamma, as taught by the Buddha, was profound and penetrating; his approach to it modern and scientific. His was not mere conventional acceptance of the teaching of the Buddha; his was a whole-hearted embrace of Dhamma with firm conviction and faith as a result of personal realization through actual practice.

He learned Vipassana meditation at the feet of the great meditation master Saya Thetgyi. When he reached a certain stage of proficiency, Saya Thetgyi felt certain that Guruji U Ba Khin was destined to play the role of the torch-bearer after he had passed away.

But it was only in 1941, after he had met and paid homage to Webu Sayadaw, believed by many to be an *arahant* (a liberated being), that he finally decided to help people find the path laid down by the Buddha. In his technique, he did not make the slightest deviation from the Buddha's teaching but, after ceaseless practical research and experimentation, he developed instructions of his own, more suited to the demands of modern times.

He felt the need of a course of instructions particularly for householders, rather than strictly for *bhikkhus* (monks) and recluses who had given up worldly life. A discipline for *bhikkhus* could not ideally be suitable for laymen. The Vipassana Research Association, initiated by Sayagyi while he was the Accountant General of Burma, undertook research and experiments in Vipassana meditation. Results and findings from these studies carried out in a special shrine room at the A.G.'s office enabled Sayagyi to present the Buddha's Dhamma to laymen in a systematic, scientific manner, thus appealing to the modern mind. His regimen of Vipassana exercises encompasses completely the three requisites laid down by the Buddha (namely *sīla, samādhi* and *paññā*), but is so streamlined and disciplined that satisfactory results could be expected within a short period of endeavour.

Foreign intellectuals and organizations first became acquainted with Sayagyi when he gave a series of lectures to a religious study group composed of members of a special technical and economic mission from America, in 1952. The lectures, rendered in booklet form, soon found their way to various Burmese embassies abroad and Buddhist organizations the world over.

Sayagyi made a few more expositions of the life and teachings of the Buddha, but mere interpretation of the Dhamma had never been his main object. He applied himself solely to the task of helping sincere workers to experience a state of purity of mind and realize the truth of suffering resulting in "the peace within" through practising Vipassana meditation. He achieved astounding results with the presentation he developed to explain the technique. To his last breath Guruji remained a preceptor rather than a preacher of Vipassana meditation.

—U Ko Lay, *former Vice Chancellor of Mandalay University*

Ever since I read a booklet containing lectures on Buddhism delivered in 1952, I had admired Sayagyi U Ba Khin. In 1956 or thereabouts I was able to visit the annual meeting of the Vipassana Association of the A. G.'s office held at I.M.C. to present a magazine published by the Rangoon University Pāli Association and to speak with Sayagyi for awhile.

Sayagyi seemed to notice my interest in his lectures on Buddhism. He said, "You are a writer and a theoretician and I am a practical man. So it is very difficult for me to explain the practice of meditation. Come and practise it yourself and you will get a better understanding than my explanation."

Sayagyi served concurrently as officer on special duty, trade development minister, chairman of the state agricultural marketing board, and member of the advisory board of the national planning commission. Foreigners hearing of these splendid achievements often raise the question: "Where do you get such energy from?" The following was Sayagyi's reply: "Because I practise Buddhist meditation, I can handle many important tasks simultaneously. If you want to purify your mind and be happy, healthy and energetic like me, why don't you make an attempt to take a course in Buddhist meditation?"

—*by Maung Ye Lwin, excerpted from an article appearing in the Burmese magazine* Thint Bawa, *December* **1960**

I once considered Sayagyi U Ba Khin an old, dry and uninteresting person who taught something which was fit only for aged people who had little interest and activity in the things the outside world offered. I regarded him with awe and fear, for I had heard much about his outbursts of anger. I visited him at the centre with the elders of my family very seldom, and only when I had to.

All these feelings evaporated, one by one, when I stayed with him for ten days and learned meditation under his guidance.

I found Sayagyi to be a very affectionate person. He was like a father to me. I could freely discuss with him any problem that faced me, and be sure not only of a sympathetic ear but also of good advice. All his anger which was talked about was only surface-deep; the core was filled with unbounded love. It was as though a hard crust had formed upon a liquid material. The hard crust was necessary—rather, very important for the work he was doing.

It was this hardness which enabled him to maintain strict discipline at the centre. Sometimes people took undue advantage of his loving nature and neglected the purpose for which they were there. They would walk around the place and talk with other students, thus wasting not only their own time, but disturbing others as well. Sayagyi's hard nature was required to set them on the right track. Even when he got angry, it was loving anger. He wanted his students to learn as much as possible in the short time available. He felt such negligent students were wasting a precious opportunity which might never come again, an opportunity of which every second was so precious.

He was very generous. He wanted to teach all he knew. He was so keen upon giving away his knowledge and experience that he made untiring efforts to teach a student. He gave freely. It was only the student's capacity to absorb his instructions which was the limiting factor.

He was very patient in his teaching too. If a person found difficulty in understanding the process, he would explain thoroughly with examples and illustrations. But he never believed in too much talking. He loved practical work, and was of the opinion that experience in the training itself will take care of all the theoretical doubts. Discussing only theories will not land us anywhere. The practical aspect was most important. How right he was! Not only in Dhamma but even in our day-to-day affairs, practical work gives better results than mere discussion.

He himself had a great zeal for work. He held six or seven highly important executive posts in the government with grave responsibilities and also conducted the classes of meditation in his free time. In fact he had no free time at all! He was always busy. He had such a large capacity for work at an age when other people think of resting and leading a quiet life. He found peace and calmness in his work.

Even with so much work to do he devoted some time to gardening. It was his favourite hobby. He loved to grow flowers and plants. The centre had such a pleasing colourful look with all the greenery around.

The beauty and peace he created at the centre will always linger in my heart. He taught a rare thing which is of great value to old and young alike. He was a great teacher and a very affectionate man indeed.

—*Mrs. Vimala Goenka,*
senior assistant teacher to S.N. Goenka

His was a fine personality: majestic, sober, noble and impressive. He always bore a faint smile and the look of a calm, satisfied mind. When with him, you felt as if he cared for you and loved you more than anybody else. His attention, love, mettā was the same for all, big or small, rich or poor; in return he did not want anything but sincerity of purpose and a truthful nature.

He tolerated all religions. He never criticized or ridiculed any faith or belief. But he preached Buddhism, as he understood it, and he understood it well above many others. He never asserted anything, never forced any idea on you. He followed what he preached or taught and left it to you to think over and accept his view, in part or in full as you wished.

He did not smoke or take alcohol or any narcotics. He took tea and coffee in moderation; liked milk, Ovaltine, etc., especially towards the later part of his life. His love of "life" was extreme. He would not allow even mosquitoes to be killed at the centre. Even the use of pesticides and insecticides was prohibited there.

He had a great aesthetic and artistic sense, loved flowers very much, and took special care about getting rare varieties. He had a nice and beautiful collection of flower plants, which were all over the garden around the pagoda. He knew all his plants well and would talk about them at length with the centre's visitors.

He had a good sense of humour and was witty. He was fond of making little jokes, and laughing, laughing very loudly. Just as he would shout loudly, he would laugh loudly!

He kept himself well-informed about world politics and the modern advances in science and technology, and was a regular listener to radio and a reader of foreign periodicals. He was especially fond of **Life** and **Time** magazines.

He had a great desire (a desire which was never fulfilled) to go abroad, especially to the U.S.A. He wanted to teach his method of meditation which he believed—and very correctly so—to be the easiest and most logical way to practise meditation. He had the means to go, had many invitations from foreign disciples, but some technical formalities in obtaining passports and so on always stood in his way. Excepting this one desire, he had all his desires and wishes in the world fulfilled. He led a full life.

He bore disease and illness bravely and well, and was a very intelligent and cooperative patient. He never took a pessimistic view of life; he was always optimistic and took a hopeful view. He took suffering and disease as a result of past *karma* and said it is the lot of one born into the world. Even his last illness which came and took him away from us suddenly, he treated very lightly.

He was a very pious and great soul; pure of mind and body, and lovable to everyone.

—*Dr. Om Prakash, former consulting physician, United Nations Organization, Burma; senior assistant to S.N. Goenka.*

My wife and I first met U Ba Khin in 1959. In all his Buddhist devotion there was none of that searing intensity or dry, brittle hardness that sometimes accompanies strong religious conviction. For U Ba Khin was genuinely and delightfully human. He loved the roses about the centre and watched the growth of a special tree with pride and joy. It was a wonderful experience to hear him tell various of the Buddhist stories. He told them with hearty and humorous enjoyment, but there was no mistaking the depth of his feeling for them and his devotion to their truth. His experience was profound enough that it could afford the reverent joke without fear of

offense. And his genuine authority as a meditation master came from this same depth of experience. There was no need for a superficial "cracking of the whip."

Thus when I think of him now, it is as a man who was eminently sane and finely human in a universal sense; who could be completely Burmese, thoroughly Buddhist, and intensely human all at once, without confusion, pretence or strain.

—*Dr. Winston King, former professor of history and philosophy of religion, Grinnell College and Vanderbilt University, U.S.A.*

Before the ten-day course was over, I knew that my most deep-lying fear was that my own body would perish and rot away, forever gone. I could not face death with equanimity. Sayagyi's help was essential in this crisis. Then, instead of being through with the whole thing and regarding it as an "interesting Burmese experience," I found myself coming back for another course while my husband had to be away on business, and then later for still another before we left Burma to return to the U.S. I did

not decide that Sayagyi should be my teacher. Rather, I discovered that he was my teacher.

Since that time I have not ever been out of touch with him. He has never failed to help me. And even with his death I cannot feel out of touch when I remember so well what he taught and was. His healing generosity and compassionate interest in all human beings, he learned only from the Enlightened One. He embodied that which he constantly taught to others—the calm center in the midst of *anicca*.

—*Jocelyn B. King, U.S.A.*

I doubt whether an ordinary being can point to so many periods in his lifetime that further his inner development as much as these ten brief days under your guidance. No doubt due to my insufficient pāramīs [virtues from the past], my achievements here may have fallen somewhat short of what they could have been. By perseverance I hope, however, to improve. And I already take back with me considerable added strength and composure.

You yourself are the finest example of what you set out to obtain in your pupils. Your wisdom, your tolerance and patience, and your deep, loving devotion leave a profound impact on the personalities of those who come and sit at your feet. To yourself and to your dedicated helpers goes my true gratefulness.

—From a letter to Sayagyi from Mr. Eliashiv Ben-Horin, former Israeli ambassador to Burma

On May first 1954, the Venerable Webu Sayadaw honoured the International Meditation Centre with a visit. In his simple, gentle way he expounded the Dhamma and then told us that Sayagyi had put us on the right path; it was left to us to walk along it steadfastly and diligently toward the goal. If we stood and stared at the scenery or strange objects on the way or tried to follow by-paths, of course it would take a long, long time. We were so elated by the Sayadaw's approval of our practice, and our gratitude and respect for Sayagyi knew no bounds. He was a true *ācariya*—a Teacher of Dhamma and Vipassana meditation, ready to advise and help all those who came to the centre. He had a clear understanding of the many types of students, their different approaches to the practice of meditation and the latent forces within each one of them. Now and again, he invited learned Sayadaws and submitted to them his findings in Vipassana research and accepted their advice and suggestions.

It was in early 1954 that I began to feel the need for training in spiritual development. No sooner had I heard about U Ba Khin and the International Meditation Centre than I met him for the first time at a tea party given by the Sāsana Council in honour of Western scholars of

Pāli. I had been impressed by his lectures at the Methodist Church. Now his presence filled me with confidence and I asked him for permission to visit the centre the following Sunday. There I learnt that the next ten-day course would begin on Friday; it coincided with the private study period at the university. So I requested U Ba Khin to accept me as a trainee. Not only did he accede to my request but he also gave me the *Ānāpānakammaṭṭhāna* (the meditation object of Anapana) on that very day and told me to practise at home before coming to the centre.

The eight trainees in the February 1954 course came from different walks of life, yet Sayagyi was able to guide and help each one of us. He was still an active government servant and although he stayed at the centre for the ten days, he had to attend to his office and meetings during the day. On his return, he would sit in the centre room and speak to us individually about our experiences, our difficulties, our progress or otherwise. At about 6:00 pm. after we had had cold drinks and stretched our legs, he would explain the Dhamma or tell appropriate stories from the *Suttas* to all of us in the main hall. We returned to our cubicles and meditated till 9:00 pm. Sayagyi was patient and painstaking, but very strict and stern when he found sloth and torpor in the trainee. Unlike foreign seekers after truth, the Burmese trainees felt that they could always go back for another ten-day course. A few felt it was a pleasant and peaceful interlude from their daily cares and worries. The vegetarian food was delicious and wholesome and, in spite of the eight precepts, one tended to put on weight. Sayagyi then told us to eat less, keep the vow of silence and remain in the cubicle as much as possible till he returned.

Although I had made frequent stays at the centre in the early days, my journeys abroad and my work and domestic involvements had left little time for more than short visits to pay my respects to Sayagyi. Nearly seventeen years had passed since my first course, when I again became a constant visitor to the centre.

On Tuesday, 19 January 1971, Sayagyi left us. He appeared to be so strong and healthy yet, "Decay is inherent in all component things, but the truth will remain forever." As instructed by him, our duty now is to be vigilant and diligent in our search for truth and become worthy disciples of Sayagyi U Ba Khin and true followers of the Buddha.

—*Daw Mya Sein, M.A., B.Lit (Oxon),*
Rangoon, Burma

Discourses of Sayagyi U Ba Khin

The Essentials of Buddha-Dhamma in Meditative Practice

by Thray Sithu Sayagyi U Ba Khin

Several years before he died, Sayagyi composed the following discourse in English particularly for his Western students. He read it to students on a number of occasions. After his death, the discourse was transcribed from an audio recording, and published under the above title.

Anicca, dukkha and anattā — impermanence, suffering and egolessness — are the three essential characteristics of things in the teaching of the Buddha. If you know anicca correctly, you know dukkha as its corollary and anattā as ultimate truth. It takes time to understand the three together.

Impermanence (*anicca*) is, of course, the essential fact which must be first experienced and understood by practice. Mere book-knowledge of the Buddha-Dhamma will not be enough for the correct understanding of *anicca* because the experiential aspect will be missing. It is only through experiential understanding of the nature of *anicca* as an ever-changing process within yourself that you can understand *anicca* in the way the Buddha would like you to understand it. As in the days of the Buddha, so too now, this understanding of *anicca* can be developed by persons who have no book-knowledge whatsoever of Buddhism.

To understand impermanence (*anicca*), one must follow strictly and diligently the Eight-fold Noble Path, which is divided into the three groups of *sīla, samādhi* and *paññā*—morality, concentration and wisdom. *Sīla* or virtuous living is the basis for *samādhi* (control of the mind, leading to one-pointedness). It is only when *samādhi* is good that one can develop *paññā*. Therefore, *sīla* and *samādhi* are the prerequisites for *paññā*. By *paññā* is meant the understanding of *anicca, dukkha* and *anattā* through the practice of Vipassana, i.e., insight meditation.

Whether a Buddha has arisen or not, the practice of *sīla* and *samādhi* may be present in the human world. They are, in fact, the common denominators of all religious faiths. They are not, however, sufficient means for the goal of Buddhism—the complete end of suffering. In his search for the end of suffering, Prince Siddhārtha, the future Buddha, found this out and worked his way through to find the path which would lead to the end of suffering. After solid work for six years, he found the way out, became completely enlightened, and then taught men and gods to follow the path which would lead them to the end of suffering.

In this connection, we should understand that each action—whether by deed, word or thought—leaves behind an active force called *saṅkhāra* (or *kamma* in popular terminology), which goes to the credit or debit account of the individual, according to whether the action is good or bad. There is, therefore, an accumulation of *saṅkhāras* (or *kamma*) with everyone, which functions as the supply-source of energy to sustain life, which is inevitably followed by suffering and death. It is by the development of the power inherent in the understanding of *anicca, dukkha* and *anattā* that one is able to rid oneself of the *saṅkhāras* accumulated in one's own personal account. This process begins with the correct understanding of *anicca* while further accumulations of fresh actions and the reduction of the supply of energy to sustain life are taking place simultaneously, from moment to moment and from day to day. It is, therefore, a matter of a whole lifetime or more to get rid of all one's *sankhāras*. He who has rid himself of all *sankhāras* comes to the end of suffering, for then no *sankhāra* remains to give the necessary energy to sustain him in any form of life. On the termination of their lives the perfected saints, i.e. the Buddhas and the *arahants*, pass into *parinibbāna*, reaching the end of suffering. For us today who take to Vipassana meditation it would suffice if we can understand *anicca* well enough to reach the first stage of an *ariya* (a noble person), that is, a *sotāpanna* or stream-enterer, who will not take more than seven lives to come to the end of suffering.

The fact of *anicca*, which opens the door to the understanding of *dukkha* and *anattā* and eventually to the end of suffering, can be encountered in its full significance only through the teaching of a Buddha for as long as that teaching relating to the Eightfold Noble Path and the thirty-seven factors of enlightenment (*bodhipakkhiya dhammā*) remains intact and available to the aspirant.

For progress in Vipassana meditation, a student must keep knowing *anicca* as continuously as possible. The Buddha's advice to monks is that they should try to maintain the awareness of *anicca, dukkha* or *anattā* in all postures, whether sitting, standing, walking or lying down. Continuous awareness of *anicca*, and so of *dukkha* and *anattā*, is the secret of success. The last words of the Buddha just before he breathed his last and passed away into *mahāparinibbāna* were: "Decay (or *anicca)* is inherent in all component things.

> The real meaning of *anicca* is that impermanence or decay is the inherent nature of everything that exists in the universe— whether animate or inanimate.

Work out your own salvation with diligence." This is in fact the essence of all his teachings during the forty-five years of his ministry. If you will keep up the awareness of the *anicca* that is inherent in all component things, you are sure to reach the goal in the course of time.

As you develop in the understanding of *anicca*, your insight into "what is true of nature" will become greater and greater, so that eventually you will have no doubt whatsoever of the three characteristics of *anicca, dukkha* and *anattā*. It is then only that you will be in a position to go ahead for the goal in view. Now that you know *anicca* as the first essential factor, you should try to understand what *anicca* is with real clarity, as extensively as possible, so as not to get confused in the course of practice or discussion.

The real meaning of *anicca* is that impermanence or decay is the inherent nature of everything that exists in the universe—whether animate or inanimate. The Buddha taught his disciples that everything that exists at the material level is composed of *kalāpas. Kalāpas* are material units very much smaller than atoms, which die out almost immediately after they come into being. Each *kalāpa* is a mass formed of the eight basic constituents of matter: the solid, liquid, calorific and oscillatory, together with colour, smell, taste, and nutriment. The first four are called primary qualities, and are predominant in a *kalāpa*. The other four are subsidiaries dependent upon and springing from the former. A *kalāpa* is the minutest particle in the physical plane—still beyond the range of science today. It is only when the eight basic material constituents unite together that the *kalāpa* is formed. In other words, the momentary collocation of these eight basic elements of behaviour, which makes a mass just for that moment, is known in Buddhism as a *kalāpa*. The life-span of a *kalāpa* is termed a "moment," and a trillion such moments are said to elapse during the wink of a man's eye. These *kalāpas* are all in a state of perpetual change or flux. To a developed student in Vipassana meditation they can be felt as a stream of energy.

The human body is not, as it may appear, a solid stable entity, but a continūm of matter (*rūpa*) coexisting with mentality (*nāma*). To know that our body is tiny *kalāpas* all in a state of change is to know the true nature of change or decay. This change or decay (*anicca*) occasioned by the continual breakdown and replacement of *kalāpas,* all in a state of combustion, must necessarily be identified as *dukkha,* the truth of suffering. It is only when you experience impermanence (*anicca*) as suffering (*dukkha*) that you come to the realization of the truth of suffering, the first of the Four Noble Truths basic to the doctrine of the Buddha.

Why? Because when you realize the subtle nature of *dukkha* from which you cannot escape for a moment, you become truly afraid of, disgusted with, and disinclined towards your very existence as mentality-materiality (*nāma-rūpa*), and look for a way of escape to a state beyond *dukkha,* and so to *nibbāna,* the end of suffering. What that end of suffering is like, you will be able to taste, even as a human being, when you reach the level of a *sotāpanna,* a stream-enterer, and develop well enough by practice to attain the unconditioned state of *nibbāna,* the peace within. But even in terms of everyday, ordinary life, no sooner than you are able to keep up the awareness of *anicca* in practice will you know

for yourself that a change is taking place in you for the better, both physically and mentally.

Before entering upon the practice of Vipassana meditation (that is, after *samādhi* has been developed to a proper level), a student should acquaint himself with the theoretical knowledge of material and mental properties, i.e., of *rūpa* and *nāma*. For in Vipassana meditation one contemplates not only the changing nature of matter, but also the changing nature of mentality, of the thought-elements of attention directed towards the process of change going on within matter. At times the attention will be focused on the impermanence of the material side of existence, i.e., upon *anicca* in regard to *rūpa;* and at other times on the impermanence of the thought-elements or mental side, i.e., upon *anicca* in regard to *nāma*. When one is contemplating the impermanence of matter, one realizes also that the thought-elements simultaneous with that awareness are also in a state of transition or change. In this case one will be knowing *anicca* in regard to both *rūpa* and *nāma* together.

All I have said so far relates to the understanding of *anicca* through bodily feeling of the process of change of *rūpa* (or matter) and also of thought-elements depending upon such changing processes. You should know that *anicca* can also be understood through other types of feeling as well. *Anicca* can be contemplated through feeling:

1. by contact of visible form with the sense organ of the eye;

2. by contact of sound with the sense organ of the ear;

3. by contact of smell with the sense organ of the nose;

4. by contact of taste with the sense organ of the tongue;

5. by contact of touch with the sense organ of the body;

6. and by contact of mental objects with the sense organ of the mind.

One can thus develop the understanding of *anicca* through any of the six sense organs. In practice, however, we have found that of all types of feeling, the feeling by contact of touch with the component parts of the body in a process of change, covers the widest area for introspective meditation. Not only that, the feeling by contact of touch (by way of friction, radiation and vibration of the *kalāpas* within) with the component parts of the body is more evident than other types of feeling. Therefore a beginner in Vipassana meditation can come to the understanding of *anicca* more easily through bodily feeling of the change of *rūpa*, or matter. This is the main reason why we have chosen bodily feeling as a medium for quick understanding of *anicca*. It is open to anyone to try other means, but my suggestion is that one should be well-established in the understanding of *anicca* through bodily feeling before any attempt is made through other types of feeling.

There are ten levels of knowledge in Vipassana, namely:

1. *sammasana*: theoretical appreciation of *anicca*, *dukkha* and *anattā* by close observation and analysis.

2. *udayabbaya*: knowledge of the arising and dissolution of *rūpa* and *nāma* by direct observation.

3. *bhaṅga*: knowledge of the rapidly changing nature of *rūpa* and *nāma* as a swift current or stream of energy; in particular, clear awareness of the phase of dissolution.

4. *bhaya*: knowledge that this very existence is dreadful.

5. *ādīnava*: knowledge that this very existence is full of evils.

6. *nibbidā*: knowledge that this very existence is disgusting.

7. *muñcitakamyatā*: knowledge of the urgent need and wish to escape from this very existence.

8. *paṭisaṅkhā*: knowledge that the time has come to work for full realization of deliverance with *anicca* as the base.

9. *saṅkhārupekkhā*: knowledge that the stage is now set to get detached from all conditioned phenomena (*saṅkhāra*) and to break away from egocentricity.

10. *anuloma*: knowledge that would accelerate the attempt to reach the goal.

These are the levels of attainment which one goes through during the course of Vipassana meditation. In the case of those who reach the goal in a short time, they can be known only in retrospect. Along with one's progress in understanding *anicca*, one may reach these levels of attainment—subject, however, to adjustments or help at certain levels by a competent teacher. One should avoid looking forward to such attainments in anticipation, as this will distract from the continuity of awareness of *anicca* which alone can and will give the desired reward.

Let me now deal with Vipassana meditation from the point of view of a householder in everyday life and explain the benefit one can derive from it—here and now—in this very lifetime.

The initial object of Vipassana meditation is to activate the experience of *anicca* in oneself and eventually to reach a state of inner and outer calmness and balance. This is achieved when one becomes engrossed in the feeling of *anicca* within. The world is now facing serious problems which threaten all mankind. It is just the right time for everyone to take to Vipassana meditation and learn how to find a deep pool of quiet in the midst of all that is happening today. *Anicca* is inside of everybody. It is within reach of everybody. Just a look into oneself and there it is—*anicca* to be experienced. When one can feel *anicca*, when one can experience *anicca*, and when one can become engrossed in *anicca*, one can and will cut oneself off from the world of ideation outside. *Anicca* is, for the householder, the gem of life which he will treasure to create a reservoir of calm and balanced energy for his own wellbeing and for the welfare of the society.

The experience of *anicca*, when properly developed, strikes at the root of one's physical and mental ills and removes gradually whatever is bad in him, i.e., the causes of such physical and mental ills. This experience is not reserved for men who have renounced the world for the homeless life. It is for the householder as well. In spite of drawbacks which make a householder restless in these days, a competent teacher or guide can help a student to get the experience of *anicca* activated in a comparatively short time. Once he has got it activated, all that is necessary for is him to try to preserve it; but he must make it a point, as soon as time or opportunity presents itself for further progress, to work for the stage of *bhaṅgañāṇa* (knowledge of *bhaṅga*).

However, there is likely to be some difficulty for one who has not reached the stage of *bhaṅga*. It will be just like a tug-of-war for him between *anicca* within, and physical and mental activities outside. So it would be wise for him to follow the motto of "Work while you work, play while you play." There is no need for him to be activating the experience of *anicca* all the time. It should suffice if this could be confined to a regular period, or periods, set apart in the day or night for the purpose. During this time, at least, an attempt must be made to keep the attention focused inside the body, with awareness devoted exclusively to *anicca*.

That is to say, his awareness of *anicca* should go on from moment to moment so continuously as not to allow for the interpolation of any discursive or distracting thoughts, which are definitely detrimental to progress. In case this is not possible, he will have to go back to respiration-mindfulness, because *samādhi* is the key to the contemplation of *anicca*. To get good *samādhi*, *sīla* (morality) has to be perfect, since *samādhi* is built upon *sīla*. For a good experience of *anicca*, *samādhi* must be good. If *samādhi* is excellent, awareness of *anicca* will also become excellent.

There is no special technique for activating the experience of *anicca* other than the use of the mind adjusted to a perfect state of balance and attention projected upon the object of meditation. In Vipassana the object of meditation is *anicca*, and therefore in the case of those used to focusing their attention on bodily feelings, they can feel *anicca* directly. In experiencing *anicca* in relation to the body, it should first be in the area where one can easily get his attention engrossed, changing the area of attention from place to place, from head to feet and from feet to head, at times probing into the interior. At this stage it must clearly be understood that no attention is to be paid to the anatomy of the body, but to the formations of matter—the *kalāpas*—and the nature of their constant change.

If these instructions are observed, there will surely be progress, but the progress depends also on *pāramī* (i.e., one's disposition for certain spiritual qualities) and devotion of the individual to the work of meditation. If he attains high levels of knowledge, his power to understand the three characteristics of *anicca*, *dukkha* and *anattā* will increase and he will accordingly come nearer and nearer to the goal of the *ariya* or noble saint—which every householder should keep in view.

This is the age of science. Man of today has no utopia. He will not accept anything unless the results are good, concrete, vivid, personal, and here-and-now.

When the Buddha was alive, he said to the people of Kālāma:

"Now look, you Kālāmas. Be not misled by report or tradition or hearsay. Be not misled by proficiency in the scriptural collections, or by reasoning or logic, or reflection on and approval of some theory, or because some view conforms with one's inclinations, or out of respect for the prestige of a teacher. But when you know for yourselves: these things are unwholesome, these things are blameworthy, these things are censured by the wise; these things, when practised and observed, conduce to loss and sorrow—then do ye reject them. But if at any time you know for yourselves: these things are wholesome, these things are blameless, these things are praised by the intelligent; these things, when practised and observed, conduce to welfare and happiness—then, Kālāmas, do ye, having practised them, abide."

The time clock of Vipassana has now struck—that is, for the revival of Buddha-Dhamma Vipassana in practice. We have no doubt whatsoever that definite results would accrue to those who would with an open mind sincerely undergo a course of training under a competent teacher—I mean results which will be accepted as good, concrete, vivid, personal, here-and-now—results which will keep them in good stead and in a state of well-being and happiness for the rest of their lives.

May all beings be happy and may peace prevail in the world.

The word "Buddha" means a person who is fully enlightened. "Dhamma" means nature. Hence, "Buddha-Dhamma" means the nature of an enlightened person.

All persons—whoever they may be, if they are really and fully enlightened—must have the same nature: that is, total freedom from craving, aversion, delusion.

When we practise *Buddha-Dhamma,* we are not getting involved in a particular sect. Rather we are actually working to develop in ourselves the nature of a Buddha—to attain freedom from craving, aversion, delusion. And the means by which we develop this nature is the practise of *sīla, samādhi, paññā,* which is universally acceptable to all.

—*S.N. Goenka*

W hat Buddhism Is

by Thray Sithu Sayagyi U Ba Khin

In 1951, when Sayagyi was the Accountant General of Burma, he was requested by a religious study group to lecture on Buddhism. The study group was headed by the information officer and the economic and finance officer of the Special Technical and Economic Division of the U.S. government. Sayagyi presented a series of three lectures in Rangoon (at the Methodist Church, Signal Pagoda Road) which were later published as a booklet entitled "What Buddhism Is." The following is abridged.

Lecture No. 1 (23 September 1951)

I consider it a great privilege to be in your midst today and to have this opportunity of addressing you on the subject of "What Buddhism Is." At the outset, I must be very frank with you. I have not been to a university, and I have no knowledge of science except as a man on the street. Nor am I a scholar in the theory of Buddhism with any knowledge of the Pāli language in which the Tipiṭakas (known as, literally, the "Three Baskets" of Buddha Dhamma) are maintained. I must say, however, that I have read in Burmese to some extent the treatises of Buddhism by well-known and learned Buddhist monks. As my approach to Buddhism is more by practical than by theoretical means, I hope to be able to give you something of Buddhism which is not easily available elsewhere. I must admit, however, that for the time being I am just a student of practical Buddhism and also an experimentalist trying to learn through Buddhism the truth of the nature of forces. As this has to be done as a householder and within a limited time available amidst the multifarious duties of a responsible officer of government, the progress is rather slow, and I do not claim for a moment that what I am going to say is absolutely correct. I may be right or wrong. But when I say a thing, I assure you that it is with sincerity of purpose, with the best of intentions and with conviction.

Lord Buddha said in the ***Kālāma Sutta***:

Do not believe in what ye have heard;

> do not believe in the traditions, because they had been handed down for generations;
>
> do not believe in anything because it is rumoured and spoken by many;
>
> do not believe merely because a written statement of some old sage is produced;
>
> do not believe in conjectures;
>
> do not believe in that as truth to which you have become attached by habit;
>
> do not believe merely the authority of your teachers and elders.

After observation and analysis, when it agrees with reason and is conducive to the good and gain of one and all, then accept it and live up to it.

Pray do not, therefore, believe me when I come to the philosophical issues until and unless you are convinced of what I say, either as a sequel to proper reasoning or by means of a practical approach.

To abstain from evil;
To do good;
To purify the mind:
These are the teachings of all the Buddhas.

This extract taken from the **Dhammapada** gives in brief the essence of Buddhism. It sounds simple but is so difficult to practise. One cannot be a true Buddhist unless he puts the doctrine of Buddha into practice. Buddha said:

> Ye, to whom the truths I have perceived have been made known by me, make them surely your own; practise them, meditate upon them, spread them abroad; in order that the pure religion may last long and be perpetuated for the good and the gain and the weal of gods and men.

Before I take up the teachings of Buddha, which form the basic foundation of Buddhism, I propose to acquaint you, first of all, with the life story of Gotama Buddha. For this purpose, I feel it my duty to give you a background of certain Buddhist concepts which may be foreign to most of you. I propose, therefore, to give you a short and descriptive explanation of such concepts in Buddhism, as to the universe, the world system, the planes of existence, etc. These will, no doubt give you some food for thought. I would however, appeal to you to give a patient hearing and to pass over these matters for the time being, i.e., until we come to the question time for discussion.

Universe

The Buddhist concept of the universe may be summed up as follows:

There is the **Okāsa Loka** (the universe of space) which accommodates **nāma** and **rūpa** (mind and matter). In this mundane world it is **nāma** and **rūpa** which predominate under the influence of the law of cause and effect. The next is the **Saṅkhāra Loka** (the universe of mental forces), creative or created. This is a mental plane arising out of the creative energies of mind through the medium of bodily actions, words and thoughts. The third and the last is the **Satta Loka** (the universe of sentient beings). These beings are the products of mental forces. We may rather call these three as a "three-in-one" universe, because one is inseparable from another. They are, so to say, interwoven and interpenetrating.

What will interest you most are the *cakkavālas* or world systems, each with its thirty-one planes of existence. Each world system corresponds to the human world with its solar system and other planes of existence. There are millions and millions of such world systems, simply innumerable. Ten thousand such world systems closest to us are within the **Jāti-Khetta** (or the field of origin) of a Buddha. In fact when the renowned *sutta* (or sermon) **Mahā Samaya** (meaning the "Great Occasion") was preached by Buddha in the Mahāvana (forest) near the town of Kapilavatthu, not only the *brahmās* and *devas* of our world system, but of all of the ten thousand world systems were present to listen to the teachings of Buddha. Lord Buddha can also send his thought-waves charged with boundless love and compassion to the sentient beings of a hundred crores (thousand million) of such world systems within the **Anākhetta** (or the field of influence). The remainder of the world systems are in the **Visaya Khetta** (or infinite space) beyond the reach of Buddha's effective thought waves. You can very well imagine from these concepts of Buddhism the size of the universe as a whole. The material insignificance of our world in the **Okāsa loka** (universe of space) is simply terrifying. The human world, as a whole, must be just a speck in space.

Now I will give you an idea of the thirty-one planes of existence in our world system which, of course, is the same as in any of the other world systems. Broadly they are:

(i) *Arūpa Loka*—immaterial world of *brahmās*;

(ii) *Rūpa Loka*—fine material world of *brahmās*;

(iii) *Kāma Loka*—sensuous world of *devas*, mankind and lower beings.

The *Arūpa Loka* is comprised of four *brahmā* worlds of immaterial state, i.e., without *rūpa* or matter. The *Rūpa Loka* is comprised of sixteen *brahmā* worlds of fine material state. The *Kāma loka* is comprised of:

(a) Six *deva lokas* (or celestial worlds), viz.:

  (i) *Catumahārājika*

  (ii) *Tāvatiṃsa*

  (iii) *Yāmā*

  (iv) *Tusita*

  (v) *Nimmāṇarati*

  (vi) *Paranimmita-vasavatti*

(b) The human world

(c) The four lower worlds, viz:

  (i) *Niraya*   (hell)

  (ii) *Tiricchāna*   (animal world)

  (iii) *Peta*   (ghost world)

  (iv) *Asura*   (demon world)

These planes of existence are pure or impure, cool or hot, luminous or dark, light or heavy, pleasant or wretched—according to the character of the mental forces generated by the mind or the volition (*cetanā*) of a series of actions, words and thoughts. For example, take the case of a religious man who suffuses the whole universe of beings with boundless love and compassion. He must be generating such mental forces as are pure, cooling, luminous, light and pleasant—forces which normally settle down in the *brahmā* worlds. Let us now take the reverse case of a man who is dissatisfied or

angry. As the saying goes, "Face is the indication of mind": the impurity, heat, darkness, heaviness and wretchedness of his mind are immediately reflected in the person, visible even to the naked eye. This is due, I may say, to the generation of the evil mental forces of *dosa* (anger) which go down to the lower world of existence. The same is the case with the mental forces arising out of *lobha* (greed) or *moha* (delusion). In the case of meritorious deeds such as devotion, morality and charity which have, at their base, attachment to future wellbeing, the mental forces generated are those that will normally be located in the sensuous planes of *devas* and of mankind. These, ladies and gentlemen, are some of the concepts in Buddhism relevant to the life story of Gotama Buddha which I will presently begin.

Preparation

Gotama Buddha is the fourth of the five Buddhas to rise in the world cycle which is known as *bhadda-kappa*. His predecessors were Buddhas Kakusandha, Koṇāgamana and Kassapa. There were also innumerable Buddhas who had arisen in earlier *kappas* (ages) and who had preached the self-same Dhamma which gives deliverance from suffering and death to all matured beings. Buddhas are all compassionate, glorious and enlightened.

A hermit by the name of Sumedha was inspired by Buddha Dīpaṅkara; so much so, that he took the vow to make all the necessary preparations to become a Buddha in the course of time. Buddha Dīpaṅkara gave him his blessings and prophesied that he would become a Buddha by the name of Gotama. From then onwards, existence after existence, the *Bodhisatta*, i.e., would-be Buddha, conserved mental energies of the highest order through the practice of ten *pāramīs*, or virtues towards perfection, viz.:

1. *dāna*	(virtue in alms-giving)
2. *sīla*	(morality)
3. *nekkhamma*	(renunciation)
4. *paññā*	(wisdom)
5. *viriya*	(perseverance)
6. *khanti*	(forbearance)
7. *sacca*	(truthfulness)
8. *adhiṭṭhāna*	(determination)
9. *mettā*	(all-embracing love)
10. *upekkhā*	(equanimity)

It is, therefore, a most enduring task to become a Buddha. Utmost strength of will-power is necessary to even think of it. The **Bodhisatta's** preparatory period came to an end with the life of King Vessantara who excelled any living being in alms-giving. He gave away his kingdom, his wife and his children and all his worldly possessions, for the consummation of his solemn vow taken before the Dīpaṅkara Buddha. The next existence was in **Tusita** (one of the celestial planes) as glorious Setaketu Deva, until he got his release from that plane and took conception in the womb of Māyā Devi, the Queen of King Suddhodana of Kapilavatthu, a place near modern Nepal.

When the time was drawing nigh for her confinement, the Queen expressed her desire to go to the place of her own parents for the event. King Suddhodana accordingly sent her there with befitting retinues and guards. On the way, a halt was made at the Lumbinī *sāla* forest. She got down from the palanquin and enjoyed the cool breeze and fragrance of the *sāla* flowers. While holding out her right hand to a branch of the nearby *sāla* tree for a flower, all of a sudden and unexpectedly, she gave birth to a son who was to become the all-enlightened Buddha. Simultaneously, the natural order of things in the cosmos was revolutionized in many respects and thirty-two wonderful phenomena were vivified. All material

worlds were shaken from the foundation. There were unusual illuminations in the solar system. All the beings of material planes could see each other. The deaf and dumb were cured. Celestial music was heard everywhere, and so on.

At that moment, Kāḷa Devala, the hermit teacher of King Suddhodana, was having a discourse with celestial beings of **Tāvatiṃsa**. He was a hermit of fame who had mastery of the eight *samāpattis* (attainments) which gave him supernormal powers. Knowing of the birth of a son to the King due to the rejoicing in all the *rūpa* and *kāma* worlds, he hurried back to the palace and desired the baby to be brought before him for blessings. When the King placed the baby before his teacher for the occasion, Devala at once understood that the baby was no other than the embryo Buddha. He smiled at this knowledge but cried almost immediately thereafter, because he foresaw that he would not live to hear his teachings, and that even after his death he would be in the *arūpa brahmā loka* (immaterial plane of *brahmās*) whence he would have no relationship with any of the material planes. He missed the Buddha and his teachings miserably.

On the fifth day, the child was named Siddhattha in the presence of renowned astrologer-palmists who agreed that the child had all the characteristics of a Buddha to come. The mother Queen, however, died a week after confinement and the child was taken care of by his maternal aunt, Pajāpati Gotamī.

Siddhattha spent his early years of life in ease, luxury and culture. He was acclaimed to be a prodigy both in intellect and strength. The King spared no pains to make the course of his life smooth. Three separate palaces were built to suit three seasons with all the necessities that would make the Prince sink in sensuality. That was because the King, out of paternal affection, desired his son to remain in worldly life as a king rather than as an enlightened Buddha. The King Suddhodana was overly watchful that his son be in such environments as would give him no chance of higher philosophical ideas. In order to make sure that the thought of the Prince never turned in this direction, he ordered that nobody serving him or in his association was ever to speak a single word about such things as old age, sickness or death. They were to act as if there were no unpleasant things in this world. Servants and attendants who showed the least sign of becoming old, weak or sickly were replaced. On the other hand, dancing, music and enjoyable parties were held right through, to keep him under a complete shade of sensuality.

The Great Renunciation

As days, months and years passed, however, the monotony of the sensual surroundings gradually lost hold of the mind of Prince Siddhattha. The mental energies of virtue conserved in all his innumerable earlier lives for the great goal of Buddhahood were automatically aroused. At times, when the world of sensuality lost control over his mind, his inner self worked its way up and raised his mind to a state of purity and tranquillity with the strength of *samādhi*. The war of nerves began.

An escape from sensuality and passion was his first consideration. He wanted to know what existed outside the walls of the palace beyond which he had not even once visited. He wished to see nature as it is, and not as man has made it. Accordingly he decided to see the royal park, outside the palace walls. On the way to the park, in spite of precautions taken by the King to clear the roads of unpleasant sights, he saw in the very first visit an old man bent with age. Next he saw a sick person in the agony of a fatal malady.

Thereafter he encountered a human corpse. On the last trip he came across a monk.

All these set his mind to serious thinking. His mental attitude was changed. His mind became clear of impurities and tuned up with the forces of his own virtues conserved in the *saṅkhāra*

> He came to the realization of the perpetual change of mind and matter in himself (*anicca*) and as a sequel thereto, the truth of suffering (*dukkha*).

loka (plane of mental forces). By then his mind had become freed from hindrances, and was tranquil, pure and strong. It all happened on the night when a son had been born to his queen, a new fetter to bind him down. He was, however, immune from anything which would tend to upset the equilibrium of his mind. The virtues of determination worked their way towards a strong resolve, and he made up his mind to seek the way of escape from birth, old age, suffering and death. It was midnight when the solemn determination was made. He asked his attendant Channa to keep his stallion Kanthaka ready. After a parting look at his wife and the newly-born babe, Prince Siddhattha broke away from all the ties of family and of the world and made the Great Renunciation. He rode across the town to the river Anomā which he crossed, never to return until his mission had been achieved.

The Search for Truth

After this Great Renunciation, Prince Siddhattha went around in the garb of a wandering ascetic with a begging bowl in his hand in search of possible teachers. He placed himself under the spiritual guidance of two renowned brahmin teachers, Āḷāra and Uddaka. Āḷāra laid stress on the belief in *ātman* (soul) and taught that the soul attained perfect release when freed from material limitations. This did not satisfy the Prince. He next went to Uddaka who placed too much emphasis on the effect of *kamma* and the transmigration of soul. Both could not get out of the conception of "soul," and the Prince ascetic felt that there was something else to learn. He therefore left both of them to work out the way to emancipation on his own. By that time, of course, he had learned the eight *samāpattis* and had become an adept in the exercise of all supernormal powers, including the ability to read events of many *kappas* to come, as well as a similar period from the past. These were all in the mundane field and they did not much concern the Prince ascetic, whose ambition was an escape from this mundane field of birth, suffering and death.

He was later joined by five ascetics, one of whom (Koṇḍañña by name) was the astrologer-palmist who had foretold on the fifth day of his birth that Siddhattha would surely become a Buddha. These ascetics served him well throughout the six years, during which he was engaged in fasting and meditation, subjecting himself to various forms of rigorous austerities and discipline until he was reduced to almost a skeleton. One day, in fact, he fell down in a swoon through exhaustion. When he survived this condition, he changed his method, followed a middle course and found that the way for his enlightenment was clearer.

Attainment of Buddhahood

It was on the eve of the full moon of **Vesākha** [equivalent to the month of May] just 2,562 years ago, that Prince Siddhattha, wandering ascetic, sat cross-legged beneath a *bodhi* tree on the bank of the river Nerañjarā in the forest of Uruvelā (near present-day Bodh Gayā), with the strongest of determinations not to rise from that posture on any account until he gained the truth and enlightenment, the Buddhahood, even if the attempt might mean the loss of his very life.

The great event was approaching. The Prince ascetic mustered up all his strength of mind to secure that one-pointedness of mind which is so essential for the discovery of truth. The balancing of the mind, the Prince found on this occasion, was not so easy as hitherto. There was not only the combination of the mental forces of the lower planes with those of the higher planes all around him, but also interferences strong enough to upset, off and on, the equilibrium of his mind. The resistance of the impenetrable masses of forces against the radiation of the light normally secured by him was unusual (perhaps because it was a final bid for Buddhahood and Māra, the supreme controller of evil forces, was behind the scene). The Prince, however, worked his way through slowly but surely, backed up by the mental forces of virtues which must inevitably have come back to him at the right moment.

He made a vow and called upon all the *brahmās* and *devas* who had witnessed the fulfilment of his ten great perfections to join hands with him in the struggle for supremacy. This done, the association with the transcendingly pure mental forces of the *brahmās* and *devas* had a salutary

> Buddhism is not a religion. It is a system of philosophy coordinated with a code of morality, physical and mental. The goal in view is the extinction of suffering and death.

effect. The thick masses of forces, which seemed impenetrable, broke away; and with a steady improvement in the control over the mind, they were wiped out once and for all. All the hindrances having been overcome, the Prince was able to raise his power of concentration and put the mind into a state of complete purity, tranquillity and equanimity. Gradually, the consciousness of true insight possessed him. The solution to the vital problems which confronted him made its appearance in his consciousness as an inspiration. By introspective meditation on the realities of nature in his own self, it came vividly to him that there is no substantiality, as there seems to be, in the human body, and that it is nothing but the sum total of innumerable millions of *kalāpas* (subatomic particles), each about 1/46,656th part of a particle of dust from the wheel of a chariot in summer. On further investigation, he realized that this *kalāpa* also is matter in constant change or flux; and, similarly, that the mind is a representation of the mental forces (creative) going out and the mental forces (created) coming into the system of an individual continually and throughout eternity.

Buddha then proclaimed that his eye of wisdom had arisen when he got over the substantiality of his "own self." He saw by means of the lens of *samādhi* the *kalāpas* on which he next applied the law of *anicca* (impermanence), and reduced them to non-entity or habitual behaviour patterns—doing away with what we in Buddhism call *paññatti* (apparent truth); and coming to a state of *paramattha* (nature of forces) or, in other words, "ultimate reality."

Accordingly, he came to a realization of the perpetual change of mind and matter in himself (*anicca*) and as a sequel thereto, the truth of suffering (*dukkha*). It was then that the egocentrism in him broke down into the void and he got over to a stage beyond "suffering," i.e., *dukkha-nirodha* (the extinction of suffering) with no more traces of *attā* (attachment to self) left behind. "Mind and matter" were to him but empty phenomena which roll on forever, within the range of the law of cause and effect and the law of dependent origination. The truth was realized. The inherent qualities of embryo Buddha then developed, and complete enlightenment came to him by the dawn of the **Vesākha** day.

"Verily, Prince Siddhattha attained *sammā sambodhi* and became the Buddha, the Awakened One, the Enlightened One, the All-knowing One. He was awake in a way compared with which all others were asleep and dreaming. He was enlightened in a way compared with which all other men were stumbling and groping in the dark. His knowing was with the knowledge compared with which, what all other men know is but a kind of ignorance."

Ladies and gentlemen, I have taken so much of your time today. I thank you all for the patient listening. I must also thank the clergy of the church for their kind permission given to me for this address.

Lecture No. 2 (30 September 1951)

Last Sunday, I gave you a brief outline—a very brief one, too—of the life of our Lord Buddha up to the moment of his attainment of Buddhahood. I am going to tell you today what his teachings are.

Buddhist teachings are preserved in what we call the *Tipiṭakas,* consisting of *Suttas* (discourses), *Vinaya* (laws of discipline for the Sangha (monks) and *Abhidhamma* (philosophical teachings). We have the *Tipiṭakas* in Pāli in several volumes which will require an intelligent Pāli scholar some months just to read through. I propose, therefore, to confine myself today only to essentials, i.e., the fundamental truths of Buddhism.

Before Lord Buddha took upon himself the task of spreading the Dhamma, he remained in silent meditation for a continuous period of forty-nine days—seven days under the *bodhi* tree, and seven days each in six other spots

> Pleasure born of sensuality is nothing compared with the *pīti* (rapture) born of the inner peace of mind which can be secured through a process of Buddhist meditation.

nearby, enjoying from time to time the peace of supreme *nibbāna* and at other times going deeper, in investigation, into the most delicate problems of *paramattha dhamma* (ultimate realities). On the complete mastery of the law of *paṭṭhāna* (the law of relations) in which infinite modes of relations between thought-moments are dealt with, there emerged from his body brilliant rays in six colours, which eventually settled down as a halo of six coloured rays around his head. He passed these seven-times-seven days of meditation without food. It is beyond us all to be without food for forty-nine days. The fact remains that throughout the period he was on a mental plane, as distinct from the physical plane wherein mankind normally resides. It is not the material food that maintains the fine material and life continūm of beings in the fine material worlds of *brahmās,* but the *jhānic pīti* (rapture arising from deep meditation), which in itself is a nutriment. This was the case with the Buddha whose existence during this long period was on a mental rather than physical plane. Our experiments in this line of research have firmly convinced us that for a man of such high intellectual and mental development as the Buddha, this is a possibility.

It was at daybreak on the fiftieth day of his Buddhahood when he arose from this long spell of meditation. Not that he was tired or exhausted, but, as he was no longer in the mental plane, he felt a longing for food. At that time, two traders from a foreign land were travelling in several carts loaded with merchandise through the Uruvelā forest. A *deva* of the forest who was their relative in one of the previous existences advised them to take the opportunity of paying homage to the all-enlightened Buddha who had just arisen from his meditation. They accordingly went to the place where the Buddha was seated, illumined by the halo of six coloured rays. They could not resist their feelings. They lay prostrate in worship and adoration before Buddha and later offered preserved rice cakes with honey for the first meal of the Buddha. They were accepted as his lay disciples. Upon requesting that they might be given some tokens for their worship, Buddha presented them with eight strands of hair from his head.

You will be surprised to know that these two traders were Tapussa and Bhallika of Okkalāpa, which today is known as Rangoon where you are at this moment. And the renowned Shwedagon, which you have all probably visited, is the pagoda in which was enshrined all the eight hair relics of Buddha under the personal direction of the then ruler of Okkalāpa, 2,540 years ago. It has been preserved and renovated until now by successive Buddhist kings and devotees. Unfortunately, however, these two traders of Okkalāpa, who had the privilege of becoming the first lay disciples of the Buddha, were disciples only by faith, without a taste of the Buddha Dhamma in actual practice which alone could give them deliverance from suffering and death. Faith is, no doubt, a preliminary requisite; but it is the practice of the teachings which really counts. The Buddha therefore said:

> The path must be trodden by each individual; Buddhas do but point the way.

Teachings of Buddha

Buddhism is not a religion according to its dictionary meaning because it has no centre in God, as is the case in all other religions. Strictly speaking, Buddhism is a system of philosophy coordinated with a code of morality, physical and mental. The goal in view is the extinction of suffering and death.

The Four Noble Truths taught by the Buddha in his first sermon known as **Dhamma-cakka-pavattana Sutta** (the discourse to set in motion the Wheel of Dhamma) form the basis on which is founded this system of philosophy. In fact, the first three of the Four Noble Truths expound the philosophy of Buddha while the fourth (the

Eightfold Noble Path, which is a code of morality-cum-philosophy) serves as a means for the end. This first sermon was given to the five ascetics, led by Koṇḍañña, who were his early companions in search of truth. Koṇḍañña was the first disciple of the Buddha to practise to become an *arahat* (a holy one gone beyond the limitations of all fetters).

Now we come to the Four Noble Truths. They are as follows:

1. *dukkha-sacca* (truth of suffering)
2. *samudaya-sacca* (truth of the origin of suffering)
3. *nirodha-sacca* (truth of the extinction of suffering)
4. *magga-sacca* (truth of the path leading to the extinction of suffering).

To come to a complete understanding of the fundamental concepts in the philosophy of Buddha, emphasis is laid on the need for the realization of the truth of suffering. To bring home this point, Lord Buddha tackled the problem from two different angles.

First, by a process of reasoning, he made his disciples understand that life is a struggle. Life is suffering; birth is suffering; old age is suffering; illness is suffering; death is suffering. The influence of sensuality, however, is so strong in mankind that they are normally apt to forget themselves, to forget what they will have to pay thereby. Just think for a moment how life exists in the prenatal period; how from the moment of birth the child has to struggle for existence; what preparations he has to make to face life; what he has to struggle with as a man until he breathes his last.

You can very well imagine what life is. Life is indeed suffering.

The more one is attached to self, the greater is the suffering. In fact, what pains and sufferings a man has to undergo are suppressed in favour of momentary sensual pleasures, which are but occasional spotlights in darkness. But for the *moha* (delusion), which keeps him away from the truth, he surely would have worked out his way for emancipation from the rounds of life, suffering and death.

Secondly, the Buddha made it known to his disciples that the human body is composed of *kalāpas* (subatomic units), each dying out simultaneously as it arises. Each *kalāpa* is a mass formed of the following nature-elements:

1. *paṭhavī* extension (lit., earth)
2. *āpo* cohesion (lit., water)
3. *tejo* radiation (lit., heat and cold)
4. *vāyo* motion (lit., air)
5. *vaṇṇo* colour
6. *gandho* smell
7. *raso* taste
8. *ojā* nutritive essence

The first four are called *mahā-bhūtas*, i.e., essential material qualities which are predominant in a *kalāpa*. The other four are merely subsidiaries which are dependent upon and born out of the former. A *kalāpa* is the minutest particle noticeable in the physical plane. It is only when the eight nature-elements (which have merely a characteristic of behaviour) are together that the entity of a *kalāpa* is formed. In other words, the coexistence of these eight nature-elements of behaviour makes a mass, which in Buddhism is known as a *kalāpa*. These *kalāpas*, according to the Buddha, are in a state of perpetual change or flux. They are nothing but a stream of energies, just like the light of a candle or an electric bulb. The body (as we call it), is not an entity as it seems to be, but is a continuum of matter and life-force coexisting.

To a casual observer a piece of iron is motionless. The scientist knows that it is composed of electrons all in a state of perpetual change or flux. If this is so with a piece of iron, what will be the case with a living organism, say a human being? The changes taking place inside a human body must be more violent. Does man feel the rocking vibrations within himself? Does the scientist who knows that all the electrons are in a perpetual state of change or flux ever feel that his own body is but energy and vibration? What will be the repercussion on the mental attitude of the man who introspectively sees that his own body is mere energy and vibration?

To quench thirst one may easily just drink a glass of water from a village well. Supposing his eyes are as powerful as microscopes, he would surely hesitate to drink the very same water in which he must see the magnified microbes. Similarly, when one comes to the realization of perpetual change within himself (*anicca*—impermanence), he must come to the understanding, as a sequel thereto, of the truth of suffering as a consequence of the sharp sense of feeling the radiation, vibration and friction of the atomic units within. Indeed life is suffering, both within and without, to all appearances and in ultimate reality.

When I say "life is suffering," as the Buddha taught, please be so good as not to run away with the idea that, if it is so, life is miserable, life is not worth living and the Buddhist concept of suffering is a terrible concept which will give you no chance of a reasonably happy life. What is happiness? For all that science has achieved in the field of materialism, are the peoples of the world happy? They may find sensual pleasures off and on, but in their heart of hearts they are not happy when they realize what has happened, what is happening and what may happen next. Why? This is because, while man has mastery of matter, he is still lacking in mastery over his mind.

Pleasure born of sensuality is nothing compared with the *pīti* (rapture) born of the inner peace of mind which can be secured through a process of Buddhist meditation. Sense pleasures are preceded and followed by troubles and pains as in the case of a rustic who finds pleasure in cautiously scratching the itches over his body, whereas *pīti* is free from such troubles and pains either way. Looking from a sensual field, it will be difficult for you to appreciate what that *pīti* is like. But, I know, you can also enjoy and have a taste of it for comparative valuation. There is therefore nothing to suppose that Buddhism teaches something which will make you feel miserable with the nightmare of suffering. But please take it from me that it will give you an escape from the normal conditions of life, a lotus as it were, in a pond of crystal water, immune from its fiery surroundings. It will give you that "peace within" which will satisfy you that you are getting beyond not only the day-to-day troubles of life, but slowly and surely beyond the limitation of life, suffering and death.

What, then, is the origin of suffering? The origin of it, the Buddha said, is *taṇhā* (craving). Once the seed of desire is sown, it grows into greed and multiplies into craving or lust, either for power or material gains. The man in whom this seed is sown becomes a slave to these cravings; and he is automatically driven to strenuous labours of mind and body to keep pace with them until the end comes. The final result must surely be the accumulation of the evil mental force generated by his own actions, words and thoughts which are motivated by the *lobha* (desire) and *dosa* (aversion) inherent in him.

Philosophically speaking again, it is the mental forces of actions (*saṅkhāra*) which react in the course of time on the person originating them, which are responsible for the stream of mind and matter, the origin of suffering within.

Path Leading to the Extinction of Suffering

What, then, is the path leading to the extinction of suffering? The path is none other than the Noble Eightfold Path taught by the Buddha in his first sermon. This Eightfold Path is divided into three main stages, namely: *sīla, samādhi* and *paññā*.

Sīla (precept)

1. right speech
2. right action
3. right livelihood

Samādhi (concentration of mind)

4. right exertion
5. right attentiveness
6. right concentration

Paññā (wisdom-insight)

7. right aspiration
8. right understanding

Sīla

The three characteristic aspects of *sīla* are as follows:

1. *sammā-vācā*   (right speech)
2. *sammā-kammanta* (right action)
3. *sammā-ājīva*   (right livelihood)

By right speech is meant: speech which must be true, beneficial and neither foul nor malicious.

By right action is meant: fundamentals of morality which are opposed to killing, stealing, sexual misconduct and drunkenness.

By right livelihood is meant: ways of living by trades other than those which increase the suffering of all beings (such as slave trading, the manufacturing of weapons, and traffic in intoxicating drugs).

These represent generally the code of morality as initially pronounced by the Buddha in his very first sermon. Later, however, he amplified it and introduced separate codes for monks and lay disciples.

I need not worry you with what has been prescribed for monks. I will just let you know what the code of morality (the precepts for a Buddhist lay disciple) is. This is called the **Pañca Sīla** (Five Precepts). They are:

1. *pāṇātipātā*—abstention from killing any sentient beings. (Life is the most precious for all beings; and in prescribing this, Buddha's compassion extends to all beings.)

2. *adinnādānā*—abstention from taking what is not given. (This serves as a check against improper desire for possessions.)

3. *kāmesu-micchācāra*—abstention from sexual misconduct. (Sexual desire is dormant in man. It is irresistible to almost all. Unlawful sexual indulgence is therefore one which the Buddha prohibited.)

4. *musāvādā*—abstention from telling lies. (This precept is included to fulfil, by the way of speech, the essence of truth.)

5. *surāmeraya*—abstention from intoxication. (Intoxication causes a man to lose his steadfastness of mind and reasoning power so essential for the realization of truth.)

The **Pañca Sīla** are therefore intended to control actions and words and to serve as a foundation for *samādhi* (concentration of mind).

Samādhi

Ladies and gentlemen, we now come to the mental aspect of Buddhism which I'm sure will greatly interest you. In the second stage of the Eightfold Noble Path (that is, *samādhi*) are included:

1. *sammā-vāyāma*   (right exertion)
2. *sammā-sati*   (right attentiveness)
3. *sammā-samādhi*   (right concentration)

Right exertion is of course the prerequisite for right attentiveness. Unless one makes a concerted effort to narrow down the range of thoughts of his wavering and unsteady mind, he cannot expect to secure that attentiveness of mind which in turn helps him bring the mind by right concentration to a state of one-pointedness and equanimity. It is here that the mind becomes freed from hindrances, pure and tranquil; illumined within and without. The mind in such a state becomes powerful and bright. Outside, it is represented by light which is just a mental reflex, with the light varying in degrees from that of a star to that of the sun. To be plain, this light which is reflected before the mind's eye in complete darkness is a manifestation of the purity, tranquillity and serenity of mind.

The Hindus work for it. To go from light into the void and come back to it, is truly **Brāhmanic**. The New Testament, in Matthew, speaks of "body full of light." We also hear of Roman Catholic priests meditating regularly for this very miraculous light. The holy Qur'an, too, gives prominence to the "manifestation of divine light."

This mental reflex of light denotes the purity of mind within, and the purity of mind forms the essence of a religious life whether one be a Buddhist, Hindu, Christian or Muslim. Indeed the purity of mind is the greatest common denominator of all religions. Love, which alone is the means for the unity of mankind, must be supreme, and it cannot be so unless the mind is transcendently pure. A balanced mind is necessary to balance the unbalanced minds of others: "As a fletcher makes straight his arrow, a wise man makes straight his trembling and unsteady thought, which is difficult to guard, difficult to hold back." So said the Buddha. Exercise of mind is as necessary as exercise of the physical body. Why not, then, give exercise to mind and make it strong and pure so that you may enjoy the *jhānic* peace within? When inner peace begins to permeate the mind, you will surely progress in the knowledge of truth.

> It is our experience that under a proper guide, this inner peace and purity of mind can be secured by one and all, irrespective of their religion or creed.

Believe it or not, it is our experience that under a proper guide, this inner peace and purity of mind can be secured by one and all, irrespective of their religion or creed, providing they have sincerity of purpose and are prepared to submit to the guide for the period of trial.

When by continued practice, one has complete mastery over his mind, he can enter into *jhānic* states (meditative states of deep absorption) and gradually develop himself to acquire *samāpattis* (attainments) which will give him supernormal powers the same as those exercised by Kāḷa-Devala, the hermit teacher of King Suddhodana. This, of course, must be tried in penance and away from human habitations, but is rather dangerous for those who still have traces of passion in them. Anyway, such a practice, which gives supernormal powers in this mundane field, was not encouraged by Buddha, whose sole object of developing *samādhi* was to have the purity and strength of mind essential for the realization of truth. We have in Buddhism forty different methods of concentration of which the most outstanding is Anapana, i.e., concentration on the incoming and outgoing breath, the method followed by all Buddhas.

Paññā

Ladies and gentlemen, I will now take up the philosophical aspect of Buddhism in the third stage of the Noble Eightfold Path: *paññā* (insight).

The two characteristic aspects of *paññā* are:

1. *sammā-saṅkappa* (right aspiration)
2. *sammā-diṭṭhi* (right understanding)

Right understanding of the truth is the aim and object of Buddhism. Right aspiration is the analytical study of mind and matter, both within and without, in order to come to the realization of truth.

You have heard of *nāma* and *rūpa* (mind and matter) so many times, I owe you a further explanation.

Nāma is so called because of its tendency to incline towards an object of the senses. *Rūpa* is so called because of its impermanence due to perpetual change. The nearest terms in English to *nāma* and *rūpa* therefore are mind and matter. I say "nearest" because the meaning is not exact.

Nāma, strictly speaking, is the term applied to the following:

1. consciousness (*viññāṇa*)
2. feeling (*vedanā*)
3. perception (*saññā*)
4. volitional energies (*saṅkhāra*)

These together with *rūpa* in the material state make what we call the *pañca-khandhas* (five aggregates). It is with the five aggregates that the Buddha summed up all the mental and physical phenomena of existence (which in reality is a continūm of mind and matter coexisting, but which to a layman is his personality or ego).

In *sammā-saṅkappa* (right aspiration), the disciple who, by then, has developed the powerful lens of *samādhi,* focuses his attention into his own self and by introspective meditation makes an analytical study of the nature: first, of *rūpa* (matter) and then of *nāma* (mind and mental properties). He feels (and at times he also sees) the *kalāpas* in their true state. He begins to realize that both *rūpa* and *nāma* are in a constant state of change—impermanent and fleeting. As his power of concentration increases, the nature of forces in him becomes more and more vivified. He can no longer get out of the impression that the *pañca khandhas* (five aggregates) are suffering within the law of cause and effect. He is now convinced that, in reality, all is suffering within and without, and that there is nothing such as ego. He longs for a state beyond suffering. So eventually getting out of the bonds of suffering, he moves from the mundane to the supramundane state and enters the stream of *sotāpanna,* the first of the four stages of *ariyas* (noble ones). Then he becomes free from: (1) ego; (2) doubts; (3) attachment to rules and rituals. The second stage is *sakadāgāmi,* on coming to which, sensuous craving and ill will become attenuated. He

ceases to have any passion or anger when he reaches the third stage of *anāgāmi.* The stage of *arahat* is the final goal.

Each of the *ariyas* can feel what *nibbāna* is like, even as a human being, for any number of times as he may choose, by going into the fruition stage of *sotāpanna,* etc., which gives him the *nibbānic* peace within.

This peace within which is identified with *nibbāna* has no parallel because it is supramundane. Compared to this, the *jhānic* peace within (which I mentioned earlier in dealing with *samādhi*) is negligible because, while the *nibbānic* peace within takes one beyond the thirty-one planes of existence, the *jhānic* peace within will still keep him within these planes—for example, in the fine material world of the *brahmās.*

Ladies and gentlemen, just a word more. What I have said here are just some of the fundamental aspects of Buddhism. With the time at my disposal, I hope I have given you my best.

To come to a state of purity of mind with a light before you; to go to the *jhānic* state at will; to experience, for yourselves, *nibbānic* peace within: these are all within your reach.

Why not, then, try for the first two at least which are within the confines of your own religion? I am prepared to give any help that you may require.

May I again express my gratitude to you all for the patient listening.

Lecture No. 3 (14 October 1951)

My talk on "What Buddhism Is" will not be complete without a reference, though in brief, to the law of *paṭicca samuppāda* (the Law of Dependent Origination) and the law of *paṭṭhāna* (the law of relations, or cause and effect).

It will be recalled that in summing up my first lecture, I mentioned how Prince Siddhattha, the wandering ascetic, realized the truth and became Buddha. Lest you forget, I will repeat that portion again.

"Verily, Prince Siddhattha attained *sammā sambodhi* and became Buddha, the Awakened One, the Enlightened One, the All-knowing One. He was awake in a way compared with which all others were asleep and dreaming. He was enlightened in a way compared with which all other men were stumbling and groping in the dark. His knowing was with the knowledge compared with which, what all other men know is but a kind of ignorance."

All religions, no doubt, claim to show the way to truth. In Buddhism, as long as one has not realized the truth, i.e., the Four Noble Truths, he is in ignorance. It is this ignorance (*avijjā*) that is responsible for the generation of mental forces (*saṅkhāra*) which regulate the life continūm (*viññāṇa*) in all sentient beings. Just as the life continūm is established in a new existence, mind and matter (*nāma* and *rūpa*) appear automatically and correlatively. These, in turn, are developed into a vehicle or body with sense centres (*saḷāyatanā*).

These sense centres give rise to contact (*phassa*); and the contact of these sense centres with sense objects gives rise to sense impressions [sensations] (*vedanā*) which have the effect of arousing desire (*taṇhā*) followed closely by attachment or clinging to desire (*upādāna*). It is this attachment or clinging to desire which is the

cause of becoming (*bhava*) or existence, with the attendant birth, old age, illness, death, anxiety, agony, pains, etc., all of which denote "suffering." In this way Buddha traced the origin of suffering to ignorance.

The Buddha said:

> Ignorance is the origin of mental forces; mental forces, the origin of the life continūm; life continūm, the origin of mind and matter; mind and matter, the origin of sense centres; sense centres, the origin of contact; contact, the origin of impression [sensation]; impression [sensation], the origin of desire; desire, the origin of attachment; attachment, the origin of becoming (existence); becoming (existence), the origin of birth; birth, the origin of old age, illness, death, anxiety, agony, pains, etc. (which are all suffering).

This chain of origination is called the Law of Dependent Origination. The root cause for all these is therefore *avijjā* or ignorance, i.e., ignorance of the truth. It is true superficially that desire is the origin of suffering. This is so simple. When you want a thing, desire is aroused. You have to work for it or you suffer for it. But this is not enough. The Buddha said, "The five aggregates which are nothing but mind and matter also are suffering." The truth of suffering in Buddhism is complete only when one realizes the truth by seeing mind and matter as they really are (both within and without) and not as they seem to be.

The truth of suffering is therefore something which must be experienced before it can be understood. For example, we all know from science that everything that exists is nothing but vibration caused by the whirling movement of an infinite number of electrons. But how many of us can persuade ourselves to believe that our own bodies are subject to the same law? Why not then try to feel them as they really are, in so far as it relates to yourself? One must be above the mere physical condition for this purpose. He must develop mental energy powerful enough to see things in their true state. With developed mental power, one can see through-and-through, more than what one can see with the help of the latest scientific instruments. If that be so, why should one not see what is happening precisely in his own self—the atoms, the electrons and whatnot—all changing fast and yet never ending. It is, of course, by no means easy.

In reality our "suffering within" is a sequel to the keen sense of feeling the vibration, radiation and friction of the atomic units experienced through the process of introspective meditation called Vipassana, with the aid of the powerful lens of *samādhi*. Not knowing this truth is indeed ignorance. Knowing this truth in its ultimate reality means destruction of the root cause of suffering: that is, ignorance, with all the links in the chain of causation ending with what we call "life," with its characteristics of old age, illness, anxiety, agony, pains, and so on.

So much for the Law of Dependent Origination and the root cause of suffering.

Let us now turn our attention to the causal law of relations as expounded by the Buddha in the law of *Paṭṭhāna* of the **Abhidhamma Piṭaka**. This is the law, in the course of the analytical study of which, six coloured rays emerged from the person of Buddha during his uninterrupted meditation for forty-nine days (soon after the attainment of Buddhahood). We have five volumes of about five hundred pages of Pāli text on this very delicate subject. I will give here only just an idea of the law.

There are twenty-four types of relations on which the fundamental principles of cause and effect in Buddhism are based. These are as follows:

1. condition (*hetu*)
2. object (*ārammaṇa*)
3. dominance (*adhipati*)
4. contiguity (*anantara*)
5. immediate contiguity (*samanantara*)
6. coexistence (*sahajāta*)
7. reciprocity (*aññamañña*)
8. dependence (*nissaya*)
9. sufficing condition (*upanissaya*)
10. antecedence (*purejāta*)
11. consequence (*pacchājāta*)
12. succession (*āsevana*)
13. action (*kamma*)
14. effect (*vipāka*)
15. support (*āhāra*)
16. control (*indriya*)
17. ecstasy (*jhāna*)
18. means (*magga*)
19. association (*sampayutta*)
20. dissociation (*vippayutta*)
21. presence (*atthi*)
22. absence (*natthi*)
23. abeyance (*vigata*)
24. continuance (*avigata*)

I will explain to you now about the correlation of *hetu* (condition) and *kamma* (action) and the effect produced by their causes as I understand them.

Hetu is the condition of the mind at one conscious moment of each *kamma* action, whether physical, vocal or mental. Each *kamma* therefore produces a condition of mind which is either moral, immoral or neutral. This is what in Buddhism we call *kusala dhamma, akusala dhamma and abyākata dhamma*. These *dhammas* are mere forces (i.e., mental forces), which collectively create the universe of mental forces.

Moral *(kusala)* forces are positive forces generated from *kammas* (actions, words and thoughts) motivated by such good deeds as alms-giving, welfare work, devotion, purification of mind, and so on.

Immoral *(akusala)* forces are negative forces generated from *kammas* (actions, words and thoughts) motivated by desire, greed, lust, anger, hatred, dissatisfaction, delusion, and so on.

Neutral *(abyākata)* forces are neither moral nor immoral, as in the case of an *arahat* who has got rid of all traces of ignorance *(avijjā)*. In the case of an *arahat*, contact *(phassa)* of sense objects with sense centres produces no sense impressions *(vedanā)* whatsoever, just as no impression is possible on flowing water which is ever-changing. To him, the whole framework of the body is but an ever-changing mass and any impression thereon automatically breaks away with the mass.

Let us now address the moral and immoral forces generated by conditioned actions with the planes of existence. For this purpose, I will classify the planes of existence roughly as follows:

Arūpa and *Rūpa Brahmā* Planes

These are beyond the range of sensuality. Supreme love, supreme compassion, supreme joy at the success and greatness of others, and supreme equanimity of mind are the four qualities of mind which generate transcendently pure, brilliant and extremely pleasing, cool and light mental forces which find their location in the highest of the planes of existence. This is the reason why in these planes matter is superfine and there is nothing but radiance. The vehicles or bodies of the *brahmās* cannot be identified with matter, but with radiation or light.

Sensuous Planes

These consist of:

1. planes of celestial beings
2. human world
3. planes of lower forms of existence

Planes of Celestial Beings

All good or meritorious deeds, words or thoughts which have a taint of desire for future well-being create moral mental forces which are considerably pure, luminous, pleasant and light. These find their location in the higher planes of celestial beings where matter is fine, luminous, pleasant and light. These celestial beings therefore have astral bodies varying in fineness, luminosity and colour according to the planes to which they belong. Ordinarily they live in heavenly bliss until their own moral mental forces are consumed; then they revert to the lower planes of existence.

Planes of the Lower Forms of Existence

(I will come to the human world last.)

All malicious, evil, demeritorious actions, words and thoughts create mental forces which are by nature impure, dark, fiery, heavy and hard. The most impure, dark, fiery, heavy and hard mental forces should therefore find their place in hell, the lowest of the four planes of existence.

The matter in these planes must therefore be hard, crude, unpleasant and hot. The human world is just above the concentration of these forces, which are meant for consumption (to be experienced) by those beings destined for the lower forms of existence. These beings, with the exception of those in the animal world, are invisible to the ordinary human eye but visible to those who have developed the higher powers of *samādhi* and secured the divine eye. Here suffering—both physical and mental—predominates. This is just the reverse of what happens in the planes of celestial beings.

Human World

Now I come to the human world, this half-way house between heaven and hell. We experience pleasure and pain mixed together in degrees, as determined by our own past *kamma*. From here, we can, by developing our mental attitude, draw in our own mental forces from the higher planes. It is also from here that we can go down to the depths of depravity and tune up with the forces of the lower order.

There is no such constancy as in the other planes of existence. One may be a saint today, but he can be a rogue thereafter. He may be rich today, but he may soon become poor. The vicissitudes of life here are very conspicuous. There is no man who is stable, no family which is stable, no community which is stable, no nation which is stable.

All are subject to the law of *kamma*. As this *kamma* comes out of "mind" which is ever-changing, the effects of *kamma* must necessarily also be changing.

As long as man has inherent impurities in him and dies with the mental attitude tuned up with the mental forces of a plane of lower existence; then, at the last moment of his death, the next existence is automatically in that lower plane (to clear, one might say, his debit account of mental forces there).

On the other hand if, at the moment of death, his mental attitude is associated with the forces in the human world, the next existence can be in the human world again. If, however, his mental attitude at the last moment of death is associated with the reminiscence of his good deeds, the next existence will normally be in the celestial world (where one enjoys the credit balance of his own mental forces in that plane). One goes to the *brahmā* world, if at the moment of death his mind is not sensual, but is pure and tranquil.

This is how *kamma* plays its role in Buddhism with mathematical precision.

These, ladies and gentlemen, are the essential teachings of Buddha. How these teachings affect the individual depends on how one takes them.

The same applies to the family, the community or the people in general. We have Buddhists in faith and Buddhists in practice. Yet there is another class of Buddhists who are simply labelled "Buddhists" at birth. Only Buddhists in actual practice can secure the change in mental attitude and outlook. Let them only observe the five precepts; they are the followers of the teachings of Buddha. If this were followed by all the Buddhists in Burma, there would be no internecine strife such as we are having here in Burma. But there is another disturbing factor: that is, the bodily requirements. One must have the bare necessities of life. Life is more precious to him than anything else. The tendency therefore is to break the laws of discipline, whether religious or governmental, for one's self-preservation and for the preservation of others depending on him.

What is most essential is the generation of pure and good mental forces to combat the evil mental forces which dominate mankind. This is by no means easy. One cannot rise to the level of pure mental attitude without the help of a teacher. If we want effective power to combat these forces, we must work for it according to Dhamma. Modern science has given us, for what it is worth, the atomic bomb, the most wonderful and yet at the same time the most dreadful product of man's intelligence. Is man using his intelligence in the right direction? Is he creating good or bad mental forces, according to the spirit of Buddhism? It is our will that decides how and upon what subject we shall use intelligence. Instead of using intelligence only for the conquest of atomic energy in matter without, why not use it also for the conquest of atomic energy within?

This will give us the "peace within" and enable us to share it with all others. We will then radiate such powerful and purified mental forces as will successfully counteract the evil forces which are all around us. Just as the light of a single candle has the power to dispel darkness in a room, so also the light developed in one man can help dispel the darkness in several others.

To imagine that good can be done by the means of evil is an illusion, a nightmare. The case in point is that of Korea. For all the loss of lives on both sides, now over one million, are we nearer to, or further away, from peace? These are the lessons which we have learned. Change of mankind's mental attitude through religion alone is the solution. What is necessary at the moment is mastery over the mind and not only mastery over matter.

In Buddhism we differentiate between *loka dhātu* and *dhamma dhātu*. By *dhātu* is meant the nature-elements or forces. *Loka dhātu* is therefore matter (with its nature-elements) within the range of the physical plane. *Dhamma dhātu*, however, comprises mind, mental properties and some aspects of nature-elements which are not in the physical but in the mental plane. Modern science deals with what we call *loka dhātu*. It is just a base for *dhamma dhātu* in the mental plane. A step further and we come to the mental plane; not with the knowledge of modern science, but with the knowledge of Buddha-Dhamma in practice.

At least Mr. H. Overstreet, author of *The Mature Mind* (W.W. Norton & Co., Inc., New York) is optimistic about what is in store for mature minds. He writes:

> The characteristic knowledge of our century is psychological. Even the most dramatic advances in physics and chemistry are chiefly applications of known methods of research. But the attitude toward human nature and human experience that has come in our time is new.

This attitude could not have come earlier. Before it came, there had to be long preparation. Physiology had to be a developed science; for the psychological person is also physiological. His makeup, among other things, is a matter of brain tissue, of nerves, of glands, of organs of touch, smell and sight. It was not until about seventy years ago that physiology was sufficiently developed to make psycho-physical research possible, as in the laboratories of the distinguished German psychologist, William Wundt. But before physiology there had to be a developed science of biology. Since brain, nerves, glands and the rest depend upon all processes, the science of the living cell had to have its maturing before a competent physiology could emerge.

But before biology, there had to be chemistry; and before chemistry, physics; and before physics, mathematics. So the long preparation goes back into the centuries.

There is, in short, a time clock of science. Each science has to wait until its hour strikes. Today, at least, the time clock of science strikes the hours of psychology, and a new enlightenment begins.

To be sure, the interests explored by this latest of the sciences are themselves old; but the accuracy of research is new. There is, in brief, a kind of iron logic that is in control. Each science has to wait for its peculiar accuracy until its predecessor has supplied the data and tools out of which its accuracy can be made.

The time clock of science has struck a new hour: a new insight begins to be at our service.

May I say that it is the Buddha-Dhamma which should be studied by one and all for a new insight into the realities of human nature. In Buddhism we have the cure for all the mental ills that affect mankind. It is the evil forces of the mind, past and present, that are responsible for the present state of affairs all over the world.

Nowadays, there is dissatisfaction almost everywhere. Dissatisfaction creates ill feeling. Ill feeling creates hatred. Hatred creates enmity. Enmity creates war. War creates enemies. Enemies create war. War creates enemies, and so on. It is now getting into a vicious cycle. Why? Certainly because there is lack of proper control over the mind.

What is man? Man is after all mental forces personified. What is matter? Matter is nothing but mental forces materialized, a result of the reaction of the moral (positive) and immoral (negative) forces.

Buddha said: Cittena niyate loko (the world is mind-made). Mind therefore predominates everything. Let us then study the mind and its peculiar characteristics and solve the problem that is now facing the world.

There is a great field for practical research in Buddhism. Buddhists in Burma will always welcome whoever is anxious to have the benefit of their experience.

Ladies and gentlemen, I have made an attempt to give you the best of what I know about Buddhism. I shall be glad to give any interested person further explanation on any point that he may wish to discuss. I am grateful to you for the kind attendance and the interest taken in my lectures. May I again thank the clergy of the church for the permission so kindly given for this series of lectures.

Peace to all beings.

The depth of my profound respect and feeling of gratitude towards Gotama Buddha, the master teacher, the Dhamma, his teaching universal, and the Sangha, who have preserved the teachings and followed them, is unfathomable.

—S. N. Goenka

The Real Values of True Buddhist Meditation

by Thray Sithu Sayagyi U Ba Khin

In December 1961, the Prime Minister of the State of Israel, David Ben Gurion, visited Burma. A delegation of Israeli press representatives also came to Burma to report on this event. Sayagyi was invited to address a gathering of these journalists, who were invited to tea at the International Meditation Centre. Those who attended the talk were already acquainted with the booklet "What Buddhism Is" by Sayagyi. From discussions with one of the journalists prior to the talk, Sayagyi concluded that the Israelis were more interested in the present values of Buddhist meditation than in what would be gained in an afterlife. Accordingly, he named his paper "The Real Values of True Buddhist Meditation," and drew from the wealth of his own personal experiences, and those of his students, to illustrate this point. Included was an extensive set of charts, graphs and examples drawn from Sayagyi's active career in government service, demonstrating the productive potential of a calm and balanced mind. Presented here is the slightly abridged introductory portion of the paper, which was published by the Buddha Sāsana Council Press, Rangoon, in 1962.

Preface

Man needs rest and peace of mind, which means and includes living a full life. The best means of attaining the real peace of mind is meditation.

The main object of Buddhist meditation is the realization of the ultimate goal of life leading to nirvana. Experience, however, proves that the process of meditation inevitably involves the importance of the two aspects of present-day life, namely, acquisition of mental equilibrium and of physical fitness.

A man who has undergone courses of Buddhist meditation is able to make quick decisions, correct and sound judgment and concerted effort—mental capabilities which definitely contribute to success in life. And at the same time, by the same process of purification of mind, the physical body becomes cleansed and physical fitness is ensured. To attain these objectives, the correct method or technique of meditation is essential.

Herein lies the simple and yet efficient technique of U Ba Khin, who is the founder of the International Meditation Centre, which is, so far as experience goes, one of the best of all meditation centres.

Those who are willing to enjoy a full life involving mental bliss of peace and physical well-being without, of course, dedicating themselves to self [importance], are well-advised to visit the centre and take a course under his guidance.

—Lun Baw
Chairman, Public Service Commission, Burma

The Foundation of a Buddhist

A Buddhist is a person who takes refuge in the Buddha, the Dhamma and the Saṅgha.

We have four categories of Buddhists, namely:

1. *bhaya* (a Buddhist because of danger);

2. *lābha* (a Buddhist because of need for gratification);

3. *kula* (a Buddhist because of birth);

4. *saddhā* (a Buddhist because of faith).

Buddhists may be further divided into two classes, namely:

1. those who intend to make a bid for release in this very life;

2. those who are just accumulating the virtues (*pāramī*) with a view to becoming:

a) **Buddha** (enlightened person; one who has discovered the way to liberation, has practised it, and has reached the goal by his own efforts);

b) **Pacceka Buddha** ("lone" or "silent" Buddha, who is unable to teach the way he has found to others);

c) *agga sāvaka* (chief disciples);

d) *mahā sāvaka* (leading disciples);

e) *arahat* (liberated being; one who has destroyed all his mental impurities)

For the consummation of the vow to become a Buddha, *pacceka* Buddha, and so on, the length of time that is required for the accumulation of virtues is roughly:

1. For

(a) **Viriyādhika Buddha**: sixteen *asaṅkheyyas* and one hundred thousand *kappas* (world cycles).

(b) **Saddhādhika Buddha**: eight *asaṅkheyyas* and one hundred thousand *kappas*.

(c) **Paññādhika Buddha**: four *asaṅkheyyas* and one hundred thousand *kappas*.

2. For a **Pacceka** Buddha: two *asaṅkheyyas* and one hundred thousand *kappas*.

3. For an *agga sāvaka*: one *asaṅkheyya* and one hundred thousand *kappas*.

4. For a *mahā sāvaka*: one hundred thousand *kappas*.

5. For an *arahat*: one hundred to one thousand *kappas* or thereabouts.

The predominating factor of *viriyādhika*, is effort; of *saddhādhika*, faith; of *paññādhika*, wisdom.

Once a person becomes a Buddhist, he acquires the seed of Buddha-Dhamma which he is to develop according to his capacity. Every Buddhist is expected to walk on the Noble Eightfold Path to attain the goal of *nibbāna* in his capacity as a Buddha or a *pacceka* Buddha, or *agga sāvaka*, etc.

Amongst those who intend to make a bid for release in the same lifetime, there are four types of individuals, namely:

1. *ugghāṭitaññu*

2. *vipañcitaññu*

3. *neyya*

4. *padaparama*

An *ugghāṭitaññu* is an individual who encounters a Buddha in person and who is capable of attaining the holy path and holy truth through the mere hearing of a short discourse.

A *vipañcitaññu* is an individual who can attain the Path and the Fruits only when a discourse is expounded to him at some considerable length.

A *neyya* is an individual who has not the capability of attaining the Path and the Fruits through the hearing of either a short or long discourse, but who must make a study of the teachings and practise the provisions contained therein for days, months and years in order that he may attain the Path and the Fruits.

In this connection, to a question raised by Bodhi Rājakumāra, Buddha said:

"I cannot say what exactly should be the time for the complete realization of the truth. Even assuming that you renounce the world and join the order of my Saṅgha, it might take you seven years or six years or five years or four years or three years or two years or one year as the case may be. Nay, it can be six months or three months or two months or one month. One the other hand, I do not also discount the possibility of attainment of *arahat*-ship in a fortnight or seven days or in one day or even in a fraction of a day. It depends upon so many factors."

A *padaparama* is an individual who, though he encounters a Buddha *sāsana* (era when Buddha's teachings are available), and puts forth the utmost possible effort in both the study and practice of the Dhamma, cannot attain the Paths and the Fruits within this lifetime. All that he can do is to accumulate habits and potentials. Such a person cannot obtain release from *saṃsāra* (the cycle of rebirth) within his lifetime. If he dies while practising *samatha* for *samādhi* (calm), or Vipassana for *paññā* (insight), and secures rebirth either as a human being or a *deva* in his next existence, he can attain the Path and the Fruits in that existence within the present Buddha *sāsana,* which is to last for five thousand years from the date of the passing away of the Buddha into *mahā parinibbāna* (final great extinction, freedom from suffering).

It is therefore to be assumed that only those quite matured in the accumulation of virtues (*pāramī*), such as those of the four types of individuals referred to above, will be inclined to make that bid for release and take seriously to courses of Buddhist meditation. As a corollary, we have no doubt that whoever is determined to follow strictly and diligently the Noble Eightfold Path through a course of Buddhist meditation under the guidance of a qualified teacher, is an individual of either a *neyya* or *padaparama* type.

The Essence of Buddha-Dhamma

The Buddha-Dhamma is subtle, deep, and difficult to understand. It is by strictly and diligently following the Noble Eightfold Path that one can:

1. come to the realization of the truth of suffering or ill,

2. annihilate the cause of suffering and then

3. come to the end of it.

Only the accomplished saint, only the *arahat,* can fully understand the truth of suffering or ill. As the truth of suffering is realized, the causes of suffering become automatically destroyed, and so, one eventually comes to the end of suffering or ill. What is most important in the understanding of the Buddha-Dhamma is the realization of the truth of suffering or ill through a process of meditation in accordance with the three steps of *sīla, samādhi* and *paññā* of the Noble Eightfold Path. As the Buddha put it:

"It is difficult to shoot from a distance, arrow after arrow, through a narrow keyhole and miss not once. It is more difficult to shoot and penetrate with the tip of a hair, split a hundred times, a piece of hair similarly split. It is still more difficult to penetrate to the fact that 'all this is suffering or ill.' "

He, who has by the practice of Buddha-Dhamma passed into the four streams of sanctity and enjoyed the four fruitions, can appreciate the six attributes of the Dhamma, namely:

1. The Dhamma is not the result of conjecture or speculation, but the result of personal attainments, and it is precise in every respect.

2. The Dhamma produces beneficial results here and now for those who practise it in accordance with the techniques evolved by the Buddha.

3. The effect of Dhamma on the person practising it is immediate in that it has the quality of simultaneously removing the causes of suffering with the understanding of the truth of suffering.

4. The Dhamma can stand the test of those who are anxious to do so. They can know for themselves what the benefits are.

5. The Dhamma is part of one's own self, and is therefore susceptible of ready investigation.

6. The fruits of Dhamma can be fully experienced by the eight types of noble disciples, namely:

   a) one who has attained the first path of sanctity, called *sotāpatti magga*;

   b) one who has attained the first fruition of sanctity, called *sotāpatti phala*;

   c) one who has attained the second path of sanctity, called *sakadāgāmi magga*;

   d) one who has attained the second fruition of sanctity, called *sakadāgāmi phala*;

   e) one who has attained the third path of sanctity, called *anāgāmi magga*;

   f) one who has attained the third fruition of sanctity, called *anāgāmi phala*;

   g) one who has attained the fourth path of sanctity called *arahatta magga*;

   h) one who has attained the fourth fruition of sanctity and thus becomes an arahat.

On the Path (Training at the Meditation Centre)

Whoever is desirous of undergoing a course of training in Buddhist meditation must go along the Noble Eightfold Path. This Noble Eightfold Path was laid down by Buddha in his first sermon to the five ascetics (*pañca vaggiyā*) as a means to the end, and all that is necessary for the student is to follow strictly and diligently the three steps of *sīla, samādhi,* and *paññā,* which form the essence of the said Noble Eightfold Path.

Sīla (precepts)

   1. right speech

   2. right action

   3. right livelihood

Samādhi (concentration of mind)

   4. right exertion

   5. right attentiveness

   6. right concentration

Paññā (wisdom-insight)

   7. right contemplation

   8. right understanding

Sīla

For the first step, i.e., *sīla,* the student will have to maintain a minimum standard of morality by way of a promise to refrain from killing sentient beings, stealing others' property, committing sexual misconduct, telling lies and taking intoxicating drinks. This promise is not, I believe, detrimental to any religious faith. As a matter of fact, we have noticed good moral qualities in foreigners who come to the centre for courses of meditation, and a promise of this kind was of no moment to them.

Samādhi

This is the second step for the development of the power of concentration to one-pointedness of mind. It is a way of training the mind to become tranquil, pure, and strong, and therefore forms the essence of religious life, whether one be a Buddhist, a Jew, a Christian, a Hindu, a Muslim, or a Sikh. It is, in fact, the greatest common denominator of all religions. Unless one can get the mind freed from the impurities (nīvaraṇa) and develop it to a state of purity, he can hardly identify himself with the **Brahmā** or God.

Although different methods are used by people of different religions, the goal for the development of mind is the same, i.e., a perfect state of physical and mental calm. The student at the centre is helped to develop the power of concentration to one-pointedness by being encouraged to focus his attention to a spot on the upper lip at the base of the nose, synchronizing the inward and outward motion of respiration with silent awareness of in-breath and out-breath.

Whether the induction of life is from the mental forces (saṅkhāra) of one's own actions as in Buddhism, or from God as in Christianity, the symbol of life is all the same. It is the rhythm, pulsation, or vibration latent in man. Respiration is, in fact, a reflection of this symbol of life. In the Anapana meditation technique (i.e., that of respiration mindfulness) which is followed at the centre, one great advantage is that the respiration is not only natural, but also available at all times for the purpose of anchoring one's attention to it, to the exclusion of all other thoughts. With a determined effort to narrow down the range of thought waves firstly to the area around the nose with respiration mind-

> **W**hoever is desirous of undergoing a course of training in Buddhist meditation must follow strictly and diligently the three steps of *sīla, samādhi,* and *paññā,* which form the essence of the **N**oble **E**ightfold **P**ath.

fulness and gradually with the wavelength of respiration becoming shorter and shorter to a spot on the upper lip with just the warmth of the breath, there is no reason why a good student in meditation should not be able to secure the one-pointedness of mind in a few days of training.

There are always pointers to the progress of this meditation when steered in the right direction, by way of symbols which take the form of something "white" as opposed to anything "black." Rather, they are in the form of clouds or cotton wool, and sometimes in shapes of white as of smoke or cobwebs or a flower or disc; but when the attention becomes more concentrated, they appear as flashes or points of light or as a tiny star or moon or sun. If these pointers appear in meditation (of course with eyes closed), then it should be taken for granted that *samādhi* is being established.

What is essential, then, for the student is to try after each short spell of relaxation to get back to *samādhi* with the pointer of "light" as quickly as possible. If he can do this, he is quite ready to be switched on to Vipassana meditation to gain insight into the ultimate truth and enjoy the great peace of **nibbāna**. If he is able to focus his attention to one point at the base of the nose with a minute point of light remaining stationary for some time, it is all the better, because at that time he reaches the **upacāra samādhi** or "neighbourhood concentration."

"Mind is intrinsically pure," said the Buddha. "It becomes polluted, however, by the absorption of impurities (*akusala forces*)." In the same way as salt water can be distilled into pure water, so also a student in Anapana meditation can eventually get his mind distilled of impurities and brought to a perfect state of purity.

Paññā

Paññā means insight into what is true of nature and is realized only when one has attained the Paths of sanctity (*magga*) and enjoyed the Fruits (*phala*) of his endeavours in Buddhist meditation. Meditation is inseparable from the development of the power of mind towards *samādhi* and the intimate study of what is true of nature towards the realization of the truth.

When the student has reached a certain level of *samādhi*, preferably the *upacāra samādhi*, the course of training is changed to Vipassana or insight. This requires the use of the powerful lens of *samādhi* already developed and involves an examination of the inherent tendencies of all that exists within one's own self. He is taught to become sensitive to the ongoing processes of his own organism, which in other words are atomic reactions ever taking place in all living beings. When the student becomes engrossed with such sensations, which are the products of nature, he comes to the realization, physically and mentally, of the truth that his whole physical being is after all a changing mass. This is the fundamental concept of *anicca* in Buddhism—the nature of change that is ever taking place in everything, whether animate or inanimate, that exists in this universe. The corollary is the concept of *dukkha*—the innate nature of suffering or ill—which becomes identified with life. This is true because of the fact that the whole structure of a being is made up of atoms (*kalāpas* in Buddhism) all in a state of perpetual combustion.

The last concept is that of *anatta*. You call a "substance" what appears to you to be a substance. In reality there is no substance as such. As the course of meditation progresses, the student comes to the realization that there is no substantiality in his so-called self, and there is no such thing as the core of a being. Eventually he breaks away the egocentrism in him—both in respect to mind and body. He then emerges out of meditation with a new outlook—ego-less and self-less—alive to the fact that whatever happens in this universe is subject to the fundamental law of cause and effect. He knows with his inward eye the illusory nature of the separate self.

The Fruits of Meditation

The fruits of meditation are innumerable. They are embodied in the discourse on the advantages of a *samaṇa's* life (*Sāmaññaphala Sutta*). The very object of becoming a *samaṇa* or monk is to follow strictly and diligently the Noble Eightfold Path and enjoy not only the Fruits (*phala*) of *sotāpatti, sagadāgāmi, anāgāmi* and *arahata,* but also to develop many kinds of faculties. A layman who takes to meditation to gain insight into the ultimate truth, also has to work in the same way; and if his potentials are good, he may also enjoy a share of those fruits and faculties.

Only those who take to meditation with good intentions can be assured of success. With the development of the purity and the power of the mind backed by the insight into the ultimate truth of nature, one might be able to do a lot of things in the right direction for the benefit of mankind.

Buddha said:

O monks, develop the power of concentration. He who is developed in the power of concentration sees things in their true perspective.

This is true of a person who is developed in *samādhi*. It must be all the more so in the case of a person who is developed not only in *samādhi* but also in *paññā* (insight).

It is a common belief that a man, whose power of concentration is good and can secure a perfect balance of mind at will, can achieve better results than a person who is not so developed. There are, therefore, definitely many advantages that accrue to a person who undergoes a successful course of training in meditation, whether he be a religious man, an administrator, a politician, a businessman or a student.

My own case may be cited as an example. If I have to say something here about myself, it is with a sincere desire and with no other motive whatsoever, to illustrate just what practical benefits can accrue to a person practising Buddhist meditation. The events are factual and, of course, one cannot deny the facts.

These are as follows:

I took up Buddhist meditation seriously from January 1937. My life sketch in "Who is Who" of the *Guardian* Magazine, December 1961 gives an account of the duties and responsibilities of government, which I have been discharging from time to time. I retired from the service of government from 26 March 1953 on attaining the age of fifty-five years, but was re-employed as from that date until now in various capacities, most of the time holding two or more separate posts equivalent to those of heads of departments. At a time I was holding three separate sanctioned appointments of the status of head of a department for nearly three years, and on another occasion four such sanctioned posts simultaneously for about a year.

In addition, there were also a good number of special assignments either as member of standing committees in the departments of Prime Minister and National Planning or as chairman or member of ad hoc committees.

Dr. Elizabeth K. Nottingham in her paper entitled "Buddhist Meditation in Burma" asked,

> May it (meditation) not possibly help to create a reservoir of calm and balanced energy to be used for the building of a 'welfare state' and as a bulwark against corruption in public life?

To this question, my answer would definitely be "Yes." I can say this with conviction, because the achievements in all spheres of work happened to be most outstanding in spite of the fact that each of the posts (viz., Director of Commercial Audit, Chairman of the State Agricultural Marketing Board, and Principal, Government Institute for Accounts and Audit) is a challenge to any senior officer of government.

I was appointed Director of Commercial Audit (i.e., as head of the Directorate of Commercial Audit with effect from 11-6-56 to reorganize the Directorate which was formed on 4-10-55) with a staff of just fifty men including only three qualified accountants. The problem was to reorganize the Directorate and raise the standard of its efficiency to cope with the work of audit of transactions of the developing Boards and Corporations of Burma, the annual receipts and payments of which were roughly 150 and 180 crores (ten millions) of *kyats* (Burmese currency) respectively in 1955–56.

Next, I was appointed as Chairman of the State Agricultural Marketing Board on 21-6-56 (just ten days after appointment as Director of Commercial Audit) to take charge of the affairs of the Board, which were found to be deteriorating with the accounts in arrears for five years, the surplus stock at the end of the preceding year at 1.7 million tons and the market price of rice fallen from 60 pounds per ton in 1953 to 34 pounds per ton in 1956. There was also the problem of disunity between the officers and members of the subordinate ranks.

In 1958, acting upon the recommendation of Boards Enquiry Commission (headed by the Prime Minister) of which I was a member, the establishment of a Government Institute for Accounts and Audit was mooted. Burma was extremely short of accountants and account clerks. The result was that with the exception of two organizations of pre-war origin, the accounts of boards and corporations were badly in arrears, i.e., for two to four years, apart from a large number of irregularities which came to

> With the development of purity and the power of the mind backed by the insight into the ultimate truth of nature, one might be able to do a lot of things in the right direction for the benefit of mankind.

notice. I was accordingly charged, in addition to my own existing duties, with the responsibility of establishing a State Institute of Government Accounts and Audit for the purpose of giving training to the officers and staff of all the boards and corporations in Burma. I assumed charge of the post of Principal of this institute with effect from 1-4-58 for spade work, and the Institute was formally opened by the Prime Minister on eleventh of July 1958.

The results of these undertakings will surely illustrate what "a reservoir of calm and energy" one can create with Buddhist meditation to be used for the building of a "welfare state."

Human Relation

The attitude towards life of a Buddhist who makes a bid for release during this lifetime differs

from the attitude of one who is in the process of accumulation of virtues for consummation of his vow to become a Buddha. For example, Rājagaha and Sāvatthi were the chief seats of the Buddha during his lifetime. Rājagaha was the kingdom of Bimbisāra, who had made a bid for release during the same lifetime and had attained the first Path of sanctity and become an *ariya*. He was very devoted to the Lord Buddha and built a stupendous monastery known as the Veḷuvana Monastery for the Buddha and his disciples. He accorded pardon to all the citizens who had committed crimes, if they joined the order of the Buddha's Sangha (order of monks). He was known as King Abhaya (the Harmless King). He would not himself harm anybody and would avoid encouraging others to harm anybody. His power in administration was his love for humanity.

On the other hand, Sāvatthi was the kingdom of Pasenadi Kosala, who was a king also very much devoted to the Lord Buddha. In fact, Buddha stayed at Sāvatthi longer than elsewhere. This king was in the process of accumulation of virtues to become a Buddha and although he would by all possible means try to avoid doing harm to others, where occasion demanded, he would be prepared to suffer himself the consequences of saving those depending upon him. Once he stopped at the Buddha's monastery on his way back to the palace after his conquest of the enemy in a battle which took place at the border of his kingdom. He led the army to fight the enemies to save his country and his people from the invaders, failing which, his countrymen would have suffered their maltreatment and tortures. When he mentioned to the Buddha his conquest over the enemies the Buddha smiled and told him,

"You have made more enemies than you had before the incident."

It can therefore, be understood that those who are in the process of accumulation of virtues cannot, at times, avoid committing an offence which would take them to the subhuman planes of existence, and in consequence are prepared to suffer themselves for the offence for the sake of humanity. As to how loving-kindness reinforced with the power of truth could do something tangible in the matter of human relations, let me cite a few of my own experiences.

I was required by the Prime Minister to investigate into the many irregularities suspected in the State Agricultural Marketing Board, and was accordingly appointed on 15-8-55 as chairman of the S.A.M.B. Special Enquiry Committee. The reports made by me led to further enquiries by the Bureau of Special Investigations, and their enquiries led to the arrest of four officers of the Board (including the General Manager) during the time of the annual conference of the Board's officers.

This was so much resented by the officers in conference that they submitted resignations en masse from their appointments under the Board. This action by the officers created an impasse, and the situation became aggravated when the Union of Employees of the Board gave support to their cause through the medium of their all-Burma annual conference being held at Pegu. The government decided to accept their resignations, and this decision upset most of the officers, who half-heartedly had taken that course of action. Eventually, after some negotiations by third parties, they withdrew their resignations and surrendered themselves to the government for a token penalty.

It was in this atmosphere that I had to join the State Agricultural Marketing Board as its chairman, before I could forget their slogans denouncing the Special Enquiry Committee and the Bureau of Special Investigations. However, I had no grudge against anybody, because I had worked for the best interests of the country and was sure that I could prevail upon them my point of view that my acceptance of the offer of the post of Chairman of the Board was to save the situation of the Board and the country at that critical juncture, and to work for the efficiency and welfare of the employees, as well as other people connected with the business of the Board.

In point of fact, after a few meetings with the representatives of these bodies, I should say I had really turned the tide. There was a reunion between the officers and the staff, and coordination between the Board and the millers and

This is not the age for showing miracles, which would be of no direct benefit to the people in general. But if the physical and mental ills of men could be removed through meditation, it should be something for one to ponder.

other traders. New plans were drawn up and improved techniques introduced. The results happened to be what nobody would have dared even to think of. I recommended very strongly two officers of the Board for their wholehearted cooperation and unrelenting efforts which made for the success of the undertaking. The government was very kind to grant the title of *Wunna Kyawhtin* (a title given to acknowledge meritorious government service) to them, one of whom was the Deputy General Manager (administration) and the other, President of the State Agricultural Marketing Board Employees' Union. Employees' unions normally run counter to government, and I presume such a case in which the president of an employees' union was awarded a title, must be rare.

For the Directorate of Commercial Audit, the case is not at all difficult. There is a Buddhist Society, many of the members of which are my disciples in meditation, and there is also a social club, where there is brotherly feeling between all the officers and staff of the Directorate. Religious functions are held annually where one and all join hands for the common objective, and twice a year they pay homage to the Directorate, both as teacher and as the head of the organization. The social club arranges annual trips in a chartered launch or other means to out-stations for relaxation where members of the employees' families also join, and a pleasant atmosphere is created for all. All these help to promote understanding with each other and pave the way for efficiency in the Directorate.

For the Institute of Accounts and Audit where teachers with extraordinary patience and good-will are required, apart from their qualifications and teaching experience, the vice-principal and the lecturers are mostly those who have taken courses of meditation at the centre. To whatever types the students may belong, the good intentions of the teachers prevail upon them and the response of the students in all the classes has been consistently excellent. From the date of the inception of the Institute, there was not a single complaint from the students. On the other hand, at the close of each course of study there are parties held by the students in honour of the principal and the teachers, where they invariably express their gratitude for the kindness shown to them and the pains taken to help them understand their lessons thoroughly.

I have no doubt, therefore, that meditation plays a very important role in the development of the mind to enable one to have the best in human relations.

By-products

In the section "Fruits of Meditation," I have explained what the advantages of meditation can be. Particularly, I would refer to the advantages of meditation as mentioned in the *Sāmaññaphala Sutta* (Discourse on the Advantages of a Samaṇa's Life), and the records of appreciation by foreigners who have come to the International Meditation Centre. What I am going to state here is about the very minor by-products of meditation relating to physical and mental ills. This is not the age for showing miracles, such as rising into the air, or walking on the surface of water, which would be of no direct benefit to the people in general. But if the physical and mental ills of men could be removed through meditation, it should be something for one to ponder.

According to the Buddhist way of thinking, each action, whether by deed, word or thought, produces and leaves behind a force of action (*saṅkhāra*) which goes to the credit or debit account of the individual according to its good or bad objective. This invisible something which we call *saṅkhāra* is the product of the mind with which each action is related. It has no element of extension. The whole universe is permeated with the forces of action of all living beings. The inductive theory of life has the origin, we believe, in these forces, each individual absorbing continually the forces of his own actions, at the same time releasing new forces of actions by deeds, words and thoughts; creating, so to say, an unending cycle of life with pulsation, rhythm and vibration as its symbol.

Let us take the forces of good actions as positive and the forces of bad actions as negative. Then we get what we may call the positive and negative reaction, which is ever taking place everywhere in the universe. It is taking place in all animate and inanimate objects, in my body, in your body and in the bodies of all living beings. When one can understand these concepts through a proper course of meditation, he knows nature as it truly is. With the awareness of the truth of *anicca* and or *dukkha* and or *anattā*, he develops in him what we may call the sparkling illumination of *nibbāna dhātu,* a power that dispels all impurities or poisons—the products of bad actions, which are the sources of his physical and mental ills. In the same way as fuel is burnt away by ignition, the negative forces (impurities or poisons) within are eliminated by the *nibbāna dhātu,* which he generates with the true awareness of *anicca* in the course of meditation. This process of elimination should go on until such time as both the mind and body are completely cleansed of such impurities or poisons.

Among those who have taken courses of meditation at the centre are some who were suffering from complaints such as hypertension, T.B., migraine, thrombosis, etc. They became relieved of these even in the course of ten days. If they maintain the awareness of *anicca* and take longer courses at the centre, there is every likelihood of the diseases being rooted out in course of time. Since anything which is the root cause of one's own physical and mental ills is *samudaya* (an arisen phenomenon), and this *samudaya* can be removed by the *nibbāna dhātu* which one generates in true Budddhist meditation, we make no distinction between this or that disease. One aspect of meditation is *samudaya pahātabba,* which literally means "for the removal of the causes of suffering."

A note of caution is necessary here. When one develops *nibbāna dhātu,* the impact of this *nibbāna dhātu* upon the impurities and poisons within his own system will create a sort of upheaval, which must be endured. This upheaval tends to increase the sensitivity of the radiation, friction, and vibration of the atomic units within. This will grow in intensity, so much so that one might feel as though his body were just electricity and a mass of suffering. In the case of those who have diseases such as those mentioned above, the impact will be all the stronger and, at times, almost explosive. Nevertheless, enduring it, he becomes alive to the fact that a change is taking place within himself for the better, and that the impurities are gradually diminishing, and that he is slowly but surely getting rid of the disease.

Mankind, today, is facing the danger of radioactive poisons. If such poisons absorbed by a man exceeds the maximum permissible concentration (m.p.c.), he enters the danger zone.

I have a firm belief that the *nibbāna dhātu* which a person develops in true Buddhist Meditation, is power, which will be strong enough to eradicate the radioactive poisons, if any, in him.

The Buddha is the Teacher who shows the way. I am an individual who continues to show the way, having received the inheritance of Dhamma from the Buddha.

The Buddha is not a person who can give nibbāna but only one who shows the way. Do not come and ask me to get the results for you; I cannot do that. How can U Ba Khin do what even the Buddha cannot? You have to practise yourself.

—*Sayagyi U Ba Khin*

The Ten Soldiers of Māra

by Thray Sithu Sayagyi U Ba Khin

The following is condensed from a translation of a discourse by Sayagyi U Ba Khin. The discourse, in Burmese, was addressed to Vipassana students during a course.

You have to be very careful. You have to stand firm and face many difficulties, so that you can know true anicca (impermanence) with your own experience. You must work very hard—that is why we repeatedly remind you. Difficulties come at this stage of the course. During the time of our great benefactor, Saya Thetgyi, students would experience various difficulties in meditation, such as not being able to feel the object of meditation at all. When asked to focus their attention on the top of their heads, they couldn't feel anything. During Anapana they couldn't feel the area around the nostrils. Some could not feel their breath while they were breathing. Some said that they could not feel their bodies. While you are here, you too will find these things happening. Sometimes you will not be able feel sensations and you won't be able to maintain your attention.

Some think that they have attained *nibbāna* (the ultimate reality) when they cannot feel their bodies. If you cannot feel the presence of your body, just hit it with your hand, or punch yourself and see. There is no need to ask the Teacher. You will know if your body is there or not. These uncertainties are rather disconcerting, aren't they?

The nature of *vipallāsa* (mental distortion, corruption) makes fools of you. These are undesirable defilements hidden inside people. They are present in every one of us. When there is understanding of *anicca* the defilements have to leave; but they don't want to—they want this understanding to leave instead. The *nibbāna*

nature of *anicca* is very potent, so Māra (the negative forces) fights against it. The *Padhāna Sutta* describes the ten soldiers of Māra. We have to be careful of these ten soldiers, as they are the destroyers of meditation.

The first soldier of Māra is the desire to enjoy sense pleasures. Some people have come to meditate but not to attain *nibbāna* at all. They come with ulterior motives such as, "If I become close to Sayagyi, who knows so many people in high positions, I may get a promotion in my job." There are some persons like that. They come with greed in their hearts. They cannot be successful in their meditation. There must be no greed. When you asked for the technique of Vipassana you said, "*Nibbānassa sacchikaranatthāya me bhante*"—in order to realize *nibbāna*... I will teach you to understand the Four Noble Truths, but if you are not interested, and intend to take your time about it, what can I do?

The second soldier of Māra is unwillingness to reside or be happy in a quiet place such as a forest dwelling.

Yesterday somebody planned to run away. He got up early and packed his belongings. He planned to sit at half past seven with you all, and then leave while I was checking the students at eight. He was planning to run like mad, catch a bus, and get home. He thought he would collect his bags at some later date. Luckily, I don't know why, I gave the one hour *adhiṭṭhāna* (strong determination) sitting earlier, and he had to sit that one hour. There he was—trapped! After the *adhiṭṭhāna* sitting, Māra left him, and he doesn't want to leave anymore.

When unwillingness to reside in a arises, the person wants to leave an[d] He may inform us that he wishes he may just quietly leave. The sec does not want to stay in a quiet se because of the turmoil inside.

The third soldier of Māra is hu[ng]ing satisfied with food. Are you al Sao Shwe Theik was one of th ones. He came with boxes full o that he could not stay without "In that case you may eat, but three days and see for yourself. and cajole him; however, he w all during the ten days.

Myanma Alin U Tin said th[at] days of eating only twice a da[y] shaky, and that in all his life, that for more than three day for permission to eat and I needed." When he got he first day, the second day, ar hungry at all. One does meditation is progressin meditation is not going is making one hungry. One cannot hunger then. Once the meditator is established in meditation, he does not feel hunger anymore.

The fourth soldier of Māra is the craving for various tastes and foods. You haven't eaten chicken curry for sometime, you want to eat a kebab? Can't stay! Chicken is not served here, but we provide the best food we can. That is why they work so hard to prepare the food here, so that everyone will enjoy it and eat well.

What happens when very tasty, delicious food is eaten? Doesn't this stimulate more craving for food? Is it possible to eat without any appreciation of the taste of the food? …Only the *arahant* (fully liberated person) can do this. Wasn't the purpose of your coming here for this course to get rid of the *kilesa* (mental impurities), to get [tan]hā (craving)? If you keep your eyes o you will not be objects. The same ne here with a tape ngs by May Shin. hem. It is the same es around wearing be any craving and ell. There is nothing ill give you pleasant tongue—can it avoid eat, and in that case a ve you glucose injec- te will occur when food ne tongue. If you eat less g and clinging for taste

ne here to get rid of your g, we should help you by nvironment so that they ldn't we? You are trying to Ve don't want to eradicate and, and increase it by food do not provide an evening ding it we have so much less or us and better for you too, because yo[u] ure to become drowsy if you eat an evening meal. So you can do without it. If you eat well in the morning and at lunchtime the two meals will provide enough for your body's requirements.

The fifth soldier of Māra is drowsiness, sloth and torpor. You can understand this. Even Mahā Moggallāna (one of Buddha's chief disciples) suffered from it. Some of you can fall asleep while sitting. When I used to go for my meditation retreats, there was an old man who accompanied me. We sat in Saya Thetgyi's meditation centre in the meditation room and he sat behind me wearing a big yogi shawl. A little while later, he started snoring aloud. Normally there are not many people who can sit and snore, but there are many meditators who can do this—sit and snore, then wake up! This is called *thīna-middha* (sloth and torpor). *Thīna-middha* cannot be avoided. When insight and wisdom become sharpened, the peaceful nature of *nibbāna* is felt; and when the wholesome and unwholesome natures clash, a reaction occurs and produces heat. Then the person becomes drowsy and sleepy.

If you feel drowsy at times, just breathe a bit harder; you've lost your *samādhi* (concentration). This is a kick from within. Your *samādhi* has gone. If you lose your *samādhi*, focus your attention on the nostrils again, breathe harder and try to calm down. Sometimes when the *aniccavijjā* (the wisdom of impermanence) becomes stronger, you experience the meeting of physical and mental experience in your body and your insight-intuition becomes very sharp and very strong. Then there's a very strong kick from within and you lose your understanding of *anicca* and become disoriented. You can't understand what happened and you ask the Teacher. If such a thing happens suddenly, there are two ways to cope with it. One method is to try and work to get re-established in *samādhi*, as I have told you. Or, you can go outside and wake yourself up and the reaction will pass away. Do not go and sleep when this reaction happens. I am giving you methods to cope. They are important from the practical aspect. Drowsiness always occurs when *saṅkhāras* (impurities) come up. Then we have to apply *anicca* firmly. It should not be just paying lip service to *anicca*, not just from the mouth. It should be the actual knowledge of the changing nature of the body with the awareness of sensations. If you practise in this way, you will overcome and win.

The sixth soldier of Māra is not wishing to be alone and being afraid of solitude. Some can-

not sit in one room but keep changing rooms, looking for company and feel frightened when alone. Win Min Tham was among those who were afraid of solitude. Her house is very big but she dared not stay by herself in any room; she needed a companion at all times. She came here to meditate and brought a maid with her. She asked my permission to keep the lights on when she meditated in her room, so I allowed her to do so. Not only that, but somebody had to sit quite close to her when she meditated. She did not dare to stay alone. When she was by herself she felt flushes all over her body. After staying for a course, she got a little better. After the next course she was in the little cell by herself in the dark. She came regularly for ten days every month and benefited quite well from it. She was first class in being afraid but her fear is gone now. Isn't that nice?

The seventh soldier of Māra is doubt about whether one can be successful in meditation. I suppose this is true of everybody—wondering if his or her meditation will be successful or not. (That girl is laughing.) You *can* succeed. The important thing is to wash away the *akusala* (unwholesome conditioning), and *kilesa* (mental defilements) embedded in us. That is important.

The eighth soldier of Māra is becoming proud and arrogant when the meditation is successful. When the meditation improves, one can feel it inside. The defilements become lighter and one tends to get conceited and arrogant, and think, "That fellow does not seem to be doing too well. I'd better help him." I am saying this from my personal experience. A long time ago when I started this meditation centre, for instance, we did not have a Dhamma hall then. There was a ten-foot square hut that was here when we bought the land. We used to sit in there and talk. One day U Hla Maung came out after the morning sitting and said, "Look." He hitched up his *longyi* and there were little lumps all over his thighs and legs just like the skin of a plucked duck. The kick from within was so strong that all those lumps appeared. He hitched his *longyi* up and showed us saying, "Please look. See how strong the kick from within was. You too, please try hard, please try hard."

This is why I'm telling you all not to preach. If there is anything that you want to ask, ask me. If there is anything that you want to say, tell me. When he preached, there was ego in it, the "I" was in it, "I am doing well. These people don't seem to be getting anywhere." He played very good soccer, was very short-tempered, ready to hit, strike and punch. When a very bad-tempered person with a lot of heat has a kick from inside, it shows up on the body surface. The next day U Hla Maung could not meditate. He could not feel any sensations and had to approach Sayagyi for guidance.

I am talking about others because I want to talk about the nature of things. If you progress in your practice, just stay quiet and proceed with your own meditation.

The ninth soldier of Māra refers to the Teacher and concerns becoming well known, receiving many offerings, gaining much respect and homage. I receive a lot of homage and offerings. I have to control myself to not get conceited. Look here, isn't it likely to cause conceit? I have to guard myself. We started this work here for the people of the Accountant General's office so they could meditate in their free time, but there are so few of them here now. We started this not on the basis of money, but on the basis of Dhamma. Any office worker who meditates for ten days becomes a member. The admission fee is ten days of meditation. Isn't it good? No need to pay a cent of subscription. Just meditate steadily, guard your practice, do not lose it. We started from that and have come to this. Money

can't do it. It was Dhamma that did it. We believe in this, and we do not have any money either.

This centre does not belong to me. U Ba Khin should not get conceited, saying this is U Ba Khin's centre. I do not own it. It belongs to the Vipassana Association of the Accountant General's office. I will have to leave if they drive me out. See, how nice! I do not own it. I have to be re-elected each year. Only if they re-elect me will I be here. If they say that they have found someone better than me, and elect that person, it's over for me. Or some members from the committee may not like me, they may say I talk too much and elect someone else. Then I would have to leave. I do not own the place.

The tenth soldier of Māra is following a false Dhamma, creating a new and special Dhamma, in order to acquire abundant offerings, praising oneself and looking down on others. This is why I do not want to say too much about others. Let others speak as they like about us, isn't that right? Some teachers get attached to receiving offerings, so as to get more students. They teach what the students would like—false teachings, teachings that are not Buddha's teachings—simply because they want the homage and offerings. They stop working with true Dhamma. That is the tenth soldier of Māra.

Dhamma dissolves sorrows and miseries and gives happiness. Who gives this happiness? The Buddha does not give it, it is the *aniccavijjā* (wisdom of impermanence) inside you that gives it. We should practise Vipassana so that the *aniccavijjā* will neither stop nor disappear. How do we practise? Focus your attention on the four elements, be calm, cultivate *samādhi* and do not let *sīla* (moral precepts) be broken. Telling lies is the one that I am afraid of among the precepts. I am not afraid of the others, because, by lying the basis of *sīla* is weakened. When sīla is weakened, *samādhi* will get weakened and *paññā* (wisdom) will also get weakened. Speak truthfully, work regularly, build up *samādhi* and pay attention to what is happening in your body; then the nature of *anicca* will come up naturally.

Our benefactor Saya Thetgyi said, "Very fast, vibrating incessantly, helter-skelter, broken up, burnt down, the destruction of the body—these are the signs of impermanence." It is the body that is changing. The thought that knows that the *rūpa* (matter) is changing is the *nāma* (mind). When the *rūpa* changes and has gone, the *nāma* which knew about the changed-and-gone *rūpa*, also is changed and goes. Both *rūpa* and *nāma* are *anicca*. Keep this in your mind, be aware of it.

Focus your attention on the top of your head, and move down through the whole body, from the top of the head to the forehead and then the face, from the face to the neck, the neck to the shoulders, from the shoulders along to the hands. Wherever the mind goes it may be like touching with a small torch and feeling the heat wherever the torch touches, wherever the mind goes. Why? Because there is burning and annihilation taking place inside; it is the innate nature of combustion of atomic units within. This is certainly present. Learn to be sensitive to it so that you can feel it. Try it with an attentive mind and you will know.

Once the meditation is practised and once one becomes aware and observes with Vipassana knowledge, the defilements, the evil *samudaya akusala* (arisen unwholesomeness) cannot remain much longer. They have to leave gradually and when they are all gone, the person becomes controlled and stable, and able to live well.

How long will one have to work? Until all the immeasurable, uncountable old *akusala kamma* (unwholesome actions) accumulated along one's journey through the *saṃsāra* (cycle of rebirth) are eradicated by observing the nature of *anicca*. Then one becomes *sotāpanna* (one who has reached the first stage of saintliness, has experienced *nibbāna),* and *ariyapuggala* (noble person). This cannot be achieved easily.

To reach the final *nibbāna* where all the *saṅkhāras* are abolished is very far off, but wouldn't you like to try and see for yourself the minor *nibbāna?* If it could be tasted only after death, these foreigners would never practise this meditation. They have tasted a bit, liked it and have kept coming back from near and far. They send their friends and acquaintances who also come from afar. Why is this? Because they have experienced the taste of Dhamma.

It is important that there is a Teacher to help students to have a taste of Dhamma. But students have to work to experience the taste. What is this taste called? It is called the *dhamma rasa.* "*Sabba rasaṃ dhamma rasaṃ jināti*"—of all the tastes, the taste of Dhamma is the most noble, the best.

You have to try to work hard to get that taste. Just as the human monarch enjoys human pleasures, the *deva* (celestial being) monarch enjoys the *deva* pleasures and *brahmā* (a higher celestial being) enjoys *brahmā* pleasures; the noble *ariyas* (saintly persons) such as the Buddha and *arahants* can also enjoy the taste of the Dhamma that they have obtained. You must try hard until you too can enjoy this taste, but please do not work to the extreme, without moderation. Try to work according to the schedule we have given, work at the right time, to the fullest, with great care and effort.

Response from the students: "*Sādhu. Sādhu. Sādhu.*"

Revolution with a View to Nibbāna

by Thray Sithu Sayagyi U Ba Khin

The following has been reproduced and abridged from the Burmese magazine The Light of the Dhamma. This discourse was given by Sayagyi in 1950 on the full moon day of July, the day known as Dhammacakka day. This day is celebrated because it was during this time of year that the Buddha gave his first discourse to his five companions: the Dhammacakka Pavattana Sutta (lit., revolving the wheel of Dhamma). In this discourse the Buddha outlines the Four Noble Truths explaining in detail the Eightfold Noble Path; in other words, the very core of his teaching.

The Discourse on the Revolution

The discourse I am going to deliver tonight is a discourse on revolution that is apt and proper for the occasion of Dhammacakka day. Some may think that it is a discourse that supports the revolution of a group of persons to free themselves from being suppressed by another group of persons. It is not so. The discourse on revolution that I am going to deliver is a supramundane revolution against one's own polluted mind for the attainment of freedom from the rounds of birth and death, which leads to the realization of nibbāna (the ultimate reality).

It will not be taken wrongly if it is said that the **Dhammacakka** discourse was delivered by the Buddha who personally revolted against the bondage of the mundane world to gain enlightenment and reach the full extinction of defilements (*sa-upādisesa nibbāna*) so that all the beings—human, **deva** and **brahmā**—might be able to revolt against the bondage of their mundane worlds and reach **nibbāna**.

To Gain Freedom from the Three Types of Mundane Worlds

The Buddha revolted against the three types of mundane worlds and gained enlightenment in the early hours of Vesākha day (the full moon of May). He was not satisfied with this achievement only, for because of the perfections (*pāramīs*) that he had fulfilled for the benefit of all beings,

he also had to impart the method of revolt for all beings to fight for the attainment of their freedom from the three worlds.

Nibbāna—Freedom in Reality

In this revolution with the view to *nibbāna,* there are so many obstructions which are on the side of ignorance (*avijjā*) that there seems to no way of escape for us. With the perfections accumulated the Buddha had to defend and fight against the five divisions of Māra's army, viz., the evil (*devaputta māra*), the defilements (*kilesa māra*), the aggregates (*khandha māra*), the death (*maccu māra*), and the *kamma* formations (*abhisaṅkhāra māra*). They suppress and imprison us, so that there is no outlet of escape for us.

Before the Buddha delivered the first sermon, during the seven weeks after the enlightenment, he took no nourishment. He was in deep contemplation on the profound details of the Dhamma. It is not an easy matter to save beings from the world entwined in ignorance (*avijjā*). When all the beings were viewed with the Buddha's eye, after the seventh week, he deliberated whether to deliver the profound Dhamma to beings enmeshed in the defilements. That is why the great **brahmā** Sahampati, accompanied by **devas** and **brahmās**, offered the jewelled garland

and entreated the Buddha to deliver the Dhamma, beginning with the Pāli words: **Desetu Bhagavā dhammaṃ, desetu sugato** (O Lord, may the blessed one teach the Dhamma; may the supremely good one teach the Dhamma).

After promising the great **brahmā** Sahampati that he would teach the Dhamma, he looked to see who among the living human beings had the ability to understand and benefit by the Dhamma. He saw the five ascetics who served him while he practised **Dukkharacariya** (the rigorous ascetic practices). So the Buddha went to the deer park near Vārānasi where the five ascetics were, and during the first watch of the night delivered the **Dhammacakka** discourse beginning with **Dveme bhikkhave antā pabbajitena nasevitabbā** (These two extremes, **bhikkhus**, should not be followed by one who has given up the world). This discourse is the way to the transformation of a new personality. In other words, the Noble Path revolts against the mundane path and leads to **nibbāna**. At the end of the discourse the leader of the five ascetics, Koṇḍañña, became a **sotāpanna** (stream-enterer), i.e., transformed into a new being as a noble person.

At that time the **devas** and **brahmās** who came from the ten thousand universes also became established in their lives as noble beings **(ariyas)**. To become an **ariya** means to grasp the true essence of the elements of **nibbāna** and to be free from mental defilements. The realization of **nibbāna** is becoming a new being, changing from an ordinary worldling to a noble being. It is not possible to transform a person to such a new life by ordinary means of preparation. The Buddha

> The mind that gives rise to unwholesome bodily actions and verbal actions, should be securely restrained. Then it cannot run amok but will stay calm and collected.

achieved this by the fulfilment of the perfections **(pāramīs)** developed through countless aeons. This culminated in the wisdom of omniscience and other wisdoms, and the turning of the wheel of Dhamma.

Why Is It called **Dhammacakka?**

The reason why this very first discourse is called the **Dhammacakka** discourse is this, as mentioned in the **Dhammacakka Kathā** of **Paṭisambhidā-magga:**

> **Dhammapavatanti kenatthena dhammacakkaṃ, dhammañca pavatteti cakkañcati.**

In what sense is the setting going of Dhamma called **dhammacakka?** It is the setting going of truth **(dhamma)** and the wheel **(cakka)** of the teaching.[1]

It is the origin of the Four Noble Truths and it also causes the continuous rotation of the noble Dhamma of the Four Noble Truths. The rotation of the wheel of Dhamma is called the **Dhammacakka.**

The essence of the **Dhammacakka** is the Four Noble Truths, which are: **dukkha sacca** (the truth of suffering); **samudaya sacca** (the truth of the origin of suffering); **nirodha sacca** (the truth of

---

1 Here, according to the commentaries, the word *cakka* (literally, "wheel") has the additional meaning of "the dispensation of Buddha." Therefore this line from *Paṭisambhidā-magga* is indicating that the first discourse of Buddha, in which the basic outline of the entire teaching is laid out, is called **Dhammacakka-pavattana** because two things are set forth or set going: *dhammañca pavatteti* (the truth is set forth) and *cakkañca pavatteti* (the dispensation is set going.) The usual translation, "the rotation of the wheel of Dhamma," implies these two meanings metaphorically.

the cessation of suffering); *magga sacca* (the truth of the noble path that leads to the cessation of suffering).

Of these Four Noble Truths, the noble path (*magga sacca*) which constitutes the Eightfold Noble Path is of the utmost importance. Although the Buddha delivered eighty-four thousand discourses, as occasions arose during the forty-five years of his ministry, the basic practical aspect of his teaching is the Eightfold Noble Path.

The Path of Revolution

The Eightfold Noble Path is composed of three aspects of practical work: morality, concentration and wisdom (*sīla, samādhi,* and *paññā*).

The path of morality (*sīla*) consists of three subdivisions: right speech (*sammā vācā*), right action (*sammā kammanta*) and right livelihood (*sammā ājīva*).

The path of concentration (*samādhi*) consists of three subdivisions: right effort (*sammā vāyāma*), right mindfulness (*sammā sati*), right concentration (*sammā samādhi*).

The path of wisdom (*paññā*) consists of two subdivisions: right thought (*sammā saṅkappa*) and right view (*sammā diṭṭhi*).

As soon as *sīla, samādhi* and *paññā*—with *paññā* as the leading factor— are properly combined in practice, one is sure to reach the noble path. If one has not reached the path, it is because *sīla, samādhi* and *paññā* are not yet properly balanced. The path prepared with these three aspects of practice, is the revolutionary path of the Buddha.

Mind is Supreme

In the path of morality, consisting of right speech, right action and right livelihood, the bodily actions and speech should be bound and restrained. Bodily actions and speech are usually controlled by greed, hatred and delusion (*lobha, dosa* and *moha*) which are in turn the servants of craving, conceit and wrong view (*taṇhā, māna* and *micchā-diṭṭhi*). These unwholesome qualities have accompanied us as our habitual inclinations through the cycle of births (*saṃsāra*). The bodily action (*kāya kamma*) and verbal action (*vaci kamma*) are the paths of the revolution that should really and truly be revolted against.

Here, as the saying goes, **Mano pubbaṅgamā dhammā** (mind is the master of the bodily actions and verbal actions). Again, as it is said: **Papasmiṃ ramati mano** (the mind delights in dwelling in evil). It cannot be revolted against by ordinary means but only with great zeal.

May all beings be able to muster immense zeal!

Discipline the Mind

In the Noble Path of right effort, right mindfulness and right concentration, the mind that gives rise to unwholesome bodily actions and verbal actions, should be securely restrained. Then it cannot run amok but will stay calm and collected.

Right concentration cannot be achieved unless there is right effort and right mindfulness, to keep the mind calm and still. To achieve right concentration, mindfulness should be developed with right effort. I want you to believe that with the help and guidance of a person who is competent to help, *samādhi* (concentration) can be rapidly established. The Buddha had to resist and fight against the evil (*devaputta māra*) while he was establishing the first stage of *samādhi* under the *bodhi* tree. After conquering the evil with the *samādhi* thus established, he subjugated the defilements (*kilesa māra*) and the death (*maccu māra*) with ease. Similarly, nowadays under the guidance and guardianship of a person who is highly developed in the perfections (pāramīs) and who can, to a certain degree, guard against the dangers of the evil (devaputta māra), samādhi can be established within a short period.

There are six types of character or nature (carita) affecting all human beings, but it is not possible to know which type a person belongs to, since we do not have the ability to do so. But it is a sure fact that no one is free from delusion (mohacarita), which is none other than ignorance itself. That is why one cannot argue that it is an unnatural process to establish samādhi by practising ānāpāna sati (awareness of the in and out breathing). This practice is suitable for persons with the nature and habitual inclination of delusion (moha). But people may not believe that it is relatively easy to establish samādhi by the practice of Anapana.

It is true that it will be difficult to subjugate the mind, to keep it refined and proper and to make it stay where one keeps it—the mind that throughout this cycle of rebirth (saṃsāra) has freely and wantonly wandered, the mind without a custodian, the incessantly restless, mercurial mind. But for those who do not look forward to worldly benefits, but want only the attainment of nibbāna, should they meet the right teacher, it becomes an easy matter.

There are many people who have experienced the clearly shining acquired image (uggaha nimitta) after the first attempt at meditation and the counter image (paṭibhāga nimitta) quite soon afterwards. That is why I would like to request those persons who are practising Dhamma for the realization of nibbāna, not to overlook the sīla-samādhi-paññā triad.

The True Nature

Right thought (sammā saṅkappa) is the contemplation of the true nature of the aggregates, sense bases and elements. The knowledge of the true nature after such contemplation is to be called the path of right view (sammā diṭṭhi). Then the problem arises: what is meant by "true nature"?

The true nature is this: the mind and matter (nāma and rūpa) of the five aggregates are incessantly and infallibly breaking down and passing away. This is the true nature of impermanence (anicca). The mind and matter of the five aggregates does not possess even a particle of satisfactoriness and is totally unsatisfactory. This is the true nature of unsatisfactoriness (dukkha). The mind and matter of the five aggregates has nothing to indicate that there is any substantiality such as me, mine and self. This is the true nature of egolessness, impersonality (anattā).

These true natures are all within the body (which is but one fathom long) of the people who are now listening to this discourse. One must penetrate with one's basic concentration and insight wisdom into this body. One must look critically at the true nature of mind and matter, to remove the conceptual beliefs that are blocking the path. One must repeatedly study the true nature of impermanence, the true nature of suffering, the true nature of egolessness of the five aggregates. And one must develop the ten insight knowledges[2] of Vipassana. This process is called vipassanā.

After that, from the knowledge gained at the conjunction of the internal and external senses (ajjhatāyatana and bahiddhāyatana) to the contemplation of the eighteen kinds of insight knowledge, is also vipassanā.

---

2 For an explanation of the ten insight knowledges, see The Essentials of Buddha Dhamma in Meditative Practice, pp. 33–4.

Attano sabhāvaṃ dhāretī ti dhātu (contemplation of all kinds of elements which are carrying their own nature is also *vipassanā*).

These practices are said to be insight wisdom which removes conceptual truth to reach the ultimate truth (from *paññatti* to *paramattha*). Fundamentally, it is to be believed that if the triad of *sīla, samādhi* and *paññā* is diligently practised, the Four Noble Truths will be comprehended and *nibbāna* will be realized. At the present time when Vipassana is more widely practised, if there is a strong base of *samādhi*, it is certain that *nibbāna* is not far off.

But those persons who are dazed by the evil (*devaputta māra*) will think that nothing can be done; they will give up and take the easy way out. When the Buddha saw and admonished the monk Kolita (who was later known as Mahā Moggallāna) for being drowsy during meditation, he said, "Kolita, for a person who is looking for the happiness of *nibbāna,* why do you want to associate with such undesirables as *thīna-middha* and *pamāda* (sloth, torpor and indolence)?"

So get rid of sloth, torpor and indolence with their repercussions and practise the Eightfold Noble Path, the Noble Path which is annunciated in the *Dhammacakka*.

Throughout *saṃsāra* (the cycle of rebirth), for the mind which believes that the compounded mind and body (*nāma-rūpa*) is:

nicca (permanent)—revolt against such a mind to open up the realization and knowledge of impermanence (*anicca vijjā ñāṇa*)

sukha (pleasurable)—revolt against such a mind to open up the realization and knowledge of suffering (*dukkha vijjā ñāṇa*)

attā (self)—revolt against such a mind to open up the realization and knowledge of non-self (*anattā vijjā ñāṇa*).

To Peace and Tranquillity

In brief, from today onwards, may you be able to practise with the utmost effort, to accomplish the supramundane wisdom (*lokuttara ñāṇa*), by revolting against the conceptualized mundane world (*loka*).

May those persons who make the effort and practise, receive and be engulfed by the *dhammadhātu, bodhidhātu,* and *nibbānadhātu* (the vibration of Dhamma, *bodhi,* or enlightenment, and *nibbāna,* respectively) of the Buddha.

May they, by their established *sīla, samādhi* and *paññā,* utterly destroy the evils who are the colonizers of *saṃsāra,* viz., craving, conceit, and wrong view (*taṇhā, māna* and *micchā-diṭṭhi*) and attain swiftly and directly the full extinction of defilements (*sa-upādisesa nibbāna*), which is beyond all the nature of compounded things (*saṅkhāra dhamma*).

May they, with the radiant rays of *nibbāna* that they have received, deliver peace and tranquillity throughout this universe.

The Chain of Teachers

The Ven. Ledi Sayadaw (1846–923)

Venerable Ledi Sayadaw (1846–1923)

by Vipassana Research Institute

The Ven. Ledi Sayadaw1 was born in 1846 in Saing-pyin village, Dipeyin township in the Shwebo district (currently Monywa district) of northern Burma. His childhood name was Maung Tet Khaung. (Maung is the Burmese title for boys and young men—equivalent to "master." Tet means "climbing upward" and Khaung indicates "roof" or "summit.") It proved to be an appropriate name since young Maung Tet Khaung indeed climbed to the summit in all his endeavours.

In his village he attended the traditional monastery school where the *bhikkhus* (monks) taught the children to read and write in Burmese as well as how to recite many Pāli texts: Maṅgala Sutta, Mettā Sutta, Jātaka stories, and so on. Because of these ubiquitous monastery schools, Burma has traditionally had a very high literacy rate.

At the age of eight he began to study with his first teacher U Nanda-dhaja Sayadaw, and he ordained as a *sāmaṇera* (novice) under the same Sayadaw at the age of fifteen. He took the name Ñāṇa-dhaja (the banner of knowledge). His monastic education included Pāli grammar and various texts from the Pāli canon with a specialty in *Abhidhammattha-saṅgaha,* a commentary which serves as a guide to the *Abhidhamma*[2] section of the canon.

Later in his life he wrote a somewhat controversial commentary on *Abhidhammattha-saṅgaha,* called *Paramattha-dīpanī* (Manual of Ultimate Truth), in which he corrected certain mistakes he had found in the earlier, widely accepted commentary. His corrections were eventually accepted by the *bhikkhus* and his work became the standard reference.

During his days as a *sāmaṇera,* in the middle part of the nineteenth century (before modern lighting), he would routinely study the written texts during the day and join the *bhikkhus* and other *sāmaṇeras* in recitation from memory after dark. Working in this way he mastered the *Abhidhamma* texts.

When he was eighteen, Sāmaṇera Ñāṇa-dhaja briefly left the robes and returned to his life as a layman. He had become dissatisfied with his education, feeling it was too narrowly restricted to the *Tipiṭaka.*[3] After about six months his first teacher and another influential teacher, Myinhtin Sayadaw, sent for him and tried to persuade him to return to the monastic life; but he refused.

Myinhtin Sayadaw suggested that he should at least continue with his education. The young Maung Tet Khaung was very bright and eager to learn, so he readily agreed to this suggestion.

"Would you be interested in learning the *Vedas* (ancient sacred writings of Hinduism)?" asked Myinhtin Sayadaw.

---

1 The title Sayadaw means "venerable teacher." It was originally given to important elder monks (Theras) who instructed the king in Dhamma. Later on it became the title of highly respected monks in general.

2 Abhidhamma is the third section of the Pāli canon in which the Buddha gave detailed technical descriptions of the reality of mind and matter in a profound form.

3 Tipiṭaka is the Pāli name for the entire canon. It means "three baskets," i.e., the "basket" of the Vinaya (rules of the monks); the "basket" of the Suttas (or discourses); and the "basket" of the Abhidhamma (see footnote 2, above).

"Yes, venerable sir," answered Maung Tet Khaung.

"Well, then, you must become a *samanera,*" the Sayadaw replied. "Otherwise Sayadaw U Gandhama, of Yeu village, will not take you as his student."

"I will become a *samanera,*" he agreed. In this way, he returned to the life of a *samanera,* never to leave the robes of a monk again. Later on, he confided to one of his disciples, "At first I was hoping to earn a living with the knowledge of the **Vedas** by telling peoples' fortunes. But I was more fortunate in that I became a *samanera* again. My teachers were very wise; with their boundless love and compassion, they saved me."

The brilliant Sāmaṇera Ñāṇa-dhaja, under the care of Gandhama Sayadaw, mastered the **Vedas** in eight months and continued his study of the **Tipiṭaka.** At the age of twenty, on 20 April 1866, he took the higher ordination to become a *bhikkhu* under his old teacher U Nanda-dhaja Sayadaw, who became his preceptor (one who gives the precepts).

In 1867, just prior to the monsoon retreat, Bhikkhu Ñāṇa-dhaja left his preceptor and the Monywa district where he had grown up, in order to continue his studies in Mandalay.

Mandalay was the royal capital of Burma at that time, during the rule of King Min Don Min (who ruled from 1853–1878), and was the most important centre of learning in the country. He studied there under several of the leading Sayadaws and learned lay scholars as well. He resided primarily in the Mahā-Jotikārāma monastery and studied with Ven. San-Kyaung Sayadaw, a teacher who is famous in Burma for translating the **Visuddhimagga** (Path of Purification) into Burmese.

During this time, Ven. San-Kyaung Sayadaw gave an examination of twenty questions for two thousand students. Bhikkhu Ñāṇa-dhaja was the only one who was able to answer all the questions satisfactorily. These answers were later published in 1880, under the title **Pāramī-Dīpanī** (Manual of Perfections). This was the first of many books to be published in Pāli and Burmese by Ven. Ledi Sayadaw.

During the time of his studies in Mandalay, King Min Don Min sponsored the Fifth Council, calling *bhikkhus* from far and wide to recite and purify the **Tipiṭaka.** The Council was held in Mandalay in 1871, and the authenticated texts were carved into 729 marble slabs that stand today (each slab housed under a small pagoda) surrounding the golden Kuthodaw Pagoda at the foot of Mandalay hill. At this Council, Bhikkhu Ñāṇa-dhaja helped in the editing and translating of the **Abhidhamma** texts.

After eight years as a *bhikkhu,* having passed all his examinations, Ven. Ñāṇa-dhaja was qualified as a beginning Pāli teacher at the San-Kyaung monastery (also known as the Mahā-Jotikārāma monastery) where he had been studying.

For eight more years he remained there, teaching and continuing his own scholastic endeavours, until 1882 when he moved to Monywa. He was now thirty-six years old. At that time Monywa was a small district centre on the east bank of the Chindwin River, which was renowned as a place where the teaching method included the entire **Tipiṭaka,** rather than just selected portions.

While he was teaching Pāli to the *bhikkhus* and *samaneras* at Monywa, his habit was to come to town during the day for his teaching duties. In the evening he would cross to the west bank of the Chindwin river and spend the nights in meditation in a small **vihāra** (monastery) on the side of Lak-pan-taung mountain. Although we do not have any definitive information, it seems likely that this was the period when he

> All who have come into contact with the path of Dhamma in recent years owe a great debt of gratitude to this scholarly, saintly monk who was instrumental in re-enlivening the traditional practice of Vipassana.

began practising Vipassana in the traditional Burmese fashion: with Anapana (respiration) and *vedanā* (sensation).

The British conquered upper Burma in 1885 and sent the last king, Thibaw (who ruled from 1878–1885), into exile. The next year, 1886, Ven. Ñāṇa-dhaja went into retreat in Ledi forest, just to the north of Monywa. After awhile many *bhikkhus* started coming to him there, requesting that he teach them. A monastery to house them was built and named Ledi-tawya monastery. From this monastery he took the name by which he is best known: Ledi Sayadaw. It is said that one of the main reasons that Monywa grew to be a larger town, as it is today, was because so many people were attracted to Ledi Sayadaw's monastery there. While he taught many aspiring students at Ledi-tawya, he retained his practice of retiring to his small cottage *vihāra* across the river for his own meditation.

When he had been in the Ledi forest monastery for over ten years, his main scholastic works began to be published. The first was *Paramattha-Dīpanī* (Manual of Ultimate Truth), mentioned above, published in 1897. His second book of this period was *Nirutta Dīpanī*, a book on Pāli grammar. Because of these books he gained the reputation as one of the most learned *bhikkhus* in Burma.

Though Ledi Sayadaw was based at the Ledi-tawya monastery, he travelled throughout Burma at times, teaching both meditation and scriptural courses. He is indeed a rare example of a *bhikkhu* who was able to excel in both *pariyatti* (the theory of Dhamma) as well as *paṭipatti* (the practice of Dhamma). It was during these trips up and down Burma that many of his published works were written. For example, he wrote the *Paṭicca-samuppāda Dīpanī* in two days while travelling by boat from Mandalay to Prome. He had with him no reference books; but, because he had a thorough knowledge of the *Tipiṭaka*, he needed none. In the *Manuals of Buddhism* there are seventy-six manuals (*dīpanīs*), commentaries, essays, and so on, listed under his authorship, but this is not a complete list of his works.

Later he also wrote many books on Dhamma in Burmese. He said he wanted to write in such a way that even a simple farmer could understand. Before his time, it was not usual to write on Dhamma subjects so that lay people could have access to them. Even while teaching orally, the *bhikkhus* would commonly recite long passages in Pāli and then translate the passage literally, which was very hard for the ordinary person to understand. It must have been that the strength of Ledi Sayadaw's practical understanding and the resultant *mettā* (loving-kindness) overflowed in his desire to spread Dhamma to all levels of society. His *Paramattha-saṅkhepa*, a book of 2,000 Burmese verses which translates the *Abhidhammattha-saṅgaha*, was written for young people and is still very popular today. His followers started many associations which promoted the learning of *Abhidhamma* by using this book.

In his travels around Burma Ledi Sayadaw also discouraged the use of cow meat. He wrote one book called *Go-maṃsa-mātikā* which urged people not to kill cows for food and promoted a vegetarian diet in general.

By 1911 his reputation both as a scholar and meditation master had grown to such an extent that the British government of India, which also ruled Burma, conferred on him the title of *Aggamahā-paṇḍita* (foremost great scholar). He was also awarded a Doctorate of Literature from the University of Rangoon. During the years 1913–1917 he had a correspondence with Mrs. Rhys-Davids of the Pāli Text Society in London, and translations of several of his discussions on points of **Abhidhamma** were published in the "Journal of the Pāli Text Society."

In the last years of his life Ven. Ledi Sayadaw's eyesight failed him because of the years he had spent reading, studying and writing, often with poor illumination. At the age of seventy-three he went blind and devoted the remaining years of his life exclusively to meditation and teaching meditation. He died in 1923 at the age of seventy-seven at Pyinmana, between Mandalay and Rangoon, in one of many monasteries that had been founded in his name as a result of his travels and teaching all over Burma.

The Venerable Ledi Sayadaw was perhaps the outstanding Buddhist figure of his age. All who have come into contact with the path of Dhamma in recent years owe a great debt of gratitude to this scholarly, saintly monk who was instrumental in re-enlivening the traditional practice of Vipassana, making it more available for renunciates and lay people alike. In addition to this most important aspect of his teaching, his concise, clear and extensive scholarly work served to clarify the experiential aspect of Dhamma.

Birds are first delivered from their mothers' wombs in the form of eggs. By breaking through the shells, they are delivered for a second time. Finally when they become full fledglings, endowed with feathers and wings, they are delivered from their nests and can fly wherever they please.

Similar is the case of meditators. They are first delivered from the distractions of the mind which have accompanied them throughout the beginningless saṃsāra (cycle of rebirth), through successfully setting up mindful body contemplation (mindfulness of the body—kāyānupassanā), or by accomplishing the work of tranquillity meditation.

Secondly, when they attain insight (vipassanā) into body, mind, aggregates (rūpa, nāma, khandhā) and so on, they are free from coarse forms of ignorance.

Finally, when the seven factors of enlightenment (bojjhaṅga), develop and mature, they become fully fledged by attaining the knowledge of the supramundane path (lokuttara-magga-ñāṇa) called sambodhi. Thus are they delivered from the state of worldlings (puthujjana), attaining the state of Noble Ones (ariya) – the supramundane (lokuttara): nibbāna.

—from *The Requisites of Enlightenment*
(BodhiPakkhiya Dīpanī)
by Ven. Ledi Sayadaw

Saya Thetgyi (1873–1945)

Saya Thetgyi (1873–1945)

by Dhammācariya U Htay Hlaing

The following account is partially based on a translation of the book Saya Thetgyi by Dhammācariya U Htay Hlaing, Myanmar.

Saya Thetgyi (pronounced Sa ya' taji in Burmese) was born in the farming village of Pyawbwegyi, eight miles south of Rangoon, on the other side of the Rangoon river. He was born on 27 June 1873 and was given the name Maung Po Thet. He had two brothers and a sister, and his father died when he was about ten years old, leaving Maung Po Thet's mother to care for the four children.

His mother supported the family by selling vegetable fritters. The little boy was made to go around the village selling leftover fritters, but he often came home having sold none because he was too shy to advertise his wares by calling out. So his mother dispatched two children: Maung Po Thet to carry the fritters on a tray on his head, and his younger sister to call out.

Because he was needed to help support the family, his formal education was minimal—only about six years. His parents did not own any land or paddy (rice) fields, and used to collect the stalks of the paddy which were left over after harvesting. One day on the way home from the paddy fields, Maung Po Thet found some little fish in a pond that was drying up. He caught them and brought them home so that he could release them into the village pond. When his mother saw the fish, she was about to beat her son for catching them, but when he explained his intentions to her, she instead exclaimed, **"Sādhu, sādhu!"** (well-said, well-done). She was a kind, good-hearted woman who never nagged or scolded, but did not tolerate any *akusala* (immoral) deed.

When he was fourteen years old, Maung Po Thet started working as a bullock driver of a cart carrying paddy. He gave his daily wages to his mother. He was so small at the time that he had to take along a special box: standing on it enabled him to get in and out of the cart.

The village of Pyawbwegyi is on a flat cultivated plain, fed by many tributaries which flow into the Rangoon river. When the rice fields are flooded, navigation is a problem, and one of the common means of travel is by sampan (long, flat-bottomed boats). Maung Po Thet's next job was as a sampan oarsman. The owner of a local rice mill observed the small boy, working so diligently, carrying loads of paddy, and hired him as a tally-man in the mill, at a wage of six rupees per month. At this time he lived by himself in the mill and ate very simple meals, such as a few split pea fritters and rice.

At first he bought rice from the Indian watchman and other labourers. They told him he could help himself to the sweepings of milled rice which were kept for pig and chicken feed. Maung Po Thet refused, saying that he did not want to take the rice without the mill owner's knowledge. The mill owner found out about this, and gave his permission. As it happened, Maung Po Thet did not have to eat the rice debris for long. The sampan and cart owners gave rice to him because he was such a helpful and willing worker. Maung Po Thet continued to collect the sweepings, however, giving them to poor villagers who could not afford to buy rice.

After one year, his salary was increased to ten rupees, and after two years, to fifteen. The mill owner offered him money to buy quality rice, and allowed him free milling of one hundred baskets of paddy per month. His monthly salary increased to twenty-five rupees, which supported his mother quite well.

Maung Po Thet married Ma Hmyin when he was about sixteen years old, as was customary. His wife was the youngest of three daughters of a well-to-do landowner and paddy merchant. The couple had two children, a daughter and a son. Following the Burmese custom, they lived in a joint family with Ma Hmyin's parents and sisters. Ma Yin, the younger sister, remained single and managed a successful small business. She was later instrumental in supporting U Po Thet in practising and teaching meditation.

Ma Hmyin's eldest sister Ma Khin married Ko Kaye and had a son, Maung Nyunt. Ko Kaye managed the family paddy fields and business. Maung Po Thet, now called U Po Thet or U Thet (Mr. Thet), also prospered in the buying and selling of paddy.

As a child, U Thet had not had the opportunity to become a novice monk. (Ordination as a novice is a common and important practice in Burma). It was only when his nephew Maung Nyunt became a novice at twelve years of age that U Thet became a novice himself and later, for a time, an ordained *bhikkhu* (monk).

When he was around twenty-three, he began to practise meditation with a lay teacher, Saya Nyunt, from whom he learned Anapana. He practised Anapana for seven years.

U Thet and his wife had many friends and relatives living close by in the village. So, with many uncles, nephews, nieces, cousins and in-laws, they led an idyllic life of contentment in the warmth and harmony of family and friends.

This rustic peace and happiness was shattered when a cholera epidemic struck the village in 1903. Many villagers died, some within a few days. They included U Thet's son and young teenage daughter (who, it is said, died in his arms). His brother-in-law Ko Kaye and his wife also perished from the disease, as well as U Thet's niece (who was his daughter's playmate).

This calamity affected U Thet deeply, and he could not find refuge anywhere. He desperately wanted to find a way out of this misery. He asked permission from his wife and sister-in-law Ma Yin and other relatives to leave the village in search of "the deathless."

U Thet wandered all over Burma in his fervent search, visiting mountain retreats and forest monasteries, studying with different teachers, both monks and laymen. Finally he followed the suggestion of his first teacher, Saya Nyunt, to go north to Monywa to practise with Ven. Ledi Sayadaw. U Thet was accompanied in his wanderings by a devoted companion and follower, U Nyo.

During these years of his spiritual searching, U Thet's wife and sister-in-law remained in Pyawbwegyi and managed the rice fields. In the first few years he returned a few times to see that all was well. But when he found that the family was prospering, he began to meditate more continuously. U Thet stayed with Ledi Sayadaw for seven years in all, during which time his wife and sister-in-law supported him by sending money each year from the harvest of the family farmland.

After seven years, accompanied by U Nyo, he returned to his village, but he did not return to his former householder's life. Ledi Sayadaw had advised him at the time of his departure to work diligently to develop his *samādhi* (concentration) and *paññā* (purifying wisdom) so that eventually he could begin to teach.

Accordingly, when U Thet and U Nyo reached Pyawbwegyi, they went straight to the *sālā* (rest-house) at the edge of the family farm, which they used as a Dhamma hall. Here they began to meditate continuously. They arranged for a woman who lived near the Dhamma hall to cook two meals a day while they continued their retreat.

U Thet continued in this way for one year. He made rapid progress in his meditation, and at the end of the period he felt the need for advice from his teacher. He could not speak to Ledi Sayadaw himself, but he knew that his teacher's books were in a cupboard at his home. So he went there to consult the manuals.

His wife and her sister had become quite angry with him for not returning to the house after such a long absence. His wife had even decided to divorce him. When the sisters saw U Po Thet approaching the house, they agreed neither to greet nor welcome him. But, as soon as he came in the door, they found themselves welcoming him profusely. They talked for awhile, and U Thet asked for their forgiveness, which they freely granted.

They invited him for tea and a meal. He procured the books and explained to his wife that he was now living on eight precepts and would not be returning to the usual householder's life. From now on they would be as brother and sister.

His wife and sister-in-law invited him to come to the house each day for his morning meal and happily agreed to continue supporting him. He was extremely grateful for their generosity and told them that the only way he could repay them was to give them the Dhamma.

Other relatives including his wife's cousin, U Ba Soe, came to see and talk with him. After about two weeks, U Thet said that he was spending too much time coming and going for lunch, so Ma Hmyin and Ma Yin offered to send the noon meal to the *sālā*.

At first the people in the village were reluctant to come to him for instruction. They misinterpreted U Thet's zeal, thinking that perhaps after the grief of his losses and his absence from the village, he had lost his senses. But slowly they realized from his speech and actions that he was indeed a transformed person, one who was living in accordance to Dhamma.

Some of U Thet's relatives and friends requested that he teach them meditation. U Ba Soe offered to take charge of the fields and household responsibilities. U Thet's sister and a niece took responsibility for preparing the meals.

U Thet started teaching Anapana to a group of about fifteen people in 1914, when he was forty-one years old. The students all stayed at the *sālā*, some of them going home from time to time. He gave discourses to his meditation students, as well as to interested people who were not practising meditation. His listeners found the talks so learned that they refused to believe that U Thet had very little theoretical knowledge of the Dhamma.

Due to his wife and sister-in-law's generous financial support, and the help of other family members, all the food and other necessities were provided for the meditators who came to U Thet's Dhamma hall—even to the extent, on one occasion, of compensating workers for wages lost while they took a Vipassana course.

After teaching for a year, in about 1915, U Thet took his wife and her sister and a few other family members to Monywa to pay respects to Ledi Sayadaw, who was about seventy years old at that time. When U Thet told his teacher about his meditation experiences and the courses he had been offering, Ledi Sayadaw was very pleased.

It was during this visit that Ledi Sayadaw gave his staff to U Thet, saying, "Here, my great pupil, take my staff and go. Keep it well. I do not give this to you to make you live long, but as a reward, so that there will be no mishaps in your life. You have been successful. From today onwards, you must teach the Dhamma of *rūpa* and *nāma* (mind and matter) to six thousand people. The Dhamma known by you is inexhaustible, so propagate the *sāsana* (era of the Buddha's teaching). Pay homage to the *sāsana* in my stead."

The next day Ledi Sayadaw summoned all the *bhikkhus* (monks) of his monastery. He requested U Thet to stay on for ten or fifteen days to instruct them. The Sayadaw told the gathering of *bhikkhus*, "Take note, all of you. This layperson is my great pupil U Po Thet from lower Burma. He is capable of teaching meditation like me. Those of you who wish to practise meditation, follow him. Learn the technique from him and practise. You, **Dāyaka Thet** (lay supporter of a monk who undertakes to supply his needs such as food, robes, medicine, etc.), hoist the victory banner of Dhamma in place of me, starting at my monastery."

U Thet then taught Vipassana meditation to about twenty-five monks learned in the scriptures. It was at this point that he became known as Saya Thetgyi (*saya* means "teacher;" *gyi* is a suffix denoting respect).

Ledi Sayadaw encouraged Saya Thetgyi to teach the Dhamma on his behalf, but his student was somewhat discouraged because of his lack of theoretical knowledge. Saya Thetgyi knew many of Ledi Sayadaw's prolific writings by heart, and was able to expound on the Dhamma with references to the scriptures, in a way that most learned Sayadaws (monk teachers) could not find fault with. Nevertheless, Ledi Sayadaw's exhortation to him to teach

Vipassana in his stead was a solemn responsibility, and Saya Thetgyi was apprehensive. Bowing to his teacher in deep respect, he said, "Among your pupils, I am the least learned in the scriptures. To dispense the *sāsana* by teaching Vipassana as decreed by you is a highly subtle, yet heavy duty to perform, sir. That is why I request that, if at any time I need to ask for clarification, you give me your help and guidance. Please be my support, and please admonish me whenever necessary."

Ledi Sayadaw reassured him by replying, "I will not forsake you, even at the time of my passing away."

Saya Thetgyi and his relatives returned to their village in southern Burma. They discussed with other family members the plans for carrying out the tall order from Ledi Sayadaw. Saya Thetgyi considered travelling around Burma, thinking that he would have more contact with people that way. But his sister-in-law said, "You have a Dhamma hall here, and we can support you in your work by preparing food for the students. Why not stay here and give courses? There are many who will come here to learn Vipassana." He agreed and began holding regular courses at his *sālā* in Pyawbwegyi.

As his sister-in-law had predicted, many did start coming, and Saya Thetgyi's reputation as a meditation teacher spread. He taught simple farmers and labourers as well as those who were well-versed in the Pāli texts. The village was not far from Rangoon, which was the capital of Burma under the British, so government employees and urbanites, like U Ba Khin, also came.

As more and more meditators came to learn meditation, Saya Thetgyi appointed as assistant teachers some of the older, experienced meditators like U Nyo, U Ba Soe, and U Aung Nyunt.

The centre progressed year by year and there were up to two hundred students, including monks and nuns, in the courses. There was not enough room in the *sālā,* so the more experienced students practised meditation in their homes and came to the *sālā* only for the discourses.

From the time he returned from Ledi Sayadaw's centre, Saya Thetgyi lived by himself and ate only one meal a day, in solitude and silence. Like the *bhikkhus,* he never discussed his meditation attainments. If questioned, he would never say what stage of meditation he or any other student had achieved, although it was widely believed in Burma that he was an *anāgāmi* (person having achieved the last stage before final liberation). He was known in Burma as "Anagam Saya Thetgyi."

Since lay teachers of Vipassana were rare at that time, Saya Thetgyi faced certain difficulties that monk teachers did not face. For example, he was opposed by some because he was not as learned in the scriptures. Saya Thetgyi simply ignored these criticisms and allowed the results of the practice to speak for themselves.

On one occasion some of the rice labourers who worked on his farm took advantage of him, accusing him of withholding their share of the harvest. Although he had retired from any direct involvement in the farm management, he went out of his way to settle the affair so that the accusers would not continue to generate anger and thereby create more unwholesome conditioning for themselves.

For thirty years he taught meditation to all who came to him, guided by his own experience and using Ledi Sayadaw's manuals as a reference. By 1945, when he was seventy-two, he had fulfilled his mission of teaching thousands. His wife had died; his sister-in-law had become paralyzed; and his own health was failing. So he distributed all his property to his nieces and nephews, setting aside fifty acres of rice paddy for the maintenance of his Dhamma hall.

He had twenty water buffaloes that had tilled his fields for years. He distributed them to people who he knew would treat them kindly, and sent them off with the invocation, "You have been my benefactors. Thanks to you the rice has been grown. Now you are free from your work. May you be released from this kind of life for a better existence."

Saya Thetgyi moved to Rangoon both for treatment and to see his students there. He told some of his pupils that he would die in Rangoon and that his body would be cremated in a place where no cremation had taken place before. He also said that his ashes should not be kept in holy places because he was not entirely free from defilements—that is, he was not an *arahant* (fully enlightened being).

One of his students had established a meditation centre at Arzanigone, on the northern slope of the Shwedagon Pagoda. Nearby was a bomb shelter that had been built during the Second World War. Saya Thetgyi used this shelter as his meditation cave. At night he stayed with one of his assistant teachers. His students from Rangoon (including the Accountant General, U Ba Khin, and the Commissioner of Income Tax, U San Thein) came to see him as much as time permitted.

He instructed all who came to see him to be diligent in their practice; to treat the monks and nuns who came to practise meditation with respect; to be well-disciplined in body, speech and mind; and to pay respects to the Buddha in everything they did.

Saya Thetgyi was accustomed to go to Shwedagon Pagoda every evening, but after about a week he caught a cold and fever from sitting in the dugout shelter. Despite being treated by physicians, his condition deteriorated. As his state worsened, his nieces and nephews came from Pyawbwegyi to Rangoon. Every night his students, numbering about fifty, sat in meditation together. During these group meditations, Saya Thetgyi himself did not say anything, but silently meditated.

One night at about 10:00 pm., Saya Thetgyi was with a number of his students. (U Ba Khin was unable to be present.) He was lying on his back, and his breathing became loud and prolonged. Two of the students were watching intently, while the rest were silently meditating. At exactly 11:00 pm., the breathing became deeper.

It seemed as if each inhalation and expiration took about five minutes. After three breaths of this kind, the breathing stopped altogether, and Saya Thetgyi passed away.

His body was cremated on the northern slope of Shwedagon Pagoda and Sayagyi U Ba Khin and his disciples later built a small pagoda on the spot. But perhaps the most fitting and enduring memorial to this singular teacher is the fact that the task given him by Ledi Sayadaw of spreading the Dhamma in all strata of society is continuing.

In a Buddhist country, from the time the mother gives birth, and one becomes a human being, the Buddhists have faith in the Buddha, Dhamma and Sangha.

Since childhood one repeats "Buddhaṃ saranaṃ gacchāmi. Dhammaṃ saranaṃ gacchāmi. Saṅghaṃ saranaṃ gacchāmi."—I take refuge in the Buddha. I take refuge in the Dhamma. I take refuge in the Saṅgha. This is the Triple Gem. Of the Triple Gem, the primary importance is that of the Gem of Dhamma.

—Sayagyi U Ba Khin

Saya Thetgyi: Anecdotes

by S. N. Goenka

The Farmer Teacher

In a village across the river from Rangoon lived a farmer by the name of U Thet (Mr. Thet). Every year, after harvesting his crop, this farmer travelled up and down the country in search of someone to teach him meditation. Finally he found a teacher who showed him how to concentrate the mind by observing respiration (Anapana). For seven years he went to this teacher, spending months at a time with him. He achieved great mastery in concentration. Then he went in search of someone to teach him Vipassana, and fortunately he encountered Ledi Sayadaw. This well-respected monk found him to be a worthy pupil, and taught him the technique. For another seven years U Thet kept going to Ledi Sayadaw, and attained proficiency in insight as well. Now he could not resist teaching what he had learned to others. With the permission of Ledi Sayadaw, he returned to his village and offered to show the technique to others.

At first, however, no one would come to him. "What can this man know about the Dhamma?" people scoffed. "He is a layman like us. His head is not shaven, and he does not wear the yellow robe of a monk. What can he know about Vipassana?"

Saya Thetgyi (respected teacher Thet) was not disconcerted. On his farm were some hired labourers. He called them and said, "Ordinarily you work in the fields, but if you are willing, I will give you the same wages for working in my house."

"As you like, sir. It's all the same to us so long as we are paid." Saya Thetgyi led them to a cur-tained room. "All right, now," he told them, "Sit down, close your eyes, and focus your attention on your breath."

The men were astonished. "Is this the work we have to do here?" They thought to themselves, "Our master has gone crazy! He says that he will pay and feed us just to watch our breath! Well, if that is what he wants us to do, we'll do it!" And so they followed the instructions of Saya Thetgyi. These men passed through the process of Vipassana and emerged smiling and happy. Whether one is an illiterate labourer or a highly educated professor, the technique works for one and all.

After the course the labourers began to tell others, "Our master can teach a wonderful technique of meditation that brings real peace of mind!" But others would not listen to them, thinking that U Thetgyi had paid his workers to sing his praises, in an effort to lure students to him.

After a few months, however, it became clear to the whole village that a big change had come to the workers of U Thetgyi. Many of them had been rough and rowdy characters, always drinking and fighting, but now they were mild-mannered and peaceable. Becoming curious, the villagers began to ask these men, "What was it that your master taught you?" The men explained as best they could, and the villagers could not help but be impressed: "Well, that is what the Buddhist scriptures say. Perhaps this man really does know something. Let us go to him just to see what he teaches."

Whatever the motives that bring people to courses, if they work in the proper way they are bound to get results. So the renown of Saya Thetgyi began to spread, and he became the foremost disciple of Ledi Sayadaw.

Playing with Fire

Among those who came to learn meditation from Saya Thetgyi was a Buddhist scholar, a very learned man. Unfortunately he seemed to be more interested in the theory of Vipassana than in experiencing it himself. Still, he completed his ten-day course successfully, and left well-pleased with what he had accomplished.

A few months later this man returned to visit Saya Thetgyi, and respectfully placed before him one or two volumes. "Sir," he said, "I have written a book explaining how to meditate, and I have dedicated it to you as my teacher."

Saya Thetgyi asked, "Are only these copies that you brought here dedicated to me?"

"Oh no, sir! All contain the dedication."

"Well, if you wish to dedicate them all to me, bring all the copies of your book here." The scholar happily agreed to do so, thinking perhaps that Saya Thetgyi would perform a ceremony to bless his work. After a few days he returned with a cartload of books.

"Are these all the copies of your book?" asked Saya Thetgyi.

"Yes, sir," the man replied proudly.

"Very well," said Saya Thetgyi, "Put them in the fallow field over there." The scholar did as Saya Thet directed, arranging the books in a neat pile.

"Now," said the teacher, "Go the kitchen and get a bottle of kerosene and some matches."

"Kerosene, sir? Matches?" The man was bewildered. What use could Saya Thetgyi have for these in the ceremony?

"Yes, kerosene and matches." Once again the scholar did as he was told, though somewhat reluctantly. When he returned with the bottle and matches, Saya Thetgyi said, "Good! Now sprinkle the kerosene over the books and set them alight."

The scholar could restrain himself no longer. "What, sir! You must be joking! I have laboured so many months to write this book."

Saya Thetgyi replied, "You would have better used your time to meditate. How can you explain meditation to others unless you have meditated deeply yourself? And even if you yourself had understood it properly, how could you expect others to learn meditation from a book? They would only burn themselves as surely as children playing with fire. Better to burn the books!"

The Venerable
Webu (Vipula) Sayadaw

(1896–1977)

The Ven. Webu Sayadaw and Sayagyi U Ba Khin at the International Meditation Centre, Rangoon.

Venerable Webu Sayadaw & Sayagyi U Ba Khin

by Vipassana Research Institute

Ven. Webu Sayadaw was one of the most highly respected monks of this century in Burma. (Sayadaw is a title used for monks. It means "respected teacher monk.") He was notable in giving all importance to diligent practice rather than to scholastic achievement.

Webu Sayadaw was born in the village of Ingyinpin in upper Burma on 17 February 1896. He underwent the usual monk's training in the Pāli scriptures from the age of nine, when he became a novice, until he was twenty-seven. In 1923 (seven years after his ordination), he left the monastery and spent four years in solitude.

He practised (and later taught) the technique of ānāpāna-sati (awareness of the in-breath and out-breath). He said that by working with this practice to a very deep level of concentration, one is able to develop vipassanā (insight) into the essential characteristics of all experience: anicca (impermanence), anattā (egolessness) and dukkha (unsatisfactoriness).

Webu Sayadaw was famous for his unflagging diligence in meditation and for spending most of his time in solitude. He was reputed to be an arahant (fully enlightened one), and it is said that he never slept.

For the first fifty-seven years of his life, Webu Sayadaw stayed in upper Burma, dividing his time among three meditation centres in a small area. After his first trip to Rangoon, at the invitation of Sayagyi U Ba Khin, in 1953, he included southern Burma in his travels, visiting there to teach and meditate from time to time. He also went on pilgrimage to India and Sri Lanka.

Webu Sayadaw spent his final days at the meditation centre in the village where he was born. He passed away on 26 June 1977, at the age of eighty-one. The following describes Sayagyi's first meeting and subsequent contact with this noble person.

At the beginning of 1941, U Ba Khin had been promoted to the post of Chief Accounts Officer, Burma Railways Board. One of his duties was to travel on the Rangoon-Mandalay line auditing the accounts of local stations. He travelled in a special carriage for the Chief Accountant, with full facilities for office work and sleeping overnight. His carriage would be attached to the main train, then detached at various stations.

One day in July, by error his carriage was detached at a station in the town of Kyaukse, forty miles south of Mandalay. Although he was not scheduled to audit the accounts here, as Accounts Officer he was permitted to check the accounts of any station, and he proceeded to do this.

After his work was over, he decided to visit the nearby Shwetharlyaung Hill and set out with the local station master. Sayagyi had heard that a monk named Webu Sayadaw, who had reached a high stage of development, was residing in the area. From the top of the hill they could see a cluster of buildings in the distance. They recognized this as the monastery of Webu Sayadaw and decided to go there.

At about 3:00 pm. they arrived at the compound. An old nun sat pounding chillies and beans, and they asked her if they could pay respects to the Sayadaw.

"This is not the time to see the reverend Sayadaw," she said. "He is meditating and will not come out of his hut until about six o'clock. This monk does not entertain people. He only comes out of his hut for about half an hour in the evening. If there are people here at this time, he may give a discourse and then return to his hut. He will not meet people at times they may wish to meet him."

U Ba Khin explained that he was a visitor from Rangoon and that he did not have much time. He would like very much to meet Webu Sayadaw. Would it not be possible to pay respects outside?

The nun pointed out the hut, a small bamboo structure, and the visitors went there together. Sayagyi knelt on the ground and said, "Venerable Sir, I have come all the way from lower Burma, Rangoon, and wish to pay respects to you."

To everyone's astonishment, the door to the hut opened and the Sayadaw emerged, preceded by a cloud of mosquitoes. Sayagyi paid respects, keeping his attention in the body with awareness of *anicca*.

"What is your aspiration, layman?" Webu Sayadaw asked Sayagyi.

"My aspiration is to attain *nibbāna*, sir," U Ba Khin replied.

"*Nibbāna?* How are you going to attain *nibbāna?*"

"Through meditation and by knowing *anicca*, sir," said Sayagyi.

"Where did you learn to be aware of this *anicca?*"

Sayagyi explained how he had studied Vipassana meditation under Saya Thetgyi.

"You have been practising Vipassana?"

"Yes, sir, I am practising Vipassana."

"What sort of Vipassana?" Webu Sayadaw questioned him closely and Sayagyi gave the details. The Sayadaw was very pleased.

He said, "I have been meditating in this jungle alone for years in order to experience such stages of Vipassana as you describe." He seemed astonished to encounter a householder who had reached advanced proficiency in the practice without being a monk.

Webu Sayadaw meditated with Sayagyi, and after some time said, "You must start teaching now. You have acquired good *pāramī* (accumulated merit), and you must teach the Dhamma to others. Do not let people who meet you miss the benefits of receiving this teaching. You must not wait. You must teach—teach now!"

With a Dhamma injunction of such strength from this saintly person, U Ba Khin felt he had no choice but to teach. Back at the railway station, the assistant station master became his first student. Sayagyi instructed him in Anapana meditation in his railway carriage, using the two tables of the dining compartment as their seats.

Although Sayagyi did not begin to teach in a formal way until about a decade later, this incident was a watershed. It marked the point at which Sayagyi began to share his knowledge of meditation with others.

In 1953, at a time when there was much conflict and strife in lower Burma, some government officials suggested that they should invite some of the saintly monks of the country to visit the capital, Rangoon. There was a traditional belief that if a highly developed person visited in a time of trouble, it would have a beneficial effect and the disturbances would calm down. Webu Sayadaw was not well-known in Rangoon because prior to this time he had strictly confined his travels to his three meditation compounds at Kyaukse, Shwebo and Ingyinpin, never leaving this small area of northern Burma. Sayagyi, however, felt strongly that this saintly monk should be invited to visit Rangoon.

Even though he had not seen nor communicated with Webu Sayadaw since 1941, Sayagyi felt confident that he would accept the invitation, so he sent one of his assistants to upper Burma to ask the Sayadaw to come and visit his centre in Rangoon for one week. This was during the time of the monsoon retreat when the monks, according to their monastic rules, must spend their time in meditation rather than in travel. Monks are not ordinarily permitted to travel during the monsoon retreat; however, for a special purpose, a monk may leave his retreat for up to seven days.

When U Ba Khin's messenger reached Mandalay and people heard what his mission was, they scoffed. "Webu Sayadaw never travels," they told him. "Especially not now during the rainy season. He will not go out for even one night, let alone seven days. You are wasting your time." Nevertheless, Sayagyi had sent him on this errand, so he persevered. He hired a taxi to Shwebo and sought an audience with the Ven. Sayadaw. When the assistant told Webu Sayadaw that he had been sent by Sayagyi U Ba Khin and extended Sayagyi's invitation, the monk exclaimed, "Yes, I am ready. Let us go." This response was a great surprise to everyone.

Webu Sayadaw, accompanied by some of the monks from his monastery, then paid a visit to the International Meditation Centre. This visit, coming after more than a decade since the two

men had first met, demonstrated Webu Sayadaw's high regard for Sayagyi. Moreover, it was unusual for a monk to stay at the meditation centre of a lay teacher.

Between the years of 1954 and his death in 1977, Webu Sayadaw made regular annual visits to towns in southern Burma to teach Dhamma. During Sayagyi's lifetime, he periodically visited I.M.C. as well. The Sayadaw was held to have attained high attainments in meditation, and it was a great honour for I.M.C. to receive him.

When Webu Sayadaw visited Sayagyi's centre, he usually gave a short Dhamma talk every day. He once mentioned, "When we first visited this place it was like a jungle, but now what progress has been made in these years. It resembles the time of the Buddha when many benefited! Can one count the number? Innumerable!"

At one time, Sayagyi decided to fulfil the Burmese tradition of becoming a monk at least once in one's lifetime. Without notifying anyone in advance, he and one of his close disciples, U Ko Lay (the ex-Vice-chancellor of Mandalay University) went to Webu Sayadaw's centre at Shwebo and, under the Sayadaw's guidance, took robes for a period of about ten days.

After Sayagyi's death, Webu Sayadaw visited Rangoon and gave a private interview to about twenty-five students from Sayagyi's centre. When it was reported to him that Sayagyi had died, he said, "Your Sayagyi never died. A person like your Sayagyi will not die. You may not see him now, but his teaching lives on. Not like some persons who, even though they are alive, are as if dead—who serve no purpose and who benefit none."

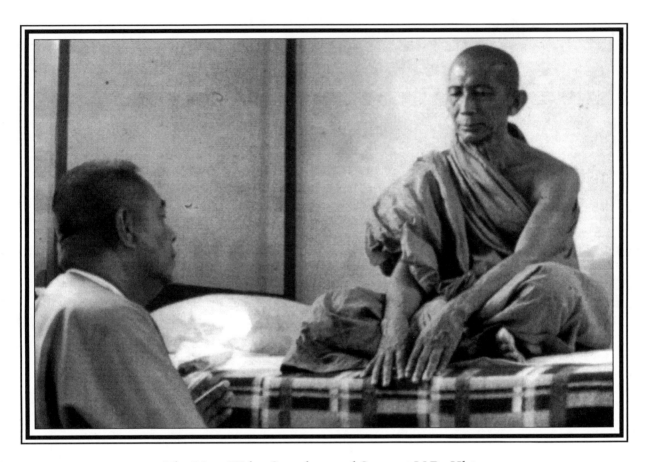

The Ven. Webu Sayadaw and Sayagyi U Ba Khin

Now Is the Time

translated by Ven. Ñāṇissara

Discourse by Ven. Webu Sayadaw addressing Sayagyi U Ba Khin and his students

Ven. Webu Sayadaw: *Dakagyis* and *dakamagyis* (gentlemen and ladies)!

You should establish your minds on the straight path to liberation (*vimutti*), and you should endeavour to possess *sovacassataguṇa* (receptivity to the teachings of Buddha). You should pay respect to the Sangha and give donation to them in order to honour the peerless dispensation of the Buddha. When you gain merits in this way, you must wish well for yourselves in this manner: "May I enter into *nibbāna* by attaining *bodhiñāṇa* (knowledge of enlightenment)."

By *bodhi* I mean penetration of the Four Noble Truths. There are three kinds of *bodhi*:

1. *sammā sambodhi* (full enlightenment)

2. *paccekabodhi* (solitary enlightenment)

3. *sāvakabodhi* (the enlightenment of a disciple)

Wishing well for yourselves means that you determine to attain one of these three enlightenments. If you analyse it, there are also three types of *sāvakabodhi*:

1. *agga-sāvakabodhi* (foremost disciple's enlightenment)

2. *mahā-sāvakabodhi* (great disciple's enlightenment)

3. *pakati-sāvakabodhi* (normal disciple's enlightenment)

So, you have many ways and many destinations in this peerless dispensation; you can go to your destination as you like, according to your wishes.

There were countless noble beings who attained enlightenment in these ways. Why were their determined wishes achieved? Because the time was right, the place was right and the endeavour was right.

From the time when the Buddha attained enlightenment, so many *devas* (deities) and men came to him, paid respect and listened to the teaching. From that time, those who have known and followed the teaching of the Buddha, who have endeavoured rightly, have accomplished their wishes.

They were not satisfied by seeing the splendid physical appearance of the Buddha, nor by merely listening to the noble Dhamma taught by him. Having developed unshakable confidence and clear understanding, they entered into the teaching and took the teaching as their shelter. The compassionate Buddha delineated the truth for them. He instructed them in how to know the truth which he had discerned. As soon as they understood the teaching of the Buddha, they followed and practised the Dhamma tirelessly, with strong endeavour, in all the four postures of the body. This is right endeavour: to practise tirelessly, successively, sorrowlessly in order to dispel the defilements and fulfil the wholesome qualities.

When a pious man accomplishes his right wish (*sammā-chanda*) by striving with diligence, he is glad in the fullness of happiness. This real happiness, free from defilements, has overcome continual suffering in successive lives. This is the happiness of freedom. Such persons are never envious or grasping, so they always share the happiness of their freedom with others. Sharing of merits is their duty. It is good to be glad!

So, for the gladdening of good people and for the happiness of all beings, all of you must propagate and maintain the teachings in your hearts. You lay people, you support the teachings by giving the requisites to the monks. And the monks support the people with the teaching. How good, how very glad!

One who possesses right effort and strives diligently, one who possesses clear faith, who is generously supported, one who possesses this quality of gentle receptivity (sovacassataguṇa); he gains the benefits. This is the great effect of the teaching.

In this way, from the time of the Buddha until now, good people with right wishes, right effort and strong faith have taken up the duties of the Buddha-sāsana (dispensation of Buddha). It is so good and joyous to be happily carrying the teachings from generation to successive generation. These are excellent opportunities that can be attained from the teachings by a pious person who endeavours when the time and place are right.

When the Buddha began to teach the Dhamma on his Dhamma journey, the king of Rājagaha (Bimbisāra), who ruled the kingdom of Magadha, attained wisdom, real happiness and liberation. The king was so keen and so wise that he donated the Veluvana grove for the accommodation of the Sangha. The Buddha taught many different sorts of discourses there to many different beings: devas and men. From that day to the present, countless beings have enjoyed real peace and happiness because of the teachings.

What is the teaching of the Buddha?

Sayagyi U Ba Khin: It is the three baskets of the teachings, bhante [venerable sir: term used to address a monk].

What are these?

Sutta (discourses), *Vinaya* (discipline), *Abhidhamma* (subtle, sublime teaching), bhante.

Oh, yes. These are for learning. But, when someone learns the three baskets in essence, he gets sīla (morality), samādhi (concentration), and paññā (wisdom). What is this for?

This is to follow, undertake and practise.

When someone follows and practises them, what benefit can he attain?

He can attain real happiness, peace and liberation, bhante.

The attainment of the benefits: is it here or hereafter?

Here and now, bhante! It is not delayed.

Aye! That is sandiṭṭhika, akālika: the nature of Dhamma is worthy of seeing by yourself, here and now, without delay. Ah, very excellent! So wonderful! How many kinds of *dhammas* (characteristics) are in the *Tipiṭaka* (scriptures)?

Three, bhante.

Sutta, Vinaya and *Abhidhamma*. And then, how many kinds are in *paṭipatti* (practice)?

Sīla, samādhi and paññā, bhante, in *paṭipatti*.

In *paṭipatti*, and how many in the penetration (*paṭivedha*)?

Magga (path), *phala* (fruition) and *nibbāna*. Three, bhante.

Though the *dhammas* are many in number, nevertheless in the characteristic of liberation, there is only one: that is *vimutti*. And in the aspect of practice there is only one, unique way: that is *sati* (awareness). Therefore men and *devas* who have followed the unique method have attained the unique Dhamma: *vimutti* equals *nibbāna*.

This is *eko* Dhamma (one Dhamma), that is taught by the Buddha. In analytical details there are countless *dhammas*, but if you learn only one of these *dhammas*, it is enough for you to practise.

For a person who wants to get liberated from the cycle of suffering, the requirements are the qualities of receptivity and gentleness (*sovacassa-taguṇa*), ardent energetic will (*āraddha-vīriya*) and penetrative wisdom (*paṭividdha paññā*). When he possesses these qualities, he will get liberated from the round of becoming without fail.

So, you should seize the instructions of the Teacher in the peerless dispensation. When you have grasped the teaching exactly, you have to place your attention in the body. You should fix the mind on the body, keeping it there steadily to train the mind to become tame.

What is the fixing of the mind?

It is mindfulness (*sati*).

What is keeping the mind steady?

It is concentration (*samādhi*).

What is the training of the mind?

It is effort (*viriya*).

What is the taming of the mind?

It is wisdom (*paññā*), bhante.

Oh *dakagyi* (gentleman): *sādhu, sādhu,...* good, quite right! How is it? Excellent! So wonderful!

Right! *Evaṃ*, bhante (it is so, sir). This is the wonder of the excellent *sāsana* (dispensation).

There is a great deal of hearing, learning-knowledge (*suta-mayā paññā*). Lots! But it needs to persist firmly in the mind. For this the learning-knowledge should lead to development-knowledge (*bhāvanā-mayā paññā*) which can penetrate the mass of defilements. Only this penetrative knowledge can bring you to liberation. It is right?

Yes, bhante.

Right! This is the only real merit. When the real merit is persistently present in one's mind, then greed, anger, delusion, sorrow,

lamentation, etc., are absent in him and he will enjoy real happiness and peace. It is so good, isn't it?

Yes, reverend bhante.

So, the absence of desire is called happiness. The absence of hatred is called happiness. The absence of delusion is called wisdom. These benefits come in this life. Do not delay their development! *Asoka* (non-sorrow), *virāga* (absence of desire): these are the only real joy, peace and cessation.

Your strong wish—aspiring to liberation from these defilements—is the road to power (*chanda-iddhi-pāda*). When you possess this strong wish as the basis, your effort becomes very energetic. This becomes energetic-will as the road to power (*viriya-iddhi-pāda*). Then your mind becomes strong and steady, straight and concentrated. This is called the consciousness which is the road to power (*citta-iddhi-pāda*). When these three—wishes, effort and consciousness—become strengthened, concentrated and energetic; at that time reason, investigation, complete wisdom is achieved. This wisdom is called a road to power (*vimaṃsa-iddhi-pāda*).

In this way, the Buddha expounded: *kevalaṃ paripuṇṇaṃ, satthu sāsanaṃ* (the whole dispensation is complete in its entirety). Now, like this, is it wholly completed?

It is actually completed, in all tasks, bhante.

He who has entirely completed all tasks has achieved happiness here and now, with no delay. This is the incomparable happiness in which tangled, perturbed defilements have passed away, ceased without exception. Such happiness, firmly seated in the meditator, never retreats, never changes. You should pay respect to and think highly of this supra-mundane happiness.

In the worldly happiness, happiness arising from sensual pleasures, there are many tangles, perturbations, interruptions, opponents, sorrows, and so on. Is this right?

Right, bhante.

Consider, for example: the happiness of human beings, the happiness of human kings, the happiness of gods and goddesses, the happiness of kings of gods and goddesses. These happinesses are but names, mere designations. They are insubstantial; there is no core inside them. When one enjoys any of these happinesses, how are they enjoyed?

They are enjoyed by feeling, bhante.

So, these are called happiness enjoyed by feeling *(vedayita sukha)*. Sensual happiness is always changing, never lasting *(vipariṇāma, anicca)*. When men and gods enjoy this worldly happiness of sensation, does defilement lie dormant in the feelings?

Bhante, if they enjoy the happiness with pleasure, then surely greed, desire and lust lie dormant in the feeling.

Suppose these enjoyers of sensual pleasure are afraid of five enemies (i.e., fire, water, a bad king, robbers, fools); or they must give up their enjoyments because they have consumed the results of previous good actions; or they are near death because they have consumed their life-span. At times like these, how do they enjoy their sense pleasures?

On the eve of these events, they could not enjoy their sensual pleasures with a feeling of happiness. **They would surely feel sorrow, lamentation, worry, anxiety and so on.**

Meanwhile, what kind of defilements lie dormant in their feelings?

Bhante, anger or hatred lies dormant in their sensations of misery.

So, the happiness of pleasant-feeling exists only for a moment, a very short period of time. It is in constant flux. It has no substantial core. The peaceful happiness *(santisukha)* never changes, is not in flux and lasts forever. Why? *Santisukha* has no defilements; it eradicates all defilements which are the roots of various miseries. It uproots them without exception. This is the cessation of defilements. This is the cessation of suffering. These are the benefits of the Dhamma.

Therefore, O *upāsakas* and *upāsikas* (laymen and laywomen disciples), now, while you can seize the excellent opportunity, during the dispensation of the peerless Teacher, try hard, endeavour ardently, with strong wishes, right effort, straight consciousness and bright wisdom to attain the peaceful happiness here and now, without delay.

May all of you be peaceful.

All listeners in attendance: *Sādhu! Sādhu! Sādhu!* (Well said! Well said! Well said!)

This discourse was translated from Burmese by Ven. Ñānissara (Sagaing, Myanmar) at V.I.A. Dhamma Giri, in October 1991.

Webu Sayadaw does not talk much with others, but he spoke a lot to me. He said, "You have pāramī. You will have to disperse the sāsana. Remember, spreading the sāsana means sending a person onto the Noble Eightfold Path—to make a person secure in sīla, samādhi and paññā. This is called dispersion of the sāsana.

To donate the four articles of the monks such as the monastery, food, robes, medicines, is to support the sāsana. It is just an act of sāsananugala and not dispersion of the sāsana. You will have to spread the sāsana. Do not delay; do it now. If you delay, the people who are in contact with you now will miss the Dhamma. So start right now."

When I got back to the station, I started teaching Dhamma to the assistant station master who was with me, right there in the railway carriage. Since then, I became a meditation teacher.

—*Sayagyi U Ba Khin*

Vipassana Students Meet with the Venerable Webu Sayadaw

In January 1976, on the fifth anniversary of Sayagyi's demise, a number of Goenkaji's Western Vipassana students travelled to Rangoon, Burma to meditate at Sayagyi's centre. During their stay, they met with the Ven. Webu Sayadaw, whose remarks were conveyed through a translator.

Translator: These are the disciples of Sayagyi U Ba Khin: fifteen foreign disciples, men and women. Today [19 January 1976] is the fifth anniversary of Sayagyi U Ba Khin's death. Fifty monks were offered breakfast very early this morning, and about one hundred fifty disciples were invited to the feeding ceremony. These foreign disciples have been coming during the whole month for their Vipassana course at the centre. These people can stay in Burma only for seven days; so they do meditation for seven days, and leave for Bangkok or Calcutta, and then come back here again. Some of them are on their second trip. More will be coming for the third trip. The meditation course is arranged for the whole of this month to commemorate the passing away of Sayagyi.

Some are from America, some from England, France and New Zealand—very far away places—representing many nationalities. Some have come from Australia; and there is one disciple from Malaysia.

Webu Sayadaw: This is just like the time of our Lord Buddha. Then, also, they arrived at the presence of the Buddha, all at the same time. Not from the same country, not from the same town, same place; but from different countries, different towns—all men of noble hearts, arriving simultaneously at the same place to pay respect to Lord Buddha. No beings, whether human or celestial, ever tired of giving homage to the Lord Buddha. Gladdened at heart, they worshipped the Buddha in great adoration.

The Buddha, having unbounded love, pity and compassion for all beings, showed them the way. They followed and practised his teachings with meekness and in all humility, being good and disciplined students. Wandering forlornly the whole of *saṃsāra* (cycle of rebirths), looking for a way out, they had now reached the end of their journey, they had now found what they have been searching for the whole of *saṃsāra*.

Innumerable are those who attained *nibbāna* (freedom from suffering) by following Buddha's advice.

You all are just like those seekers of the old days. And, just like them, if you are determined to acquire what they did; are equipped with the noble zeal and earnestness, having now reached a place of sanctity where Buddha's teachings are perpetuated; doing all that is necessary to be done; following the teachings with meekness and humility, without wasting time; working hard in this way—being able to work hard in this way, you will achieve what you have been working for, the supreme goal of the holy life. This is something you should all feel happy about.

Do they understand what I have said? I wonder if they do.

Translator: One or two might understand, Sir. They have learned some Burmese in America.

Sayadaw: Have they really? Well, very good! I am glad. The ones who understand can then pass on the teachings of the Buddha to the rest, thus benefiting many. Isn't it so?

Who is the one who can speak Burmese fluently? So *dakagyi* (gentleman)—you understand Burmese, you understand me? Only a little? Well, a little will be useful! Understanding even a little of what Buddha taught will be a great help. Just a few of Buddha's words is not really little; it means a great deal.

There is something which you have longed for, worked for throughout the *saṃsāra*. When you understand the teachings of Buddha and follow his advice, you will achieve what you have been looking for. Now, what is it that you all wish for, now and for always, throughout the lengthy *saṃsāra*? What do I mean by "now"? I mean the immediate present—right this moment.

You all want happiness, relief from suffering, right now—don't you all? And you all want to

> **I**nnumerable are the holy ones who have trod the path and reached the nibbāna. If you set up sufficient *viriya* and work diligently with all humility, you also will arrive at your goal.

be assured of happiness in *saṃsāra*, too. Well, going the rounds of *saṃsāra* means you are all the time subjected to old age, illness and death. It means great suffering. You all are afraid of old age, illness and death, aren't you? Yes, you all are, I'm sure. Being frightened, you don't want to have anything to do with that, do you?

What you really long for is a place where these sufferings don't exist, a place of happiness because these sufferings are not existent—where old age, illness and death are unknown. Where all these sufferings cease; in short, *nibbāna*. This is what you are striving for. If you follow Buddha's instructions with due meekness and in all humility, you will achieve your goal, won't you? You will have accomplished all your work, having gained success, having gained what you always longed for.

So, what you understand may be very little—only a short, brief teaching. But if you follow it diligently, the achievement will not be small. It is what you have been striving for throughout the ages. Can it be regarded as only a small reward? Not at all! It is indeed a big reward.

Once you understand the instructions, however brief and concise, and follow it carefully, ceaselessly, happiness will be yours. Happiness will be for all the universe, for all the humans, the **devas** and the **brahmās** (celestial beings). Although the teaching is little, the achievement is great. All that you want is achieved. Is it not so? Indeed, it is so.

So, *dakagyi*, you can manage to follow and practise that little instruction? Can you? Very good!

Like you all, at the time of our Blessed One, there were people who wandered forth, looking for peace and happiness for all time. They were looking for it before the Enlightened One had made his appearance yet. Who were they? Oh, you can say, the whole world! But I will single out for you the example of Sāriputta and Mogallāna, the auspicious pair who later became the two chief disciples of the Blessed One. Maybe you are acquainted with the story of their going forth.

Sāriputta and Mogallāna were living the holy life as wanderers, looking for the deathless. It was Sāriputta who first came into contact with one of the five disciples who had learned the law from the Blessed One. The wanderer Sāriputta saw him going round for food. Seeing his faculties serene, the colour of his skin clear and bright, Sāriputta at once knew that he possessed the knowledge of the way he had been looking for.

Sāriputta followed the holy man until he had finished his round and left him alone with his alms food. He waited at a respectable distance while the holy man ate his meal, then went up to him, paying courteous respect, and asked him about his teacher and the law he taught. (All this is in the *Piṭakas* [Buddhist scriptures], but I will give you just a short summary, just a little.)

The holy monk replied that he had gone forth under the Blessed One who was his teacher, and it was the Blessed One's law that he confessed. When Sāriputta pressed for exposition of the law, the holy monk said, "I have only recently gone forth. I have only just come to this law and discipline. I cannot teach you the law in detail. I can tell you its meaning in brief."

This holy monk had actually reached the supreme goal, so he must actually have known the whole law; but he confessed in all humility that he knew only a little. Then Sāriputta—the one who later became the chief exponent of the Blessed One's law—said that he did not want much; he wanted to hear only a little of what the Buddha taught.

The holy monk granted his request. He gave him only a sketch of the law. How little was it? So little that it was not even a full stanza. When Sāriputta heard the short statement of the law, he said that it was sufficient for him; for the spotless, immaculate vision of the whole Dhamma had arisen in him after hearing just a little of it.

So the teaching was very little. But the understanding by Sāriputta was not little at all! He understood the whole law.

So also, *dakagyi*, you understand that little, don't you, now?

Well, if you do and follow the Blessed One's advice, your achievement will be very great.

I, of course, cannot speak your language. So you, *dakagyi*, if you understand a little, pass it onto your friends, so all of you will know a little of Dhamma. Can you do this? I am sure you can.

You all have accumulated, each one of you, great *pāramīs* (virtues, perfections). That's why you are all here, coming from various countries, distant lands, far, far away from here. But, because you have acquired sufficient *pāramīs*, you all arrived here at the same time, simultaneously from different countries.

And then, having reached here, you want to know the law, so you have heard the law; you have learnt the Buddha's advice. And you do not remain satisfied with just hearing the law and just remembering it. You want to practise it. So you strive energetically and begin to walk the path. You establish necessary *viriya* (effort) and, in time, you must surely enjoy the fruits of your effort. Even now—you know of course, don't you?—you are getting results commensurate with your applications and diligence.

You all are here now because you have acquired sufficient *pāramīs* to do so. The Blessed One said that if you stay with Dhamma and follow the law, you are dwelling near him, although physically you may be at the other end of the universe, far away from him.

On the other hand, if you reside near him—so near, so close that you could hold the end of his robes with your hand—yet, if you don't follow his advice and practise the law according to his instructions, there is the whole distance of the universe between him and you.

So, now, you live in such-and-such countries, far far away; and yet with the Blessed One you all are so close to him. And following his advice, diligently with due meekness, you will have your wish achieved. You will have won the goal which you have strived for throughout the *saṃsāra*.

Innumerable are the holy ones who have trod the path and reached the *nibbāna*. So also you from different countries, different towns, all holy people, arriving simultaneously at the place of sanctity. If you set up sufficient *viriya* and work diligently with all humility, you also will arrive at your goal.

This is really an occasion for happiness and joy! We all can't help being buoyant in spirit and cheering and admiring you, seeing your wonderful devotion and zeal. I wish you all success. Well done, well done!

Have you all strived, without interruption, in all the four postures, whether you are lying down, sitting, walking or standing? Have you all strived in that manner, continuously, without interruption?

Students: (Laughter)

You are trying at all times? Not at all times?

Not continuously.

It is not difficult or hard to strive with *viriya*, neither does it cause any pain. (**Laughter.**) If you are striving with complete *viriya*, doesn't it cause happiness?

Yes.

If you are not striving, do you feel happy?

No.

Which do you prefer, happiness or suffering?

(Laughter.)

Our *samādhi* (concentration) is like a candle in the wind…Our problems are effort, awareness and concentration. Our *samādhi* is very weak.

If you are going forward, you are progressing. The only thing is: don't stop! Strive diligently, with *viriya*. Do you know what *viriya* is?

Effort.

The noble ones of the olden days strived with *viriya*, without any interruption, and happiness set in. If you follow the teachings of Lord Buddha with attention and without interruption, you will experience the result of your noble aspirations. Just remember one thing: strive without interruption, and happiness will be immediate.

How many hours is it since your arrival in Burma?

Twenty-four hours.

Since your arrival here, have you striven to the fullest?

Not every hour, no.

In the hours that you have tried, haven't you been happy?

Sometimes when I meditate I fall asleep, and then I'm not happy.

Great happiness sets in the inner self of one who strives. Is striving difficult? If it is not difficult nor causes pain, then don't relax, become happy!

And if it is difficult and painful?

If you strive diligently, will you experience anything which causes suffering?

The striving itself may be painful, but the result of striving would not be painful.

By striving with total *viriya*, isn't the aim and objective to achieve happiness? Happiness will certainly be achieved. So, does striving cause pain?

The pain is when we fall asleep.

Do you fall asleep when your *viriya* is small or large? You should use all the *viriya* that you possess.

Everybody here has got a certain amount of *viriya*, but not all the time.

Everybody has got *viriya*. Are you saving a portion of it for a future time? **(Laughter.)** Do you strive to the fullest, utmost efforts?

I don't strive like that every moment. Sometimes I fall asleep.

Falling asleep is *thīna-middha* (sloth and torpor). Does this set in when *viriya* is small or when it is large?

When *viriya* is small.

If you strive to follow the noble teachings of Lord Buddha, to get your mind to stay where you want it to, do you need small *viriya* or big *viriya*?

Big *viriya*.

Yes. For a child to climb the Himalayas takes a long time. He must use all his effort, but still, he will fall at times. We are like children trying to climb the Himalayas, so we fall from time to time. If you know you are falling you must strive with *sati* (awareness).

Our *sati* is like a candle flame in a windy room. It's never still.

If you stay in an enclosed place where the breeze cannot get in, will the flame flicker? So, you must stay in a place where it will not be possible for the breeze to enter.

Where can we find such a place?

Viriya! Now, if you come here from another place, don't you have to strive to get here? Ask yourself, do you wish to get here quickly or slowly?

Quickly.

If you want to arrive quickly will you walk slowly?

No.

Would it be possible for anyone to ask that person who wants to arrive quickly to walk slowly? Do you understand now? You all have got good *viriya*. You have come here from so far away, so you have got lots of *viriya*. Utilize all of that *viriya*. If you leave aside a portion of that *viriya*, won't the enemies (namely *thīna-middha*) set in? If you use all the *viriya* that you possess, what will be the result?

We will fulfil our aspirations.

If one strives with all the *viriya* one possesses without keeping aside any portion of the *viriya*, the noble aspirations will be fulfilled, just as the noble ones of the olden days achieved their aspirations.

Essays by S.N. Goenka

The Art of Living: Vipassana Meditation

by S.N. Goenka

The following is based on a public talk given by S.N. Goenka in July 1980 in Bern, Switzerland.

Everyone seeks peace and harmony, because these are what we lack in our lives. From time to time we all experience agitation, irritation, disharmony, suffering; and when we suffer from agitation, we do not keep this misery limited to ourselves. We keep distributing it to others as well. The agitation permeates the atmosphere around the miserable person. Everyone else who comes into contact with him becomes irritated, agitated. Certainly this is not the proper way to live.

One ought to live at peace within oneself, and at peace with others. After all, a human being is a social being. One has to live in society—to live and deal with others. How to live peacefully? How to remain harmonious within ourselves, and to maintain peace and harmony around us, so that others also can live peacefully and harmoniously?

When one is agitated, then, to come out of it, one has to know the basic reason for the agitation, the cause of the suffering. If one investigates the problem, it soon becomes clear that whenever one starts generating any negativity or defilement in the mind, one is bound to become agitated. A negativity in the mind—a mental defilement or impurity—cannot coexist with peace and harmony.

How does one start generating negativity? Again investigating, it becomes clear. I become very unhappy when I find someone behaving in a way which I don't like, when I find something happening which I don't like. Unwanted things happen, and I create tension within myself. Wanted things do not happen, some obstacles come in the way, and again I create tension within myself; I start tying knots within myself. Throughout one's life, unwanted things keep happening, wanted things may or may not happen, and this process of reaction, of tying knots—Gordian knots—makes the entire mental and physical structure so tense, so full of negativity. Life becomes miserable.

Now one way to solve the problem is to arrange things such that nothing unwanted happens in my life, and that everything keeps on happening exactly as I desire. I must develop such a power—or somebody else must have the power and must come to my aid whenever I request it—that everything I want keeps happening. But this is not possible. There is no one in the world whose desires are always fulfilled, in whose life everything happens according to his wishes, without anything unwished-for happening. Things keep occurring that are contrary to our desires and wishes. So, in spite of these things which I don't like, how not to react blindly? How not to create tension? How to remain peaceful and harmonious?

In India as well as in other countries, wise saintly persons of the past studied this problem—the problem of human suffering—and they found a solution. If something unwanted happens and one starts to react by generating anger, fear, or any negativity, then as soon as possible one should divert one's attention to something else. For example, get up, take a glass of water, start drinking—your anger will not multiply; you'll be coming out of your anger.

Or start counting: one, two, three, four. Or start repeating a word, a phrase, or perhaps some mantra. It becomes easy if you use the name of a deity or a saintly person in whom you have devotion. The mind is diverted, and to some extent you'll be out of the negativity, out of anger.

This solution was helpful; it worked. It still works. Practising this, the mind feels free from agitation. In actuality, however, this solution works only at the conscious level. By diverting one's attention one in fact pushes the negativity deep into the unconscious, and at this level one continues to generate and multiply the same defilement. At the surface level there is a layer of peace and harmony, but in the depths of the mind is a sleeping volcano of suppressed negativity, which keeps erupting in violent explosions from time to time.

Other explorers of inner truth went still further in their search. By experiencing the reality of mind and matter within themselves, they recognized that diverting the attention is only running away from the problem. Escape is no solution; one must face the problem. Whenever a negativity arises in the mind, just observe it, face it. As soon as one starts observing any mental defilement, then it begins to lose all its strength. Slowly it withers away and is uprooted.

A good solution, avoiding both extremes of suppression and of free license. Keeping the negativity in the unconscious will not eradicate it, and allowing it to manifest in physical or vocal action will only create more problems. If one just observes, then the defilement passes away: one has eradicated that negativity, is free from that defilement.

This sounds wonderful, but is it really practical? When anger arises, it overpowers us so quickly that we don't even notice. Then, overpowered by anger, we commit certain actions which are harmful to us and to others. Later,

when the anger has passed, we start crying and repenting, begging pardon from this or that person or god: "Oh, I made a mistake. Please excuse me!" Again the next time, in a similar situation, we react in the same way. All this repenting does not help at all.

The difficulty is that I am not aware when a defilement starts. It begins deep at the unconscious level of the mind, and by the time it reaches the conscious level, it has gained so much strength that it overwhelms me. I cannot observe it.

Then I must keep a private secretary with me, so that whenever anger starts, he says, "Look master! Anger is starting!" Since I don't know when this anger will start, I must have three private secretaries for three shifts, around the clock; or rather, four of them to give staggering holidays!

Suppose I can afford that, and the anger starts to arise. At once my secretary tells me, "Oh, master, look! Anger has started." Then the first thing I do is slap and abuse him: "You fool! Do you think you are paid to teach me?" I am so overpowered by anger that no good advice will help.

Suppose that wisdom prevails and I do not slap him. Instead I say, "Thank you very much. Now I must sit down and observe the anger." Is it possible? As soon as I close my eyes and try to observe the anger, immediately the object of anger comes into my mind, the person or incident because of which I became angry. Then I am not observing the anger. Rather, I am observing the external stimulus of the emotion. This will only multiply the anger. This is no solution. It is very difficult to observe any abstract negativity, abstract emotion, divorced from the external object which aroused it.

However, one who reached the ultimate truth in full enlightenment found a real solution. He discovered that whenever any defilement arises in the mind, simultaneously, two things start happening at the physical level. One is that the breath loses its normal rhythm. I start breathing hard whenever a negativity comes into the mind. This is one reality which everyone can experience, though it be very gross and apparent. At the same time, at a subtler level, some kind of biochemical reaction starts within the body—some sensation. Every defilement will generate one sensation or the other inside, in one or another part of the body.

This is a practical solution. An ordinary person cannot observe abstract defilements of the mind—abstract fear, anger or passion. But with proper training and practice, it is very easy to observe the respiration and the sensations, both of which are directly related to the mental defilements.

The respiration and the sensations will help me in two ways. First, they will be my private secretaries. As soon as a defilement starts in the mind, my breath will lose its normality. It will start shouting: "Look, something has gone wrong!" I cannot slap the breath; I have to accept the warning. Similarly, the sensations tell me: "Something has gone wrong." I must accept this. Then, having been warned, I start observing the respiration, the sensations, and I find very quickly that the defilement passes away.

This mental-physical phenomenon is like a coin with two sides. On the one side is whatever thoughts or emotions arise in the mind. On the other side are the respiration and sensation in the body. Any thought or emotion (whether conscious or unconscious), any mental defilement manifests in the breath and sensation of that moment. Thus by observing the respiration or sensation, I am indirectly observing the mental defilement. Instead of running away from the problem, I am facing the reality as it is. Then I will find that the defilement loses its strength; it can no longer overpower me as it did in the past. If I persist, the defilement eventually disappears altogether and I remain peaceful and happy.

In this way, the technique of self-observation shows us reality in its two aspects, outside and inside. Previously, one always looked with open eyes, missing the inner truth. I always looked outside for the cause of my unhappiness. I always blamed and tried to change the reality outside. Being ignorant of the inner reality, I never understood that the cause of suffering lies within, in my own blind reactions.

It is difficult to observe an abstract negativity when it arises. But now, by training, I can see the other side of the coin: I can be aware of the breathing and also of what is happening inside me. Whatever it is, the breath or any sensation, I learn to just observe it, without losing the balance of the mind. I stop multiplying my miseries. Instead, I allow the defilement to manifest and pass away.

The more one practises this technique, the more one will find how quickly he or she can come out of the negativity. Gradually the mind becomes freed of defilements; it becomes pure. A pure mind is always full of love, detached love for all others; full of compassion for the failings and sufferings of others; full of joy at their success and happiness; full of equanimity in the face of any situation.

When one reaches this stage, then the entire pattern of one's life starts changing. It is no longer possible for one to do anything vocally or physically which will disturb the peace and happiness of others. Instead, the balanced mind not only becomes peaceful in itself, it helps others to become peaceful also. The atmosphere surrounding such a person will become permeated with peace and harmony, and this will start affecting others too.

This is what the Buddha taught, an art of living. He never established or taught any religion, any "ism." He never instructed followers to practise any rites or rituals, any blind or empty formalities. Instead, he taught to just observe nature as it is, by observing the reality inside. Out of ignorance, one keeps reacting in a way which is harmful to oneself and to others. Then when wisdom arises—the wisdom of observing the reality as it is—one comes out of this blind reaction. When one ceases to react blindly, then one is capable of real action, action proceeding from a balanced, equanimous mind, a mind which sees and understands the truth. Such action can only be positive, creative, helpful to oneself and to others.

What is necessary, then, is to "know thyself"—advice which every wise person has given. One must know oneself not just at the intellectual level, at the level of ideas and theories. Nor does this mean to know oneself at the devotional or emotional level, simply accepting blindly what one has heard or read. Such knowledge is not enough.

Rather, one must know reality at the actual level. One must experience directly the reality of this mental-physical phenomenon. This alone is what will help us to come out of defilements, out of sufferings.

This direct experience of reality within one's own self, this technique of self-observation, is what is called Vipassana meditation. In the language of India in the time of the Buddha, *passanā* meant to look, to see with open eyes, in the ordinary way. But *vipassanā* is to observe things as they really are, not just as they seem to be. Apparent truth has to be penetrated, until one reaches the ultimate truth of the entire mental and physical structure. When one experiences this truth, then one learns to stop reacting blindly, to stop creating defilements. Naturally the old defilements are gradually eradicated. One comes out of all miseries, and experiences happiness.

There are three steps to the training which is given in a Vipassana course. First, one must

abstain from any action, physical or vocal, which disturbs the peace and harmony of others. One cannot work to liberate oneself from defilements in the mind while at the same time continuing to perform deeds of body and speech which only multiply those defilements. Therefore a code of morality is the essential first step of the practice. One undertakes not to kill, not to steal, not to commit sexual misconduct, not to speak lies, and not to use intoxicants. By abstaining from such actions, one allows the mind to quiet down.

The next step is to develop some mastery over this wild mind, by training it to remain fixed on a single object, the breath. One tries to keep one's attention on the respiration for as long as possible. This is not a breathing exercise; one does not regulate the breath. Instead one observes the natural respiration as it is, as it comes in, as it goes out. In this way one further calms the mind, so that it is no longer overpowered by violent negativities. At the same time, one is concentrating the mind, making it sharp and penetrating, capable of the work of insight.

These first two steps of living a moral life and controlling the mind are very necessary and beneficial in themselves. But they will lead to self-repression unless one takes the third step: purifying the mind of defilements, by developing insight into one's own nature. This, really, is Vipassana: experiencing one's own reality, through the systematic and dispassionate observation of the ever-changing mind-matter phenomenon manifesting itself as sensations within oneself. This is the culmination of the teaching of the Buddha: self-purification through self-observation.

This can be practised by one and all. The disease is not sectarian, therefore the remedy cannot be sectarian: it must be universal. Everyone faces the problem of suffering. When one suffers from anger, it is not Buddhist anger,

Hindu anger, Christian anger. Anger is anger. Due to anger, when one becomes agitated, it is not a Christian agitation, or Hindu, or Buddhist agitation. The malady is universal. The remedy must also be universal.

Vipassana is such a remedy. No one will object to a code of living which respects the peace and harmony of others. No one will object to developing control of the mind. No one will object to developing insight into one's own reality, by which it is possible to free the mind of negativities. It is a universal path. It is not a cult. It is not a dogma. It is not blind faith.

Observing the reality as it is, by observing truth inside—this is knowing oneself at the actual, experiential level. And as one practises, one starts coming out of the misery of defilements. From the gross, external apparent truth, one penetrates to the ultimate truth of mind and matter. Then one transcends that and experiences a truth which is beyond mind and matter, beyond time and space, beyond the conditioned field of relativity: the truth of total liberation from all defilements, all impurities, all suffering. Whatever name one gives this ultimate truth is irrelevant. It is the final goal of everyone.

May all of you experience this ultimate truth. May all people everywhere come out of their defilements, their misery. May they enjoy real happiness, real peace, real harmony.

What is necessary is to "know thyself"— advice which every wise person has given. ...

One must experience directly the reality of this mental-physical phenomenon. This alone is what will help us to come out of defilements, out of sufferings.

—S.N. Goenka

Buddha's Path Is to Experience Reality

by S.N. Goenka

The following has been condensed from a public talk given by S.N. Goenka in Bangkok, Thailand in September, 1989.

Most Venerable Bhikkhu Saṅgha, friends, devotees of Lord Buddha:

You have all assembled here to understand what Vipassana is and how it helps us in our day-to-day lives; how it helps us to come out of our misery, the misery of life and death. Everyone wants to come out of misery, to live a life of peace and harmony. We simply do not know how to do this. It was Siddhattha Gotama's enlightenment that made him realize the truth: where misery lies, how it starts, and how it can be eradicated.

There were many techniques of meditation prevailing in those days, as there are today. The *Bodhisatta* Gotama tried them all, but he was not satisfied because he found that he was not fully liberated from misery. Then he started to do his own research. Through his personal experience he discovered this technique of Vipassana, which eradicated misery from his life and made him a fully enlightened person.

There are many techniques that give temporary relief. When you become miserable you divert your attention to something else. Then you feel that you have come out of your misery, but you are not totally relieved.

If something undesirable has happened in life, you become agitated. You cannot bear this misery and want to run away from it. You may go to a cinema or a theatre, or you may indulge in other sensual entertainments. You may go out drinking, and so on. All this is running away from misery. Escape is no solution to the problem—indeed the misery is multiplying.

In Buddha's enlightenment he realized that one must face reality. Instead of running away from the problem, one must face it. He found that all the types of meditation existing in his day consisted of merely diverting the mind from the prevailing misery to another object. He found that practising this, actually only a small part of the mind gets diverted. Deep inside one keeps reacting, one keeps generating *saṅkhāras* (reactions) of craving, aversion or delusion, and one keeps suffering at a deep level of the mind. The object of meditation should not be an imaginary object, it should be reality—reality as it is. One has to work with whatever reality has manifested itself now, whatever one experiences within the framework of one's own body.

In the practice of Vipassana one has to explore the reality within oneself—the material structure and the mental structure, the combination

> **W**hen you become miserable you divert your attention to something else. Then you feel that you have come out of misery, but you are not totally relieved.

of which one keeps calling "I, me, mine." One generates a tremendous amount of attachment to this material and mental structure, and as a result becomes miserable. To practise Buddha's path we must observe the truth of mind and matter. Their basic characteristics should be directly experienced by the meditator. This results in wisdom.

Wisdom can be of three types: wisdom gained by listening to others, that which is gained by intellectual analysis, and wisdom developed from direct, personal experience. Before Buddha, and even at the time of Buddha, there were teachers who were teaching morality, were teaching concentration, and who were also talking about wisdom. But this wisdom was only received or intellectualized wisdom. It was not wisdom gained by personal experience. Buddha found that one may play any number of intellectual or devotional games, but unless he experiences the truth himself, and develops wisdom from his personal experience, he will not be liberated. Vipassana is personally experienced wisdom. One may listen to discourses or read scriptures. Or one may use the intellect and try to understand: "Yes, Buddha's teaching is wonderful! This wisdom is wonderful!" But that is not direct experience of wisdom.

The entire field of mind and matter—the six senses and their respective objects—have the basic characteristics of *anicca* (impermanence), *dukkha* (suffering) and *anattā* (egolessness). Buddha wanted us to experience this reality within ourselves. To explore the truth within the framework of the body, he designated two fields. One is the material structure: the corporeal structure, the physical structure. The other is the mental structure with four factors: consciousness; perception; the part of the mind that feels sensation; and the part of the mind that reacts. So to explore both fields he gave us *kāyānupassanā* (observation

of the body) and *cittānupassanā* (observation of the mind).

How can you observe the body with direct experience unless you can feel it? There must be something happening in the body which you feel, which you realize. Then you can say, "Yes, I have practised *kāyānupassanā*." One must feel the sensations on the body: this is *vedanānupassanā* (observation of body sensations).

The same is true for *cittānupassanā*. Unless something arises in the mind, you cannot directly experience it. Whatever arises in the mind is *dhamma* (mental content). Therefore *dhammānupassanā* (observation of the contents of the mind) is necessary for *cittānupassanā*.

This is how the Buddha divided these practices. *Kāyānupassanā* and *vedanānupassanā* pertain to the physical structure. *Cittānupassanā* and *dhammānupassanā* pertain to the mental structure. See from your personal experience how this mind and matter are related to each other. To believe that one understands mind and matter, without having directly experienced it, is delusion. It is only direct experience that will make us understand the reality about mind and matter. This is where Vipassana starts helping us.

In brief, understand how we practise Vipassana. We start with Anapana, awareness of respiration—natural respiration. We don't make it a breathing exercise or regulate the breath as they do in *prāṇāyāma*. We observe respiration at the entrance of the nostrils. If a meditator works continuously in a congenial atmosphere without any disturbance, within two or three days some subtle reality on this part of the body will start manifesting itself: some sensations—natural, normal bodily sensations. Maybe heat or cold, throbbing or pulsing or some other sensations. When one reaches the fourth or fifth day of practice, he or she will find that there are sensations throughout the body, from head to feet.

One feels those sensations, and is asked not to react to them. Just observe; observe objectively, without identifying yourself with the sensations.

When you work as Buddha wanted you to work, by the time you reach the seventh day or the eighth day, you will move towards subtler and subtler reality. The Dhamma (natural law) will start helping you. You observe this structure that initially appears to be so solid, the entire physical structure at the level of sensation. Observing, observing you will reach the stage when you experience that the entire physical structure is nothing but subatomic particles: throughout the body, nothing but *kalāpas* (subatomic particles). And even these tiniest subatomic particles are not solid. They are mere vibration, just wavelets. The Buddha's words become clear by experience:

> *Sabbo pajjalito loko,*
> *sabbo loko pakampito.*

The entire universe is nothing but combustion and vibration.

As you experience it yourself, your *kāyānupassanā,* your *vedanānupassanā,* will take you to the stage where you experience that the entire material world is nothing but vibration. Then it becomes very easy for you to practise *cittānupassanā* and *dhammānupassanā.*

Buddha's teaching is to move from the gross, apparent truth to the subtlest, ultimate truth, from *oḷārika* to *sukhuma.* The apparent truth always creates illusion and confusion in the mind. By dividing and dissecting apparent reality, you will come to the ultimate reality. As you experience the reality of matter to be vibration, you also start experiencing the reality of the mind: *viññāṇa* (consciousness), *saññā* (perception),

vedanā (sensation) and *saṅkhāra* (reaction). If you experience them properly with Vipassana, it will become clear how they work.

Suppose you have reached the stage where you are experiencing that the entire physical structure is just vibration. If a sound has come in contact with the ears you will notice that this sound is nothing but vibration. The first part of the mind, consciousness, has done its job: ear consciousness has recognized that something has happened at the ear sense door. Like a gong which, having been struck at one point, begins

> The so-called "unconscious" mind is not unconscious. It is always conscious of body sensations, and it keeps reacting to them. If they are unpleasant, it reacts with aversion. If they are pleasant, it reacts with craving.

vibrating throughout its structure, so a contact with any of the senses begins a vibration which spreads throughout the body. At first this is merely a neutral vibration, neither pleasant nor unpleasant.

The perception recognizes and evaluates the sound, "It is a word—what word? Praise! Oh, wonderful, very good!" The resulting sensation, the vibration, will become very pleasant. In the same way, if the words are words of abuse the vibration will become very unpleasant. The vibration changes according to the evaluation given by the perception part of the mind. Next the third part of the mind starts feeling the sensation: pleasant or unpleasant.

Then the fourth part of the mind will start working. This is reaction; its job is to react. If a pleasant sensation arises, it will react with craving. If an unpleasant sensation arises, it will react with aversion. Pleasant sensation: "I like it. Very good! I want more, I want more!" Similarly, unpleasant sensation: "I dislike it. I don't want it." Generating craving and aversion is the part played by the fourth factor of the mind—reaction.

Understand that this process is going on constantly at one sense door or another. Every moment something or the other is happening at one of the sense doors. Every moment the respective consciousness cognizes; the perception recognizes; the feeling part of the mind feels; and the reacting part of the mind reacts, with either craving or aversion. This happens continuously in one's life.

At the apparent, surface level, it seems that I am reacting with either craving or aversion to the external stimulus. Actually this is not so. Buddha found that we are reacting to our sensations. This discovery was the enlightenment of Buddha. He said:

Saḷāyatana-paccayā phasso
phassa-paccayā vedanā
vedanā-paccayā taṇhā.

With the base of the six senses, contact arises with the base of contact, sensation arises with the base of sensation, craving arises.

It became so clear to him: the six sense organs come in contact with objects outside. Because of the contact, a sensation starts in the body that, most of the time, is either pleasant or unpleasant. Then after a pleasant or unpleasant sensation arises, craving or aversion start—not before that. This realization was possible because Buddha went deep inside and experienced it himself. He went to the root of the problem and discovered how to eradicate the cause of suffering at the root level.

Working at the intellectual level of the mind, we try to suppress craving and aversion, but deep inside, craving and aversion continue. We are constantly rolling in craving or aversion. We are not coming out of misery through suppression.

Buddha discovered the way: whenever you experience any sensation, due to any reason, you simply observe it:

Samudaya dhammānupassī vā
kāyasmiṃ viharati
vaya dhammānupassī vā kāyasmiṃ viharati
samudaya-vaya-dhammānupassī vā
kāyasmiṃ viharati.

He dwells observing the phenomenon of arising in the body.
He dwells observing the phenomenon of passing away in the body.
He dwells observing the phenomenon of simultaneous arising and passing away in the body.

Every sensation arises and passes away. Nothing is eternal. When you practise Vipassana you start experiencing this. However unpleasant a sensation may be—look, it arises only to pass away. However pleasant a sensation may be, it is just a vibration—arising and passing. Pleasant, unpleasant or neutral, the characteristic of impermanence remains the same. You are now experiencing the reality of *anicca*. You are not believing it because Buddha said so, or some scripture or tradition says so, or even because your intellect says so. You accept the truth of *anicca* because you directly experience it. This is how your received wisdom and intellectual understanding turn into personally experienced wisdom.

Only this experience of *anicca* will change the habit pattern of the mind. Feeling sensation in the body and understanding that everything is impermanent, you don't react with craving or aversion; you are equanimous. Practising this continually changes the habit of reacting at the deepest level. When you don't generate any new conditioning of craving and aversion, old conditioning comes on the surface and passes away. By observing reality as it is, you become free from all your conditioning of craving and aversion.

Western psychologists refer to the "conscious mind." Buddha called this part of the mind the *paritta citta* (a very small part of the mind). There is a big barrier between the *paritta citta* and the rest of the mind at deeper levels. The conscious mind does not know what is happening in the unconscious or half-conscious. Vipassana breaks this barrier, taking you from the surface level of the mind to the deepest level of the mind. The practice exposes the *anusaya kilesa* (latent mental defilements) that are lying at the deepest level of the mind.

The so-called "unconscious" mind is not unconscious. It is always conscious of body sensations, and it keeps reacting to them. If they are unpleasant, it reacts with aversion. If they are pleasant, it reacts with craving. This is the habit pattern, the behaviour pattern, of the so-called unconscious at the depth of the mind.

Here is an example to explain how the so-called unconscious mind is reacting with craving and aversion. You are in deep sleep. A mosquito bites you and there is an unpleasant sensation. Your conscious mind does not know what has happened. The unconscious knows immediately that there is an unpleasant sensation, and it reacts with aversion. It drives away or kills the mosquito. But still there is an unpleasant sensation, so you scratch, though your conscious mind is in deep sleep. When you wake up, if somebody asks you how many mosquito bites you got during the night, you won't know. Your conscious mind was unaware but the unconscious knew, and it reacted.

Another example: Sitting for about half an hour, some pressure starts somewhere and the unconscious mind reacts: "There is a pressure.

I don't like it!" You change your position. The unconscious mind is always in contact with the body sensations. You make a little movement, and then after some time you move again. Just watch somebody sitting for fifteen to twenty minutes. You will find that this person is fidgeting, shifting a little here, a little there. Of course, consciously he does not know what he is doing. This is because he is not aware of the sensations. He does not know that he is reacting with aversion to these sensations. This barrier is ignorance.

Vipassana breaks this ignorance. Then one starts understanding how sensations arise and how they give rise to craving or aversion. When there is a pleasant sensation, there is craving. When there is an unpleasant sensation, there is aversion, and whenever there is craving or aversion, there is misery.

If one does not break this behaviour pattern, there will be continual craving or aversion. At the surface level you may say that you are practising what Buddha taught, but in fact, you are not practising what Buddha taught! You are practising what the other teachers at the time of Buddha taught. Buddha taught how to go to the deepest level where suffering arises. Suffering arises because of one's reaction of craving or aversion. The source of craving and aversion must be found, and one must change one's behaviour pattern at that level.

Buddha taught us to observe suffering and the arising of suffering. Without observing these two we can never know the cessation of misery. Suffering arises with the sensations. If we react to sensations, then suffering arises. If we do not react we do not suffer from them. However unpleasant a sensation may be, if you don't react with aversion, you can smile with equanimity. You understand that this is all *anicca*, impermanence. The whole habit pattern of the mind changes at the deepest level.

Through the practice of Vipassana, people start to come out of all kinds of impurities of the mind—anger, passion, fear, ego, and so on. Within a few months or a few years the change in people becomes very evident. This is the benefit of Vipassana, here and now. In this very life you will get the benefit.

This is the land of Dhamma, a land of the teaching of Buddha, a land where you have such a large Sangha. Make use of the teaching of Buddha at the deepest level. Don't just remain at the surface level of the teaching of Buddha. Go to the deepest level where your craving arises:

Vedanā paccayā taṇhā;
vedanā-nirodhā taṇhā-nirodho;
taṇhā-nirodhā dukkha-nirodho.

Sensations give rise to craving.
If sensations cease, craving ceases.
When craving ceases, suffering ceases.

When one experiences the truth of *nibbāna*—a stage beyond the entire sensorium—all the six sense organs stop working. There can't be any contact with objects outside, so sensation ceases. At this stage there is freedom from all suffering.

First you must reach the stage where you can feel sensations. Only then can you change the habit pattern of your mind. Work on this technique, this process, at the very deepest level. If you work on the surface level of the mind you are only changing the conscious part of the mind, your intellect. You are not going to the root cause, the most unconscious level of the mind; you are not removing the *anusaya kilesa*—deep-rooted defilements of craving and aversion. They are like sleeping volcanoes that may erupt at any time. You continue to roll from birth to death; you are not coming out of misery.

Make use of this wonderful technique and come out of your misery, come out of the bondages and enjoy real peace, real harmony, real happiness.

May all of you enjoy real peace,
real harmony, real happiness.

Vedanā and Sampajañña Seminar: Closing Address

by S.N. Goenka

A seminar on the Importance of Vedanā and Sampajañña was held at Dhamma Giri in February 1990. Eminent Pāli scholars from around the world participated.

Respected Bhikkhu Saṅgha and Dhamma friends:

We have come to the happy conclusion of this Dhamma seminar—a unique seminar in the sense that you have practised Vipassana and you have started understanding its theory. Practice and theory: both are equally important.

If someone practises, certainly he or she will reach the final goal. Someone who has not read even one word of the *Tipiṭaka* and yet practises, will reach the final goal. But (except in the case of a *pacceka* Buddha) to show the path there must be an Enlightened One, a Buddha. Only by walking on the entire path will the final goal be reached. And when an Enlightened One is not there to personally guide us, his words are there to show the path.

There has been a gap of twenty-five centuries since the Buddha showed the path. Due to this gap someone walking on the path may feel skeptical as to whether one is walking correctly. Doubts may arise: "What am I doing? Is it correct? Did the Buddha really teach this?" To remove doubts, to get a clear picture of the path, *pariyatti* (theory) is very helpful. But if one remains only limited to *pariyatti,* I would say that this person is very unfortunate.

Pariyatti is to give us inspiration, to show us the path, but *paṭipatti* (practice) will take us to the final goal. Sometimes *pariyatti* can cause confusion due to incorrect translation or interpretation; or because the student who is reading it does not have the capacity to understand what is being said. These problems can be removed by *paṭipatti.* If one does not practise, one cannot understand *pariyatti* as one should: that is, as guidance and inspiration for liberation. To me *paṭipatti* is of utmost importance.

I come from a very staunch, conservative Hindu Sanātani tradition. When I first went to my teacher Sayagyi U Ba Khin, he explained what the path was. I listened to his discourses, and I kept on meditating. I didn't find anything new. *Sīla* (morality) is given importance in my tradition—that was nothing new. *Samādhi* (concentration): yes, *samādhi* should be practised. Unless the mind is under control, concentrated, how can one get the benefit of Dhamma? I had been reading about *paññā* (wisdom) in the scriptures, in the tradition in which I was born. It is full of *paññā, pragya* (wisdom), *sthitapragya* (established in wisdom). I had been reading, "Get established in *paññā.*" That was nothing new. And yet it was new, so new and so wonderful.

Now a blind person could see. It was so wonderful. In the darkness a light came. I had been involved in only intellectual, devotional or emotional games. Nobody had told me, "This is how you can become *sthitapragya.* This is how you will become established in *paññā.*" The entire tradition had no technique. This was quite clear to me, even after taking my first course. A thirsty person, lost in a desert wants water; he is so thirsty, so miserable. Someone comes to him and gives him a sermon, "Oh, you miserable person, you should drink water." But he doesn't give any water to drink! He doesn't show how to find water! Here I found someone who gave water.

The need to be free from *rāga* (craving), *dosa* (aversion) and *moha* (delusion) was not new to me, but the technique whereby I could become free from them was new. That was the biggest contribution Buddha made to suffering humanity. He gave a path, a technique. He continued to teach people for forty-five years, day and night. He would lie down for two or three hours a night, just to give rest to the body, remaining with *sati* (awareness) and *sampajañña* (understanding of impermanence). Twenty-four hours a day for forty-five years this person continued distributing Dhamma to suffering people, without expecting anything in return. He was filled with compassion. He did not teach in order to establish a particular sect, or philosophy; not at all. Otherwise he would not have been a Buddha. He taught just to give a path to people so that they could come out of their miseries.

He gave *sammā diṭṭhi* (right view of reality), not a *diṭṭhi* (philosophical belief). And he said that it is only with *jānato passato* (knowledge, seeing correctly) that one can have *sammā diṭṭhi*. Otherwise, however correct something may be, however logical something may be, if there is not *jānato passato* then it is *micchā diṭṭhi* (wrong view). It is only *sammā diṭṭhi* which can liberate, and *sammā diṭṭhi* is the *diṭṭhi* which you personally experience yourself, within yourself. Only then it is *sammā* (correct); otherwise it cannot be right, cannot be correct.

You have heard about something and you may contemplate or imagine it; but if you ha-

ven't experienced it, how can you really know what it is? *Yathā-bhūta* (as it is): your understanding has to develop with your personal experience. Otherwise it is not *yathā-bhūta*. It is *yathā-shruta*—you have just heard about it. Or *yathā-kalpita*—you have imagined it. Or *yathā-vāñchita*—you want it to happen in a certain way. This is not *yathā-bhūta*. *Yathā-bhūta* must happen within you, with experience: "Oh, yes! This is *yathā-bhūta ñāṇa dassanaṃ* (the wisdom of reality as it is understood by direct experience)." You are to experience the truth within you as it is, and the *ñāṇa* (wisdom) that arises because of that is the *sammā ñāṇa, samyak gyāna* (right wisdom). Otherwise again it is the *ñāṇa* from a book, a *ñāṇa* of others, but not your own *ñāṇa*. *Agama* (book knowledge) is good for inspiration. But when you start experiencing it yourself, then it is *adhigama* (attainment). You have then walked the Path, you have experienced it; and only that liberates, nothing else.

That was the beauty of this enlightened person. At the time of Buddha, and before Buddha, *samādhi* was practised, but it was not *sammā samādhi* (right concentration). The teaching of *paññā* was also there, but it was all mere talk. Each particular sect or tradition, had its own beliefs. But it was only talk; nobody was actually practising wisdom. There were some practices wherein people were going to extremes, without understanding things properly, so they didn't benefit from these practices.

Gotama was not the only Buddha. Countless Buddhas had come before him. We don't even know the names of all of them. Everyone who gains enlightenment and breaks the shackles of impurities is a Buddha, is an *arahant* (a liberated person). Whoever becomes a Buddha, or an *arahant,* cannot have any clinging. If he has any clinging there is something wrong; this person cannot be liberated. If he is motivated by the wish that, "I must have a large number of followers. After my death people must remember me, build temples and statues in honour of me, praise me saying, 'Buddha was great.' People should call themselves Buddhists..." No—this is not the volition of a Buddha. Compassion is the only volition: "Look, all around people are suffering. I rediscovered this noble path, and I practised it, and by practising it I became liberated. May more and more people come out of their misery." If this is the volition, then yes, this person is a Buddha. This is the difference in volition between one who is a Buddha and one who is not a Buddha.

At the time of Gotama the Buddha, and even before, there were many who claimed that they had become a Buddha. This was a common name for all these mendicants. They called themselves "Buddha"; but what is a Buddha? If one is not totally liberated from all impurities, one is not a Buddha. And to tell whether one is really liberated from all impurities, the yardstick is that this person has now become compassionate, infinitely compassionate. He cannot have compassion only for the people who call themselves Buddhists. His compassion is infinite. Only then is he a Buddha.

That is why he taught the truth to one and all. He was not interested in sectarianism. He told people: "Experience for yourself." Someone came to him and Buddha questioned him: "What do you believe? This *nāma* (mind), this *rūpa* (matter), is it *anicca* (impermanent) or not?"

"Yes sir, it is *anicca!*"

"Do you believe it is a source of *sukha* (happiness), or *dukkha* (misery)?"

"Oh sir, it is *dukkha!*"

"Do you believe, this is 'I,' 'mine' or 'my soul'?"

"No, no sir! How can mind and matter be 'I,' 'mine' or 'my soul'?"

Understand, the person who answered those questions was not a follower of Buddha. He had come from outside.

Buddha asked the outsider, *"Kiṃ maññasi?* (What do you believe?)" and he replied in that way.

That means he believed in *anicca*, *dukkha* and *anattā*. The Buddha continued: *"Passa jāna* (experience for yourself to gain understanding)." Whatever you believe now, you must realize this truth with Vipassana at the experiential level. This alone will help you, nothing else. Merely believing there is a sun in the sky will not give you light or warmth—you must experience it.

This was Buddha's contribution. It is such a wonderful contribution. *"Yathā vādī, tathā kārī"*—whatever he taught, he practised, and he taught only practice.

The entire teaching of Buddha is *passa jāna, passa jāna*—experience for yourself and then you will understand. Don't believe just because a particular scripture, tradition or teacher says so. Experience the truth yourself, and when you find that, yes, it is beneficial—then accept it and live that life. Only that life will help you: this alone, nothing else.

It is rare to find such a practical person. It is easy to give sermons, to say, "I am such a wise person." But to live your life free from all impurities is very difficult. A person who has practised and then teaches others to practise it, is indeed a unique person, a wonderful person. This was something which attracted me to Buddha. To be very frank, when I took my first course with my Sayagyi U Ba Khin, I had not even read the *Dhammapada*, which is very well-known. I started *pariyatti* only after my first course, and then it seemed as if Buddha were talking directly to me. Every word carried such a deep meaning. Because we can only understand by experience what Buddha really meant. That is why my teacher used to say that theory and practice should go together: *paṭipatti* and then *pariyatti*. The Path then becomes so clear.

When one progresses on the Path, two rare qualities naturally start developing in the mind. One is *pubbakārī*—taking the initiative to do good for others, without expecting anything in return. If, before you do something, you think you should receive this or that benefit, then this is not *pubbakārī*. The first thing that must arise in the mind is, "I must help others," without thinking of what you will receive in return. This is a quality which someone walking on the Path of Dhamma has to keep on measuring himself by. Then *kataññutā, katavedī*— a feeling of gratitude. This is the second rare quality which should develop if someone is really practising Dhamma. With the feeling, "I have received this wonderful Dhamma which takes all the misery out of life," if gratitude does not arise, then certainly one is not developing in Dhamma.

When I came to this country and started teaching, I kept saying that "I am teaching Dhamma, not Buddhism." This was not a question of strategy. Buddha never taught Buddhism; he taught Dhamma. He called those walking on the path *dhammiko, dhammaṭṭho, dhamma-cārī, dhamma-vihārī*. Can I improve on the teaching of Buddha? He did not teach in the name of Buddhism. He made people "dhammic." I felt I should teach Dhamma to people in the same way—*sīla, samādhi* and *paññā*—the practical applied Dhamma. If I had only given sermons, then the people of this country would have said, "No thank you. We already have this; we have our *Gītā*."

The *Gītā's* concept of *sthitapragya* became very clear to me through the teaching I received from Sayagyi. Before then it had only been a word in the *Gītā*. Now I understood *sthitapragya* to be the quality of an *arahant* (fully liberated person), and now I was shown the way: *ṭhita pañño* (to

get established in wisdom). This is to be *sampajāno*. We must be aware of *anicca* from moment to moment, then we are getting established in *paññā*, or as the *Gītā* says, *sthitapragya*. But it must be practised, otherwise the words remain empty. *Paññā* is to understand the reality of the world of mind and matter and what lies beyond.

This field of mind and matter, the field of the six sense doors is the field of *anicca*, constantly arising and passing. But we must experience it. Otherwise it is only a *diṭṭhi* (view) which has nothing to do with *sammā diṭṭhi* (right view). Only with experience is it *paññā*, and if it is continuous in every action—sitting, standing, walking, eating, drinking—then one becomes *ṭhita pañño*—established in wisdom.

This teaching of the Buddha made *sthitapragya* so clear to me: *vedanā* and *sampajañña*; this is *dukkha*, and this is the way out of *dukkha*. We must learn to observe *dukkha* objectively by developing *sampajañña*, and this will take us beyond the field of *dukkha*, beyond the field of *vedanā*.

Many people come and say they are so grateful for the Dhamma, for the teaching that has come from the wonderful country of Burma. Initially people may hesitate. They may think, "This is Buddhism! This person is bringing nothing but Buddhism. He wants to convert us to another religion in an indirect way. He is a businessman, so he knows how to do it cunningly." But I smile at that. Yes, I was a businessman, no doubt. But understand—by converting you to a particular religion, what would I get? Tell me! If the President of the country said, "You must all call yourselves Buddhists," what would happen? Would people be liberated from their misery? No! But if only a small percentage of them start practising *sīla, samādhi, and paññā*, no matter what they call themselves, they will come out of their misery. This is more important—they should get pure Dhamma, free from all kinds of sectarianism. This was my conviction, and this has remained my conviction because I myself came to Dhamma in this way.

If my teacher, Sayagyi U Ba Khin, had told me, "Come Goenka, I'll make a Buddhist out of you. I'll convert you to Buddhism," then I would not have learned Dhamma. Everyone has so much attachment to one's own tradition. And I come from a tradition where the ego is very strong: "We Hindus, our **Veda** is the source of all the wisdom of the world." To ask such a person to convert to another religion—impossible! Fortunately I found a wonderful teacher who was only interested in Dhamma. He said, "Come Goenka, I will teach you *sīla, samādhi* and *paññā*—a way out of your misery. Don't you agree that this *moha, rāga,* this *dosa,* makes you very miserable?" "Yes sir, I do." Because I myself was a bundle of miseries, of anger, passion and ego. In spite of all the understanding of the *Gītā,* in spite of all the devotion, blind devotion, not a trace of my impurities had gone away.

After I passed through this technique, I don't say that it made me a fully liberated person, but what a great change started happening! One has to be grateful. But if someone comes and tells me, "You teach *sīla, samādhi and paññā,* and this is wonderful, but please don't use the name of Buddha, because when you say Buddha, people will think, 'Oh, this is Buddhism. Look, he is converting us to Buddhism.'" I feel only pity for such a person, because even after a few courses he or she has not understood what Dhamma is. *Kataññutā* (gratitude) is a part of Dhamma; it is a yardstick to measure whether one is really progressing on the path of Dhamma or not.

A wonderful person discovered this noble path by which he liberated himself. And then he distributed it compassionately, without any discrimination. He taught people to reach the stage where they could teach others—*bahuja-na hitāya, bahujana sukhāya lokānukampāya* (for the benefit of many, for the happiness of many, out of compassion for the world)—without expecting anything in return. His followers were not interested in starting a sect in the name of Buddha. Their only motivation was to help people to come out of their misery. One feels great gratitude towards those people.

This wonderful technique was kept in its pristine purity from generation to generation through a chain of Teachers culminating in Sayagyi U Ba Khin—a brilliant star in the galaxy of stars, who gave me this wonderful Dhamma. How could I forget him? How could I not have gratitude towards Buddha? How could I not have gratitude toward this line of Teachers who kept it in its pristine purity? How can I not have gratitude towards my Sayagyi, U Ba Khin?

And then the country of Myanmar which kept the technique in its pristine purity. Where not only *paṭipatti,* but the entire *pariyatti* was also kept in its pristine purity. A feeling of gratitude is bound to come. How carefully *paṭipatti* and *pariyatti* were maintained from one generation to another, without anything being added or subtracted. That is why we are getting them today. If *pariyatti* had not been kept available, then there might have been some doubt whether it was really Buddha's word or not. A feeling of gratitude is bound to come on the Path, even if one has taken only a few steps. Certainly one has to be grateful, very grateful.

Those who come to practise pure Dhamma should understand they are not converting themselves to an organized religion, not at all. But they are certainly converting themselves to Dhamma, and Dhamma is purity of mind. Purity of mind must contain these qualities: love, compassion, selfless service and gratitude. These are the yardsticks which one can use to measure whether or not one is really purifying the mind.

One may belong to any sect or tradition—whatever one has obtained from that tradition, one should remember: Whatever good qualities one has developed, one should remain grateful for.

Remember the qualities of all good saintly people and try to adopt those qualities yourself. Then you will be a Dhamma person. Use this wonderful path to liberate yourself from all bondages. Don't just develop pride that you have got this wonderful path which others don't have. This pride will not help at all. You have to practise. Use *pariyatti* to support your practise. We are glad that the *pariyatti* in *Tipiṭaka, Aṭṭhakathā,* and the *Ṭīkā,* were all maintained by the neighbouring country. India had lost it totally, and now it has returned. We must make good use of it.

The Vipassana Research Institute is for research work, both for *pariyatti* and for *paṭipatti.* With the research work and the translations, we must understand that every language, however rich it may be, has its own limitations. Technical terms, such as those we have explored in this seminar, can only be understood by experience. The equivalent terms in some other language might create confusion in the minds of people.

But when they practise and then listen to a word, try to understand a word, the meanings become so clear. So *pariyatti* and *paṭipatti,* theory and practice, should go together.

Keep moving on the Path of Dhamma. Keep moving on the Path of liberation. Get enlightenment, your own enlightenment. Get wisdom, your own wisdom. Get the Dhamma which will arise in you, and which will manifest in your daily life.

May all of you who have come to this Dhamma seminar reach the goal of final liberation; may all of you come out of your miseries. We receive inspiration from *pariyatti,* and all the fruit from *paṭipatti.* For those who have not yet tasted the nectar of Dhamma, may they get the opportunity to come in contact with pure Dhamma, the path of liberation. May they also taste the Dhamma's nectar of liberation.

May all of you be happy. May all others be happy. May all of you be peaceful. May all others be peaceful. May all of you be liberated. May all others be liberated.

Bhavatu sabba maṅgalaṃ.
(May all beings be happy.)

A Hindu who learns Vipassana may continue to call himself a Hindu; a Muslim a Muslim, and so on for a Jain, a Christian, a Buddhist. The important point is to become a good person, living a happy and harmonious life. Dhamma helps everyone to become a good human being.
—S. N. Goenka

Proper Veneration of the Buddha

by S.N. Goenka

For over seventeen years, the Patrikā (Hindi language Vipassana newsletter) has been sent monthly to thousands of people in India. Each newsletter has featured an article—short or long—by Goenkaji. The following article has been extracted from different issues of the Patrikā, and slightly adapted.

Incidents from the Life of the Buddha

An announcement had been made that the Buddha would breathe his last when the full moon night of Vesākha[1] came to an end. He was eighty years old. He lay underneath the twin sāla trees. Devotees were flocking in large numbers to pay their respects, carrying handfuls of flowers. Even the gods, out of their devotion, began to shower celestial flowers and celestial sandalwood powder. Divine musical instruments began to be played, and divine songs could also be heard. The Buddha said to Ānanda (who was attending him):

"Ānanda! A Buddha is not honoured by such showering of flowers, or the sounds of musical instruments and celestial singing! The Buddha is honoured when some monk, or nun or lay meditator establishes himself or herself on the path of the bounteous Dhamma, and begins to live a life of truth and purity. Ānanda, let the people take note of this!"

On another occasion the Buddha had been asked whether a *cetiya* (stupa) could be built as a memorial during his lifetime. The Buddha answered that a *cetiya* could be built during the Buddha's lifetime, but that planting a *bodhi* tree was a more appropriate memorial for him; for, under its shade, seekers would feel inspired to meditate and work for *nibbāna* (freedom from suffering).

Ānanda once asked the Buddha, "What will be done with your dead body?" The Buddha explained: "Many devotees of the Buddha will prepare a mound (stupa) on the remnants of the body after it is consumed by fire. They will honour it with flowers, incense, garlands, and so on. By these acts they will purify their minds to an extent and, as a consequence, will be blessed with enjoyment for a long time. They will be reborn in a happy world."

Even so, the Buddha's serious teaching was not merely to afford his followers a happy birth in the next life. His teaching was to take them beyond all lives, beyond the wheel of suffering and rebirth. He used to tell serious meditators, therefore, to keep themselves apart from honouring his body in the conventional way. They should, instead, engage themselves in the realization of the ultimate truth.

Other instances illustrating the proper way to revere the Buddha involved his mother, Mahāpajāpati Gotami. Siddhattha Gotama's birth mother, Mahāmāyā, died on the seventh day after giving birth. Mahāmāyā's younger sister, Mahāpajāpati, brought him up. On the death of her older sister, Mahāpajāpati entrusted her own son to the care of a wet nurse, and fed Siddhattha at her own breast.

---

1 The full moon of May, the day the Buddha was born, enlightened and passed into *parinibbāna* (death of a fully enlightened being).

In her old age, Mother Gotami was ordained by the Buddha and joined the order of *bhikkhunis* (nuns). Ardently practising Vipassana, she became an *arahant* (fully enlightened person).

All those who received Dhamma from the Buddha were called his own "sons" and "daughters." Age and worldly relationships did not matter at all. This is why, at a very old age, Mother Gotami proclaimed: "O, Sugata! I am your mother. And you, O brave one, are my father!"

Shortly before her demise, Mother Gotami became very joyful, knowing that this was to be her last demise. Filled with gratitude, she remembered the Buddha: "O father! You gave me birth in the true Dhamma. O son! I quenched your thirst for short periods by feeding you at my breast. But, father! You have quenched my thirst for life-after-life by making me taste the nectar of Dhamma. Son! I fed you at my breast for your physical growth. In return, O father, you gave me the nectar of Dhamma for the growth of my Dhamma-body. It may be easy for a woman to be called Queen or Mother Queen, but it is a rare thing to be called Buddha's mother."

Thus Mother Gotami, overflowing with gratitude, properly venerated the Buddha. She also taught others how to pay proper respect. When some of the monks and nuns who had not yet experienced the stage of liberation came to know of her impending demise, they became highly perturbed and started wailing. Mother Gotami, Dhamma person that she was, then explained to them, "This is an auspicious time, a time for rejoicing! An opportunity to come out of the rounds of birth and death is an auspicious occasion. This cannot be an occasion for moistening of the eyes." Then she told them that if they had true reverence for her, the only way to express it would be to strive to get established in the noble Dhamma.

Preserving the Tradition of Proper Veneration

The tradition of honouring the Buddha in the proper manner was preserved in Burma by a limited number of people. Students of Sayagyi U Ba Khin used to pay respect to the Dhamma by bowing down before him three times, in accordance with the local tradition. But he taught serious meditators how to pay respect to the Teacher correctly. He taught them to observe the sensations of *anicca* (arising and passing away) at the top of the head when they bowed for the first time. The second time they were to experience *dukkha* (the truth of suffering), and the third time *anattā* (the truth of egolessness). Reverence expressed in this manner is the proper reverence; otherwise it is merely an empty ritual.

The real benefit accrues to a meditator only if he or she honours the Buddha in the proper way.

Emulating the Wise

If one wishes to honour one's favourite saint or deity, one should recollect his or her good qualities and, getting inspiration from these, try to emulate them in one's life. This alone constitutes true veneration.

Similarly, anyone desiring to pay respects to the Buddha should recall his qualities. Inspired by these qualities, one should try to emulate them. Then one avoids becoming entangled in a sectarian net.

When venerating the Buddha, one should express: "Salutation to the one who is *bhagavā* (an exalted being), *arahant* (liberated being), *sammā sambuddha* (self-enlightened being of surpassing magnitude)!" This recognition means that one honours the qualities of enlightenment, whether possessed by Gotama Buddha, Kassapa Buddha, or anyone else. One does not revere any particular person, but all people who attain enlightenment.

This is why in the field of true Dhamma, proper respect is demonstrated by acknowledging,

"The Buddhas of the past, the Buddhas of the future, the present Buddhas—I honour at all times."

A being who becomes perfectly enlightened radiates infinite compassion for all suffering beings. An Enlightened One realizes that many people who are deeply entangled in sectarianism, rites, ritual and philosophical speculations may not grasp the true Dhamma (law of nature). But at least some—who are less engrossed in these—may get benefited by Dhamma. Such a person therefore distributes Dhamma with open hands, without any distinction of caste or creed. This is why he is called *satthā* (the teacher). He is the teacher of the rich and poor, the well-read and the illiterate, male and female, rulers and subjects, gods and men!

Whenever one wishes to honour the Buddha, one should understand that true veneration occurs when one remembers the Enlightened One's qualities, and works to develop these qualities oneself.

Qualities of the Triple Gem

Followers of the Buddha take refuge in the Triple Gem: the Buddha, Dhamma and Sangha. How did the Buddha himself define these three?

Gotama Buddha once defined a **buddha** as follows: "A **buddha** is one who, having discriminatory knowledge of the entire field of suffering, understands the arising and passing of all miseries, is completely free from mental defilements, is pristinely pure and will not be reborn."

A Buddha is always known by the following qualities:

He is an exalted one (*bhagavā*) because, having vanquished all craving, aversion

and delusion, he lives the life of a liberated person.

He is a conqueror of enemies (*arahaṃ*) because he has annihilated all his enemies, in the form of mental impurities.

Having become fully enlightened by his own rightful efforts (*sammā sambuddho*), he is a perfectly enlightened being.

He is perfect in both wisdom and conduct (*vijjā-caraṇa-sampanno*).

He has gone to the ultimate truth (*sugato*) because he has become pure in body, speech and mind.

He is the knower of worlds (*loka-vidū*) because he understands them through personal experience.

He is the unsurpassed charioteer of tameable men (*anuttaro purisa-damma-sārathi*)

He is teacher of gods and men (*satthā deva-manussānaṃ*).

Anyone who acquires these qualities will become a Buddha. And whoever is a Buddha will have these qualities.

Buddha is not the name of a person, community, or sect. There are many other appellations of Buddha, expressing his qualities, such as:

Lord (*bhagavā*), conqueror (*jina*), valorous (*mahāvīra*), omniscient (*sabbaññū*), truth-discoverer (*tathāgata*), possessor of ten strengths (*dasa-bala*), one having exhausted all defilements (*khīṇāsavo*), highly compassionate (*mahā-kāruṇiko*), free from passion (*vīta-rāgo*), free from aversion (*vīta-doso*), free from delusion (*vīta-moho*), free from craving (*vīta-taṇho*), truth-perceiver (*sacca-dassī*), nibbāna-perceiver (*nibbāna-dassī*), Dhamma-bodied (**Dhamma-kāyo**), and many more.

All these names signify qualities, characteristics—the nature of Buddha. They are, therefore, universal. There is nothing sectarian about these terms.

Such a person teaches Dhamma as follows:

This is *sīla*, this is *samādhi*, this is *paññā*.

After *sīla* is perfected, *samādhi* proves highly beneficial.

After *samādhi* is perfected, *paññā* proves highly beneficial.

After *paññā* is perfected, the mind becomes free from all impurities.

Dhamma taught by a Buddha has the following attributes:

It is well-explained (*svākkhāto*).

It can be experienced in this life (*sandiṭṭhiko*).

It gives immediate results (*akāliko*).

It invites people to "come and see" (*ehi-passiko*).

Every successive step takes one towards the final goal of full liberation (*opanayiko*).

It is to be experienced by each person of average intelligence, for oneself (*paccattaṃ veditabbo viññūhīti*).

Dhamma is not sectarian. It is called by several other names:

Eternal dhamma (*esa dhammo sanantano*); noble eightfold path (*ariyo aṭṭhaṅgiko maggo*); true dhamma (*saddhammo*); pure dhamma (*visuddhi-dhammo*); dhamma leading to full liberation (*vimutti-dhammo*); noble dhamma (*ariyo-dhammo*); stainless dhamma (*sukka dhammo*); foremost dhamma (*aggo dhammo*); ancient dhamma (*purāṇo dhammo*).

The Sangha characterized by the Buddha comprises those who, practising Dhamma according to his teachings, have become stream-enterer, once-returner, non-returner or fully enlightened ones. This is not an assembly of ordinary people.

Like Buddha and Dhamma, Sangha is characterized by universal qualities such as:

Being worthy of invitation (*āhuneyyo*); worthy of hospitality (*pāhuneyyo*); worthy of offerings (*dakkhiṇeyyo*); worthy to be saluted with folded hands (*añjali-karaṇīyo*); field of merit par excellence (*anuttaraṃ puññakkhettaṃ*); temperate, tranquil (*danto, santo*); free from passion, spotless (*virajo, vimalo*); composed, not diffused (*nippapañco*).

When we take refuge in the Triple Gem, when we honour Buddha, Dhamma and Sangha, let us remember their qualities, and work diligently to develop these very qualities ourselves.

By Living a Life of Purity, We Properly Honour the Buddha

True veneration of the Buddha occurs only when we practise the following:

Abstention from killing.

Abstention from stealing.

Abstention from sexual misconduct.

Abstention from speaking lies, backbiting, slander, bitter and frivolous talk.

Abstention from the use of intoxicants.

Abstention from trafficking in weapons, liquor, poison, meat and animals.

Abstention from reflection on malevolence, passion and anger.

Mindfulness of natural, normal respiration.

Awareness of physical sensations arising as a result of mental defilements.

Realizing the impermanent nature of the mind-matter phenomena at the base of physical sensations.

Self-realization that all sensations, however pleasant, are impermanent in nature and, ultimately, turn into suffering.

Feeling disenchantment towards the free flow of pleasant, subtle vibrations throughout the body, realizing that relishing them is hideous, horrible and perpetuates the wheel of suffering.

Self-realization that the notion of "I," "mine," "my soul" in the mind-matter

phenomena (which occur as a result of cause and effect) is fictitious.

Self-realization that the sense doors and their objects are impermanent, the cause of suffering and bereft of any substance.

Complete objectivity towards craving, aversion and delusion after realizing that the sense doors and their objects are impermanent, the cause of suffering and bereft of any substance.

Eradication of the old stock of *saṅkhāras* by remaining equanimous and preventing the formation of new *saṅkhāras* by observing the body sensations as *anicca*.

Leading a life of *sati* (awareness) and *sampajañña* (constant thorough understanding of impermanence) in all situations, such as standing, sitting, walking, eating, bathing, sleeping, waking, etc.

Self-realization of the path and fruit of the stages of a stream-enterer, once-returner, non-returner, and fully enlightened one after actual experience of the stage of stream-enterer, through unceasing practice of *sati* and *sampajañña*.

Leading a life of loving-kindness, compassion, sympathetic joy and holy detachment; and working ceaselessly for the good of all beings.

What Happens at Death?

by S.N. Goenka

To understand what happens at death, let us first understand what death is. Death is like a bend in a continuous river of becoming. It appears that death is the end of a process of becoming, and certainly it may be so in the case of an arahant (a fully liberated being) or a Buddha; but with an ordinary person this flow of becoming continues even after death. Death puts an end to the activities of one life, and the very next moment starts the play of a new life. On the one side is the last moment of this life and on the other side is the first moment of the next life. It is as though the sun rises as soon as it sets with no interval of darkness in between, or as if the moment of death is the end of one chapter in the book of becoming, and another chapter of life begins the very next moment.

Although no simile can convey the exact process, still one might say that this flow of becoming is like a train running on a track. It reaches the station of death and there, slightly decreasing speed for a moment, carries on again with the same speed. It does not stop at the station even for a moment. For one who is not an *arahant,* the station of death is not a terminus but a junction from where thirty-one different tracks diverge. The train, as soon as it arrives at the station, moves onto one or another of these tracks and continues. This speeding "train of becoming," fuelled by the electricity of the *kammic* reactions of the past, keeps on running from one station to the next, on one track or the other, a continuous journey that goes on without ceasing.

This changing of "tracks" happens automatically. As the melting of ice into water and the cooling of water to form ice happens according to laws of nature, so the transition from life to life is controlled by set laws of nature. According to these laws, the train not only changes tracks by itself, it also lays the next tracks itself. For this train of becoming the junction of death, where the change of tracks takes place, is of great importance. Here the present life is abandoned (this is called *cuti*—disappearance, death). The demise of the body takes place, and immediately the next life starts (a process which is called *paṭisandhi*—conception or taking up of the next birth). The moment of *paṭisandhi* is the result of the moment of death; the moment of death creates the moment of conception. Since every death moment creates the next birth moment, death is not only death, but birth as well. At this junction, life changes into death and death into birth.

Thus every life is a preparation for the next death. If someone is wise, he or she will use this life to the best advantage and prepare for a good death. The best death is the one that is the last, that is not a junction but a terminus: the death of an *arahant.* Here there will be no track on which the train can run further; but until such a terminus is reached, one can at least ensure that the next death gives rise to a good birth and that the terminus will be reached in due course. It all depends on us, on our own efforts. We are makers of our own future, we create our own welfare or misery as well as our own liberation.

How is it that we are the creators of the tracks that receive the onrushing train of becoming? To answer this we must understand what *kamma* (action) is.

The healthy or unhealthy volition of our mind is *kamma.* Before performing any action at the mental, vocal, or physical level, whatever wholesome or unwholesome volition arises in the mind is the root of that action. The consciousness arises due to a contact at a sense door, then the *saññā* (perception and recognition) evaluates the experience, sensations *(vedanā)* arise, then a *kammic* reaction *(saṅkhāra)* takes place. These volitional reactions are of various kinds. How strong is the volition? How slow, deep, shallow, heavy or light? According to this the intensity of these reactions will vary. Some are like a line drawn on water, some like a line drawn on sand and some a line on rock. If the volition is wholesome, then the action will be the same and the fruits will be beneficial; and if the volition is unwholesome, then the action will be the same—it will give fruits of misery.

Not all of these reactions result in a new birth. Some are so shallow that they do not give any substantial fruits. Some are a bit heavier but will be used up in this lifetime. They do not carry over into the next life. Others being still heavier continue with the flow of life into the next birth, but they themselves do not give new birth. Nevertheless they can continue to multiply during this life and the next. Many *kammas* however, are *bhava-kammas*, or *bhava-saṅkhāras*, those that give a new birth, a new life. Each one of these *bhava-kammas* (actions that give rise to the process of becoming) carries a magnetic force that is in tune with the vibrations of a particular plane of existence. The vibrations of a particular *bhava-kamma* will unite with the vibrations of the *bhava-loka* (world, plane) that has the same intensity, and the two will attract each other according to the universal laws pertaining to forces of *kamma.*

As soon as one of these *bhava-kammas* is generated, this "railway train of becoming" gets attracted to one or the other of the thirty-one tracks at the station of death. Actually these thirty-one tracks are the thirty-one fields of existence. They are the eleven *kāma lokas* (realms

of sensuality: the four lower realms of existence, and the seven human and celestial realms); the sixteen *rūpa-brahma lokas* (where fine material body remains), and the four *arūpa-brahma lokas* (non-material realms, where only mind remains).

At the last moment of this life, a specific *bhava-saṅkhāra* will arise. This *saṅkhāra* capable of giving a new birth will get connected with the vibrations of the related realm of existence. At the moment of death the whole field of thirty-one realms is open, so it depends on which *saṅkhāra* arises as to which track the train of existence runs on next. In the same way a train gets shunted onto a new track, the force of the *bhava-kamma* reaction provides the push to the flow of consciousness into the next existence. For example, the *bhava-kamma* of anger or malice, being of the nature of heat and agitation, will unite with some lower field of existence. Similarly, one with the nature of *mettā* (compassionate love), having peaceful and cool vibrations can only unite with some *brahma-loka*. This is the law of nature, and these laws are so perfectly "computerized" that there is never any flaw in the operation.

At the moment of death, generally, some intense *saṅkhāra* will arise; it may be either of a wholesome nature or an unwholesome nature. For example, if one has murdered one's father or mother, or perhaps some saintly person, in this lifetime, then the memory of this episode will arise at the moment of death. Likewise if one has done some deep meditation practice, a similar state of mind will arise.

When there is no such dense *bhava-kamma* to arise, then a comparatively less dense *kamma* will arise. Whatever memory is awakened will manifest as the *kamma*. For example, one may remember a wholesome *kamma* of giving food to a saintly person, or one may remember killing someone. Reflections on such past *kammas* as these may arise. Otherwise, objects related to the particular *kamma* may arise. One may see the plate full of food that was offered as *dāna*, or the gun that was used to kill another. These are called the *kamma-nimittas* (signs).

In another case, a sign or a symbol of the next life may appear. This is called *gati-nimitta* (departing sign). These *nimittas* correspond to whichever *bhava-loka* the flow is being attracted towards, such as the scene of some celestial world, or perhaps of an animal world. The dying person will often experience one of these signs as a forewarning, just as the train's headlight illuminates the track ahead. The vibrations of these *nimittas* are identical to the vibrations of the plane of existence of the next birth.

A good Vipassana meditator has the capacity to avoid the tracks leading to the lower realms of existence. He clearly understands the laws of nature, and practises to keep himself ready for death at all times. If he has reached an advanced age, there is all the more reason to remain aware every moment. What preparations are undertaken? One practises Vipassana, remaining equanimous to whatever sensations arise on the body and thereby breaking the habit pattern of reacting to the unpleasant sensations. Thus the mind, which is usually generating new unwholesome *sankhāras,* develops a new habit of remaining equanimous. Very often at the time of death, if there are no very heavy *sankhāras* to arise, habitual reactions occur; and as the new *sankhāra* is being made, an old one from the storehouse might get stirred up onto the surface, gaining in strength as it arises.

At the approach of death, it is very likely that one will experience very unpleasant sensations. Old age, disease and death are *dukkha* (misery). They produce unpleasant sensations of a grosser type. If one is not skilful in observing these sensations with equanimity, then one will be likely to react with feelings of anger, irritation, maybe malice, which provides an opportunity for a *bhava-sankhāra* of like vibration to arise. However, as in the cases of some well developed meditators, one can work to avoid reacting to these immensely painful sensations by maintaining equanimity at the time of death. Then, even those related *bhava-sankhāras* lying deep in the *bhavanga* (seat of birth-producing *kamma*) will not have an opportunity to arise. An ordinary person will usually remain apprehensive, even terror-stricken at the approach of death and thus will give occasion for a fearful *bhava-sankhāra* to surface. In the same way, grief, sorrow, depression, and other feelings may arise at the thought of separation from loved ones, and the related *sankhāra* will come up and dominate the mind.

A Vipassana meditator, by observing all his or her sensations with equanimity, weakens the *sankhāra* and thus does not allow it to arise at the time of death. The real preparation for death is this: developing a habit pattern of repeatedly observing the sensations manifesting in the body and mind with equanimity and with the understanding of *anicca*.

At the time of death, this strong habit of equanimity will automatically appear and the train of existence will link up with a track on which it will be possible to practise Vipassana in the new life. In this way, one saves oneself from birth in a lower realm and attains one of the higher realms, which is very important because Vipassana cannot be practised in the lower realms.

A meditator who is on the point of death is fortunate to have close relatives or friends nearby who can help maintain a good Dhamma atmosphere, free from lamenting and gloom; people who can practise Vipassana and generate vibrations of *mettā,* which are most favourable for a peaceful death.

At times a non-meditator will attain a favourable rebirth at the time of death due to the the manifestation of wholesome *bhava-saṅkhāras* such as generosity, morality and other strong wholesome qualities. But the special achievement of an established Vipassana meditator is that he enables himself to attain an existence where he can continue to practise Vipassana. In this way, by slowly decreasing the stock of accumulated *bhava-saṅkhāras* stored in the *bhavaṅga* of his flow of consciousness, one shortens one's journey of becoming and reaches the goal sooner.

One comes into contact with the Dhamma in this life because of great merits one has performed in the past. Make this human life successful by practising Vipassana. Then whenever death comes, it will come with the experience of an equanimous mind, bringing with it well-being for the future.

N.B.: *The analogy of a running train changing tracks should not be mistaken for transmigration, as no entity goes from one life to the next. Nothing passes to the next life except the force of the accumulated kamma saṅkhāras.*

What Wonderful People

by S.N. Goenka

U Chan Htoon

Before coming in contact with the Buddha, Sāriputta met Assaji, one of the first five disciples of the Buddha. It was from this saintly person that he first heard the benevolent words of pure Dhamma:

> *Ye Dhammā hetuppabhavā*
> *tesaṃ hetuṃ Tathāgato āha,*
> *Tesaṃ ca yo nirodho*
> *evaṃ vādī mahāsamaṇo.*

> Those phenomena which arise due to some cause, that cause has been explained by the Buddha.
> And also its cessation. Such is the teaching of the Great Monk (Ascetic).

With these words arose the wisdom of *anicca* (impermanence) at the depth of Sāriputta's mind. He thereupon attained the stage of *sotāpanna* (stream-enterer).

With this direction from Assaji, Sāriputta went to the Buddha to take refuge, and accomplished all that has to be accomplished in this life. Although he attained the status of **Dhamma Senāpati** (Commander-in-Chief of Dhamma), Sāriputta always remembered Ven. Assajit with a feeling of deep gratitude. He paid respects to him mentally everyday.

There can be no comparison with those great *arahants* (liberated beings) of the Buddha's day; yet I can never forget my feeling of gratitude towards U Chan Htoon, the ex-Judge of the Supreme Court of the Union of Burma. It was he who pointed me in the direction of the late Sayagyi U Ba Khin, from whom I received the wonderful path of liberation.

I had known U Chan Htoon since the days when he was the Attorney General of Burma. In time, we became very close friends. He became Judge of the Supreme Court and General Secretary of the Buddha Sāsana Council, as well as President of the World Fellowship of Buddhists. It was while he was General Secretary of the Buddha Sāsana Council that the meritorious, historical Chaṭṭha Saṅgāyana (Sixth Synod) was held. In those days, I had the opportunity to render him some small services related to this work. I also had the wonderful opportunity of coming into contact with many very high, respected monks of the country.

At that time, I was a victim of unbearable outbreaks of migraine. Every fortnight, severe migraine attacks would strike, and no medicine could help me. The doctors started giving me morphine injections. Then a fear arose that I might become a morphine addict. The best doctors in Burma had no cure, so I decided to visit some Western countries in search of a treatment to at least break my dependency on morphine.

I went to Switzerland, Germany, England, America, and Japan for these treatments. U Chan Htoon had friends in the Burmese embassies of each of these countries—either the ambassador or the first secretary or the military attaché. He gave me letters of introduction to these people. U Chan Htoon was really worried about my incurable disease. His friends gave me very good assistance. They arranged prompt appointments with the best doctors in each of the countries.

After being treated for many months, I returned home with neither improvement nor relief. Freedom from the disease of migraine was far away. I could not even get rid of morphine, as no other painkiller tried on me would work. I was greatly disappointed and depressed.

At that time, U Chan Htoon suggested that I meet U Ba Khin and take a ten-day Vipassana course with him. He was very confident that I would be benefited. He said, "The Lord Buddha gave a path to come out of all the miseries of countless lives. Why not give a trial to this path? Quite possibly you may get relieved from your physical misery."

The Bhikkhu Saṅgha of Myanmar

The Buddha experienced the peace of *nibbāna* (the ultimate reality) within himself, and throughout his life he kept teaching people the technique to experience this peace themselves. He had totally purified his own mind, and was teaching people how to do that themselves. Naturally Buddha was a peace-loving person, a purity-loving person.

He did not like noise, nor filth. This is why in the temples of Buddha and the *vihāras* (monasteries) of the monks, so much importance is given to silence and cleanliness, even today.

I grew up in Mandalay, the old capital of Burma. During my childhood and adolescence I visited many temples of Buddha, and a few *vihāras* (monasteries), where I would feel greatly inspired. In some other temples, I encountered such a great din, such clutter. In contrast, the peace and cleanliness of the Buddhist temples was very attractive to me.

In those days, in the early morning before sunrise, I would see lines of saffron-clad monks walking along the street for their morning alms round. Viewing this scene, great respect and de-

What followed is now history. It gave a new direction to my life. What a wonderful new turn to the life, what a pleasant turn, what a benevolent turn! The curse of migraine headaches turned out to be a blessing in disguise.

The company of a good friend is always beneficial, and a good friend is one who inspires and helps one to take the path of true Dhamma. In this way, U Chan Htoon was my good friend, my true friend. I always remember him with a feeling of deep gratitude for having pointed out to me the path of true Dhamma. I always feel so pleased to share my merits of **Dhamma-dūta** (work of spreading Dhamma) with him.

votion arose within me. All the *bhikkhus* (monks) walked in complete silence (*tuṇhī bhāvo*), with eyes downcast (*okkhitta cakkhu*), walking with measured steps (*pāda alolupa*). They appeared to me to be the perfect personification of peace.

The devoted Burmese householders knew very well that this was the time for the *bhikkhus* to go out for alms. The housewives would rise very early to prepare food for them, and wait respectfully at the gates of their houses for their silent arrival. The monks would approach with downcast eyes, without speaking a single word. They would accept the alms from the householders, keeping their eyes downcast the entire time. Then they would move further. They did not utter a word to beg for their alms.

In comparison to this shining example, we observe so much crying and beseeching by the begging mendicants, and so much greediness and quarrelling among the priests. The priests display such unwholesome efforts, trying to forcefully procure *dāna* (donation) by any method. At times they praise the householder's generosity to the skies; and if this method proves unsuccessful, they denounce the donor's miserliness. As if generosity can be aroused by such insults. What a great difference between the two scenes!

The rules of the *Vinaya* (guidelines of conduct for the monks) were laid down by the Buddha 2,500 years ago, and are still being scrupulously followed in our time. A sensible person will naturally develop a feeling of respect towards these monks, witnessing the ideal peace, serenity and modesty in their behaviour. Their beneficent examples made a deep impression on my young mind which continues to be there, even today.

The Service of the Bhikkhu Saṅgha to Society

The five fingers of our hands are never alike. In a flock of sheep, there are always a few black ones. But the *Bhikkhu Saṅgha* (order of monks) of Myanmar generally lives a life of morality. It is true that most of them do not practise the technique of Vipassana meditation. Nevertheless, a large number of them have a deep knowledge of the scriptures, and nearly everyone lives a moral life. There are about 200,000 monks in a population of four million in Myanmar, but this large number is not a burden to the country. The usefulness of the monks to the society is unquestionable.

In every village there is a monastery in which one or more monks reside, living on alms given very respectfully by the local villagers. The monks not only give religious instruction to the villagers, but other mundane teachings as well, such as instruction in reading, writing and mathematics to the children of the village. This is the reason why virtually the entire population of Myanmar is literate, except for a few hill tribes where the teaching of Buddha did not penetrate. The credit for this goes to the monks who serve the villages so selflessly. This was one reason why a feeling of great respect arose within me towards the Sangha.

In my teenage years I saw how these monks were also leaders in other social services. In those days, Gandhiji's movement in India was encouraging the use of locally-made products. This impulse swept the country like a tidal wave, and tens of thousands of people in villages across India began spinning their own *khādi* (homespun cotton) and weaving their own fabrics, rather than using fabric imported from Britain. Burma was also influenced by this sentiment, and the social service-minded monks were the leaders of this movement.

In those days the women of Burma wore blouses made from cotton organdy manufactured in Manchester, England. This was harmful in two ways. The policy of importing all of this cotton into the country had devastated the local weaving industry and helped to impoverish the country. In addition, the very fine imported cloth was transparent, and it was improper in this strict Buddhist culture for women to wear such revealing clothing. Unfortunately, this had become the fashion and little else was available, since there was no locally-made product to compete with it. The Burmese women stopped using organdy because the monks championed the cause of reviving homespun cotton. Seeing their combined spiritual and social service to the nation, tremendous devotion and respect towards the monks developed in me, even at a tender age.

Bhikkhu Uttama

During my childhood, there was a famous Burmese monk named Bhikkhu Uttama. He had gone to live in India, where he played a very important role in the national freedom and social movements there. Burma and India were of course one country then, under British colonial rule. At one time Bhikkhu Uttama was the president of the All India Hindu Mahāsabhā (Congress). He was a source of inspiration and encouragement to the other monks in Burma who wanted to follow India's lead in movements like the production of *khādi* cloth.

At that time I was in primary school, and this venerable monk visited Mandalay while touring Burma. A public observance was held at our school. Our teacher, Paṇḍita Kalyan Dutt Dube, was a Hindi poet as well as a teacher, and he composed a poem in praise of Bhikkhu Uttama for the occasion. This poem was taught to me and five or six students of the same age, and we sang the words of the song at the public gathering. I still remember the last few words:

"As you are **Uttama** (Great), similarly make us *uttama*."

Our teacher gave a short speech honouring Bhikkhu Uttama, describing his great services to the nation. This had a great impact on my young mind. This was yet another reason why I was attracted to the Burmese *Bhikkhu Saṅgha* at a young age.

Contact with Members of the Bhikkhu Saṅgha

After Burma gained independence in 1948, I had many occasions to have contact with the *Bhikkhu Saṅgha*. For example, I was fortunate in meeting Ven. Ananda Kosalyayana and Bhikkhu Jagdish Kashyapa. They were two important Indian *bhikkhus* who initiated the work of helping people to understand the Buddha's teaching once again in India. They did the first translations into Hindi of **Aṅguttara Nikāya** and **Saṃyutta Nikāya**. Whenever they visited Burma, they would often stay at my Mogul Street residence. Even if they stayed elsewhere, they always gave me the opportunity to invite them to my home for meals. Through them I met some of the leading monks in Rangoon. Then in 1954–56 during the Chaṭṭha Saṅgāyana (Sixth Recitation of the Buddha's teachings), I came in contact with many more monks through my friend U Chan Htoon and other Burmese friends.

During the pre-war days, when I was living in Mandalay, I had seen the **Buddhavāṇi**—words of the Buddha which had been inscribed on marble slabs during the fifth Saṅgāyana under the auspices of King Min Don Min. But in those days I had no knowledge of the subject whatsoever, and therefore it did not make any impression on me. It was only during the sixth Saṅgāyana that I came to understand that the compilation of the words of the Buddha's teachings, and the commentaries and sub-commentaries, were such a vast literature. This was a very pleasant surprise to me. A much greater surprise was to learn that this huge literature had been preserved in its pristine purity for ongoing centuries without any alteration—not only in Burma, but also in Sri Lanka, Thailand, Laos and Cambodia. This realization generated a further feeling of immense gratitude and devotion in me towards the *Bhikkhu Saṅgha*. The Buddha's words are compiled in three divisions. This is why the scriptures of the Buddha are called *Tipiṭaka* (three baskets, or containers). They contain the *Sutta-piṭaka* (the basket of discourses), the *Vinaya-piṭaka* (the basket of the rules for the monks), and the *Abhidhamma-piṭaka* (the basket of sublime theoretical teachings). One branch of the Sangha memorizes the entire literature of the *Sutta-piṭaka* from generation to generation. This branch is called *Suttadhara*. Similarly, the other branches are called *Vinayadhara* and *Abhidhammadhara*.

Through the ages there were a number of very intelligent individual *bhikkhus* who had memorized, and could recite, all the three *Piṭakas*. They were called *Tipiṭakadhara*. In postwar Burma there were three such *Tipiṭakadharas*. One of these monks was living in Mingun Monastery near my birthplace in Mandalay, on the other bank of the Irawaddy River. I remember going to Mingun on one occasion to pay respects to this venerable monk. I was astounded by the magnitude of his intellect. Currently he occupies the exalted position of *Raṭṭhaguru* (spiritual teacher of the nation).

I was also greatly influenced by Ven. Mahāthera U Thithila, who had lived in England for many years. He is extremely competent in explaining the most intricate points of Dhamma in very simple English. When I first became interested in the Buddha's teaching, I had tried to read the Pāli texts in English translation; but I was not proficient in English, and the language of the Pāli Text Society translations was too difficult for me. The Burmese translations were also too technical for my understanding in that language. I knew so little about the theory of Dhamma, and there was very little material about Dhamma available in my own language—Hindi—at that time. This monk helped me to understand Dhamma in English in simple terms, and I am so grateful to him for that.

Venerable Mahāthera U Janakābhivansa and Mahāpaṇḍita Rahula Sankrityayana

I also met the Ven. Mahāthera U Janakābhivansa who lived in a monastery in Amarapura near Mandalay. I was highly influenced not only by his great intellect, but also by his simplicity, humility and capacity for hard work. He has written scores of books on Dhamma in simple Burmese. The entire nation of Myanmar has great respect for him. What I saw was that he did not have even a trace of ego. I observed not one iota of intellectual pride. I found him to be the incarnation of simplicity, honesty and egolessness.

He had the habit of writing all of his articles while standing at a tall desk, like a lectern. I saw him at this desk working in this way, writing in a big register book. He had a large cabinet full of reference books, but his memory and intellect were so powerful, it is said that he hardly used them.

He reminded me of the famous Indian *bhikkhu* Mahāpaṇḍita Rahula Sankrityayana, who later on voluntarily disrobed (i.e., resumed the life of a householder). He was a top literary figure in India and President of the All India Peasant Organization. He was a master linguist, a Sanskrit and Pāli scholar and the first to translate the *Dīgha Nikāya* (the Long Discourses of the Buddha) into Hindi. For me it was like ambrosia to be able to read Buddha's words in my own tongue.

He was a voluminous writer on many subjects, producing over a hundred scholarly books. He did all of his writing lying down on the floor! He would write for hours in this manner, lying on his stomach. It is said that he wouldn't write well sitting up. He used to come to my house in Rangoon quite often, and I felt very close to him.

After meeting Sayagyi and coming into contact with Vipassana, I was fortunate to meet quite a few leading *bhikkhus* of Burma, such as Masoyein Sayadaw of Mandalay, Chauthagyi Sayadaw of Rangoon and Kan U Sayadaw of Bahan. Their saintly behaviour influenced me greatly.

Venerable Mahasi Sayadaw

In 1990, when I returned to my motherland, the Dhamma land of Myanmar after an interval of twenty-one years, it was a very pleasant surprise to discover that my son was living in a house which is close to Thathana Yeikta, the meditation centre of the late Ven. Mahasi Sayadaw. While I was staying there, early in the morning just before dawn, I would see a line of about one hundred fifty monks, coming out of the meditation centre and walking in front of my son's house. I was overwhelmed to behold such an inspiring sight once again. Each morning my daughter-in-law had prepared some food for the monks. As I put a portion in the begging bowl of each *bhikkhu,* my whole mind and body was filled with a feeling of great rapture.

Each monk stopped for only ten or fifteen seconds in front of a house, just to give the devoted householder the opportunity to gain the merits of *saṅghadāna* (giving donation to the order of monks) by placing some food in the begging bowls. Then they continued to walk in silence with eyes downcast.

What more pleasing meritorious deed could there be than to give the first morning food to a diligent meditator who was moving with awareness in every step? Even now as I recall it, my entire being, mind and matter, starts vibrating with happiness. The sight of this line of exemplary recluses seems to contradict the words of Saint Kabir:

> As there cannot be sacks of rubies,
> There cannot be flocks of swans;
> There cannot be packs of lions.
> Similarly, there cannot be a group
> of saints walking together.

Those who remain all the time extroverted, rolling in the pleasures of talking and intellectualizing, are not true saints. A saint is one who remains engaged in meditation all the time.

It is indeed very rare to find a large number of recluses engaged in continuous meditation for long periods. Even if they exist, it is a rare event to see them. And even if one encounters them, it is a rare opportunity to offer them their first food of the day. All these rare opportunities were available to me, and therefore I became suffused with joy.

In earlier days, I was very attracted to Ven. Mahasi Sayadaw himself. The Buddha Sāsana Council and its chairman, U Chan Htoon, used to invite people from different parts of the world to come to meditate at the Thathana Yeikta monastery where Ven. Mahasi Sayadaw was the master teacher. When Indians came and stayed there for extended periods, I would often go there to offer them Indian vegetarian food. U Chan Htoon would sometimes telephone, asking me to bring fruit and other dishes for the Indians. But before offering food to the meditators, I would take advantage of the opportunity to offer a portion to Mahasi Sayadaw. In this way I came to know him, and he would often take the time to speak with me about Dhamma and my practice. He knew very well that I was a close disciple of Sayagyi U Ba Khin, and at first I had a small fear that the venerable Sayadaw might suggest to me that I come and meditate with him. Some of my friends had insisted that I should do this, but I felt so satisfied with the practice I had learned from Sayagyi that I knew there was no point in going to another teacher.

But, if Ven. Mahasi Sayadaw himself were to suggest it, I would have been put in a very embarrassing position.

In our conversations we discussed how I was practising, and he always had very practical advice and encouragement for me. He said that what I was doing was correct and urged me to continue until I reached the final goal. He never once hinted that I should try his technique. This only increased my respect for this great *bhikkhu.*

Usually he did not go to the houses of laymen to take food; instead, people brought food to his monastery. Once, very hesitantly, I requested him to please visit my house and take a meal there. With a smile he agreed to come. He came with three of his close disciples and we served them food. On this occasion he had a long discussion with me about what I was practising, and he expressed not one word against the way Sayagyi had taught me. In fact, he expressed a deep appreciation for this method of teaching. He never held a sectarian view of the practice of meditation, and my respect for him grew with continued contact.

Mahāthera Webu Sayadaw

The greatest impact of the *Bhikkhu Saṅgha,* at the deepest level of my heart, occurred when I came into contact with Mahāthera Webu (Vipula) Sayadaw. Sayagyi had a very strong connection with this saintly monk. The Sayadaw visited his centre in Rangoon several times.

Besides seeing him, listening to him and paying respect to him at the International Meditation Centre, I was fortunate to have visited his centre in upper Burma, with Sayagyi and some other of his students. As we reached his centre, the venerable Sayadaw had just finished his meal, and I was surprised to see him sitting beside a water tap at the side of a small lane, cleaning his begging bowl. He had hundreds of disciples around him who would happily have performed such services for him, but he did not allow others to do his chores. He always swept his own room, washed his own clothes, etc., with perfect humility.

He took us to the room in his own residence where usually no outsiders were allowed to visit, and there he talked with us.

The glow and the peace on his benevolent face, his heart-catching smile, and the calm and pleasant atmosphere around him would be a source of attraction to any person, not just a Vipassana meditator.

My gratitude and respect for all the venerable *Saṅgha* was crowned with the respect I felt for this *arahant,* Ven. Webu Sayadaw.

For progressing in *Vipassana* meditation, a student must keep knowing *anicca* as continuously as possible. The Buddha's advice to monks is that they should try to maintain the awareness of *anicca*, *dukkha* or *anattā* in all postures ... Continuous awareness of *anicca*, and so of *dukkha* and *anattā*, is the secret of success.

The last words of the Buddha just before he breathed his last and passed away into Mahā Parinibbāna were: "Decay (or *anicca*) is inherent in all component things. Work out your own salvation with diligence."

This is in fact the essence of all his teachings during the forty-five years of his ministry. If you will keep up the awareness of the *anicca* that is inherent in all component things,
you are sure to reach the goal
in the course of time.

—*Sayagyi U Ba Khin*

Dhamma Is for One and All

by S.N. Goenka

Sayagyi's Decision

On behalf of the Buddha Sāsana Council, its General Secretary, U Chan Htoon, used to invite quite a few people from different countries to come to Burma to practise Vipassana. At times, some of us would get the opportunity to gain merits by giving dāna (donation) to cover the travel expenses of such Dhamma-seeking visitors.

At his suggestion, I also became a *dāyaka* (donor) for some of these Dhamma aspirants. One amongst them was a person by the name of Sri Brahmachari Munindra Prosad Barua. He was the superintendent of the Bodh Gaya Temple in India. Having fulfilled his mission of taking a course of Vipassana, he expressed his desire to stay longer in the country in order to master in detail both *pariyatti* and *paṭipatti* (theory and practice).

He was a very suitable person for this task. He had studied the whole *Tipiṭaka* with commentaries and sub-commentaries, staying with various teachers of Dhamma. He made a special study of the **Abhidhamma,** the deeper explanation of which was available only in Burma. For meditation, he practised the technique taught by the Venerable Mahasi Sayadaw at Thathana Yeikta, Rangoon. He learned many more techniques of meditation, staying with various *bhikkhus* (monks) and lay teachers at different centres, including the Ledi Yeikta, founded by Ledi Sayadaw and the Hanthawadi Center, established by Sayagyi Thet, the teacher of U Ba Khin.

He had heard much praise about the meditation teaching of Sayagyi U Ba Khin, from me and

many others, so naturally he was very eager to learn this technique also before returning home. However, Sayagyi strictly refused to accept him on a course. U Lun Baw, who was then the Deputy Prime Minister of the caretaker government and a very close and dear disciple of Sayagyi, pleaded with him to accept Munindraji as a student. But still Sayagyi would not agree. As Munindraji was in a way my Dhamma guest, I also strongly requested Sayagyi to change his decision; but again he refused. His only explanation was this: "This person has already taken Vipassana from the learned *bhikkhus* and other teachers. Why does he need to take a course with me? Let him get ripened in whatever he has learned."

I could understand the reason behind this decision which was not merely for Munindraji but for everyone who had taken a course of meditation under any *bhikkhu*. It had happened that one Bhikkhu Mahinda had come to Burma from India under a similar invitation from the Buddha Sāsana Council a few months earlier and was practising meditation at one of the meditation centres in Rangoon. Whenever an Indian vegetarian meditator happened to come for such courses, I was informed by U Chan Htoon and asked to help with providing Indian vegetarian food some of the time. In this connection, I had the opportunity to meet Bhikkhu Mahinda a few times while he was at the meditation centre.

One day I got a call from U Chan Htoon asking me to come meet with Bhikkhu Mahinda immediately. When I went to see him, I found his mental condition very unbalanced. He was behaving in a very bizarre manner. I was told by the management that he had even tried to commit suicide. As soon as he saw me, he told me of his agony and his strong desire to disrobe, begging me to get him the clothes of a layman. I was perplexed as to what to do, so I went to the main teacher of the centre and asked his permission to take the *bhikkhu* to my residence for a few days. He was accommodated at the guest house of our Mogul Street residence. Partly because of the change in environment and partly because of the service he received here, we found that in a few days his mental state returned to normal and he became healthy once again. Gradually, he started talking about meditation.

One day during these discussions, he came to know that I also practised Vipassana and that my teacher was Sayagyi U Ba Khin. The moment he heard Sayagyi's name, a glint came into his eyes as if this were a very pleasant surprise for him, and he started pressing me to take him to my teacher. I went with him to my teacher's meditation centre. When he met Sayagyi, Bhikkhu Mahinda was overwhelmed with joy. I, too, was very pleasantly surprised to learn they had known each other intimately in the past. Bhikkhu Mahinda was a former resident of Burma, and in his householder's life was a civil engineer by the name of Bahadur. He had been an important officer in the Burma Railways at the same time that Sayagyi had been Accounts Officer of Burma Railways, and this is how they knew each other.

As an engineer, Bahadur had been involved in some work at the Gotaik Bridge near Naungkio, in the Shan states. One day, people discovered that he was missing. When a search was made, it was found that he had disappeared into the dense jungle in the deep valley below. His family members and companions undertook an extensive search of the area, but all they found was his pair of sandals sitting by the bank of a rapidly flowing mountain stream. Therefore

> After trying a few techniques, one should stick to the particular technique most suitable and work on it seriously. This has been my advice and encouragement to all my students.

people thought that he had either committed suicide or had fallen into the river and drowned accidentally. Actually, he had gone from there down to the plains where he entered a *vihāra* and ordained as a *bhikkhu*. He later went to India. Now he had returned to Burma as Bhikkhu Mahinda, having come to learn Vipassana.

Sayagyi wanted to help his old friend. The next Vipassana course was to start some time later. However, with strong pressure from Bhikkhu Mahinda, he agreed to conduct a special course for him alone. Bhikkhu Mahinda worked with great devotion and enthusiasm and was highly benefited by the practice. When he came back to my house after the course, he decided to visit various parts of Burma to meet many of his old friends before returning to India.

Wherever he went on his tour of Burma, his old friends gathered and requested him to give a public talk on meditation. Out of overenthusiasm, he began praising the technique of Vipassana taught by Sayagyi U Ba Khin. This much Sayagyi could accept, but soon he began to denounce the meditation taught by his previous teacher. In his overenthusiasm, he did not realize that Sayagyi would not approve of such comparisons. A message was sent to him to abstain from such talk, but he would not comply.

All this created quite a controversy which Sayagyi did not like in the least. He used to say that a son of Buddha never gets involved in controversies. Whatever technique Sayagyi had acquired from his teacher, he was simply distributing the same to others, very humbly. These kinds of quarrels and arguments comparing techniques were totally against his nature. Therefore he made a strong decision that in the future, if anyone came to him having already taken a course of meditation with another teacher — especially a monk teacher— then he would not entertain such a person at the centre and would not allow him to take a course under him. This was only to prevent any recurrence of such unfortunate incidents. This was the reason that he was not willing to teach Vipassana to Munindraji.

When I came to India I was already in contact with my friend, Munindraji, and when I gave courses in Bodh Gaya quite a few persons, who were friends or disciples of Munindraji, participated and benefited. Because of this, he himself was also very enthusiastic to sit a course. It was a great embarrassment for me. How could I take someone in my course who was rejected by my teacher, however friendly that person might be? I immediately wrote to my teacher and was very pleased to get his permission. He explained that there was no such controversy in India. I was given permission to teach anyone and everyone who came to me. This is how the restriction on Munindraji was removed and he was able to participate in the course.

During the first course he attended, he was greatly benefited and wrote a very glowing report to Sayagyi, full of gratitude and Dhamma sentiments. Later, he attended two more courses and gained more benefits.

This incident gave me the liberty to teach Vipassana to anyone who asks for it, even those who might have taken a course with other teachers. Of course, I am very particular to see that such students are serious and not just running from one teacher to another for the sake of curiosity. I would certainly not want to encourage such behavior. After trying a few techniques, one should stick to the particular technique most suitable and work on it seriously. This has been my advice and encouragement to all my students.

Freely Given to All

After I began teaching in India, another problem arose. After conducting a few more courses in Bombay, a Sri Lankan *bhikkhu* who was residing in Bombay expressed his desire to join a camp. I was an ordinary householder. How could I teach someone who had renounced the householder's life? To resolve this situation, I contacted Sayagyi by phone. He immediately gave permission. He explained that because there was no one else in India who could teach this pure technique of Vipassana, where else could these *bhikkhus* learn it? He instructed me to give the Dhamma to anyone who requests it. With this liberty, I could serve the large number of *bhikkhus* who requested Dhamma from me, not only from India but also from Bangladesh, Sri Lanka, Nepal, Tibet, Thailand, Cambodia, Laos, Vietnam, Korea and Japan. In one of the courses at Nagpur, all the participants were *bhikkhus* and *sāmaṇeras* (novices). Courses in Sri Lanka and Nepal attracted local *bhikkhus* there to come and take advantage of this technique.

Similarly, recluses from various other sects got the opportunity to learn Vipassana. Quite a large number of Jain, Christian and Hindu monks and nuns were benefited by joining such courses. One course was organized specifically for Jesuit priests and Catholic nuns. It was held in the Christian monastery at Khandala where the church was used as the meditation hall.

Special courses were held in Delhi and Ladanu in Jain **Upāsraya** (monasteries) in which a large number of Jain monks, nuns and *sāmaṇeris* participated. At the request and with the cooperation of His Holiness the Dalai Lama, a special course was held for Tibetan *lamas* in Dharamsala.

In this way, the floodgate of Vipassana was opened for the benefit of people of every religious sect and way of life. Someone had warned me that if this technique was freely given to the leaders of various sects, there was the danger that some of these leaders would try to make use of it to strengthen their hold over their followers, by disguising it as part of their own sectarian teaching. This fear was well-founded, as later on this proved to be true in a few cases. However, I had no hesitation because for me the flow of the Ganges of Dhamma was for one and all. I have given this wonderful jewel of Dhamma to help people come out of their own misery. If they misuse it and continue to roll in misery, what can be done? On the other hand, I found that quite a few of the sectarian leaders were very sincere and have kept it in its pristine purity for their own good and for the good of others. Therefore, I never have any regrets about Sayagyi's decision encouraging me to give the Dhamma to one and all and I shall continue to do so, without any discrimination whatsoever.

Westerners Request the Dhamma

I faced one more difficulty several months after I started teaching in India. A few Western students had come to join the Vipassana camps. At that time my evening discourses and all the daily instructions were in Hindi. My knowledge of English was very limited, so I could not speak much. I would explain the theory and practice to this handful of Western students in a few simple words, so that they could work properly. Very soon the news of Vipassana began spreading, and the numbers of Westerners began increasing. The students worked very seriously, and as a result they were quite successful.

It was barely a year since I had come to India from Burma when a small group of Western students—about fifteen—invited me to give a course in English at Dalhousie. How could I give a course in English? It was impossible for me to give the evening Dhamma discourses in this language.

My education in English had been quite limited. I had completed only my high school matriculation, through which I had gained enough knowledge of English to conduct my business. I was not able to give even a short extemporaneous talk in English. Whenever I had to give a long talk in English—say, as president of the Rangoon Chamber of Commerce and Industry, or any such organization where English was used—I would dictate my ideas to my secretary. He would draft out my speech in good English, and I would simply read it aloud. I had never given a speech in English without reading it. My English vocabulary was very limited. My knowledge of technical words pertaining to Dhamma was even weaker. Therefore, I expressed my hesitation to conduct the course. I actually refused to give it.

These foreigners then wrote a letter to my revered Sayagyi in Rangoon and complained that I had declined their request. They described their difficulty: they could not go to Burma because only a three-day visa was granted at the time, and there was no one else available to teach Vipassana outside of Burma. Therefore, they were being deprived of receiving this wonderful technique.

Sayagyi immediately telephoned me and advised me to go to Dalhousie and give the course. I explained to him my difficulty with the language. But he replied very firmly that I should go to give the course without hesitation, and that Dhamma would help. I respectfully followed his instructions, and the course started.

The first evening I could speak for only fifteen minutes. This turned into one half hour the next evening, and then it started flowing. All my hesitation and doubt about my capabilities in speaking English vanished. Conversing with the Western students, my vocabulary started increasing, and very soon full courses in English became a regular occurrence. Later on the courses turned into bilingual courses where I gave instructions in both Hindi and English, one after the other. The discourses were given in one language in the morning, and the other language in the evening.

This is how, through the kind benevolence of Sayagyi, the way opened for the teaching of Vipassana in English throughout the world.

A necdotes of S.N. Goenka

I Want Divine Light

I nearly ran away from my first Vipassana course.

The early days of the course were devoted to developing concentration. I found the first instructions of my teacher easy to understand and follow: I was simply to focus my attention at the area of the nostrils, to be aware of the breath or anything else happening there. I could do this well enough. But we are always curious about others, so I was tempted to ask some of the other people participating in the course about their experiences in meditation. One of them told me, "As I sit with eyes closed in my cell, I see a light."

"A light? That is wonderful!" In India the witnessing of "divine light" is widely considered to be the highest goal of meditation. I was deeply impressed and equally disappointed that I myself had not seen any light.

Another meditator said to me, "I hear a sound as I meditate, something like the sound of the sea." "That must be divine sound!" I had read of this and knew that it was experienced by many saints. Inevitably I asked myself what I was doing wrong that I had not had such experiences. True, I could keep my mind fixed on the breath and could feel distinctly the area of the nostrils. But what good was that? I wanted to experience divine light, divine sound.

I became dejected and convinced that I could not succeed in the course. After all, it is written that it is easier for a camel to pass through the eye of a needle than for a rich man to enter the kingdom of heaven. Yet here was I, a wealthy industrialist, looking for a way into heaven!

No wonder the other meditators were more successful, I thought. They were quiet people without the twisted mind of a businessman. They were not involved in the rat race of making money, as I was.

By the evening of that day I had made up my mind to abandon the course and go back home. Every day at 5 pm. a car came from my house with fresh laundry and other necessities. I knew that the Teacher would not agree to my leaving, so I decided to slip away that evening in my car.

I went to my room and began to pack my bags. Fortunately, however, a friend came to check on me, a Burmese lady who had practised Vipassana for some time. Naturally she was surprised that I had decided to leave. I explained that despite all my efforts of two days I had not been able to experience divine light or sound.

"But were you asked by the Teacher to experience them?"

"No, his instructions were just to observe the breath at the entrance of the nostrils."

"And have you been able to do that?"

"Yes, but…"

"Then why should you be upset? Forget about these other things. Try for just one more day, and give importance only to what you actually feel within the area of the nostrils."

Abashed and heartened by her words, I returned to my meditation cell. This time I was determined to follow the instructions of the Teacher and ignore everything else. Soon my mind became concentrated, and as I sat in the darkness of my cell a bright, star-like light appeared before me. "Oh no!" I thought. "I am not interested in that. My job is just to observe the breath." I ignored it and after a little while it passed away. A few minutes later I started to hear sounds. I said to myself, "These are beyond the focus of my attention. I should not follow them in any way." I kept on resolutely observing breath, and in their turn the sounds eventually disappeared. I worked exactly according to the advice of my friend and the instructions of my teacher. And how grateful I am that I did! Visions and sounds, "divine" or otherwise, will come and go, but by the end of the course I had discovered the happiness of a mind that keeps its balance with all experiences, a mind at peace.

How to Walk, How to Eat

In a one-month course with Sayagyi U Ba Khin in Burma, I experienced a very deep stage of *bhaṅga* in which my entire body seemed to have dissolved into a mass of vibrations constantly arising and passing away. Even if by chance I happened to look at someone, I saw only the outline of that person and within it a kind of blinking or oscillation.

One day during this course my teacher said to me, "Come, Goenka, I shall teach you how to walk." Now what was this? I was not a baby crawling on all fours; I was a man of mature years! Sayagyi explained, "Walk as you do normally, neither quickly nor slowly. As you walk be aware of each movement of your body, and also be aware of what is happening within you." I had been practising that in ten-day courses, but it was different now. I tried it and found that while walking I could experience the flow of vibrations, the subtle reality within. At a superficial level I was aware of my walking, and at a deeper level I was aware of the unceasing process of change within myself—just a mass of atoms moving about, rather than a solid body.

"Now come," said Sayagyi, "I shall teach you how to eat." By this time I had understood that, though I was not an infant to be spoon-fed, there was something I needed to learn. We went to the dining room and a tray of food was placed before me, each item neatly arranged in a separate dish. "Make small pieces of all the food, and put it in a bowl," Sayagyi said. "Now, mix it all together—solid or liquid, sweet or sour, combine it all." This is the way that monks are supposed to eat. I did as he said and mixed all the food together in the bowl. "Now, remain in deep *bhaṅga.*" said Sayagyi, "Keep your eyes closed and continue. Take a morsel of food with your fingers, and feel sensations." I did this, and as I touched the food I felt strong vibrations in my fingertips. "Move your hand to your mouth feeling sensations…" I did so, feeling strong vibrations. "Place the food in your mouth and feel sensations." I did so, feeling vibrations on my lips, my tongue and gums. "Chew the food and swallow it feeling sensations." I did so, feeling vibrations throughout my mouth and throat. The taste of the food became immaterial. Instead I experienced it only as vibrations entering the vibrations of my body.

Having finished the meal in this special Vipassana way, I was asked to take rest. I went and lay down on the bed. For quite some time I kept feeling distinct movement and vibration in the stomach and intestines.

After that course, all my food preferences disappeared. I had been very fond of some of the more spicy Indian preparations. Now I eat whatever is placed before me, but if there is a choice my hand goes automatically to the simpler dish. I had indeed learned how to eat: not to satisfy cravings but to provide the nourishment this body needs to carry on its task.

Thanks to Sayagyi, thanks to Dhamma.

Conversion to Dhamma

A friend of mine, a Muslim merchant in Rangoon, had suffered for years from insomnia. Nothing could help him. His existence was an unrelieved misery. When he heard how Vipassana had changed my life for the better, he came to me and asked to know about the technique. I explained it carefully to him and he became eager to join a course. First, however, he wanted to visit the meditation centre and meet my teacher.

One evening I brought this man with me to the centre and introduced him to Sayagyi. The calmness of the place and the kindly presence of the Teacher made a strong impact on him. He declared that he wished to join the next course. We said our goodbyes to Sayagyi, and before returning home I offered to show my friend around the centre. As we were making our tour, I noticed that he suddenly lost all enthusiasm and interest. I was surprised by his sudden change in attitude and asked him what was wrong.

With hesitation he told me. As we were walking he had happened to glance through an open doorway and had seen inside a shrine, with a statue of the Buddha and someone kneeling before it. "In my religion all graven images are forbidden," my friend said, "and we must not bow to anyone but God. If I come to a course, I see that I shall have to bow down to this idol and to your teacher. It is impossible for me to come."

Instead of arguing with him I said, "Let us go and tell the problem to Sayagyi." My friend reluctantly came and repeated what he had told me.

"Well," said Sayagyi, "this being a Buddhist country, we have a statue here for traditional Buddhists simply to give them inspiration to meditate. No one will ask or expect you to bow to it, still less to me. If you find it offensive I can curtain off the statue while you are here so that you need not even see it. Don't allow this to stop you from learning Vipassana."

The man accepted Sayagyi's advice, though not without misgivings. When the next course started he joined it. Before ten days were over, the Dhamma had worked a deep change in him. He was now freed of the tensions that had made him unhappy for years. Naturally he was filled with gratitude. He came and insisted on bowing to my teacher, understanding now that he was not showing respect for any person but for the teaching of truth.

After his course this friend of mine did not start calling himself a Buddhist. He remained a devout Muslim, and at the same time he lived a life of Dhamma, practising morality, concentration and wisdom. Nor was my teacher disappointed that this man had not adopted a new label for himself. Sayagyi was not interested in converting people from one religion to another, since that has nothing to do with the Dhamma. The only conversion he wished to see was from suffering to happiness, from ignorance to wisdom, from bondage to liberation. In this sense certainly my friend had undergone a conversion, and Sayagyi was pleased that he had understood and benefited from the Dhamma.

Repaying Burma's Debt to India

My parents left Burma around 1965 and came to settle in India. In about 1968, my mother developed a nervous ailment. I knew that if she took Vipassana, she would be free of her ailment, but there was no one in India to teach her. Accordingly, I applied to the authorities in Burma to permit me to go abroad in order to serve my old ailing mother. I was pleasantly surprised when this request was granted, and I was extremely grateful to the government for having issued me the necessary passport.

When my teacher came to know that I was free to travel to India, he was very pleased, since he anticipated that along with my mother, others among my relatives and friends in India could learn Vipassana, and in this way the wheel of Dhamma would start rotating again in that land. In preparation he gave me detailed instructions about how to conduct courses and how to teach Vipassana-Dhamma.

Sayagyi was so greatly enthused, because he saw my going to teach Vipassana in India as the means by which the Dhamma debt of Burma would be repaid. Burma was deeply indebted to India because it was from this land that it had received the treasure of the Buddha's teaching.

When the time came for my departure, Sayagyi gave me a warm send-off, with all his strong *mettā*. "You are not the one going," he told me as we parted, "I am going—Dhamma is going. We must pay back the debt of Burma to India." Greatly moved, I embarked on this Dhamma pilgrimage. In July of 1969, I gave the first course in Bombay, and that is how the wheel of Dhamma started rotating. As Sayagyi began receiving my reports of successfully completed courses, he was filled with happiness at seeing his dream of many years being realized at last.

The Gem Returns to India

Following the nationalization of trade and industry in Burma, many Indian residents there were left with no means of livelihood, and therefore had to return to their native land. On leaving Burma they were forbidden to take any valuables with them. Nevertheless, to avoid the loss of their entire life savings, many departing Indians would try to smuggle out valuables, particularly in the form of gems—rubies or other stones for which Burma is famous. In order to suppress such smuggling, Burmese customs inspectors were naturally more vigilant with departing Indians.

As I was preparing to embark for India at Rangoon Airport, I passed through the emigration check and came to the customs counter. The official there was very friendly, and jokingly asked whether I was carrying any valuables with me. "Yes," I replied, "I am carrying a gem." The official became nervous. Though friendly to me, he was an honest man who would not neglect his duty. Therefore he searched all my belongings carefully without finding what he was looking for. I watched him with amusement. Finally I happily explained to the worried man, "My friend, the gem that I am taking from here will be used to pay back a debt of Burma to India. It originally came from India, and is sorely needed there today. By my taking it from here, Burma will not become any poorer. I am taking the jewel of the Dhamma." The official laughed and said, "Please go ahead—take this gem with you! I am very happy that you will use it to repay this debt." And this is what I did, bringing Dhamma back to India in fulfilment of the wishes of my teacher. According to the news I had from my friends in Burma, the

official always felt very happy whenever he heard about the success of my work here.

My Life Changed Course

I have often told the story of how a severe physical disease—migraine headaches—provided the impetus for me to go to Sayagyi U Ba Khin and to undertake a ten-day course of Vipassana meditation. While I was suffering from them, these headaches seemed so undesirable, unbeneficial. But after learning Dhamma from Sayagyi, I realized that the migraine had been a blessing in disguise. Certainly, the disease was now cured; but this benefit was only a very minor, trivial aspect of the help my teacher gave me. Immeasurably more valuable is the jewel of Dhamma received from him which has changed my life—a treasure which grows the more it is used.

Mindful of this great debt to my teacher, I often reflect on the past and consider what my life might have been had I not received this Dhamma. My successful career as a businessman and industrialist had been interrupted by the programme undertaken by the government of Burma to nationalize trade and industry. Nevertheless, I could have drawn on my years of experience and worldwide contacts to establish myself as a businessman in India. Given the huge consumer market in this country, and the government policy favourable to private enterprise, I might well have been successful in amassing wealth as great as what I had before or even greater. This is the path that many of my friends and relatives have followed who left Burma when I did. But had I given all my attention and energy to amassing money, far from helping myself by doing so, I would have been generating stronger ego, with all the resultant tensions. My life would have become much more miserable than it had been.

In Burma I had worked successfully in the field of voluntary social service; and I might have continued in this field after coming to India where the opportunity for service to the poor is so vast. I might have worked managing public institutions such as schools, hospitals, orphanages, adult education centres, and so on. But there would still have been the danger that such voluntary service might build nothing but ego and mental tensions—always expecting others to appreciate one's service, and feeling depressed if appreciation is absent. Life would still have been full of misery.

I had also worked in Burma as a leader of the Indian community in social, educational, commercial, industrial and other undertakings; and perhaps I could have manoeuvered to achieve a position of leadership in India also—had I not doubted whether such a position, with all the attendant madness, was worthwhile. Having passed through the process of truth realization as taught by Gotama the Buddha and passed on to me with such compassion by my Dhamma father, I had understood that all competition for leadership, for special position or status, is nothing but a rat race bringing endless misery.

If someone had merely advised me not to waste my time in such ways, I might have understood this at a superficial, intellectual level; but the impact of this understanding would not have been so great. However, with the practice of Vipassana, I was able to realize at the actual level, deep within myself, the dangers of all such worldly endeavours. It is only when one achieves such a direct realization that he starts working earnestly and strenuously to emerge from the miseries of a life of competition, of seeking after wealth, status, position, power.

When I recall the past before I came in contact with Sayagyi, it seems to me that it all was a previous existence, and that having received Dhamma from him, I entered a new life, far superior to the old one. The Dhamma words come to mind:

Yaṃ kiñci vittaṃ idha vā huraṃ vā
Saggesu vā yaṃ ratanaṃ paṇītaṃ
Na no samaṃ atthi Tathāgatena
Idampi Buddhe ratanaṃ paṇītaṃ
Idampi Dhamme ratanaṃ paṇītaṃ
Idampi Saṅghe ratanaṃ paṇītaṃ

Whatever treasure there may be in this world or the next,
Whatever jewels may be found even in celestial fields,
None of these can compare with the jewel in the *Tathāgata*—the jewel in the *Tathāgata* is far higher.
This is the jewel in the Teacher.
This is the jewel in the Teaching.
This is the jewel in the followers of the Teaching.

All the wealth I had amassed, whether there in Burma or here in India, could give me merely earthly pleasures. All the merits I had gained by giving service before I learned Dhamma might have given me a new life in celestial planes, where I might have enjoyed still greater pleasures. But all these pleasures, earthly or celestial, would be ephemeral, bound to pass away; and must lead to disappointment and misery when they go. They are nothing compared to the happiness I have gained in receiving the jewel of Dhamma from my teacher—a happiness which keeps growing every day of my life.

Nor was the jewel given merely for ornament, without use. Sayagyi made it so clear that pure Dhamma is applied Dhamma. Intellectual appreciation of the teachings of the Buddha might have purified my mind at the surface level. But only the practice of Dhamma through Vipassana meditation penetrates to the depths of the mind and transforms it totally.

I could never have attained real happiness, real peace without learning this technique from that great, saintly person, my Dhamma father Sayagyi U Ba Khin. He did not try to impress people with his mental powers, or to convince them intellectually of the superiority of the Buddha's teachings. He was, rather, a saint who lived the life of Dhamma, and whose every word carried the weight of his own experience. A man of such sterling character, practising pure Dhamma, full of love and compassion, devoting himself to serving others selflessly—this was my Dhamma father.

On this anniversary of his passing, I recall all his extraordinary qualities, and I bow down in deep respect to his memory and to the Dhamma which he lived and which he gave to me as an invaluable gift. May I prove worthy of his teaching. I know I still have a long way to go until I reach the final goal; but I also know that the royal road he showed me will certainly lead me there. With this confidence I keep walking on the path; and out of my own experience of Dhamma, I keep encouraging all others to take this path, and to come out of their suffering.

May all beings share this peace.
May all beings share this happiness.
May all beings share this Dhamma.

I do not wish to convert people from one organized religion to another; I have no interest in any of these organized religions. My interest is in Dhamma — the truth, the teachings of all Enlightened Ones.

If at all there is any conversion, it should be from misery to happiness, from defilement to purity, from bondage to liberation, from ignorance to enlightenment.

—*S.N. Goenka*

Homage to Baba

by S.N. Goenka

"One is always more attached to the interest one receives than to the capital one loans." This Hindi folk saying expresses the common belief that a grandfather always feels stronger attachment to a grandson than to his own son. And perhaps as a reaction, a grandson is likely to feel more attachment to his grandfather than to his father.

From my own experience, this belief seems to me to be quite correct. Perhaps it explains why the most distinct memories I have of my childhood focus on my grandfather, Basesarlalji, even though I was only seven or eight years old when he died at the ripe age of seventy-three.

Some of Baba's words etched themselves deeply on my young and impressionable heart, leaving a lasting stamp on the course of my life. He had a high regard and respect for the land of Burma and its people. To this day, some of his reminiscences of Burma live and remain fresh in my memory. Here is one incident that he often recounted.

He used to travel from place to place selling textile goods, and for transport he would hire horses and mules. One part of the country that he visited in his rounds was the mountainous Shan Plateau of eastern Burma. There each locality organized a weekly market, and for the convenience of merchants like my grandfather, the market days were staggered in adjacent areas. This made it possible to sell at the market in one town, then travel two or three days to the next place and be in time for the market there. In this way Baba gradually made his rounds, selling at all the markets along the way, and returning at last to the family home in Mandalay.

While on his travels, he would make camp every night at a public resthouse. These resthouses, called *zeyat* in Burmese, are still in use today in some parts of the country. The accommodation is quite basic: a high, roofed platform, without any enclosing walls. The traveller keeps his belongings on the platform and rests there overnight, continuing on his way in the morning. There is no charge for staying at a *zeyat*. Each is built by local villagers as a service to travellers, and in the same spirit of service the villagers keep the *zeyat* neat and clean, and provide water nearby.

In those days, Baba said, silver coins were the accepted currency in which all business transactions were conducted. He used to keep his silver in a money belt around his waist. When he went to bed at night, he would take off the belt and put it under his pillow. One morning he had planned to begin his journey before sunrise, but instead he overslept. When he awoke he hurriedly collected his belongings, loaded them on the pack animals, and started on his way. After five to six hours of travelling he suddenly realized that the money belt was not around his waist and that he must have left it behind in the *zeyat*. In a panic to recover it, he immediately asked the horsemen to turn back, but they flatly refused. "You'd better continue to the next market and then return," they insisted; "your money belt will be waiting for you when you come back."

Despite his fears, Baba had no choice but to accept the advice of the horsemen. It was only after four or five days that he was able to return to the *zeyat*. As he rode towards it, his heart pounded at the thought that he had probably sustained a heavy loss: the money belt had been full of coins, and by forgetting it he had not only wiped out the profits of the trip but had cut deeply into his capital.

An anxious moment awaited him when he reached the *zeyat*. But there was the money belt on the platform where he had left it. Baba counted the coins with growing amazement: not a single rupee was missing. No one had even touched the belt, neither the people of the village nor the hundreds of travellers who must have passed a night at the *zeyat* since the belt was forgotten there. It was no wonder that Baba always had such a high opinion of the honesty of the people of Burma.

Another incident of which he often told us occurred in the marketplace of the city of Mandalay. There a woman had dropped a diamond earring, evidently without noticing it, and it lay on the footpath in front of the shops. Every day many people passed the earring which lay in full view, but no one took it. Each morning a woman came to sweep the street; when she reached the earring she would lift it, sweep the ground below, and then put it back in the place where it had fallen. This continued for seven days until a government officer took it into safekeeping, and it was announced by public crier throughout the city that whoever had lost a diamond earring should come and claim it. Such was the honesty of the people of Burma.

Baba told us that within living memory it had been the custom never to lock the doors of houses in Burma. People would bolt their doors to keep out stray animals, but they felt no need of locks, no matter how rich they were. This custom had persisted until the overthrow of the Burmese monarch in 1885. Once control of the country passed into the hands of the British, many foreigners came to settle there and the entire social structure gradually was subverted.

Thievery began, against which people tried to protect themselves by using locks, and the next step was that burglars would smash locks to enter and rob houses. When the social order is collapsing, a lock on the door will not provide security.

I do not know whether Baba had settled in Mandalay while the Burmese King Mindon-Min was still on the throne, but certainly he was living there during the reign of the last King of Burma, Thibaw, whom he used to call the *phongyi*-king, that is, monk-king. I never knew why Baba referred to the king in this way, whether it was because he had been a monk for some time or because he had been of a very religious temperament. British historians have drawn a very black image of this king, perhaps for political reasons. The man himself may well have been quite different.

At least in the judgement of Baba, this was the case. He had witnessed the snatching of Thibaw's kingdom from him, and had seen the fallen monarch in a pitiable condition, led as a prisoner from the royal fort to the bank of the Irrawaddy, and on into exile. Baba would tell this story with real sorrow showing in his face and voice. He grieved for Burma's loss of independence, and felt that British rule was a calamity for both Burma and India.

Baba had great respect for the last Burmese king. According to him, Thibaw and his government functionaries showed such friendliness and regard for Indian traders that those from Britain and other countries became very jealous. At that time goods being brought from southern Burma up the Irrawaddy had to pass a customs inspection on their arrival at the river port of Mandalay. The Burmese customs officers would treat Indian merchants very politely, simply asking what goods they were bringing without opening or searching their boxes. Whatever the merchants said to the officers was accepted on faith, and the customs duty was fixed accordingly. People from all other countries, however, had to undergo a thorough inspection.

This preferential treatment of Indians aroused the animosity of other traders. As a result of their protests, the Burmese government officers began to open the boxes of Indian traders too. But they would look without disturbing the contents, so that actually they would see only what was on top of each box. Indian merchants received inspection in name only, and their word was still accepted without question by the customs officers.

This state of affairs continued for many years. Finally, however, a few Indian merchants started deceiving the Burmese officers and so shattered the confidence that had been placed in them. In a box full of valuable velvets these merchants would place a few pieces of cheap, unbleached cloth on top in order to fool the customs inspectors and to escape paying the full duty. Their trickery at last became known and because of

> When a businessman loses his honesty, he loses his reputation, and when he loses his reputation he has lost everything. Baba felt that honesty must be the basis for doing business. It is only honesty that can bring prosperity and peace.

the dishonesty of a few, the integrity of the entire Indian business community became suspect. One or two decaying fish will spoil the entire tank. One or two drops of vinegar will curdle a pot of milk. One or two rotten apples will spoil the whole barrel.

Baba used to say that in ancient times in Burma, people used the term *kula* (*kala*) for Indian people as a mark of their respect for them. (Perhaps this usage was in accordance with that found in old Pāli literature, for example Mahā-kula Anāthpiṇḍika and Mahā-kula Visākhā.) But now, within a few years, the foolish actions of these greedy merchants caused the usage to change totally, and the word became a pejorative. When a businessman loses his honesty, he loses his reputation, and when he loses his reputation he has lost everything.

Baba felt that honesty must be the basis for doing business. It is only honesty that can bring prosperity and peace. Although he had retired long before I was born, his views on the proper way to conduct business continued to exert influence. He used to say that the customer is the prop and support, the provider of the businessman. He was aghast at the idea of being dishonest to one's supporter; that for him was biting the hand that offers food. Everyone in the family accepted his views and followed his principles in business; one of my uncles even took them to extremes.

In many other ways Baba had a strong impact on my life. For example, he greatly enjoyed the daily newspaper, but his eyes had grown weak in his old age, and so he would ask me to read the paper to him every day. He used to follow closely political developments in Burma and also India. His interest influenced me so deeply that reading the daily newspaper has practically become an addiction for me.

Baba had a great love of literature and a vast store of folk tales and poems in his memory. He told us countless stories, and his *dohas* (rhymed couplets) in his native Rajasthani made a deep impression on me. Fortunately my teacher in elementary school, Shri Kalyan Dutt Dube, shared

Baba's love of poetry, being himself a poet. In order to introduce the Hindi language to me, he started by giving me not a children's reader but a book of *dohas*. This first book that I read in Hindi was called **Rahimana Sudha**, a collection of *dohas* of the medieval Muslim poet Rahim.

Inspired by reading this work, I composed my first *doha* at the age of seven or eight and eagerly recited it to my Baba, expecting that he would be proud of me. To my surprise, he took such pleasure in this first effort of my pen that he laughed loud and long. It was only after many years that I understood what had provoked his mirth. I had noticed that in each *doha* of **Rahimana Sudha** the name of Rahim appeared (it being a popular convention for a poet to include his name in any poem that he composed). In my youthful simplicity I thought that the name of Rahim must appear in my *doha* as well, and so I included it. No wonder Baba had laughed! Perhaps it is just as well he never knew that this naive budding poet would one day compose a collection of *dohas* in memory of his grandfather, and that every one of these poems would include the name "Baba."

About ten miles from Mandalay in the village of Tagundaing was a *goshālā*, a place where pious Hindus offered shelter and protection to cows. Every year on the auspicious day of Gopastami (the cow festival), a big fair was held at this cow shelter, to which Baba brought the children of the family. All day long we had free rein to satisfy our childish desires. In the evening would be a public meeting with many lectures and speeches, in which Baba took keen interest. One year Master Dube prepared a speech of seven or eight pages for me to read at this meeting. When Baba came to know of it he said, "Why read? You must speak from memory; that will be really impressive." Obediently I learned the speech by heart and declaimed it at the meeting without any notes. Baba was very pleased with my performance. Perhaps he was giving me training for the future.

In our home, lunch was served between twelve and one and dinner from seven to eight, as is customary in Indian households. Baba, however, preferred to eat these meals earlier, as do the Burmese, and so he would regularly have lunch at ten in the morning and dinner at 5 pm. Although this gave extra work to his daughters-in-law, they were happy to satisfy his wishes. This earlier meal schedule is followed in Vipassana courses, and it seems to me much better for the health. In fact I often feel uncomfortable if I eat too late at night.

We never saw Baba praying, or reciting scriptures, or chanting, or fasting, or performing any rites or rituals. In the city was a Hindu Satyanarayan Temple, but he was never seen inside it. On the yearly festival day of the temple people would come in crowds and elaborate decorations were erected, but Baba ignored it all. Baba's daughter lived with us, being a young childless widow. This aunt, Chanda-bai, was always very affectionate to the children, but sometimes she would become irritated with Baba over a trifling matter and would take him to task, saying, "Oh Father, for you there is no reciting the name of God, no rosary, no beads, no pilgrimage, no fasting! You will certainly waste your whole life doing nothing!"

Baba would smile at her words without replying. In fact this supposedly irreligious man would often take the children with him to visit the Arakan Pagoda, four or five miles from Mandalay, where the famous Mahāmuni statue of the Buddha is enshrined. There he would sit silently for some time. I have no idea whether he was meditating or simply sitting and doing nothing. Perhaps it was just the atmosphere of the place that appealed to him. In most places of worship it is impossible to find peace or even clean, orderly surroundings. They have been polluted by the commotion of the constant chanting and praying, the muck and rubbish left behind by countless rituals. But here at the feet of the Mahāmuni Buddha we found nothing but pure cleanliness, pure peace. This atmosphere of purity naturally affected all who came to the place; I remember that I would always feel very calm and peaceful there.

Sometimes Baba would also take the children on an outing to Mandalay Fort, in order to show us the former palace of the kings of Burma. He carefully explained all the different structures of the palace to us: throne room, audience chamber, private apartments of the royal family, etc. After inspecting the entire palace he would invariably take us to an old *bodhi* tree which grew not far away within the grounds of the Fort, and there he would rest for some time. I remember distinctly that under this tree I felt the same peaceful atmosphere as at the Arakan Pagoda. In fact I became so attracted to this place that in the ten days' study holidays before my high school matriculation examinations, I spent the time under this tree. Each morning I took my bicycle, and equipped with books and lunch box, I headed to the Fort. Although it was a long journey from my house, I was undeterred. I would spend the entire day studying under the *bodhi* tree within the Fort, returning to my home only in the evening. The peace I found under this tree left a lasting impression on me.

In this way Baba planted seeds of literary inclination and pure Dhamma in the receptive soil of my young mind, and in due season they sprouted, blossomed and bore fruit.

I was born in the auspicious land of Burma because Baba had migrated there. I was born in a family of businessmen, and might well have earned great worldly wealth in any country where I happened to live. But in that land of Dhamma I had the unique opportunity to encounter a true saint who nevertheless lived within the world: Sayagyi U Ba Khin. This great teacher helped me to earn the priceless gem of the Dhamma, which has enriched my life immeasurably.

None of this would have been possible had it not been for my grandfather. He has been a great benefactor in my life. Endless salutations to the sacred, living memory of Baba!

I Am Grateful to So Many

by S.N. Goenka

The following article was written by S.N. Goenka in 1979 to mark his completion of ten years as a teacher of Vipassana. By 1979, he had fulfilled his decision to spend the first ten years teaching only in India. In the twelve years since, many important developments have unfolded: regular trips by Goenkaji to teach Dhamma abroad, and the resulting establishment of centres and year-round Vipassana courses in countries outside of India; the appointment of assistant teachers; the establishment of the Vipassana Research Institute. Nevertheless, the article is timely today.

On 20 June 1969 my revered teacher, Sayagyi U Ba Khin, formally bestowed on me the heavy responsibility of vipassanā-ācariya (teacher of Vipassana). Two days later I was to leave my motherland, Burma, to visit India. This was a joyous and blessed occasion. It would have been natural to feel regret at leaving the noble land of my birth, which was to me a heavenly abode. But regrets were dimmed by the shining prospect of coming to the homeland of the Dhamma, the land trodden by so many Buddhas, saints and sages, the holy land of my ancestors, the land now to become the kamma-bhūmi, the scene of action of my future life.

Sayagyi had a strong Dhamma wish that Burma repay its debt of gratitude to India. More than two millennia back, Burma had received the beneficent technique of Vipassana from the land of its origin. Now, he felt, it must be returned to India in all humility; only then would Burma's obligation be discharged.

Sayagyi had hoped to perform this important task himself, but various obstacles came in the way. Therefore he looked to me to undertake this duty. In fact, he had been waiting for the appropriate moment to arise.

As I have often recounted, the opportunity came when my aged mother, who had gone earlier to India, fell sick. Although the Burmese government at that time did not usually permit their citizens to make trips abroad, they granted me a passport to visit India on compassionate grounds. The Indian government was equally helpful in issuing me the necessary visa. To both these governments I am deeply grateful.

Sayagyi was very pleased that the way was now open for me to go to India, and he entrusted to me the task of fulfilling his long-cherished wish. Although knowing my own limitations, I accepted this great responsibility since I too had a debt to repay: that to my beloved teacher.

That great saint full of pure love had taught me this wonderful technique and had helped me to break the shell of ignorance. By showing me how to develop self-realization, truth-realization within myself, he had given me a new birth. Not only that, with the tender devotion of a father he had nourished me for years in the technique, helping me to grow strong in Dhamma. To repay even a little of the great debt to my Dhamma father I was prepared to accept the heaviest responsibility, whatever my limitations might be.

Truly it was a great responsibility. Although India today respects and takes pride in the Buddha, there is widespread opposition to his teaching, purely because of misconceptions about what he actually taught. For the misunderstandings and antagonism of more than two millennia, who can

> The real nature of Dhamma is coming to light, beneficial to all and accessible to all, no matter what one's background. This pure and universal Dhamma is what the Buddha taught.

we blame? I myself was once involved in them. Out of attachment to certain philosophical beliefs, I myself had joined the opposing camp. But through Sayagyi's overflowing compassion, I was able to learn the practical aspect of Dhamma as taught by the Enlightened One, and as a result all my misconceptions melted and my resistance evaporated. This same practical aspect of the teaching of the Buddha has removed the misconceptions and opposition of many, and it continues to do so. The real nature of Dhamma is coming to light, beneficial to all and accessible to all, no matter what one's background. This pure and universal Dhamma is what the Buddha taught. He brought to light the actual practice of *Sīla, Samādhi,* and *Paññā.* Dhamma is not a matter of empty discussions or arguments, of mere beliefs or philosophies. Pure Dhamma is not a cause for establishing a sect. Dhamma is simply seeking one's own real welfare and the welfare of all others.

It is this universal, universally beneficial nature of Dhamma that attracted me to it. This is what has attracted and continues to attract a large number of intelligent people in this country. *Aho Buddha, aho Dhamma, aho Dhamma-sudhammatā!* (Great is the Buddha, great is the Dhamma, great is the nature of Dhamma!) Great is the Buddha who teaches universal Dhamma. Great is the Dhamma which applies to one and all. Great is the nature of Dhamma because of which any ordinary person of average intelligence can practise it and benefit. I am grateful

to this wonderful, universal Dhamma which transcends the narrow-mindedness of sectarianism. The strength of this pure and universal Dhamma has enabled Vipassana to become a medium for serving the general public, despite initial difficulties.

Certainly there were difficulties at first. One was that out of a population of six hundred million, there were hardly one hundred people in India whom I knew well, and of these I could count on my fingers those who might be called my intimates. Closest were naturally the members of my family who were already residing in India, but I found them to be strongly committed to a different technique of meditation that is inimical to Vipassana. Given this situation, it seemed to me that I could not expect any cooperation from my family. Nevertheless they did in fact give their cooperation, which I can never forget and for which I am always grateful. I share with them the merits of my Dhamma work.

During the last ten years thousands of people from India and abroad have come to learn Vipassana, all because of the power of the Dhamma. Many who came were apparently strangers to me, but soon they seemed to be old acquaintances whom I had known for a long time.

Among those who came were many who have performed a meritorious deed in the past, because of which they could now receive the seed of pure Dhamma—a seed which will yield good fruit when the time ripens. I am thankful to all of them. They gave me the opportunity to serve them in Dhamma and to repay even a small measure of my debt of gratitude to my teacher. But there were also those who came to learn the technique and who naturally became a part of the Dhamma work. What great service has been given by these people! When I review the last ten eventful years, a number of faces come to mind of those who dedicated themselves mentally, physically, and financially to arrange and manage Vipassana camps.

In those days there was no centre for the teaching of Vipassana. The organizers had to find the physical facilities for a camp: a resthouse (*dharmashālā*), or a school. They had to provide for the boarding and lodging of the participants. If someone fell ill during a course they had to make the arrangements for medical treatment and special regimens. For ten days the organizers had to set aside all their own affairs in order to look after the meditators, waiting on them hand and foot. And the job was not limited to ten days. Before the camp there was the work of preparation and corresponding with applicants. After the course as well, there was much to do and usually few to do it: returning and paying for rented equipment, arranging railway bookings for the participants, and so forth. Large or small, innumerable tasks awaited the organizers after a course. Despite the heavy burden, I found that they met their responsibilities smilingly, with the pure volition of serving the Dhamma.

These people derived no material advantage from their work, nor did they expect any, not even name or fame. It was simply because they had benefited from this wonderful technique that they wished more and more people to benefit.

When I recall the faces of these many dedicated servants of the Dhamma, I feel a thrill of rapture throughout my body. I ask myself whether the great work accomplished in only ten years would ever have been possible without their selfless service.

Of these dedicated people were some who undertook to establish centres at Igatpuri, Hy-

derabad and Jaipur in respect for the glorious memory of Sayagyi U Ba Khin. Many more meditators gave their cooperation in constructing facilities at the centres, and they still give it without expecting anything in return. Their service is truly selfless and pure. Others have given large donations, but they did not assume that they were therefore entitled to name or fame, or to any special treatment at the centres. All of these people who have been aiding the Dhamma work do so without the thought that because of their help some special status is due to them, some position or power in the organization. I am deeply grateful to all these selfless servants of the Dhamma.

Nor has this Dhamma service been confined to Indian meditators. Many young Western stu-

> **W**hatever portion of the journey has been completed gives the inspiration and strength to walk on. And the greatest help upon the path is gratitude. This is the support for the journey ahead.

dents of Vipassana have dedicated their lives to serving the Dhamma. Quite a few have been living the life of true recluses at Dhammagiri. Whenever needed, they willingly give *dāna* of physical work, toiling like ordinary labourers. Their devoted service gives joy and Dhamma inspiration to others.

Outside India as well, there are many engaged in freely-given Dhamma service. In different countries there are contacts to spread information about Vipassana, and places where meditators can sit together once a week. Courses are also organized regularly. These many Indian and Western meditators all deserve my thanks, although I know that none of them works expecting even thanks from me.

During the last ten years many Vipassana camps have been organized in the places of worship of different religious groups: Buddhists, Jains, Hindus, Muslims and Christians. These courses were made possible only through the magnanimity of the leaders of the various religious organizations. If they had had even a tinge of sectarian narrow-mindedness, they would not have allowed their places of worship to be used for teaching Vipassana meditation. Their broad-mindedness is all the more remarkable when it is considered that they agreed to suspend all rituals, prayers, and recitations in their places of worship for the period of the course, so as to avoid any conflict or interference with the teaching of Vipassana.

When a camp was organized at Saint Mary's Church in Khandala, the main sanctuary was used as the meditation hall. For the period of the course not only daily prayers but even the Sunday masses and sermons were suspended. Two consecutive courses were arranged in a large mosque in Ningal, Kutch (Gujarat), and for the benefit of Vipassana meditators daily worship and even the Friday congregational prayers (namaj) were stopped. In Hindu temples, even the customary practice of ringing prayer bells was suspended. Such actions are evidence of the broad-mindedness and magnanimity of the guardians of these religious establishments. All these religious groups cooperated willingly to help course participants learn the universal technique of untying the knots of the mind.

The meditation technique of Vipassana was maintained in Burma through millennia, but in its pure form it was preserved only by a small number of people who transmitted it from teacher to pupil in an unbroken chain. There are many monks there who do not know this technique

which gives such quick results (akālika), concrete results that can be experienced here and now (sandiṭṭhika). Quite a few respected bhikkhus (monks) wanted to learn this wonderful technique from Sayagyi U Ba Khin but they hesitated to do so, since it is contrary to all tradition in Burma for a monk to learn Dhamma from a layman. For this reason Sayagyi was pressed hard to take robes so that there would be no obstacle for these monks to learn from him.

Sayagyi, however, had his principles. He had to act according to his own understanding of Dhamma, even if this might restrict him in some ways. It was his ideal to live the life of a bhikkhu while remaining a layman. In this way, he felt he could enable more people to gain the benefits of Vipassana. Therefore, although many monks in Burma were convinced that here was a person who knew the technique by which one can reach the final goal of full liberation—the very goal in pursuit of which they had left worldly life—still they felt unable to break with tradition and to learn meditation from Sayagyi.

Wonderful, however is the land of India! During the last ten years a large number of monks and recluses have come to learn Dhamma from an ordinary layman, not concerning themselves with the question of possible loss of prestige in doing so. Among those who have come were leading Buddhist bhikkhus who are research scholars and teachers of great renown; prominent Jain munis and nuns who are highly respected in their community; leading Christian priests and nuns; and well-known Hindu sannyasis. For these people of reputation and standing to learn from a layman, they had to set aside considerations of ego and prestige. This they did with resolute mind, and worked with zeal to learn the technique.

The obstacles they faced were all the greater because for the period of the course they had to suspend their customary religious ceremonies; yet still they came. In fact a large number of Jain *munis* and nuns, whose discipline forbids them to use wheeled or mechanized transport, walked for hundreds of miles to join a camp. Great is their zeal to learn Dhamma, great is their zeal to become liberated, great are their efforts towards that goal, great is their renunciation! Certainly they must have performed highly meritorious deeds in the past, which have led them in the direction of Vipassana meditation. When I remember each one of them my mind fills with rapture and bows with sincere respect.

I do not devalue what has been done for the spread of Vipassana in the last ten years, since to do so would be to devalue the selfless service given by so many people. But the fact remains that up to now only a first step has been taken in the work, and a small step. A long journey lies ahead. From a firm base in India, the light of Vipassana must spread everywhere around the world.

It is a lifetime job. It is a steep ascent of the mountain. Upon the way are many obstacles and hindrances, those within and those without: not only conflicting responsibilities to family and society but also the opposition of many elements opposed to the Dhamma. To overcome these difficulties requires great strength of Dhamma, perseverance, forbearance, zeal, and egolessness.

At times when faced with great difficulties I find that I have stooped beneath their weight. Very soon, however, I have stood up, brushed the dust from my knees, and started walking with increased Dhamma strength. Whatever portion of the journey has been completed gives the inspiration and strength to walk on. And the greatest help upon the path is gratitude. This is the support for the journey ahead.

Therefore gratitude keeps overflowing in my mind, first to the Enlightened One who rediscovered this lost technique and used it for his benefit, and who with free hand and compassionate heart distributed it for the benefit of one and all. I am grateful to the entire chain of teachers from Buddha, the Enlightened One, to Sayagyi U Ba Khin who maintained this wonderful technique in its original form, thereby permitting me to learn it in its purity. I am grateful to all the members of my family whose cooperation has been so helpful in the *Dhamma-dūta* (spread of Dhamma) work. I am grateful to all my comrades and friends in the Dhamma, all who have given me their cooperation and assistance, whose companionship has given me sustenance on the path.

If during the last ten years by my deeds of body, speech, or mind I have committed any wrong action knowingly or unknowingly, intentionally or unintentionally towards anyone, I ask pardon.

Again, my gratitude to one and all.

May all beings be happy!
May all beings be peaceful!
May all beings be liberated!

Anna vastra, vāhana bhuvana
svarṇa ratna kā dāna
saba dānoṅ se ucā hai
sreṣṭha Dharma kā dāna.

Dharama ratana sā jagata meṅ
aura ratana nā koya.
Dukkha dainya sāre miṭeṅ,
saba vidhi maṅgala hoya.

Gifts may be of food, clothing,
transport or shelter;
gifts may be of gold or gems;
but greater than all of these
is the noble gift of Dhamma.

In the world there is no jewel
like the jewel of Dhamma.
It ends all suffering
and wretchedness;
all its ways are happiness.

—*Hindi dohas of S.N. Goenka*

Interviews

Mr. and Mrs. S.N. Goenka

Master of Meditation: An Interview with S.N. Goenka

by Stephan Bodian

The following article was written by Stephan Bodian, editor of Yoga Journal (Berkeley, California). It appeared in the September/October 1989 issue of the magazine, and is reprinted here in its entirety.

Next to the Dalai Lama, S. N. Goenka may be the Asian Buddhist teacher best known in the West. Several prominent American teachers have studied with him; he makes periodic visits to Europe, Australia, and the United States; and hundreds flock each year from all over the world to attend his ten-day and one-month meditation courses near Bombay.

Yet Goenka, though he claims to teach what the Buddha taught, does not call himself a Buddhist. "The Dhamma is universal and non-sectarian," he insists. In a country torn by differences of caste and belief, this ecumenical message is like salve on an open wound. Hindu temples, Christian churches, Buddhist retreat centers, and a Muslim mosque have hosted his meditation courses, and hundreds of Christian priests, monks, and nuns have studied with him as a required part of their pastoral training.

What Goenka imparts to his students is called Vipassana, often translated as insight meditation. Learned from the great Burmese master U Ba Khin, Goenka's version of this ancient technique emphasizes three aspects: moral behavior, to encourage the mind to settle; mastery of the mind through concentration on the breath; and Vipassana proper, purification of the mind through insight into one's physical and mental structure. Following in the Buddha's footsteps, Goenka claims that this is a direct path to eradicating the threefold source of all suffering: craving, aversion, and ignorance.

Nothing about Goenka's upbringing would seem to have prepared him to be a teacher of Vipassana. Born to an Indian family that had settled in Burma two generations before, Goenka was taught the elaborate rites and rituals of conservative Hinduism. As a youth he was groomed to enter the family textile business, which he did while still in his teens, and by his mid-20s he had become an extremely successful businessman and a leader of the Indian community in Burma.

But success brought with it "a lot of ego, a lot of tension," as he puts it, and he began to suffer from severe migraine headaches, for which no cure could be found except morphine. Afraid of becoming an addict, Goenka sought medical care in Europe, America, Japan, but to no avail. Then a friend suggested he take a ten-day Vipassana course with U Ba Khin, who, in addition to being a meditation master, held high government office as the Accountant-General of Burma.

"I was hesitant initially," Goenka recalls, "partially because I could not believe this meditation could help when the best doctors could not, and partially because it was Buddhist, and I come from a very staunch Hindu family." But meeting U Ba Khin changed his mind.

"He was such a saintly person. The atmosphere around him was so calm and serene, just meeting him for a few minutes persuaded me to give this technique a try." The results were dramatic, and thoroughly convinced Goenka of the value of Vipassana.

"Of course, it gave me relief for my migraine. But the biggest relief was that the stress and strain and tension that I used to build up because of my ego—all that got released." Once a "short-tempered person," Goenka found that he now got along much better with his family and staff. Dogmas and rituals became "trivial" as he came to see that the Dhamma is not a religion but an "art of living, the art of living peacefully and harmoniously within oneself and of generating nothing but peace and harmony for others."

For the next fourteen years, Goenka practised regularly with U Ba Khin—when he wasn't attending to the responsibilities of business and family. Then in 1969 he moved to India, where, with the encouragement of his teacher, he began teaching courses in Vipassana. Since 1976, Goenka has been based at the Vipassana International Academy in Igatpuri, near Bombay. Built entirely with the donations of grateful students, this center boasts a meditation hall that seats over 400, with individual meditation cells for over 250. Centres have also been established near three other Indian cities and in Nepal, Australia, New Zealand, Japan, England, France, and the US. In all, approximately one hundred assistant instructors authorized by Goenka teach this approach without charge or personal profit to all who request it.

A teddy bear of a man in his mid-sixties, Goenka gives every impression of being "the real thing"—one who has faithfully followed the path he espouses and has achieved the happiness and equanimity of which he speaks. During our interview, his voice never betrays the slightest agitation, exuberance, irritation or concern. Rather, it exudes the quiet, steady warmth and serenity one would expect of a master of one of the world's oldest forms of meditation.

Yoga Journal: In a recent interview, you are quoted as saying, "To me, Hinduism and Buddhism are both madness."

S. N. Goenka: One thing is clear: for me, Dhamma is universal; it can never be sectarian. The life of morality [*sila*] cannot be a monopoly of Hindus or Buddhists or Christians. All must live a moral life, doing nothing at the physical or vocal level to harm other beings.

Nor can mastering the mind [*samadhi*] and keeping it pure and free from all negativities [*pañña*; pronounced *"pahn-ya"*] be a monopoly of any sect or religion. These three [*sila, samadhi,* and *pañña*] are what constitute the Dhamma, the teachings of the Buddha. So the Dhamma is universal. When I teach this approach, I don't call it Buddhist, because "Buddhism" is a loaded word, like Hinduism, Jainism, Christianity. It refers to a sect, whereas what I am teaching is universal. For me, sects divide; Dhamma unites. When I used the word "madness," I was referring to the situation in India and Sri Lanka, where Hindus are killing Buddhists, and Buddhists are killing Hindus. Even beautiful Dhamma has turned into a sect and become poisonous and fanatical, and the essence of Dhamma has been lost. When one is teaching pure Dhamma, there can't be any madness.

Could you say a little more about the Dhamma? What is this Dhamma you teach?

The Dhamma is the law of nature which governs the entire universe, both animate and inanimate. If one understands the laws of nature and works in accord with them, one leads a good and proper life. Now, Dhamma wants us not to kill, not to steal, not to tell lies, not to engage in sexual misconduct, and not to get intoxicated [the five basic precepts for lay Buddhists]. At the surface level these are actually laws of society, rather than laws of nature, because they contribute to the peace and harmony of society.

But when you start practising Vipassana, deep inside you understand that every time you break any of these precepts, even before you harm others, you have started harming yourself. You can't kill without generating a lot of anger or hatred in your mind. And as soon as you generate hatred or ill will, indeed any negativity, nature starts punishing you, and you become miserable. When you generate anger, you can't possibly experience peace and harmony. You feel so agitated, so miserable.

> When we generate negativity we become miserable. When we come out of negativity, we start experiencing peace, and we start helping others because we are being helped ourselves.

Similarly, every precept that is broken creates agitation in the mind and makes one miserable. Maybe nature continues to punish us after death; I believe it does. But nature definitely punishes us here and now. This is the law. I place my hand in the fire, and it burns. If I want to keep myself free from burning, I had better keep myself away from fire. So *sīla* [morality or precepts] is practised not just to oblige the society, but for one's own sake, to keep oneself peaceful and harmonious.

When these negativities are removed and the mind becomes calm, quiet, and pure, the law of nature is such that a pure mind naturally becomes filled with love, compassion, goodwill. One does not have to cultivate these virtues deliberately; they develop quite naturally. And as

soon as I develop love, compassion, and goodwill in my mind, nature starts rewarding me then and there. I feel so peaceful, so harmonious. The reward for a pure mind and the punishment for an impure mind are universal. It works the same for Buddhists, Hindus, Christians and Jews. Because I call myself a Buddhist, nature will not favor me. The Dhamma is universal.

Another way in which Dhamma is universal is that, in the practice of *samādhi*, controlling or concentrating the mind, the object of concentration is the breath. No verbalization, no recitation of a name or mantra, no visualization of a god or goddess. Just natural breath that comes in and goes out. Now, this too can be practised without any difficulty by a Hindu, a Muslim, a Christian, or a Jain. Breath is breath. It's a natural reality that is present in every being.

In the practice of *paññā* [wisdom] mind and matter work, how they interact. When we generate negativity, an unpleasant sensation arises in the body and we become miserable. When we come out of that negativity, we start experiencing peace, and we start helping others because we are being helped ourselves. All this can be done easily by a person of any sect, because no dogma or philosophy or symbolism is involved, just the law of nature. You are just observing nature, which is the same for everyone. So, in my own experience of all three aspects, *sīla, samādhi, and paññā,* I have found that Dhamma is universal.

Much of what you have been describing sounds like the law of *karma*, the law of cause and effect. If this law is indeed universal, I wonder why all the different religions don't teach it.

Not only other religions, but Buddhism as well. Over the centuries the teachings of Buddha have also been corrupted, and the various

Buddhist sects have started giving importance to rites, rituals, sectarian beliefs, dogmas, and all kinds of different philosophies. But the essence of Dhamma is always universal. If the essence of Dhamma is lost, then every teaching degenerates into sectarian belief. We can't blame any one religion only. Every religion has degenerated into an empty shell; the essence of Dhamma has been lost everywhere.

But if we understand what the essence of Dhamma is, then there is no difference between one religion and another. Large numbers of people come to my Vipassana courses from different religions, and they find it so beneficial. At the end of one course, a Christian priest told me that I am teaching Christianity in the name of Buddha. At the end of another, a Jain monk said, "This is the essence of our teaching, which we have lost. This is what we are looking for." Hindus, Jews, Muslims, they all say the same thing, because nobody can find any defect in pure Dhamma. It is always acceptable by one and all.

Could you say a little about the Four Noble Truths?

Again, these are so universal. Nobody can deny the First Noble Truth, the reality of suffering. Association with undesirables [undesirable objects, people, situations] and disassociation from desirables bring suffering. So the First Noble Truth, the truth of suffering of misery, is universal. The Second Noble Truth, the cause of misery, looks different from the inside and from the outside. It seems that I am miserable because something happened outside that I didn't want to happen, or something didn't happen according to my wishes. But deep inside, everyone can realize that the misery I am suffering is caused by my reaction of craving or aversion. I like something, and I generate craving. I dislike something, and I generate aversion. This Second Noble Truth is common to all.

So, too, the way to come out of misery is common to all, because you have to eradicate the root of your misery, where craving and aversion start. At a gross level, a good way to do that is to practise *sīla*—that is, don't perform any action, physical or verbal, that will disturb or harm other beings, because simultaneously it will harm you. Then work with *samādhi*; control your mind. But mere control is not sufficient; you must go deep and purify your mind. Once it is purified, craving and aversion are gone, and you have reached the stage where there is no misery at all. It's all so scientific; people accept it so easily. Of course, if we keep fighting over dogma, difficulties arise. But I say, just practise and see: Are you suffering or not? Isn't this the cause of the suffering? And isn't it eradicated by practising in this way?

You talk about Vipassana meditation. What are the techniques of Vipassana, as you teach it?

The technique of Vipassana is to observe the truth of suffering within oneself, how one becomes agitated, irritated, miserable. One has to go deep within oneself to observe it objectively. Otherwise, the cause of misery always appears to be outside. Say, for example, that I'm angry, and I want to investigate this anger. Even if I close my eyes and try to understand it, the apparent external cause of the anger will keep coming to mind, and I will keep justifying my behavior. "So and so abused me, so and so insulted me, and that is why I am angry. It's no fault of mine." But the fact is, I am miserable.

The technique of Vipassana teaches you just to observe. If you are miserable, just observe misery as misery. As you start observing, the cause of misery becomes clear. Because you reacted with negativity, with craving or aversion, you are now experiencing a very unpleasant sensation in the body. But as you keep observing the sensation, it loses its strength and passes away, and the negativity passes with it.

We start with respiration because the mind doesn't become concentrated unless it has an object to focus on. For the first three days of the retreat, we observe the breath coming and going at the entrance of the nostrils. As the mind calms down a bit, we start experiencing the sensations around the nostrils and then expand to experience the sensations throughout the body. These sensations take us to the root of our minds. They take us to the root of the misery, to the root of the cause of misery, and they help us to eradicate that cause. This is what is taught in Vipassana.

If I'm not mistaken, the technique of observing sensations throughout the body is called "sweeping."

Yes, sweeping in the sense that, at a certain stage, all the solidity of the body dissolves. The apparent truth of the material body is solidity. We feel a solid body. But, as you keep observing it objectively, this solidity starts dissolving, and you start experiencing that the entire material structure is nothing but a mass of subatomic particles arising and passing away, arising and passing away. The entire body is just a mass of vibrations. At first, however, when you are still with the solidity, you can't sweep, can't get a flow of vibration throughout the body, because there are blockages here and there—pain, pressure, heaviness. Instead, you keep observing part by part, and little by little all that solidity dissolves, and you reach the stage of total dissolution, mere vibration. Then your attention can move easily from the head to the feet and back again without any obstruction. This is what I refer to as "sweeping."

So sweeping occurs when you are totally clear.

Totally—when there is no blockage anywhere. The Buddha says: "By this technique, a student learns how to feel the entire body in one breath. Breathing in, you feel the entire body. Breathing out, you feel the entire body." This happens only when the body dissolves, when all solidity disappears. Then as you breathe out, you feel from head to feet; as you breathe in, you feel from feet to head. That is what we call sweeping—a stage where the body dissolves and intense mental contents dissolve as well. If there are strong emotions, you can't get this sweeping, because strong emotions result in a feeling of solidity in the body. When emotions are dissolved at the mental level, and the solidity of the body is dissolved at the material level, nothing remains but a mass of vibration, a mass of energy moving in the body.

Ideally, one would be able to do this at all times, throughout the day.

Yes. Once one reaches this stage, one continues to work with sweeping. But certain conditionings or impurities of the past, called *saṅkhāras*, may exist at a very deep level of the mind. Through this sweeping, moving from head to feet and feet to head, these impurities get shaken and start coming to the surface. Say a certain *saṅkhāra* manifests itself as gross sensations in the body. You work on these gross sensations by just observing them, until they too dissolve and you again get a free flow.

The goal of this technique is not to achieve the free flow of vibrations, which is after all just another transitory experience, but to accept with equanimity whatever manifests

> The goal of this technique is not to achieve the free flow of vibrations, which is after all just another transitory experience, but to accept with equanimity whatever manifests itself.

itself. In this way, you eradicate your mental conditioning layer by layer, and along with it your suffering.

How is this practice different from other forms of Vipassana?

I don't want to give any opinions about others. But as I understand the teachings of the Buddha in the *Satipaṭṭhāna Sutta* and elsewhere, the starting point can be different for different people, but at a certain stage everyone must follow the same path towards *nibbāna.*

At the start of practice, Buddha gave different objects of meditation to different people, according to their mental conditioning, temperament, understanding, and capability. For example, those who have great attachment to the body and to the passions of the body, Buddha would have contemplate a corpse, so they would come to understand that their body is also like that—made up of flesh and bones and blood and pus and mucus and so forth. Someone who is so attached to the body doesn't want to accept that the body is dirty, after all. What, then, would there be to develop an attachment toward?

One can start this way, but eventually one must reach the stage where one experiences *anicca,* impermanence, how things arise and pass away. This arising and passing away should not be accepted at the intellectual or devotional level only; Buddha wanted us to experience it for ourselves. And it can be experienced only with sensation in the body. At the level of sensation, one finds, "Look, it has arisen, and look, it has passed away." Sensation arises, passes away; arises, passes away. When it is solidified, intensified, it arises and seems to stay for a while; but sooner or later it passes away.

> According to Buddha, whatever arises in the mind manifests itself as a sensation in the body. When a thought arises, simultaneously there is a sensation in the body. And the sensation is actually the root of the problem.

When all solidity dissolves, it turns into subtle vibration, and every vibration becomes a wavelet that arises and passes away. So one experiences both solid sensation and subtle sensation arising and passing, arising and passing. Unless one experiences this directly, one hasn't understood the Buddha properly. Even before the Buddha, there were those who taught that the whole universe is impermanent, arising and passing. But Buddha discovered a technique by which one can experience it. And when we experience it, attachment, craving, and aversion go away, and the mind becomes purified. At a later stage, arising and passing occur so rapidly that one can't separate the one from the other. Then, after further purification of the mind, one reaches the stage of *nibbāna.* Whether one starts with contemplating a corpse, the material parts of the body, respiration, or some other object, the rest of the path must be the same.

So this is why you stress mindfulness of sensation, as opposed to mindfulness of mental states.

Exactly. According to Buddha, whatever arises in the mind manifests itself as a sensation in the body. People don't give enough importance to this teaching. If you just observe mental states, that will help you to perfect your faculty of observation. But that is not the totality of the truth. You are observing only your own thoughts. But what is happening to the body at that time? Mind and matter—both have to be observed.

When a thought arises, simultaneously there is a sensation in the body. And the sensation is actually the root of the problem. We don't react to thoughts. It may appear that, when I have a very pleasant thought in my mind, I start craving, and when I have a very unpleasant thought in my mind, I start to develop aversion. In fact, however, according to the law of nature, what you call a pleasant thought is nothing but a pleasant sensation in the body. Displeasure is nothing but an unpleasant sensation in the body. If you miss the sensation, you are just working at the surface level. This may give you some benefit, but it won't take you to where you eradicate your impurities. The roots still remain.

> This technique does not make you inactive. A responsible person in society is full of action.

So when you are meditating, and you have a lot of mental turbulence...

Start observing the sensation in the body, and accept the fact that there is turbulence in the mind. That's all. Don't go into the details of the turbulence, and don't try to forcibly calm it down. Otherwise, you'll end up rolling around in your thoughts and not observing them objectively.

As you observe your sensation, you will find that your mind automatically calms down. Negativity is not suppressed, nor do you express it at the physical or vocal level. It just gets eradicated. If you observe the sensations with equanimity, without reacting to them, then you are purifying your mind at the deepest level. Otherwise you purify your mind at the surface level only.

Many of these ideas, which are classic Dharma, foreshadow the insights of modern mind-body theorists. For example, the German psychologist Wilhelm Reich believed that past conditioning is stored in the body and can be released by working at the physical level. And Carl Jung, the Swiss psychologist, believed that the unconscious exists in the body.

Quite so. The so-called unconscious mind is constantly reacting to the body's sensations, while the conscious mind has no idea what is happening. There is a big barrier. The conscious mind may not know what the unconscious is doing. This technique breaks the barrier between the conscious and the unconscious. Then one becomes aware of everything that is happening in the body. Little sensations here or there that the conscious mind would not otherwise have felt, it now feels. And this technique trains the mind not to react. At the root level, the unconscious mind has always reacted with craving and aversion, and this influences the conscious mind as well. The entire structure of the mind is influenced by the root. Buddha teaches us that, if we rectify things at the root, the entire mind will become perfectly all right.

Unless the sleeping impurities at the root of the mind are eradicated, one can't call oneself an enlightened person. To me, Buddha's contribution to meditation was this technique by which the unconscious impurities are eradicated. Otherwise, the unconscious mind will always be reacting to the body sensations.

We've talked quite a bit about *anicca*, impermanence. What about the teaching of *anattā*, which is ordinarily understood as "no self" or "no abiding self"? Ordinarily we think that we

need a self in order to function in the world. We have expressions like "self-esteem" and "self-confidence," and we believe that "ego strength" is a measure of a person's ability to cope with daily life. What does this "no self" teaching mean?

For those who haven't experienced the stage of "no self," it's true that in the apparent world there must be an ego, and this ego must be stimulated. If I don't crave something, I won't get the stimulation I need to function. In my courses, whenever I say that craving and attachment are harmful, people say that if there were no attachment, no craving, what would be the fun of living? There would be no life. We'd all be like vegetables.

Being a family man who has done business in the world, I can understand their concerns. But I also understand that when you work with this technique and reach the stage where the ego dissolves, the capacity to work increases many-fold. When you lead a very ego-centered life, your whole attitude is to do as much as possible for yourself. But this attitude makes you so tense that you feel miserable. When, as a result of doing Vipassana, the ego dissolves, then by nature the mind is full of love, compassion, and goodwill. You feel like working, not only for your own benefit, but for the benefit of all. When the narrow-minded ego stimulation goes away, you feel so much more relaxed, and so much more capable of working. This is my own experience, and the experience of so many who have walked on this path.

This technique does not make you inactive. A responsible person in society is full of action. What goes away is the habit of blind reaction. When you work with reaction, you generate misery. When you work without reaction, you generate positive feeling.

How do you recommend that people use this technique in their daily lives?

The first thing is to strengthen and perfect *sīla*, morality. The five precepts we teach—no killing, no stealing, no sexual misconduct, no

> As we explore this path of arising and passing, arising and passing, we experience something that is beyond arising and passing, which we call *nibbāna.*

lying, not becoming intoxicated—are the base. Once one starts slipping in any of these, *samādhi* becomes weak, and *paññā* becomes shallow. You can't work at the level of your sensations; you just end up playing intellectual games at the surface of the mind. But if *sīla* is strong, you can start going to the depths of the mind. And then, when you've gone to the depths and eradicated even some of the impurities, *sīla* and *samādhi* are both strengthened. All three help each other.

The next thing is this: while you're working, give all your attention to your work. This is your meditation at that time. But when you're free, even for five minutes, be aware of your sensations with open eyes. Whenever you have nothing else to do, observe your sensations. This will give you strength while you are going about your tasks. This is how people can use this technique in their daily life.

What about enlightenment. Where does enlightenment figure into all of this?

To me, enlightenment is progressive. It is because of ignorance that we keep on reacting deep inside with craving and aversion. When we come to understand that we are craving in reaction to a pleasant sensation and feeling aversion in reaction to an unpleasant sensation, then we have become enlightened to that reality. As we proceed, this reality becomes clearer and clearer, which means that enlightenment is increasing. And as we explore this path of arising and passing, arising and passing, we experience something that is beyond arising and passing, which we call *nibbāna.*

So enlightenment is the experience of a stage beyond arising and passing.

Yes, final, complete enlightenment is the experience beyond mind and matter, beyond the entire sensorium. All sense faculties stop working there. Eyes, ears, nose, tongue, body, mind—they cannot function. For all practical purposes, one is like a dead person. But deep inside one is aware. How one is aware, and what one is aware of, cannot be explained in words, because the experience is beyond the sensory field.

So a person like this doesn't function in the world.

Yes, while one is in that state—for a second, or a few minutes, or maybe even a few hours—one does not function. Then one comes back to the sensory field, but one is totally changed. Because now one understands everything at the experiential level.

Having had that experience, a person would then lead a very different life.

Yes. That is an important yardstick for measuring whether one is enlightened or not. Otherwise anybody can say, "I reached this or that stage." But the only way to judge is to examine how they lead their life.

Interview with Mataji

Mrs. Ilaichi Devi Goenka, who is known to her family and students as Mataji (respected mother; a respectful form of address for elderly Indian women) was born in Mandalay, Burma in January, 1930. Her ancestors migrated from Rajasthan, India to Burma about one hundred years ago. They were merchants, trading in grains and other commodities. She was one of three children, two girls and one boy.

Mataji spent the first twelve years of her childhood in Mandalay, the old capital of Burma, in the house next door to the one where Goenkaji's family lived. As was the custom in those days, the marriage was arranged and she was engaged to Goenkaji at a young age.

Near the end of 1941, the Japanese invaded Burma, and went on to occupy the country for the duration of the Second World War. Many of Burma's Indian residents, including Mataji's and Goenkaji's families, fled to their ancestral homes.

Goenkaji and Mataji were married in Mandalay in early 1942, during an aerial bombardment of the city. Almost immediately thereafter their families fled to India, where they remained for the duration of the war. Mataji's family stayed in northern India, where her father established a livelihood in Gujarat and the Punjab. Goenkaji's family stayed in southern India, where Mataji joined her husband during the war.

After the war, Goenkaji and Mataji returned to Burma and settled in Rangoon, where they were fully occupied with the householders' responsibilities of raising six sons, conducting the family businesses, and being a leading family of the Hindu community.

Goenkaji took his first Vipassana course with Sayagyi U Ba Khin in 1955. Mataji and other family members and friends also took courses and began practising under Sayagyi's guidance. In 1969, Goenkaji went to India and began conducting the first Vipassana courses there. Mataji stayed in Burma until after Sayagyi's death in 1971.

Because of the change in the Burmese government, and the work of spreading the Dhamma (first in India; later, around the world) the family settled in Bombay shortly after Sayagyi's death.

Goenkaji and Mataji have six sons, six daughters-in-law and eleven grandchildren, most of whom live together in a traditional joint family house in Bombay.

The following interview, through an interpreter, was held at the family residence in Bombay in October 1991.

Can you tell us about your first meeting with Sayagyi?

Mrs. Goenka: After Goenkaji did his first course, I went to the centre and met Sayagyi. Sayagyi gave me Anapana at that time, and sometimes I would practise it, but I used to feel very heavy in the head, practising only Anapana. Sayagyi told Goenkaji that it was important that I also sit a course, that this was very important for Goenkaji's progress also.

How old were you when you first met Sayagyi? What kind of a Dhamma teacher was he?

I was perhaps twenty-seven or twenty-eight years old when I first met him. I remember that I felt very peaceful whenever I was with Sayagyi, but I also felt something very overwhelming inside, which is difficult to put in words.

Can you tell us about your first course with Sayagyi?

It was really quite a miracle! When I went to my first course I was very ill, I could not even climb the stairs leading up to the Dhamma hall: two people had to support me and help me climb them. I was so ill that I could not even eat anything when I went. But after being given Anapana and practising it for just the first evening, I felt well again—the next day I could walk around, and eat, and do whatever was necessary unaided. The meditation was very helpful! (Laughter)

How old were your little children when you did your first course?

My youngest child, Jay Prakash, must have been four years old.

That's very young. Did you miss your children?

It was not difficult for me, I didn't suffer much from a feeling of separation, because I didn't have too much bodily clinging to the children. Also, because of our joint family, I knew that there were people to look after the children

properly at home, so I had nothing to worry about in that respect. Of course I remembered the children, but not with that much attachment.

Sayagyi spoke in Burmese and English, but you speak Hindi. How did you communicate? What were the discourses like?

Sayagyi didn't talk much. By gestures he would ask and by gestures I could reply, and that was more than enough. He gave very short Dhamma discourses, of about fifteen to thirty minutes only. Goenkaji translated just a few lines to the Indian students. The main thing was that you had been shown the path, and how to work, and then you just worked!

This was four years after Goenkaji took his first course?

Yes, three or four years later.

In those three or four years, did you notice any changes in Goenkaji?

There was a great change! (Laughter)

Did you and Goenkaji take the children to Sayagyi's centre sometimes?

In the first five or seven courses we didn't take the children, but later, when I went more often, the children used to go with me. They would sleep at the centre, and the next morning go to school from there.

How did Sayagyi respond to the children?

He loved them; he treated them very affectionately. He explained Anapana to them. Whenever it was vacation time for the children, they would stay there all day, and Sayagyi taught them Vipassana as well as Anapana. So the children were also on the path.

At home, did you have a room where your family meditated?

In the later years, there was a room for meditation on the terrace. The children also used to sit there, and they would recite the *Ratana Sutta* and *Maṅgala Sutta* with us. They would do a little bit of meditation, as much as they felt like, then go out quietly, to school or elsewhere, while the adults continued with their meditation.

> We were being trained, but we didn't realize because Sayagyi didn't explain it to us. Now we realize that he was always training us.

And otherwise did you go to Sayagyi's centre for sitting sometimes?

Sometimes, but not daily. Before nationalization, we used to go maybe once a week. But after the new government came and the businesses were nationalized, there was more time on hand, and we used to go thrice a week, sometimes in the morning, but not at fixed times.

During those years, did you know that your future would become completely devoted to spreading Dhamma?

Oh, no, I never knew anything!

Did Sayagyi talk about your spreading the Dhamma?

Sayagyi would very often say to me, "You have to work very hard! You have to do a lot of work, you have to work so much!" I always understood that my life would be filled with domestic chores, so I wondered: why was Sayagyi telling me that I had to continue to do domestic chores throughout my life? (Laughter) I didn't know what Sayagyi meant. He never mentioned to us that we would have Dhamma work to do. He was training us, giving us Dhamma training, but without telling us. We didn't know!

Sometimes Sayagyi would say, "Go and meet that student who is sitting on this course; see what you feel." And other things like that. We were being trained to be sensitive, but we didn't realize that this was part of the training, because he didn't explain it to us. Now we realize that he was always training us.

After Goenkaji went to India to teach Dhamma, you stayed in Burma for another two years?

For two and a half years.

Did you have any contact with Sayagyi at his centre during this time?

I had much more contact than before, a great deal more. When I went to Sayagyi's centre after Goenkaji had gone to India, he showed me so much love and affection. He would ask, "How are you?" just as if he was my father. He knew that I was separated from Goenkaji, and he was as concerned about me as any parent would be. He always asked about my welfare, and whether things were going well at home. I would go to his centre and meditate, and then sit and talk a little with Sayagyi, and then I would feel so much better, very relaxed. There was so much *mettā* (loving kindness) in him. I felt it at that time particularly; he was filled with so much *mettā*.

Did your own parents meet Sayagyi?

Yes, both my mother and father did two ten-day courses with Sayagyi.

When you and Goenkaji became established in Dhamma, did your parents notice a big change in your life? Were they happy for you?

When we started the Dhamma work, my parents felt a little taken aback at first, because they feared we might not be able to take care of the children, as we should, because of being absorbed in Dhamma work. But later on, when they saw that things were going well, when they saw the good results of Dhamma, and also that the children were on the right track, they also felt happy about our Dhamma work.

Was there a period when Goenkaji had just taken Dhamma, that your family felt concerned for his well-being—that he might be exploited?

When Goenkaji went for his first course, everyone in the family was really worried. The fear was, that if he turned to Buddha Dhamma perhaps he would become a monk, and then what would happen to our family? Everyone in the family was discussing their worries, and this strengthened my own concerns in that direction.

But then, gradually, as the changes in Goenkaji became apparent, and then when I did the course—and later all the others in the family also—then all of that was washed away. After that, there were no fears, no apprehension, nothing like that.

It is not money which brings happiness and contentment in the heart. One will feel so content, even if there is no money, because Dhamma is there.

Were you in Burma when Sayagyi died?

Yes, I was.

Can you tell us about the ceremony after he died, how the people said goodbye to the body?

After Sayagyi passed away, I felt so much emptiness inside, as though everything was finished. I went to the funeral, but I couldn't make myself go and see everything; it was beyond me. There was an electric cremation, and I didn't watch.

After the funeral, we went home and sat for meditation. Then I felt peaceful, and much, much happier. Before that it had been terrible; I had felt very empty. Even going to the centre to meditate became too much. It was as if the purpose of the centre was gone when Sayagyi was not there. During one of my courses there, while I was sitting, I felt—if there is no Sayagyi, there is no centre, there is no use in my coming here. Then I had the feeling as if Sayagyi were standing near me; but when I opened my eyes, there was nothing. It was just a feeling inside, feeling his presence.

After that experience, did all your confidence in Dhamma come back?

The confidence in Dhamma was always there. That wasn't lost or shattered because of Sayagyi's passing away. His passing was just the experience of when somebody very near and dear to you dies suddenly. If you lose such a person suddenly, what a traumatic experience it becomes. You feel so empty from deep inside. One feels bereft at the loss, but not because Dhamma is lost. And, with time all the wounds heal; then gradually, you become normal once again.

It must have been a big surprise when Sayagyi passed away so quickly. Did it shock everybody?

It was a great shock, because he was ill for just two days. Nobody realized that he would die so quickly. When I came to know that, at three o'clock he had passed away, it was such a big shock. He was in hospital for one or two days, but one could never think that he would pass away.

If we go back to before Sayagyi's passing, when Goenkaji was in India teaching, and you would go to the centre, did Sayagyi have any advice or guidance for you, about your return to India and teaching Dhamma? Did he talk about the role you would play?

He never told me directly that I would also go to India and then around the world on the Dhamma mission with Goenkaji. But he always said that he was very pleased and happy that Goenkaji had gone to India and was spreading Dhamma.

Were you happy living in Burma?

It was my country. I felt very happy living there because it was my country, I was born there.

Does it still feel like home?

Now, for me, it is like this: wherever I go is my home and I feel happy.

In Burma, is Mandalay or Rangoon your favourite place?

I spent my childhood in Mandalay, and afterwards when we came back to Burma, then we lived in Rangoon. I was happy in both places. Rangoon was of course a bigger city than Mandalay, but I didn't give a thought about which was better. Wherever you live is good enough! Be happy!

What was it like for you to go back to Burma after being away for twenty-one years?

I felt very happy, because the atmosphere there is charged with Dhamma vibrations. So it was a wonderful experience to go back.

In 1971, you left Burma and moved to India. What was it like to leave Burma, and settle in a new country?

When we left the house in Rangoon, then of course I felt very sad, because our family house had been established there for so many years, and now I had to leave it. But when we came to Bombay, when I saw the house there—where all our family was living—I felt quite happy and very relaxed. Now it's a better place and I feel very good. Of course there was not so much tranquillity in this country as in Burma.

In those early days, when Goenkaji was teaching the "gypsy camps," did you help teach the camps?

Yes, I used to accompany Goenkaji to the Dhamma courses at the gypsy camps.

That must have been a big contrast from Sayagyi's centre where it was so peaceful, so established. In the gypsy camps everything was so unpredictable.

Yes, it was difficult. But that was part of it, and with the strength of Dhamma, things would sort themselves out. Any upheaval which came would sort itself out, and settle down again without any problems.

In those days, the gypsy camps were quite demanding. You were travelling to different parts of India, and the foreigners who came on the courses could be somewhat wild. It seems like a huge undertaking. How did you find it?

It was a very rewarding and happy experience for me. When I found a change coming in the Western students, it was of course very rewarding. Because then we could see how much Dhamma can do for them, to change their life pattern. That was a big reward.

And you were confident that your children were well looked-after in the joint family in Bombay?

Yes. Dhamma takes care of everything.

As a loving and highly respected wife and mother and grandmother—and you are at the centre of a traditional extended Indian family—what value do you see in Vipassana for family life?

It is very, very helpful for the joint family. If somebody asks for guidance, then one sees it from the Dhamma angle: one does not find fault with others, and gives the correct advice. On the other hand, if you are not asked for any guidance, then you are also happy. It is not as if you are boosting your ego, that everybody must come and ask you for everything. If somebody asks, you give your opinion; otherwise you are content and happy within yourself. Vipassana is very helpful.

Are Anapana and Vipassana good for children?

Yes, they are a big help to children because they get the seed of Dhamma planted in their early years, and then anytime later it can grow and develop. It is good for them, very good.

We understand that it is the mother-in-law's role, when the daughter-in-law is having a baby, to be very supportive. What are your duties when your daughter-in-law is expecting a child?

It is an important duty for the mother-in-law. I must take great care of my daughter-in-law at that time—giving her proper rest, and taking full care of her. This is essential.

For how long a period?

After the child is born, for about a month or a month and a half.

How many grandchildren do you have?

Eleven.

Did you go to the birth of each grandchild?

No, for two grandchildren I wasn't there at the time of birth.

When you are present at the time of a birth, do you find that mettā helps your daughters-in-law?

If the daughter-in-law also practises Vipassana, then the *mettā* will be very helpful to her. But if she is rolling in the pain, if her mind is absorbed in pain—of course only the daughter-in-law understands how much she is rolling in pain, and how much she is able to take in the *mettā*.

But from my side of course I give *mettā*; I am always giving as much as I can. How can I say how much *mettā* I can give? (Much laughter)

Did your mother-in-law help you when you gave birth to your children?

Oh yes, she took much better care of me than I take of my daughters-in-law! She worked so much harder than I work. Now we have so much help; how much do we do on our own, with our own hands? Whereas, they didn't have so much help, they did everything themselves. They took much better care of us.

What is the role of the grandmother to the grandchildren in the extended family?

(Laughter: one sixteen year-old granddaughter is present.) We guide the children to walk on the proper path, and then it's up to them! How they take it and what they do is up to them. We just guide them onto the proper path. I feel happy because as of today the grandchildren are all on the right path. The responsibility lies on the shoulders of the elder grandchildren, because, if they walk on the right path, the rest will follow.

About my children also—they are doing their jobs well, and they understand their responsibilities. This gives me satisfaction.

How has Dhamma helped you? And, as a Dhamma teacher, how have you seen the technique help others?

I have peace of mind. I am happy, and I don't care for other things. For me, Dhamma is a benefit all around. It gives people peace of mind in all respects, and also helps them to carry out their duties in life. It is not money which brings happiness and contentment in the heart. If someone has no money, and has Dhamma, then such a person will feel "Oh, I am full." One will feel so content, even if there is no money, because Dhamma is there.

How do you feel about travelling so frequently, especially to countries where you do not speak the language?

The journeys are tiring. We get off the airplane and just for a day or two it is very tiring. Because of travelling, and the different vibrations all around, we are unsettled a little for a day. Once we start the course, and get engrossed in it, then it is very peaceful and very nice.

Although I do not understand the language, yet I feel very good within myself. The students ask questions, and although I don't understand them fully, it give me happiness to be there.

Many Westerners say that although you do not understand English, they feel that you do understand. They feel that you understand very well what they say.

(Laughter: Mataji is smiling, indicating to all that she has understood this comment.)

I don't speak much because I am very aware of the fact that nothing wrong, nothing which is not truth, should come from me. I am very aware of this fact. Even from my childhood it has been my nature to speak less about matters involving many people. It is better to watch, better to be watchful than to be actively participating, talking.

May we ask you, when Goenkaji is giving a Dhamma discourse, what are you doing?

You want to know what I do at that time? (Laughter) I meditate and keep giving *mettā* to everyone at that time.

We've come to the end of our questions. Thank you.

Be happy.

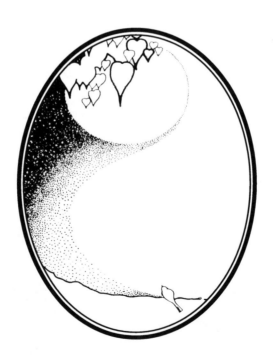

In the Tradition of Sayagyi U Ba Khin

The following is condensed from remarks made by S.N. Goenka in March, 1991, during an interview about his teacher, Sayagyi U Ba Khin.

Would you give us the outlines of U Ba Khin's teaching?

S.N. Goenka: A meditator has to start with *sīla* (morality), and then one develops *samādhi* (concentration), by cultivating awareness of the natural breath, pure breath, without anything else added to it. Next, one starts developing *paññā* (wisdom) by observing the sensations on the body with equanimity, without reacting, understanding their characteristic of *anicca* (impermanence), so that no new impurities are generated, and the old ones come on the surface and get eradicated. This is what U Ba Khin taught; this is what Buddha taught; this is what I am teaching.

What is the fundamental distinction of Vipassana meditation as taught by U Ba Khin?

All importance is given to *bhāvanā mayā paññā* (wisdom developed from direct, personal experience). In *suta mayā paññā* (wisdom gained by listening to others), or *cinta mayā paññā* (wisdom gained by intellectual analysis), one can purify the mind, but only to a certain extent. It is only *bhāvanā mayā paññā* (wisdom developed from personal experience) which can purify the

deepest level of the mind. Buddha called the deep-rooted *saṅkhāra* (mental conditioning) *anusaya kilesa*—the impurities sleeping deep inside—and he taught that unless these are eradicated, one is not fully liberated. Purification of the *anusaya kilesa* can only be done by *bhāvanā mayā paññā*. *Bhāvanā mayā paññā* can only occur when there is a direct experience of reality. And direct experience of reality is only at the level of body sensations.

Why did U Ba Khin choose such a small area below the nostrils to concentrate on? Why did he suggest feeling a sensation in this area, along with the awareness of respiration? Isn't Anapana only concentration on the breath?

If one's goal in meditation is concentration of mind using either the four *jhānas* (states of mental absorption) or the eight *jhānas*, then using the object of sensation is unnecessary. A meditator can remain with the respiration, and along with it some symbols will appear while the eyes are closed. Then the meditator concentrates on these symbols, and attains *jhānic samādhi*.

But the Buddha's teaching takes one to Vipassana, and for Vipassana, awareness of body sensation is absolutely essential. One works with the breath passing over the area of the nostrils, and the smaller the area of awareness, the sharper the mind

> **W**hen a Buddha does not change the technique of the previous Buddha, who is U Ba Khin to change the technique? Who is Goenka to change it? The technique of meditation must never be changed.

becomes. As the mind becomes more sensitive, it starts feeling sensations. If one keeps the mind scattered over a large area, it becomes difficult to feel sensations, especially the subtler ones. Therefore, after two or three days of Anapana—observing just the respiration—one is taught to feel the sensations.

Why did U Ba Khin give predominance to the observation of bodily sensations, and why predominance to the observation of the material phenomenon, with the base of sensations, more than to the observation of the mental phenomenon?

Because when we are working with bodily sensations, this is a direct, tangible experience; no imagination is involved. Buddha did not want us to work with imagination. Most of the time when meditators talk of observing the mind, they are not observing it. They are merely rolling in thoughts; they are just contemplating, thinking. When you are aware of the body sensations, it doesn't mean that you have forgotten your mind, because it is not the body that feels, it is the mind that feels. The sensation is on the body, but it is felt by the mind. So mind and matter are both involved when one observes sensations on the body.

Why did U Ba Khin use the word "sweeping" for the observation of sensation? Is this a new technique that is different from the Buddha's teaching?

This was a way of explaining things. When a meditator reaches a stage where the entire body and mind get dissolved, one's attention can move from head to feet without any obstacle. In the ancient language of Pāli this stage was called *bhaṅga*—dissolution. One's attention moves quickly from head to feet, and feet to head, like a flow. The Buddha used these words:

sabba kāya paṭisaṃvedī passasissāmi, ti sikkhati, sabba kāya paṭisaṃvedī assasissāmi, ti sikkhati. (with each breath, incoming or outgoing, one feels the entire body.)

In English we describe it as "free flow," or a "sweep." In Hindi we use the word *dhārā pravāha.* When one has reached the stage of dissolution, then—when one breathes in, one feels the whole body; when one breathes out, one feels the whole body.

> Sayagyi had to deal with Western students and had to explain things in a modern, scientific way which Westerners would understand.

We can use the word *bhaṅga,* or sweeping, or free flow for that. It is simply a way of describing an experience. This does not mean that we are changing the technique in any way. Call it by any name, but this experience of *bhaṅga ñāṇa* is a very important milestone on the path of full liberation.

How did this confusion arise?

Perhaps it all started because in one of his talks, Sayagyi said, "I have developed a technique which is very suitable for non-Buddhist English-speaking people. Everyone can work with this and get results. Come, try and you will get the same result." This was his announcement. Before U Ba Khin, the teachers were all teaching to Burmese Buddhists, who have a certain way of understanding. But U Ba Khin was dealing with non-Buddhist, non-Burmese students, so he had to develop a way of expressing the technique that they could understand.

His presentation was certainly the unique presentation of U Ba Khin, but the technique remained the technique taught by Buddha.

Who was U Ba Khin's meditation teacher?

Sayagyi was the appointed teacher of a tradition. His teacher was Saya Thetgyi, a farmer who lived on the opposite side of the Rangoon River. Saya Thetgyi's teacher was Ledi Sayadaw, a very learned monk and very renowned master teacher of Vipassana. That was a century back. The tradition stretches back before that, but we no longer know the teachers' names.

Why is your technique referred to as "in the tradition of Sayagyi U Ba Khin"? Did your teacher inaugurate a new tradition of Buddhism? If not, what tradition was he continuing?

Buddha's tradition! Buddha's teaching went from India to Myanmar, and, as I said, we do not know the names of all the teachers. But we do know the names of the last three generations: Ledi Sayadaw, then his disciple Saya Thetgyi, then his disciple U Ba Khin.

We use the name U Ba Khin because he was the most recent teacher in the tradition, and was

His presentation was certainly the unique presentation of U Ba Khin, but the technique remained the technique taught by Buddha.

known to others. If we were to use the name Saya Thetgyi, or Ledi Sayadaw, many would not know who they were. So we use U Ba Khin's name, but this does not mean that he invented the technique.

In your teaching method, are you following U Ba Khin, or have you introduced changes? If so, how can you be sure that the changes

are improvements, and are not simply creating confusion and wrong understanding?

No one can make any amendment to the teaching of Buddha unless he has become a super-Buddha. Everyone is below the status of a Buddha. Therefore no teacher should try to alter the teaching and, in the name of improving it, spoil it.

The method of explanation will of course differ. Sayagyi had to deal with Western students and had to explain things in a modern, scientific way which Westerners would understand. Similarly, when I came to India I had to face a large number of people who come from different sects and traditions. Being of Indian heritage myself, I have the background of the whole spectrum of Indian spiritual thought—before Buddha, during the time of Buddha, and after Buddha. So when I discuss Dhamma with someone from a particular sect, I have to consider that person's background, and then explain things in a way which is easily comprehensible. If the student does not understand my explanation, then the whole purpose of my teaching is lost.

When I give a discourse to Western people, the essence remains the same. But when I explain the Dhamma in Hindi, there is a big difference: the examples, stories, and so on are different. I have to consider who is listening and how I can explain the technique so that they will understand and practise properly.

If you study the *suttas* (discourses), you will find that Buddha himself when talking with a particular community—say, the *brahmin* (priests) community—would talk in one way. Then when he was talking with the *shramana* (wandering ascetics) community he would speak in the way which *shramanas* would understand. There is a term in Pāli to describe this quality of the Buddha: *upāya kosalla.* It means "skill in the use of means." Even when he had not become a

Buddha (enlightened one), when he was a **Bodhisatta** (one working to become a Buddha), we find him developing this quality. How skilfully in different situations he saved himself from slipping down in *sīla* (morality); how skilfully he helped others! When he became Buddha, he became all the more skilful.

Everyone who is walking on the path of Buddha, and everyone who is going to spread Buddha's teaching, has to be skilful. The method of expressing Dhamma differs from time to time, place to place, and person to person. But the essence of the teaching remains the same. The method of meditation does not change, even from one Buddha to another. When a Buddha does not change the technique of the previous Buddha, who is U Ba Khin to change the technique? Who is Goenka to change it? The technique of meditation must never be changed.

Did U Ba Khin call himself a Buddhist? How could he call Vipassana a universal teaching without giving it a sectarian connotation?

Sayagyi called himself a Buddhist, and felt quite satisfied and proud to do so. But it was very clear that he was not trying to convert people to a sectarian religion. His method of teaching Dhamma was always non-sectarian. In my case, for example, he never pressed me to become a Buddhist. He repeatedly said that someone who does not practise *sīla*, *samādhi* and *paññā* but calls himself a Buddhist simply because he was born into a Buddhist family, is not a Buddhist. Another person who may not call himself a Buddhist, but practises *sīla*, *samādhi* and *paññā*—for Sayagyi, that person is a true Buddhist. Following the teaching of Buddha is more important than this or that name.

How did you realize that U Ba Khin was your teacher?

I come from a very staunch Hindu background and, although I was not very highly educated—not having a college degree—my thirst for knowledge was very great. Even from a very young age I started reading many books, especially books on Hindu religion: the *Gītā*, *Vedānta*, *Upanishadas*, and so on.

These teachings attracted me so much. I felt that to free the mind from all negativities was the best thing one could achieve in human life. But I found that merely contemplating the purity of the mind, or understanding the theory of *dharma* did not help me at all. So I took to practising devotion, strong devotion, due to a friend's recommendation and also my family's tradition. I thought perhaps devotion might purify my mind, which was full of impurities, full of ego. I had not come out of these by playing an intellectual game, so I tried the emotional, devotional game. This also did not work, except for giving a temporary relief.

On my first course, the first thing which struck me was that all the teachings of the *Gītā*, *Upanishadas*, and so on, were only teachings. They offered no technique to purify the mind. The scriptures keep saying, "Purify the mind, make

When I give a discourse I have to consider who is listening and how I can explain the technique so that they will understand and practise properly.

it free from craving, make it free from aversion." But how could I make my mind free from craving and aversion? Just giving suggestions to the mind does not work.

Here, on my first course, I found a technique which started helping. So then and there, in my first course, I made the decision that this is the path for me. There was no meaning in my looking here or there for another path. The practical teaching of the Buddha, given by my teacher Sayagyi U Ba Khin I found to be so enchanting, so fascinating, so satisfying.

Traditionally meditation has been perceived as retreating from society. Why did U Ba Khin give so much importance to the role of meditation within society?

You withdraw from others and focus your attention inside to gain purity of mind and Dhamma energy. Then you must become extroverted and use this energy. When you take a long jump, you must first take some steps backward. Then you run, and make the jump. Like this, you first withdraw, observe yourself inside and get the energy. Then you make a long jump into society, to serve society. These two steps cannot be separated.

Buddha left his householder's life for six years to gain enlightenment. But once he became a Buddha he was involved in serving the society throughout his life—for forty-five years, day and night. In the same way, one who develops in Dhamma does not turn away from responsibilities towards society. Householders have more worldly responsibilities to fulfil than monks or nuns. Monks and nuns are venerable and are worthy of respect because of their renunciation. But they too keep on serving society in one way or the other.

How did U Ba Khin use meditation to combat the problem of corruption in the government?

His colleagues and subordinates who were involved in corruption naturally were full of greed and craving (*lobha*). When one practises Vipassana, craving is lessened. So after practising Vipassana, these people no longer wanted to illegally squeeze money from others. By teaching Vipassana to office workers U Ba Khin tackled the root of the problem.

Besides, not everyone was corrupt. There were many who were not, but they were inefficient. Their minds were cloudy, and they were unable to make quick, efficient decisions. With Vipassana one's mind becomes clearer and clearer. One can go to the depth of the problem, and then make quick and correct decisions. This is how efficiency was increased. Vipassana was helpful for eradicating corruption and increasing efficiency in the administration.

Could you tell us some episodes in U Ba Khin's life which you feel clearly demonstrate his approach to meditation?

There are too many incidents to describe in such a short talk. But one outstanding thing was that he would not budge an inch from the truth, whatever the temptation or pressure might be. You see, every government officer works under the pressure of his superiors, who are politicians, ministers, party leaders, and so on. Frequently these superiors are corrupt. They want to favour their friends or party supporters, so they tell the officers to make decisions which are improper or illegal.

Many officers succumb to such pressures, whereas U Ba Khin's integrity was such that he never succumbed. Whatever pressure he faced, he would not hesitate to make the correct decision, however much he displeased his superiors.

Another difficulty a government officer faces is his limited salary. One signature of his can earn hundreds of thousands of dollars to this or that merchant, importer or industrialist. Ordinary human beings fall prey to greed and think, "This fellow is rolling in money due to the permit or license that I gave him. Because of my permission he can now undertake this industrial or commercial activity. Why shouldn't I get a share of this?" Often these business people want illegal permission from the officers, and they try to instigate greed in the minds of the officers by offering bribes in larger and larger amounts. The officers have never seen this amount of money in their lives, and they could never hope to accumulate such wealth from their meagre government salary. So ordinary people may succumb to this temptation.

Here we see such a sterling quality of U Ba Khin. Whether facing pressure or temptation, he conducted his duties without fear or favour.

Namaskāra gurudeva ko
kaise santa sujāna!
Kitane karuṇā citta se,
diyā Dharama kā dāna.

Salutations to the Teacher,
what a wise and saintly man
Who with compassion overflowing
gave this gift of Dhamma.

—Hindi dohas of S.N. Goenka

On Goenkaji's Return to Myanmar (Burma)

The following is extracted from an interview with S.N. Goenka conducted at Dhamma Giri in February 1991, in which he discussed his return in November 1990 to Myanmar, after a twenty-one year absence.

Goenkaji, we know that you left Myanmar in 1969 and stayed in India for ten years. Then, in order to be able to travel abroad you took Indian citizenship in 1979. Since then you have not been able to get a visa permitting travel to Myanmar. How did it happen that suddenly you were allowed to visit Myanmar in November 1990?

S.N. Goenka: I was invited to visit Myanmar by the authorities. According to the present regulations, all those Burmese citizens who left Myanmar and changed their nationality are not allowed to go back there. Because I come in that category I could not get an ordinary visa. But during the last ten years, word has spread in Myanmar that I have been doing good work around the world. The people of Myanmar are proud that one of their countrymen, and a disciple of Sayagyi U Ba Khin, is spreading Dhamma in the world, and that many people are benefiting. There have been a number of articles in magazines in Myanmar written by people who have visited Dhamma Giri, who felt very proud seeing how the work is being done. Some government officials have also visited Dhamma Giri.

Some of the Burmese people who visited Dhamma Giri were enthusiastic that I should come to Myanmar, but there was the difficulty with the visa restriction. There was a way: I could apply for a business visa, which would be permitted since my sons are now engaged in business there. It was suggested that I visit Myanmar to help my sons in their business. But I said, no, because I am no longer in business.

I would be the last person to go for business. I can go for Dhamma.

When they got home, they discussed how they could invite me to Myanmar, and this is how it happened: There are some universities in Myanmar of *pariyatti* (theoretical study) for monks, and a number of leading monks from them have come to Dhamma Giri. They were very interested, especially in the seminar on the meaning of the words *sampajañña* and *vedanā,* that was held here in early 1990. They were pleased to see how deeply we go into Dhamma—we don't just recite the scriptures and call this *pariyatti.* We go deeply into every word that is related to the teaching, especially words related to Vipassana meditation, that is, *paṭipatti* (practice) and *paṭivedha* (penetration towards the final goal).

They thought it would be good if I could go and discuss these things with learned monks there, because my understanding of certain words is not traditional. When you practise the teachings of the Buddha, a word can carry an altogether different meaning from the accepted translation. So they wanted me to go and give a talk, and this materialized. That was why I was given the visa.

When you arrived in Yangon (Rangoon), what did you do first?

I went to pay respect to my motherland, the land where I got Dhamma. I have two birthplaces in Myanmar: the place where I was born, and the second, where the shell of ignorance was broken and a new Goenka was born.

In our tradition, when a child is born, and the umbilical cord is cut, it is not just thrown away. Somewhere near the place where one is born, the cord is buried. The land where the cord lies is my birthland. This birthland is 360 miles away from Yangon, in Mandalay.

The birthland where the real birth in Dhamma happened—I went there first and paid respect.

So you went first to the International Meditation Centre?

Yes. I paid respect, meditated and met my friends there. Fortunately it was the last day of a course. My elder Dhamma brothers U Tin Yee and U Ba Po were waiting eagerly to give me a warm welcome. They had delayed the giving of *mettā* (loving-kindness meditation) until my arrival, so that I could give *mettā* and share merits with the students. My plane was late, but they kept waiting and waiting until I came. Many of the students had heard of our work and were eager to meet us.

As you approached I.M.C., did you feel pleased? It must have been very exciting.

Naturally it was very exciting: I was returning after such a long time. Even the landing at the airport was exciting, like joy. It is not that there was an emotion; there was no emotion. But joy was there: "Oh, look. I have come back home. " Like a child coming back to the lap of the mother.

You see, although India is the land of my ancestors and the land of all the Buddhas, I don't feel more at home in India than in Myanmar. I'm not unhappy here, not at all. But compared to my happiness as I landed in Myanmar—oh, it was totally different, totally different.

How long did you stay in Myanmar?

Ten days. My visa was only for seven days, but someone from Mandalay was present at the first talk I gave to the monks at Pariyatti University,

and he informed the monks at Pariyatti University in Mandalay of my talk. They pressed me to go and speak there, so my visa was extended.

Can you tell us about the public discourses that you gave? Where were they held, and how many people attended?

There were two discourses in the Pariyatti University in Yangon, the monks' university. The first was for the student monks only, and there were about three hundred or so. Word spread after the first talk, and other monks and quite a few lay people came to the second. I am told there were eight or nine hundred at the second discourse.

Moreover, our Vipassana students had also arranged for three public talks to be held in the Gandhi Memorial Hall, one of the biggest halls in Yangon. It can hold about eight hundred people. These talks were scheduled on consecutive evenings. I give a series of consecutive talks sometimes in India too. For example, in Bombay I will give five consecutive talks—first about what Dhamma is; then what *sīla* (moral conduct) is; how to control the mind in a non-sectarian way; how to purify the mind in a non-sectarian way; and then how to use it in life. People understand more about the technique of Vipassana from these talks than if they listen to only one discourse. I've given these consecutive talks in a number of places. So this was arranged in Yangon, and the hall was full. Some had to stand as there was not enough seating.

What sorts of people came to the talks?

Some members of the audience were old friends, but a much larger number were those who had heard about the Dhamma-*dūta* work (work of spreading Dhamma). There were also quite a few intellectuals who were inquisitive about why I am successful. So after the discourses there were many questions. Many questions were also asked when I met Pāli scholars and monks individually and in groups. That was very interesting because many things were clarified.

How did the questions differ from questions that Indians or Westerners ask you?

Well, mostly they were interested to hear why our Dhamma work is so successful. People know very well that I come from a business background. And for a person who has been such a successful businessman, so busy in the mundane world, for such a person to become a Dhamma teacher—it's unbelievable. But they see the success, so they wanted to see me personally and ask how I became successful. That was one general inquiry that came.

Another was what difficulties I had faced in spreading Dhamma, especially in India, where there is no antagonism towards the person of the Buddha but there is strong antagonism about the teaching of Buddha. It's unbelievable for the Myanmar people that Hindus, Jains and people from so many religions, and monks and nuns from these religions, are coming to practise Dhamma.

And why did you say that you are successful?

(Laughs) I said people come to me because they have got *pāramīs* (accumulated virtues)! There is no specialness in me. They have got *pāramīs*! It is time for them to get Dhamma. And they get it. I just become a medium.

What obstacles did you tell them that you faced?

I explained that of course there are people who don't understand what the Buddha really taught. They mistake the teaching as that of an organized religion. They feel that I am trying to convert them to Buddhism. And, in India, nobody likes conversion, because of the forceful historical conversions. So that obstacle comes. But once they join the course it becomes so clear that no conversion is involved. They understand the Buddha's teaching as non-sectarian, universal and very inspiring, which is Dhamma, and they have no objection to being converted to Dhamma.

The Myanmar audience was interested in how you teach Dhamma in India and out in the West?

Yes. There is no difference in the actual teaching, but there is in the way of presentation. For example, I don't use the word "Buddhism" which is commonly used for the teaching of the Buddha. Nor do I use the word "Buddhist" for those who follow the teaching of Buddha.

But, you see, most of the time I have to deal with people, especially in India, who are not followers of the Buddha, who belong to different religions. For them the words, "Buddhism" or "Buddhist" have a sectarian connotation. If I used these words, they would not even come to listen to what I say—taking a course of ten days would be out of the question. Certainly I don't want to scare people and make them shy away from this wonderful teaching. If these words scare them, I do better to say "Dhamma" and "Dhammist," which sounds non-sectarian to them, which sounds universal.

> The law of cause and effect—this law, or Dhamma— is always operable, whether a Buddha exists or not. But a Buddha discovers the law and makes use of it not only for his own liberation; out of infinite compassion, he distributes it to one and all.
> He never calls it Buddhism; he calls it Dhamma.
> In the same way, he does not call his followers Buddhists.

And for me this is not some sort of strategy to use the word "Dhamma" instead of "Buddhism," but, rather, it is a matter of strong conviction. As I studied Buddha's words, nowhere could I find the word "Bauddha," which is equivalent to "Buddhist" as well as "Buddhism." I found the Buddha using the word "Dhamma" and I could locate only five words used to refer to his followers: *dhammiko, dhammattho, dhammiṃ, dhammacāri, dhammavihāri.*

Dhamma means natural law, which is universal, not sectarian. The law of *paṭicca samuppāda* (dependent origination)—cause and effect—this law, or Dhamma, is always operable, whether a Buddha exists or not. But a Buddha discovers the law and makes use of it not only for his own liberation; out of infinite compassion, he distributes it to one and all. He never calls it Buddhism; he calls it Dhamma. In the same way, he does not call his followers Buddhists.

While discussing this with the learned scholars of *Tipiṭaka* (Pāli canon), both venerable monks and lay professors, they smiled and agreed with what I said.

But the people of Myanmar are born Buddhists as Sayagyi was. It must puzzle them that you stress this non-sectarian aspect of Dhamma so much.

For me it is the actual practice of Vipassana which is the most significant contribution of Buddha to mankind. I explained to them how I got so fascinated, with a tremendous magnetic pull towards the teaching of Buddha, even during my first ten-day course with Sayagyi. This was entirely because of the practical aspect of the teaching.

At the theoretical level, there was not much that was not available in the common Indian spiritual tradition. Nearly all the different spiritual schools of India give importance to *sīla, samādhi* and *paññā.* To some extent the practice of *sīla and samādhi* has also been there. But so far as *paññā* is concerned, no such practice as that given by the Buddha is found anywhere. We find in many different scriptures the use of the word *paññā*—in Sanskrit, *prajñā, ṛtambharā prajñā,* or *sthitaprajñā.*

> **F**or me it is the actual practice of Vipassana which is the most significant contribution of Buddha to mankind.

There is so much talk about becoming *vīta rāga, vīta dosa* (Sanskrit *vīta dvesha*), *anāsavo* (*anāshrava*). But besides playing devotional and intellectual games and performing recitations, rites and rituals, there is no actual, systematic, scientific practice in the entire Indian tradition. This is what was given only by the Buddha, and this is what fascinated me.

I very much wanted to come out of mental defilements, but I found no way. Vipassana came as an answer because it is practical, not mere sermons. I keep saying that one who does not practise Vipassana does not practise the quintessence of Buddha's teaching. This statement seems shocking initially, but as people discussed it, they seemed to be fully convinced.

Basically the people of Myanmar are very intelligent and, fortunately, there is no religious fanaticism or fundamentalism as in other places. I had no difficulty in convincing them of my views.

Goenkaji, are Dhamma teachers and the people of Myanmar aware of Sayagyi U Ba Khin—his method of teaching and his importance in the spread of Dhamma?

U Ba Khin was known amongst Dhamma teachers, but not amongst the masses. He taught only a small number of students; he didn't teach large courses. However, the Vipassana teachers knew that he taught non-Buddhist foreigners.

But you said that people were aware of your work, and the spread of Vipassana.

Many articles were written. Some Burmese have visited Dhamma Giri and seen the work for themselves. And the Burmese who travel abroad—when they visit universities in different countries, at times they visit the departments of Buddhism or Pāli or Sanskrit or Indology. Many times there it is discussed that the teaching of U Ba Khin is being offered in our courses around the world. Even if they might not have heard of U Ba Khin before, and have had nothing to do with meditation, naturally they are enthusiastic to hear things like this.

Sayagyi U Ba Khin has become known around the world because his work was so good.

You told us a few years ago of your volition to return to Myanmar. From all that you've said, it sounds as if it was successful…

Yes, that volition has been fulfilled, in a very good way. Of course everybody would like to return to his motherland, his birthplace. There is a saying in Sanskrit that one's birthplace is more precious even than the celestial world; there's nothing comparable to it.

However, another reason for wanting to visit Myanmar was that I wanted to discuss my understanding of the Buddha's teaching with learned scholars who are also practising meditation.

Although I was sure that I was not deviating from the teaching of the Buddha, I have tried to understand it from my background of a spectrum of many colours of Indian spirituality of the past and present. Centuries before Buddha there was a certain spiritual understanding in India. Then Buddha came and contributed something, and this spiritual understanding continued for centu-

ries. These traditions have been passed down to today. There are different branches, but nonetheless there is a common spiritual background. How this spiritual understanding evolved, reached such a height, and then slowly deteriorated, I can understand so easily—it's as if I have lived that experience. Viewing Buddha's teaching from so many different perspectives I feel has helped me to understand and evaluate it better.

Another reason is that my mother tongue is the Rajasthani language, which seems to be a direct granddaughter of Pāli. So many words, and even the grammar, are directly in line with Pāli. And I have learned this language with "my mother's milk." So for me, it was not necessary to learn Pāli formally, with the grammar, and so on. When I read Pāli, the words spontaneously seem to give their own meaning and this helps me to understand Buddha more clearly.

The third reason I feel that the Buddha's words are very clear to me is because of my practice. I had never studied Buddha's teaching before I started to practise Dhamma. For me, *paṭipatti* was the first step, and *pariyatti* came much later. With the direct experience of Buddha's teaching, his words carry special meaning for me. So I wanted assurance that in my understanding there was no deviation from the Buddha's teaching, and I am glad to have received this assurance.

Actually, my main aim in returning to Myanmar was to find Pāli scholars there who are also meditators. In Myanmar there are deep meditators. That was a great desire in my mind to meet people who are good meditators and at the same time scholars, so that I could ask them why they give particular meanings to certain words.

And I got that opportunity in November. What a wonderful opportunity! On my first full day in Yangon, I offered a meal to a reputed monastery teaching *paṭipatti* and was able to have discussions with some chief monks. On other occasions, we invited many leading monks to meals, and I had the opportunity to talk with them about points of Dhamma.

The second day of my visit to Myanmar I went to see the most Venerable Mingun Sayadaw. He is *Tipiṭakadhara* (holder of the *Tipiṭaka) Dhamma Bhaṇḍagārika* (treasurer of Dhamma). He knows the entire *Tipiṭaka* by heart. It is not easy to memorize so many hundreds of thousands of words. (In fact, he has twice been in the *Guinness Book of Records*.) Today he is the most respected monk in Myanmar. He is known as *Abhidhaja Mahāraṭṭhaguru* (foremost spiritual teacher of the nation). He played a leading role in the *Chaṭṭha Saṅgāyana* (sixth recitation of *Tipiṭaka*, held in Burma in 1954–56) and now is a guiding light of the Myanmar Saṅgha and of the Buddha *sāsana* (dispensation of Buddha's teaching) work.

I was fortunate to have met with him previously in his monastery in Mingun, which is across the river from my birthplace, Mandalay. Although very aged and physically weak now, I found him mentally very sharp. I specially requested him to help me meet Pāli scholars to discuss certain words of Buddha. He and the Pariyatti University of monks very kindly helped this to materialize.

So a meeting was arranged with about twenty or twenty-five leading professors, who are teaching Dhamma and Pāli there in the universities. We had a long sitting, about two to three hours; and later I met with a few for a second time. That was wonderful. We went into the details of many important words. I explained to them how the Indian spiritual background gives a particular meaning for a particular word, which perfectly suits Buddha's teaching.

We went into the words chronologically and etymologically, examining the precedents of a certain word, and then the successive meanings, as we do in our research at V.R.I. (Vipassana Research Institute). They agreed with our interpretation. It was a healthy and productive meeting.

So the Burmese Pāli scholars realized that something very good is being done at V.R.I. when the discussion of such words came up.

Quite true. This is why they had invited me to Myanmar. They felt it would be helpful if I went to talk with the scholars there. And it was helpful.

In order to be certain that I was not inadvertently distorting the Buddha's teaching due to the conditioning of my background, which would be wrong, I felt that I had to discuss Dhamma with people who are not influenced by other Indian traditions. They received the pure teaching of the Buddha. They have no influence of any other teaching. So they have kept Buddha's teaching in its own pure form. I was seeking the opportunity to compare my understanding with that of others, and I received it during those discussions. It was very helpful; I felt very satisfied.

Is there anything else you wish to mention?

The present enthusiasm in Myanmar that has developed towards this technique of meditation will spread. Those who came to the discourses started understanding why we give so much importance to body sensations. This importance to body sensations is given in the schools of the Ledi Sayadaw tradition but not in all the schools of meditation there. This point, clearly expounded in Buddha's teaching, in his own words, has been put in the limelight. So I'm sure this will spread, and this means that with this teaching, more and more people will benefit by practising Vipassana.

After Goenkaji and Mataji's November 1990 visit to Myanmar, they were invited to return in September

*1991, when two ten-day courses were conducted.
These were the first independent courses conducted
by Goenkaji in the land of his birth.*

*The consecutive courses were held at the Daw Dhammethi Nunnery, in the outskirts of Yangon, from 8 to
19 September, and 20 September to 1 October. Two hundred students attended the first course, including
forty-five nuns from the nunnery. The enthusiasm for this course was such that the second (unscheduled)
course was immediately organized. One hundred thirty students attended the second course.*

*During his stay, Goenkaji again met with monks who were Pāli scholars and heads of monasteries and
discussed certain important points pertaining to the publication and research of the entire Pāli literature
being conducted at V.R.I., Dhamma Giri.*

*Before the courses, Goenkaji gave a three-day series of public talks in English at Yangon University. Each
was attended by over six hundred people, filling the hall to its maximum capacity. At the end of the last
discourse, Goenkaji commented,*

> "Years ago, after passing my high school final exam, I was admitted to this very
> university. I stayed and studied here for all of three days before I was pulled away by
> family responsibilities. So, now I am happy to be able to repay my debt of gratitude
> to this prestigious institution by giving these talks, for exactly three days, about
> Dhamma, which was my greatest gift from this country."

**Aisī jage Vipaśyanā,
samatā citta samāya.
Eka eka kara maila kī
parata utaratī jāya.**

May Vipassana thus arise,
    may equanimity suffuse the mind.
One after another, may each layer
    of dross be stripped away.

—Hindi dohas of S.N. Goenka

S. N. Goenka: Dhamma Son of Myanmar

by Dhammācariya U Htay Hlaing

The following article by Dhammācariya ("teacher of Dhamma") U Htay Hlaing, was published by Ma Hatta Maghandi Monastery (Yangon, Myanmar) in November 1990. It was written to mark the visit of S. N. Goenka, who returned to Myanmar in that same month, after an interval of twenty-one years.

Dhammācariya U Htay Hlaing is a renowned Pāli language poet in Myanmar, and his piece reflects the characteristic reverence the people of Myanmar feel for their motherland and the Dhamma, which has been preserved there for twenty-two centuries.

This prose poem was published in both Pāli and Burmese (the Burmese article being slightly longer than the Pāli). Here the Pāli verses are preceded by the English translation of the Burmese version.

Satya Narayan Goenka and his wife Mataji were born in Yadanabon, the royal city of Mandalay, in the country of Myanmar, golden in the wellbeing of the sāsana (era of the Buddha's teaching).

Because of the perfections they had fulfilled through the journey of *saṃsāra* (cycle of rebirth), both their thoughts and their deeds were in harmony, and they became wealthy and prosperous, even in their twenties. In their thirties, they began living in the peace of Dhamma. Through the power of Dhamma, they were able to face the ups and downs brought about by great wealth, with neither depression nor elation. This was a marvellous thing.

The Dhamma, indeed, gives protection from all danger to those who follow the path of Dhamma, bringing them to a state of tranquillity and peacefulness amidst the worries and flurries of this world.

At the age of forty, Mr. S. N. Goenka, reflecting on the power of Dhamma, made the following firm resolve:

From this time onwards, I will forsake worldly affairs and go round from village to village, from country to country, in order to illuminate the teachings of Buddha, and declare the Noble Triple Gems: the true Buddha, the true Dhamma, the true Sangha.

Now the gong of Dhamma has been struck: first in India, birthplace of the Buddha, where his teachings have long been absent, and then in different parts of the world. Up to now, people from many nations, from different classes, with different views, have been awakened by Mr. Goenka's energetic proclamation of the Dhamma. They have developed faith and taken refuge in the true Dhamma.

A messenger of Dhamma has been distributing the technique of Vipassana meditation around the world for the past twenty years! Who is he?

It is he, Guruji Satya Narayan Goenka by name, who was born in Myanmar and who loves his motherland, Myanmar Naing-Ngan. He is a noble disciple of Ven. Ledi Sayadaw, Ven. Webu Sayadaw, Anagam Saya Thetgyi and Sayagyi U Ba Khin.

How happy and peaceful the mother feels who gave birth to such a noble son! She will definitely be proud of having such an honourable son!

How happy and peaceful the teacher feels who produced such a noble disciple! He will definitely be proud of having such an honourable disciple!

How happy and peaceful is the motherland, who has produced such a noble son! She will

definitely be proud of having such an honourable son!

Be happy and peaceful!

Sacca Nārāyano Goyaṃko, jāto ca'ssa pajāpatī
Dhammoja Brahmaraṭṭhamhi, mantale rāja dhāniyaṃ.

Sama citta samasilā, ubho' pacita pāramī.
Yuva kālamhi te bhoga-samappitā dhanañcayā.

Aho te lokāmisesu, bhogesu nunnatonatā.
Niccalā dhamma tejena, dhammaṭṭhā brahmācarino.

Dhammo hi dhammacārīnaṃ, pāleti akuto bhayaṃ.
Dhāreti amataṃ santaṃ, ussukesu anussukaṃ.

Avajjetvā dhamma balaṃ, sanniṭṭhāna' makāsio su.
"Jahissam gihīkammāni, jotetuṃ Buddhasāsanaṃ.

So ahaṃ vicarissāmi, gāmā gāmaṃ purā puraṃ.
Namassamāno sambuddhaṃ, dhammassa ca sudhammata"nti.

Tadā so majjhimaṃ desaṃ, ciraṃ ucchinna sāsanaṃ.
Adiṃ katvā videsesu, ahanī dhamma dundubhiṃ.

Nānāraṭṭhā nānākulā, nānādhimuttikā bahū.
Pabujjha dhamma ghosena, āsuṃ dhammapparāyanā.

Vīsati vassā tikkantaṃ, saṃkhonaṃ mediniṃ pajaṃ.
Dhamma dūto dhammaghosako, ko so vipassanā guru.

Myanmā jāti sa Goyaṃko, guru no Myanmā māmako.
Ledī, Vebū Mahāthera—sissā nūsissa jeṭṭhako.

Nibbutā nūna sā mātā, nibbuto nūna so garu.
Nibbutaṃ nūna taṃ raṭṭhaṃ, yassā'yaṃ īdiso suto.

Bhavatu sabba maṅgalaṃ.

Having appreciated and experienced

the Buddha's teaching to be deep like the ocean,

broad like the vast earth and high like the Himalayas,

I feel very comfortable to accept, practise and teach

Buddha's teaching in its pristine purity.

There can be no question of practising or teaching

anything but this wonderful Dhamma.

Dhamma is paripuṇṇa—it is complete, there is nothing to add.

And it is parisuddha—so pure, there is nothing to be removed.

—*S.N. Goenka*

Assistant Teachers

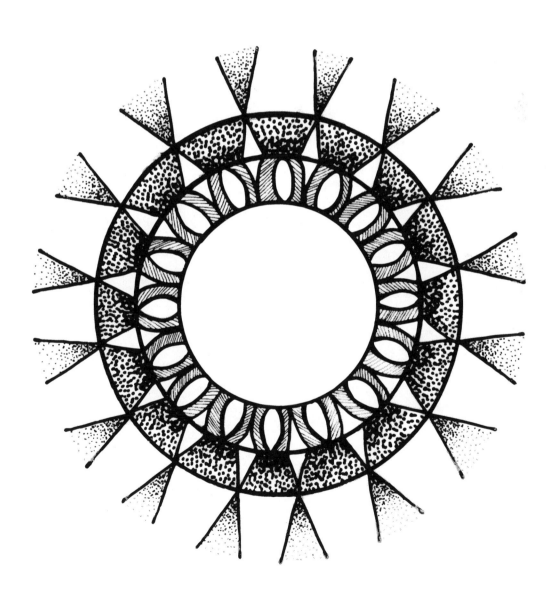

An Introduction to Vipassana Meditation

by Graham Gambie

The following introductory article was written in 1981.

Vipassana meditation is the personal purification of the mind. It is the highest form of awareness—the total perception of phenomena in their true nature here and now. It is the refuge of the real, the choiceless observation of things as they are.

Vipassana is the meditation the Buddha developed after trying all other forms of bodily mortification and mind control and finding them inadequate to free him from the seemingly endless round of birth and death, pain and sorrow.

It is a technique so valuable that in Burma it was preserved in its purity for more than 2,200 years.

Vipassana meditation has nothing to do with the development of supernormal, mystical or special powers, even though they may be awakened. Nothing magical happens. The process of purification that occurs is simply an elimination of negativities, complexes, knots and habit energies that have clouded pure consciousness and blocked the flow of mankind's highest qualities—pure love (*mettā*), compassion (*karuṇā*), sympathetic joy (*muditā*) and equanimity (*upekkhā*). There is no mysticism in Vipassana. It is a science of the mind that goes beyond psychology by not only understanding, but also purifying, the mental process.

The practice is an art of living which manifests its profound practical value in our lives—lessening and then eliminating the greed, anger and ignorance that corrupt all relationships, from the family level to international politics. Vipassana spells an end to day-dreaming, illusion, fantasy—the mirage of the apparent truth.

Like the sizzling explosion of cold water being thrown on a red-hot stove, the reactions after bringing the mind out of its hedonistic tendencies into the here and now are often dramatic and painful. Yet there is an equally spectacular feeling of release from tensions and complexes that have for so long held sway in the depths of the unconscious mind.

Through Vipassana anyone, irrespective of race, caste or creed, can eliminate finally those tendencies that have woven so much anger, passion and fear into their lives. During the training a student concentrates on only one task—the battle with his own ignorance. There is no guru worship or competition among students. The teacher is simply a well-wisher pointing the way he has charted through his own long practical experience.

With continuity of practice, the meditation will quiet the mind, increase concentration, arouse acute mindfulness and open the mind to the supramundane consciousness—the "peace of *nibbāna* (freedom from all suffering) within."

As in the Buddha's enlightenment, a student simply goes deep inside himself, disintegrating the apparent reality until in the depths he can penetrate even beyond the wheeling of subatomic particles into the absolute.

There is no dependence on books, theories and intellectual games in Vipassana. The truth of impermanence (*anicca*), suffering (*dukkha*), and egolessness (*anattā*) are grasped directly with all the enormous power of the mind rather than the crutch of the intellect. The illusion of a "self," binding the mental and physical functions together, is broken. No more the madness of cravings and aversions—the endless grasping of "I, me, mine" that has caused so much suffering and disappointment.

The prattle of conditioned thinking and the action of blind impulse stop their bitter struggle. By his own efforts the student arrives at his own truth.

The foundation of Vipassana meditation is *sīla*—moral conduct. The practice is strengthened through *samādhi*—concentration of the mind; and the purification of the mental processes is achieved through *paññā*—the wisdom of insight. We learn how to observe the interplay of the four physical elements within ourselves with perfect equanimity, and find how valuable this ability is in our daily lives.

We smile in good times, and are equally unperturbed when difficulties arise all around us, in the certain knowledge that we, like our troubles, are nothing but a flux, waves of becoming without finality, mind and body movements arising with incredible speed, only to pass away with equal rapidity.

Although Vipassana meditation was developed by the Buddha, its practice is not limited to Buddhists. There is absolutely no question of conversion—the technique works on the simple basis that all human beings share the same problems, and a technique that can eradicate these problems will have a universal application.

Hindus, Jains, Muslims, Sikhs, Jews, Roman Catholic and other Christian sects have all practised Vipassana meditation, and have reported a dramatic lessening of those tensions and complexes that affect all mankind.

Leading priests and nuns of the Roman Catholic faith have taken courses and have found no conflict with their profession of faith.

There is a feeling of gratefulness to Gotama, the historical Buddha, who showed the way to the cessation of suffering, but there is absolutely no blind devotion.

The Buddha repeatedly discouraged any excessive veneration paid to him personally. He said, "What will it profit you to see this impure body? Who sees the teaching—the Dhamma—sees me."

> There is no mysticism in Vipassana. It is a science of the mind that goes beyond psychology by not only understanding but also purifying the mental process.

The Ten-day Course

Students wishing to learn Vipassana meditation undergo a minimum ten-day course, during which time they take precepts not to kill, not to steal, not to commit sexual misconduct, not to speak lies, and to refrain from intoxicants. For the entire ten days they live within the course site, and do little else but sleep, eat, wash, and meditate. After three days' concentration of the mind by observing the inhalation and exhalation of the breath (Anapana) and the consequent sensations arising, students are shown how to penetrate their entire physical and mental makeup with the total clarity of pure insight. Each day's progress is explained during an hour's discourse in the evening.

The course closes on the last day with the practice of loving-kindness meditation (*metta-bhāvanā*), the sharing of the purity developed during the course with all beings.

The work of controlling and purifying the mind is given top priority during the course. The results are allowed to speak for themselves. Philosophical and speculative conversation is discouraged.

Each day begins at 4:30 a.m., and continues until nine at night, with the student aiming for at least ten hours of meditation (with breaks).

There is no charge whatsoever for the teachings. As for costs of board, lodging, return airfare for the teachers, and other minor expenses, these are met by the donations of grateful students of past courses who have experienced the benefits of Vipassana, and who wish to give others an opportunity to experience them. In turn, having completed a course, if one feels benefited by it and would like others also to benefit from the practice of Vipassana, he or she may give a donation for future courses.

The rate of progress of a student depends solely on his own *pāramīs* (previously acquired merits), and on the operation of five elements of effort, viz., faith, health, sincerity, energy, and wisdom.

> The work of controlling and purifying the mind is given top priority during the course. The results are allowed to speak for themselves.

More than 20,000 students from about eighty countries have already attended courses in India and abroad, and have found little difficulty in conforming to the course discipline. The vegetarian menu is designed to aid meditation as well as to suit most tastes.

The Teacher

S.N. Goenka was authorized by the late Sayagyi U Ba Khin of Burma to teach Vipassana meditation. Since 1969, he has conducted Vipassana meditation courses around the world. He is also spiritual director of the Vipassana International Academy, Igatpuri, India.

Mr. Goenka studied Vipassana for fourteen years at the International Meditation Centre in Rangoon, under the guidance of U Ba Khin. He has given more than 200 courses of ten days to people from all over the world, and has been invited by such groups as Roman Catholic seminaries and colleges, universities, Jain monks and the Dalai Lama to conduct meditation courses throughout India. He was also invited to conduct courses at the famous Nalanda Buddhist University for the staff and students, as well as at the Indian Institute of Technology, Bombay. Mr. Goenka was also at the centre of an innovative plan by the government of the State of Rajasthan to give a meditation course to 120 convicted murderers being held in prison. Following the dramatic success of this course, the government arranged a second course for senior police officers. Both these courses were subjected to scientific evaluation by university psychologists, social workers and police officials.

Mr. Goenka is a married householder with a large family. He stresses that meditation is not to encourage people to withdraw from society, but rather to face all the ups and downs of life in a calm, balanced way.

Graham Gambie was a senior assistant teacher to S.N. Goenka. He passed away in June 1986.

Jo upaje so bhaṅga ho,
Vipaśyanā se dekha.
Kaisā maṅgala śuddhi patha,
rahe na dukkha kī rekha.

Whatever arises passes away;
observe his through Vipassana.
What a pure path of happiness!
Not a trace of suffering remains.

—*Hindi dohas of S. N. Goenka*

Remain Equanimous

by N.H. Parikh

At the age of forty-two, while living the life of a good householder, there arose in me a tremendous urge to pursue the path of purification of mind. This was stirred up in me as a result of a saintly person saying to me, "There can be no progress in the spiritual life without purification of the mind." Upon hearing these words, I immediately began to search for a method by which the mind could be purified.

Two friends of mine told me about Vipassana meditation as taught by Goenkaji, but at that time I wasn't inclined to go and try. But when another friend attended the course and within a month expressed his desire to take a second course, I thought there must be something worthwhile in it. This was primarily because this man was a businessman to whom time and money were important, yet he was prepared to sacrifice both for the sake of Vipassana.

I attended my first course in July 1972, at Nasik and immediately stayed on for the following short course. In this first course, even though one gets only a glimpse of the technique, I felt that such a unique experience was just what I had been searching for. For the first time in my life I was a real meditator: really introverted, observing myself.

Despite this positive feeling, I did not want to blindly accept this technique without experimenting and putting it to the test. So I decided to practise for three months at home and then practise intensively for another three months doing courses with Goenkaji in different camps throughout India. At the end of this period I was firmly convinced that here was a wonderful technique for purification of the mind, purifi-

cation which can eradicate defilements from the deepest level of the mind. Now Vipassana has become a part of my life—not a mere rite or ritual, but a way of life.

While the experiences that can arise in meditation are not to be compared nor given any valuation, nevertheless, relating them sometimes helps to inspire confidence in others who are struggling on the same path. But if certain of these experiences are taken as something which one must attain, then they create obstacles. A few instances will illustrate this point.

One meditator who had taken twenty or twenty-five courses read somewhere that when you concentrate on a small area below the nostrils and above the upper lip, you see a light and experience warmth. She had not experienced this, so she came to me with a long, sad face.

She was worried because she was not having a particular experience. This is not Vipassana. Even after many courses this student was giving importance to certain experiences over others, with no equanimity.

In my own experience, I had initially come to understand how the sensations arise, seem to stay for some time, and then pass away. After some practice the sensations which "seem to stay for some time" begin to get disintegrated, and we reach the stage where only the arising and passing away of sensations is experienced.

When a severe pain is present somewhere in the body, we expect it to pass away quickly and naturally. After all, we're repeatedly told it is *anicca, anicca* (impermanent). But still the pain persists. One hour, two hours, two days, ten days and it still persists, so we get upset because it is not going. In my own case it remained for about two years. In my upper back there was a solid plate about eight inches by six inches and three quarters of an inch thick. It was so solid that tremendous pain began as soon as I sat for meditation. It wasn't there when I was not meditating. I patiently observed it with never a thought that it should go away. But it persisted for two years, and sometimes it became so hot it felt as if you could prepare *chapatis* on it.

This solidity started melting and became liquid and began to move about within the same area, like water moving in a hot water bag. This lasted for about four to five months; then it started to disintegrate in the form of sparks, as if a live volcano was erupting. It was really hell-fire, not for a few days but for months together. Gradually the volcano has become quiet, but that area has become so sensitive that when anything happens outside or inside, there will immediately be a reaction on that part of the body. It is like a signal (as in Goenkaji's story about the private secretary), a warning signal for me to be aware.

No one should expect a similar experience, but the point to be noted is that sensations which are intense, solidified and gross do seem to "stay for some time"; but this "staying for some time" does not necessarily mean minutes, hours or days, but maybe years or even the whole lifetime. So very patiently, quietly we just observe, observe.

Another experience which may be of help to meditators is that in my tenth or eleventh course I could not feel sensations below the nostrils and

the upper lip, nor anywhere else on the body for seven or eight days. I was equanimous with the situation and continued to do Anapana for those seven or eight days. No complaint, no advice sought. Just observe what is.

> [working with gross sensations]
> "staying for some time" does not necessarily mean minutes, hours or days, but maybe years or even the whole lifetime. So very patiently, quietly we just observe, observe.

Once it happened that after about seven or eight years of meditation, having taken a number of courses and assisting Goenkaji with the teaching work, there arose in me during one course a tremendous aversion to the discipline, rules and regulations. It began the first day at the first sitting and was so strong that it was not possible for me to do even a moment of Anapana. This continued for two full days. I had been telling students to return to Anapana when any difficulty arises. Now here I was in this predicament.

Normally I find solutions to problems which arise by myself. So what to do? Despite being unable to do Anapana, there was no worry or tension. Sitting quietly doing nothing, after a few hours on the third day, I noticed that the resistance had cleared and I began working effortlessly with enthusiasm for the remainder of the course.

All these experiences have been very helpful for me in learning how to deal with different situations equanimously. May they serve the reader likewise on the path of Dhamma.

The Path

by Ram Singh

It was in the month of March 1975 that a close friend of ours visited our home in the morning when we were taking tea. He told us that he had good news for us. He had discovered a cure for my wife's ailment. She had been suffering since early childhood from a severe headache which doctors diagnosed as migraine, notwithstanding prolonged treatment under eminent doctors. It was, indeed, good news for all of us. My wife, though anxious to know about this remedy, did not show much enthusiasm, because she had almost reconciled herself to the agony which all treatment had failed to alleviate.

However, when our friend disclosed that the remedy was nothing but Sri Goenkaji's Vipassana camp which was soon to be held at the stadium in Jaipur, our enthusiasm totally vanished. We would never attend such camps. At that time I was working as Home Secretary of the Government of Rajasthan, and I knew something of the spiritual camps that were organized then, and even now. A Vipassana camp was new to me. I had never heard the name "Vipassana" either. We politely declined the offer of our friend.

The friend met us again and explained in great detail how he himself had benefited, and he felt confident that my wife would come out of her suffering. He insisted that we could at least make a trial. Goenkaji's camp was quite a different camp, and considering the lifelong suffering to which my wife had been subjected, ten days could be spared.

After a good deal of discussion, my wife agreed to attend the camp on the condition that I also attend with her. This was an impossible proposition. The entire idea of my joining the camp looked fantastic, deeply skeptical as I was. But I had to agree ultimately, due to the preconditions that my wife imposed. Getting ten days' leave was difficult because of the law and order situation prevailing then. The Chief Secretary and the Chief Minister, when I talked to them about the problem, showed great sympathy and agreed to give leave on the condition of recall at any moment if considered necessary.

So both of us attended the camp, most reluctantly, cursing the friend for pushing us into the venture; but we decided to give it a fair trial.

Ten days' stay in the camp was, indeed, an experience. Starting from observation of our own respiration, we were asked to observe all our bodily and mental phenomena, develop awareness and maintain equanimity. No mantra was to be recited, no picture was to be observed, and no ritual was to be performed. All concepts of visualization and imagination were to be discarded and were, in fact, prohibited. The student in a Vipassana camp is asked to see things as they are from moment to moment. The entire practice is to establish oneself in *sīla* (morality); *samādhi* (control of mind); and *paññā* (wisdom.) The technique provides a practical training for self-development, leading ultimately to purification of the mind.

I felt amazed at the result that the camp brought about within a period of ten days. We returned home with great happiness and cheer. My wife's face beamed with joy and new hope. She had benefited greatly. But the benefit to me was immense. I had never realized that in such a short period one could learn a technique which had unlimited possibilities for self-improvement.

I rushed to my friend's house and thanked him profusely. Our gratitude to him for showing us the way is abiding.

From my early childhood, due to my mother's interest in spiritual matters, I had developed interest in reading scriptures. We had regular recitation of the *Rāmayana* and *Shrimad Bhāgwat* at our home. For a number of years, I continued reading the *Gītā* as a morning ritual. This interest continued throughout my education and official career. I read translations of the *Vedās* and the *Upanishads*, as well as the writings of Dayanand Saraswati, Vivekananda, Aurobindo, and Gandhi. Nanak and Kabir inspired me deeply. I made a special study of the classics of communism, my interest in which landed me in great difficulty in the early fifties! I escaped a formal inquiry due to the sympathetic Chief Minister. When I passed through the Vipassana experience, I realized that mere knowledge of things spiritual and sublime does not help. Intellectual pursuits cannot bring a change in attitude or behaviour.

I discovered that Vipassana can provide a solution to many of the problems which afflict man today. Despite great opportunities, the progress of science and technology has unleashed strain and strife, and mad competition between individuals, social groups and nations. The envy, hatred and animosity which this competition generates; the greed and lust for supremacy which are concealed in the phrase "enlightened self interest;" and the ever-widening gulf between example and precept add to the ever-growing tension in the human mind and lead to continuous misery.

The basic objective of Vipassana is purification of the mind. All human problems are mind-based; and if by some measure, purification of the mind can be achieved, most of the complex problems which confront man can be resolved. I realized that the golden period of Indian history under the Ashokan dispensation, which continued for a few centuries, was not just an accidental phenomenon and could not have been achieved by sheer might of arms. Nor could it have been achieved by exhortation of pious words or sermons, or intellectual debate. Rather, it was achieved by hard and sustained work done by individuals playing key roles in society and established in real Dhamma, in Vipassana.

> Jail officers who participated in the camps became more sensitive towards their duty and responsibility, and the condemned prisoners showed much improvement in their behaviour.

In the area of education and training, an exploration is going on all over the world to devise techniques which can bring about changes in attitude. Instruments for imparting information, knowledge and skills have been greatly refined, but no reliable method has been found which can transform the human mind and human behaviour.

The organized religious establishments, relying completely on merely preaching moral ideas, depending on rites and rituals, and advocating blind beliefs, have enslaved man. As a result of this we see so much strife and conflict and so much exploitation perpetuated in the name of religion. The recurring communal troubles in our country are a bitter reminder of the utter inadequacy and futility of these systems. I realized that a major impact could be made through Vipassana in the area of attitude change. Vipassana could further serve as an instrument for change and reform in all areas which are vital for the progress and happiness of man. I found that Vipassana could clear the darkness of ignorance which is the root cause of human misery.

On the last day of the camp I discussed with Goenkaji the possibility of Vipassana courses for government officials so that the process of reform could be initiated in the government. He said that this was a strong possibility and pointed out that in Burma, Sayagyi U Ba Khin (his teacher of Vipassana, the then Accountant General of Burma,) successfully used the Vipassana technique for reform in government departments. Pursuant to these discussions, I took up the matter with the government of the state of Rajasthan, and it was decided that an experiment be made.

Two Vipassana camps were organized in the Jaipur central jail. In each camp, over one hundred prisoners convicted of heinous crimes and sentenced to life imprisonment (including a few condemned prisoners) participated. Some jail officials also joined the camps. Vipassana had a profound impact on the participants. They felt greatly relieved of tensions. There were perceptible changes in their behaviour. Some of the prisoners who were prone to commit petty offences in jail became disciplined; crimes in jail were reduced by a considerable extent; and jail officers who participated in the camps became more sensitive towards their duty and responsibility. The condemned prisoners showed much improvement in their behaviour, having developed calmness and equanimity. A study of the impact of Vipassana was made by Professor Unnithan of Rajasthan University (who is now its Vice Chancellor). The study confirmed the positive impact.

Encouraged by the result of this experiment in the Central Jail, a decision was made to organize

a Vipassana camp for police officials. The course was organized in the Police Academy at Jaipur in which police officers of all ranks participated. A study was also made of this camp by the Rajasthan University. The experience had a great effect on the behaviour pattern of the officers. The participants got a clear perception of their functions and roles and developed greater awareness of their duty towards society. Some of the participants addicted to drinking gave it up on their own. They emerged as almost new men, their outlook changed.

Internal reforms were introduced in the Home Department of the Government of Rajasthan in which many procedural changes of far-reaching importance were carried out. Paperwork was reduced by a considerable extent. Decision-making processes became quicker, and pending work which had accumulated over many years got cleared. All this was done with full, close and active participation of all cadres working in the Home Department.

Simultaneously, substantial reforms were carried out in the functioning of the Department of Jails and Prisons. Improvements were effected in the working of the Police Department, and the training of police personnel was reorganized. A new level of efficiency was achieved in the functioning of these departments. In the process of these reforms, officers who participated in Vipassana camps played a key role.

These experiments, though carried out in a small segment of governmental activity, indicate the possibility of a major step towards change and reform in the government through Vipassana. The characters of all governments have an impact on the people they govern, but in India it is much more so because of its ancient heritage in which persons who ruled were the real pace-setters in society. The factor of under-development is also a major phenomenon in which involvement of government is all-pervasive in the life of its citizens. Therefore, good government seems to be a prerequisite for orderly and harmonious development of society.

But how to get good government? Democracy provides a good framework for government. Government is made up of people. If we have good people, we have good government. Vipassana provides a reliable instrument for making people good. And good people are needed everywhere—in education, trade and industry and in all segments of public life.

The message of Vipassana is universal. It transcends all boundaries—national, racial, communal and sectarian. Thousands of people from all walks of public life in India and abroad have benefited from Vipassana. Vipassana courses are open to all and provide a forum where people belonging to different nationalities and faiths—Hindus, Muslims, Christians, Jains, Buddhists, leaders of various religious orders, monks and nuns—join in a common endeavour to learn the technique of Vipassana with the objective of purification of the mind. These camps provide an ideal setting where one finds full expression of secularism and international brotherhood, and wherein an individual engages himself for self-improvement and comes out successful. The results are "here and now."

In bringing Vipassana from Burma back to India, the home of its origin, Goenkaji has set the wheel of Dhamma in motion once again. He has kindled the light of real Dhamma. The light dispels the darkness, the darkness of ignorance, the root cause of misery, the root cause of suffering. The light shows the path. In the course of teaching Vipassana, Goenkaji expounds the essence of Dhamma with a clarity and precision so rare as to be found nowhere in any philosophical treatise on Dhamma. He conveys the message of Vipassana in a language that is simple and clear, at once understandable and practical for one and all. This is the process of making a new man that India needs, that the world needs—the process of making the good man.

For me, the first Vipassana camp marked a turning point in life. The path is clear, no more searching now, the destination is found. The destination is "the path."

It is a common belief that a man, whose power of concentration is good and can secure a perfect balance of mind at will, can achieve better results than a person who is not so developed. There are, therefore, definitely many advantages that accrue to a person who undergoes a successful course of training in meditation, whether he be a religious man, an administrator, a politician, a businessman or a student.

—Sayagyi U Ba Khin

What Meditation Is

by William Hart

In 1976 I left my job to spend three years in a small town in India studying meditation. When they hear of my experience, people often ask me, "What do you do when you meditate?" Of course in one sense, meditation means "not-doing;" we have to stop all the things that we do in ordinary life, and start doing the opposite.

The meditation which I studied is called Vipassana. This is a word from Pāli, the language spoken in India in the time of the Buddha. Its meaning is insight—seeing the reality, the truth; understanding reality by experiencing the reality inside oneself.

All our lives we are busy looking outside. We are only interested to see what others are doing; we aren't interested in ourselves. When we meditate, we have to change all that, and start to observe ourselves.

We sit down, stop moving, and close our eyes. There is nothing to hear or see, no external thing to interest us. So we look inside, and we find that the biggest thing happening is our own breathing. We begin by paying attention to this reality: the breath entering and leaving the nostrils. We try to keep the mind fixed on the breath as long as possible, ignoring any other thoughts.

At once we find how hard this is to do. As soon as we try to keep the mind on the breath, we begin to worry about a pain in the legs. As soon as we try to stop all thoughts, a thousand things jump into the mind. As soon as we try to forget past and future and concentrate on the breath now, this moment, passing through the nostrils, at once some pleasant or unpleasant memory of the past comes up, some hope or fear for the future. Soon we forget what we are trying to do.

The fact is that the mind is like a spoiled child with too many toys. It starts to play with one toy, becomes bored, then reaches for another, and another. In the same way, the mind keeps jumping from one thought, one object of attention to another; and in this way we keep running away from reality.

Now we have to stop doing that. Instead of trying to escape, we have to face the reality, whatever it is. And so we keep trying patiently to bring the mind back to the breath. We fail and try again, and again.

After some time we find that the mind does stay a little longer on the object of the breath. We have succeeded, never mind how slightly, in changing the habit pattern of the mind, training it to remain concentrated on a single object.

Using this strong concentration, we then change the object of attention deliberately, systematically, to examine every part of the body; and because mind and body are so closely interrelated, we are at the same time examining our minds.

Usually this self-examination gives the meditator many surprises. Many complexes of the past arise from the deep, unconscious levels of the mind—all sorts of memories, forgotten thoughts and emotions. Often, especially at the beginning, these forgotten memories bring with them a lot of physical or mental discomfort, even pain.

However, we don't allow this discomfort to stop us. Our job is to observe our own reality, whatever it may be—like a scientist observing an experiment in his laboratory.

Usually we react to any thought, any feeling, any impression which forms in the mind. If it is something pleasant, we start wanting it—more, more; if unpleasant, we start hating it—how to avoid or escape it. But when we meditate, we must simply know what is happening inside us, and accept it as reality. We don't try to change it or avoid it; we just observe, without reacting.

If we persist, we soon realize that our experiences are constantly changing. Every moment, what we feel in the body changes. Every moment, the thought in the mind changes. This reality—the reality of myself—is changing every moment. Nothing remains forever—not the most pleasant or unpleasant thing.

Thus by observing ourselves, we come to understand, from our own experience, one important fact: *anicca* (Sanskrit *anitya*)—impermanence, the reality of change. Everything inside me, and similarly everything in the world outside me, is changing every moment.

Of course we have always known this, and modern scientists have proved that this is true—that the entire material universe is composed of tiny particles which arise and vanish millions of times in a second. But instead of just hearing about this reality or apprehending it intellectually, we have experienced it directly, through meditation.

We continue, and we soon realize that if nothing remains more than an instant, then there is nothing inside me to call an ego, a self—no I, no me, no mine. This "I" is really just a phenomenon, a process which is always changing. And whenever I try to hold on to something, saying "This is I, this is me, this is mine," then I make myself unhappy, I make suffering for myself—because sooner or later that something must go away, or maybe "I" go away.

All this I understand not because someone is telling it to me—I see it for myself, by observing myself.

Then how not to make myself unhappy? Simple: instead of trying to keep one experience and escape another, to pull this to me, to push that away—I just watch; I don't react. I observe with equanimity, with a balanced mind.

It sounds easy, but what to do when I sit to meditate for one hour, and after ten minutes a pain starts in the knee? At once I start hating the pain; I want the pain to go away. But it doesn't go away, and the more I hate it, the stronger it becomes.

If I can learn for one moment just to observe the pain—if I can forget, temporarily, that it is *my* pain, that *I* feel pain—if I can just examine the feeling like a scientist—then probably I shall see that the pain itself is changing. It does not remain forever. Every moment it changes, passes away, starts again, changes again.

When I understand this, by my own experience, then I am free of the pain. It does not control me. Maybe it goes away quickly, maybe not—but to me it doesn't matter. I don't suffer from the pain any more because I can observe it. I have started to liberate myself from suffering.

And all this I do by sitting still with eyes closed, trying to remain aware of anything that happens inside me.

The purpose of Vipassana meditation, then, is to purify the mind, to free the mind from suffering and its causes. Usually we don't know what is really happening. We are wandering in the past or the future, blinded by our desires or aversions; and we are always agitated, full of tension.

But by meditating we learn to face the reality of this moment, without wanting or hating it. We observe it with a smile—with equanimity, a balanced mind.

This awareness and equanimity are very useful for us in ordinary life. Instead of being ignorant of what is really happening—blindly following our unconscious desires, fears, hatred—now we can see the reality in any situation. Then instead of reacting blindly and making more tensions, it is possible for us to take real, free, creative action which will be helpful for ourselves and for other people.

Every person faces the same problems in life: things happen that we don't want; things don't happen that we want. In all these situations, if I react blindly, I make myself and others unhappy. If I keep a balanced mind, then I remain happy and I can help others to be happy.

When a sick man recovers health, naturally he feels happy. When a blind man can see again, naturally he feels happy. Similarly when we learn the way from suffering to liberation, naturally

we feel happy. Previously we forced others to share our unhappiness; now we want others to share our peace and joy.

Thus a real meditator tries to change the world, after having changed himself. Perhaps his action is no more than a smile instead of a frown—but that smile may have far reverberations if it is a real smile from the heart. On the other hand, a smile is useless if it merely hides the tensions inside.

Certainly we have a moral duty to change the world for better—and we must begin with the material nearest to hand: ourselves. Having done that, we'll be capable of anything.

This, then, is meditation as I understand it: an art of living.

A balanced mind is necessary to balance the unbalanced minds of others.

—Sayagyi U Ba Khin

Equanimity in the Face of Terminal Illness

by S. Adaviyappa

About ten years ago, my wife Parvathamma was diagnosed as having motor neuron disease, a rare condition which is considered incurable. Treatment by allopathic, homeopathic, ayurvedic and naturopathic doctors did not produce any results. She experienced a gradual wasting away of the muscles of her arms, thighs, legs and neck. She required assistance with even normal activities. Her helplessness caused her tension and strain, and she became gloomy and wept frequently.

It was a heart-rending situation for us. But everyone in the family took care that she was not put to any discomfort and that there was never any opportunity for her to feel neglected. All our efforts went toward keeping her spirits up. But she would still break down whenever a friend or relative called on her.

It was at this stage about four years into the illness, that my wife took a Vipassana course in Jaipur under the guidance of Goenkaji. She found the first day most trying. But with loving fellow meditators around her, she put up with the hardship with a smile. On Vipassana day, she was a changed person. She experienced the flow of subtle vibrations throughout the body. She was beaming with joy, and felt she had gained strength throughout her body. Her retreat proved a most beneficial sojourn.

For the following months, she practised her meditation regularly in spite of the limitations of her physical condition. I was away at Ajmer due to my official work, but I used to join her in meditation whenever I visited Jaipur. She was also helped by two tapes of Goenkaji's Pāli chanting, and visits from other local meditators.

After the Vipassana retreat, her nature changed completely. Joy emanated from her. People who came to console her went back carrying peace. She never complained about her illness to anybody. Neither did she express regret about her miserable condition. She made frequent loving and compassionate enquiries about the welfare of the visitors and their family members, wishing them happiness and joy.

The illness progressed quickly. She developed a rapid deterioration of her muscles. Her face continued to beam with a radiant smile, although her body below the neck was a pitiful heap of bones and shrunken muscles. She continued her meditation throughout this period.

On the thirteenth of January, 1985, about thirty hours before her death, Parvathamma made a fervent wish to the family members to pardon her for any harsh words she might have spoken while they were attending her. She said she was very fortunate to have such a kind family. She was given a glucose drip and oxygen for three days, and underwent extreme pain. However, she retained full control of her faculties.

On the morning of the fifteenth, she was cheerful and took some milk. But at about 7:15 am. she had a bout of coughing, which she always dreaded. She felt suffocated and asked me to send for the doctor. The doctor arrived in fifteen minutes. Just as he was at the doorstep, her last breath went out along with a cough. In her last moment, she had a clear mind and passed away peacefully, casting compassionate glances on those of us standing around her.

We have learned from Goenkaji that our practice is also a preparation for dying. Our family's experience is a testimony to this. Through her equanimity in the midst of severe suffering, my wife was in control of her faculties even during the extreme pain of dying. This has been a great inspiration to all of us, and those of us who are meditators have applied Dhamma more seriously. By determined effort and regular practice we have been helped to weather the shock of the tragic loss of this loving soul. We are regularly sending *mettā* to her with wishes for her freedom from all suffering.

Research at the Experiential Level

by Dr. Chandrasheela Shakya

Dr. (Mrs.) Chandrasheela Shakya is a Pāli scholar based in N.E. India and Nepal. She wrote this article in January 1984.

After having completed a number of courses at Dhamma Giri under the guidance of Goenkaji, I have come to a new realization concerning the intent and meaning of many of the words and teachings of the Buddha. These courses have enabled me to reassess my intellectual understanding of the Pāli language and its literature, and to see that their real meaning can only be made clear if learned through actual practice in the way in which the author wanted them to be practised.

I have completed a Ph.D. on "The Critical Study of the *Dīghanikāya*" (Collection of Long Discourses of the Buddha) at Benares Hindu University. As such, I am very familiar with the theories of this field of study and with the various commentarial, lexicological and linguistic works which have been done as well. But now, my research at the experiential level through the method taught by S.N. Goenka has convinced me that I was, in fact, far from the actual meaning of what the Buddha wanted to convey. Interestingly enough, I have found that this is also the experience of many other students who have completed these same courses, including other Pāli scholars like myself. The Buddha himself indicated this when he said that *pariyesana* (complete research) is actually *sevitabbā bhāvitabbā* (at the experiential level). I find that, until recently, all of the modern research into the Buddha's words has actually been *asevitabbā* and *abhāvitabbā* (non-experiential). Unfortunately, the experiential aspect of experimenting with the truth of the Buddha's words has been totally missing.

Although I realize that the intellect is an important factor for research, nevertheless without personal experience, the words of an enlightened person like the Buddha cannot be properly understood. Because I am a scholar and because I have made scholarship and research the central endeavour of my life and my career, I find it very exciting to learn that the academy at Dhamma Giri is taking the proper approach to this important research.

Pāli, the language of the Buddha, is already a dead language. Because of this fact, the glorious cultural heritage of our country and our countrymen is not properly understood by Indians in general. The important work being done at Dhamma Giri will bring out the glory of this invaluable cultural heritage and make it comprehensible, not only to our own countrymen, but to the world at large. From the purely linguistic point of view, this research will enrich and elucidate much of our understanding of the origin and roots as well as the historical development of our own modern Indian languages. Not only the teachings of the Buddha but the language itself is of inestimable value in understanding our cultural heritage. As a scholar, I am impressed, and at the same time pleased, that this is being done in a completely scientific and non-sectarian way.

My own orientation has been to the language and literature of the Buddha, but I believe that scholars of other religions who have done Vipassana courses have had similar experiences in their own academic disciplines. Because the method taught at by S.N. Goenka is completely devoid of any sectarian orientation, the way in which people experience the words of the Buddha inside themselves has given much understanding and special insight to people of various religions and philosophies; even into their own scriptures and saintly authors. People have found new and clearer meanings in the **Vedas,** the **Gīta,** and the **Upanishads.** Even Jain scholars have been impressed with the fresh understanding they have achieved in studying the **Āgamas.** I have also heard that Christians and Muslims who complete Vipassana courses and whose religions are not Indian in origin have been surprised by the new meanings which they find in the Bible and the Koran.

By my own research and experiments at Dhammagiri, I am convinced that reality at the experiential level is far different from reality at the intellectual level. Vipassana meditation gives us the opportunity to experience this reality for ourselves.

Physician Heal Thyself

by Dr. Geo Poland

This paper was originally presented as an address to the participants in the Vipassana Seminar on Health, held at Dhamma Giri in 1990. The audience had completed a ten-day course just prior to the presentation of the papers.

It is indeed a pleasure to see so many fellow physicians and healing professionals assembled here to discuss and practise Dhamma. Certainly we need more and more such Dhamma doctors, nurses, physiotherapists, etc., in this world. It is all the more a pleasure to see such a wide spectrum of various "pathies" [allopathy, homeopathy, naturopathy, etc.] represented here today, and to realize that for all the differences which may appear to exist between such "pathies," as regards etiology of disease, diagnosis and treatment, there is a common thread which binds us all together—the desire to help others come out of their suffering. We may disagree as to the "how," but the goal remains the same.

I feel it is an occupational hazard that as one works more and more with sick people (facing so much suffering day after day, patient after patient), that slowly, almost imperceptibly one becomes more and more distanced from the patient as a suffering human being. Naturally one has to maintain an objective outlook in order to come to the right diagnosis and treatment of the patient's disease. However, in the process one must not lose sight of the fact that

this patient is not only an interesting case, a diagnostic challenge, a therapeutic triumph, but also a vulnerable, suffering human being—someone needing not only treatment of their disease process, but also compassion and understanding of the suffering they are undergoing as a result of their illness. This becomes all the more important when one is treating someone suffering from a chronic illness, or a terminally ill patient for whom there is no "cure." Naturally it is frustrating for the medical personnel to be unable to cure the patient; one feels that one has failed somehow and often one tends to avoid interacting with such patients. It seems to me that this stems from our own inability to come to terms with all the suffering we see around us because we have not been able to deal with our own suffering.

Through the practice of Vipassana meditation one comes face to face with one's own suffering deep inside, and by understanding its impermanent nature one gradually develops equanimity. Thus little by little one is able to eliminate this suffering. The result of this self-purification or self-healing process is a deep sense of relief and resultant compassion for others who are likewise suffering. One realizes that one suffers because one keeps reacting to the sensations deep inside. Similarly our patients not only suffer from their disease but also from their mental reactions to it. This understanding and compassion goes a long way in practis-

> The result of this self-purification or self-healing process is a deep sense of relief and resultant compassion for others who are likewise suffering.

ing the art of medicine, which is a combination of not only the learned skills of diagnosis and treatment, but also a heavy dose of loving-kindness or *mettā*, as we all learned here at the end of the course.

Many years ago, after returning to Canada from India, I struck up a deep friendship with an eighty-five year old, crippled farmer patient of mine. We would while away the hours in his kitchen drinking tea and swapping stories. He was a very practical man who had been successful at almost everything he did. He told me that he only went to school for one day and learned all he needed to know. The teacher wrote on the board "Never Be Idle;" so he went back to the farm and started working!

He also told me that in the good old days he had had a doctor who was a real doctor. He said the moment you entered his office you started feeling better, and by the time you left his office you felt even more relieved although you hadn't yet taken any medicine. He then explained that it is very easy to be a good doctor—all you have to do is give the patient lots of "TLC" (tender loving care). Certainly this is not all there is to the practice of medicine, but it is a part which is gradually being replaced by our dependence on investigations, tests and so on to make the diagnosis.

Through Vipassana and the development of *mettā* we can rekindle this TLC. "Physician Heal Thyself" is a well-known phrase. We of the healing profession should take this to heart if we really want to help ourselves and likewise our patients.

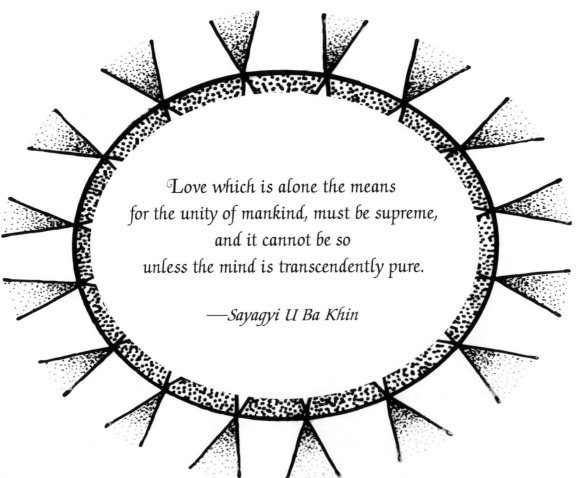

*Love which is alone the means
for the unity of mankind, must be supreme,
and it cannot be so
unless the mind is transcendently pure.*

—*Sayagyi U Ba Khin*

Vipassana and Education

by Dr. B.G. Savla

Goenkaji conducted the first ten-day children's Vipassana course in December 1970, in Bagda, Bihar at the suggestion of Vinobha Bhave, the well-known Indian educational and spiritual leader. Thirty-seven children participated and, although the results were very positive, no further children's courses were held until 1986. A fifteen year-old girl, who had completed a regular course with her parents, requested a "kids only" course. Goenkaji agreed and, in April of that year, a four-day course was held in Jamnabai Narsee School, Bombay. The children who participated, their parents and teachers all felt that the course was so successful that a regular programme of short children's courses has been held in three Vipassana centres in India since 1987. Dhamma Giri holds five or six courses annually during school vacations, each attended by about two hundred children. The centres in Jaipur and Hyderabad each hold a similar number of smaller courses.

During the courses the children are divided into small groups. Each group is assigned a "counsellor"—a trained young adult of the same sex. The counsellor sleeps in a room near the children, meditates in the hall with them, joins in playing games and guides them in all the sessions. Most importantly, twice a day the counsellor leads group discussions, where the children explore the relevance of Dhamma to their lives. Questions such as "What happens to my breath when I get angry, or when I feel peaceful?" are explored. This way of working is proving quite successful.

Recently, one-day courses have also been introduced in schools. One particularly successful program has been set up in a large school in Bombay, where all secondary level students have attended a one-day course and are given the opportunity to follow this up with daily practice in the school.

In the year 1993, more than fifty children's courses were held in Vipassana centres, schools and at other sites with more than 5000 students participating.

The following article discusses the value of these children's courses.

Education today has unfortunately been reduced to training of the intellect, taught at the school and university level. Reading, writing, memorizing, and thinking—these work only at the conscious superficial levels of the mind. This type of education is not solving the major problems of today's youth, such as drug and alcohol use, promiscuity, undisciplined rebellious behaviour, violence and other anti-social activities. Nor is it resolving the problem of academic and occupational dropping out.

Acknowledging that these problems are serious and are not being resolved, we must look for a component of education that is lacking, and see if by adding this these difficulties can be eradicated, and youth are enabled to lead happy, active lives.

True education implies the acquisition of "wisdom," i.e., knowledge based on self-experience. Perhaps it is this aspect of education that is missing.

To train the mind to live with the reality of the present moment within the body and mind is the essence of the technique of Vipassana meditation. The basis of Vipassana is morality. A moral code is given to which students must adhere in order to attend a Vipassana course, and the value of continuing to abide by this code becomes apparent as the student tries to practise meditation in daily life. The second step is Anapana meditation. This means remaining aware of the natural breath at and inside the nostrils for as long as possible, thereby increasing concentration. The third step on a Vipassana course is Vipassana meditation proper—developing insight, personally acquired wisdom of the nature of our bodies and minds. Those who sincerely undergo a course in Vipassana meditation report an appreciation of the need for morality; improved concentration, and a feeling of release from tensions and negativity; and an increase in happiness and positive activity. Hence Vipassana is not merely an art of living but also true education.

> The ideal period to begin this education in a child is before birth, in the mother's womb. During pregnancy a woman who regularly practises Vipassana creates an environment conducive to positive mental health development in the child.

The ideal period to begin this education in a child is before birth, in the mother's womb. During pregnancy a woman who regularly practises Vipassana creates an environment conducive to positive mental health development in the child.

Once the child is born, how soon can he or she be given this mental training? Optimum benefits are seen in children above eight years of age. However, some between five and seven years of age who have participated in children's courses, accepted this education well.

In India many two or three-day Anapana courses have been successfully conducted at three Vipassana centres, as well as in schools. Though a residential course of two to three days is optimum, even one-day courses conducted in schools have shown promising results. Different courses are held for different age groups (e.g., eight to ten, eleven to thirteen, and thirteen to fifteen years), the schedules varying according to the cognitive-grasping capacity of the age group. School children are taught only Anapana, the important preliminary technique in the teaching of Vipassana. Younger children work for fifteen to thirty minutes with ease; middle school children can easily meditate for thirty to forty-five minutes at a stretch. Group discussions, games and creative activities punctuate the periods of meditation. In addition, the theory and value of this meditation practice are taught in short discourses and in counselling sessions with older experienced meditators. Some middle and high school students, after learning Anapana and practising for some time, come on their own for a full ten-day Vipassana course, which they successfully complete. Recently a few schools have incorporated the teaching of Anapana into their daily curriculum. Scientific research studies are being carried out on the beneficial effects, based on parents' and teachers' reports. Preliminary findings indicate positive changes.

Some colleges and universities in India have been holding ten-day Vipassana courses or have been sending their students for regular courses, as part of their teaching programme. So far no research work has been done to evaluate the benefits of these ten-day courses, but regular requests for courses, and enthusiastic responses from the youth and teacher participants, suggest a favourable outcome.

The real benefits will come only if this meditation practice becomes an integral part of daily life. The multiple benefits are the consequence of important changes in two major spheres. First, developing concentration with awareness increases the child's mental strengths of understanding, memory and expression. This benefit manifests in his or her academic career as well as various other activities such as games, arts and crafts. Second, the technique helps to purify the mind. Negativities such as abusive or violent behaviour gradually start giving way to more peaceful, harmonious and respectful behaviour at school, home and in society. Hence, with this practice, these problems are bound to show a decline in the long run.

We are confident that more teaching of Anapana and Vipassana as a part of the regular curriculum in the field of education would lead to lasting beneficial changes in the younger generation, which would bring about a positive revolution in society.

Children Comment on Their Meditation Experiences

The following were written by children who attended courses in India.

I am a girl aged 17. I first attended a Vipassana course when I was 12 years old.

The first time I realized that Vipassana had helped me was when I took my tenth standard board exam. Basically a person who grew nervous at the slightest cause, I found myself surprisingly calm and composed as I sat in the examination. Twice-a-day meditation had brought a certain amount of confidence in me. In a state of nervousness, a student tends to forget even those facts which at one time he knew so well. But when he is calm and confident, those chapters which he had read only a few times, become so clear in his mind.

I used to pass through stages of depression (though for no obvious reason) and periods when I would grow rebellious. I still do sometimes, as most people pass through at this age. But now I see that I do not waste as much time brooding or feeling lethargic as I used to. My outlook towards my student life has also changed. Known for my rebellious nature, I have indeed calmed down. It is a practice these days among students to mock their teachers. But Vipassana has helped me build a certain respect for my elders, which though not very perceptible, is nevertheless felt inside by me. I have also developed a certain optimistic view towards things. In fact it is mainly the pessimistic view which ultimately leads teenagers to opt for drugs and other bad habits.

I feel Vipassana is an important element, essential to students. If I want to become a better person, I know Vipassana will help me.

—*Kavita, age 17*

I think that I have begun to speak less, and more or less consult with my mind before speaking or doing any actions. This has put a stop to my reflex actions.

—*Vayati, age 14*

At first I did not enjoy much what I was there for. Then I forced myself to do exactly what Goenkaji said, because I wasn't following his steps properly. Little did I know that suddenly I would break out of my passions and anger as if a cloud-burst had occurred in me to free myself from all the bad visions of life. Why don't they organize these courses in jails so that the criminals will be free from all their anger and bad life?

—*Hilaur, age 14*

I was very happy to see children of different religions coming to this camp, and to see that not only people from our country, but also from other countries, came here. I performed sādhanā (practice) with full interest, and wrong thoughts and wrong things vanished from my mind like thin air.

Here Goenkaji treats every religion equally. According to me this is the best way of national unity. I wish I was a little bigger to join in Vipassana. This is the best experience in my life.

—*Ajay, age 16*

These three days I had a rather tough time meditating for so many hours. At the end of this course I am quite determined to attend the ten-day course. I realized one thing when I was speaking with a foreigner, and that is how eager people are to learn this technique all around the world.

—*Siddhartha, age 14*

I got Vipassana at the age of 10. I consider myself very lucky to become a Vipassana meditator at such an early age.

In my studies Vipassana has been very helpful to me. I find that I concentrate better and therefore understand better. Previously I was quite nervous before examinations. Now whenever I feel nervous, I watch one breath and overcome my nervousness to a certain degree.

Whenever I get angry, I am able to get over it more quickly than before. Sometimes I feel frustrated and irritated, but then I am able to watch my breath and sensations and overcome the anger.

I believe my tolerance has increased since I became a meditator. I get easily irritated when someone does something that I don't like, but now I feel this has decreased a little.

Lastly, to a certain extent, I can take things as they are more easily than before. I have full faith that if I continue practising Vipassana, I will undoubtedly become a better human being.

—*Dipali, age 17*

Secularism and Vipassana

by Usha Modak

India is a secular state. Unlike some countries, it has no declared state religion and there is absolute freedom of religious practice. Secularism represents the concept wherein, despite religious differences, people live harmoniously and peacefully with each other. In secular countries such as India, where many religions are practised, the country shelters all of them, giving no preference to any particular one. This is an important way of impartially promoting national and emotional integration.

Here in India public institutions such as schools, colleges and universities are not allowed to teach or advocate a particular religion. However this policy of the state has contributed to a decline in moral values and standards. Students are no longer trained in these values by their teachers, and their parents are unsure what to give them in this regard.

Additionally, under the garb of secularism, the state pays lip service to promoting national integration and to maintaining peace and harmony among people of different religions. But time and again we see these differences erupting like volcanic lava, at times taking monstrous shapes and forms and causing a great deal of suffering in a world already brimming with tensions and anxieties of all kinds.

Can Vipassana meditation play a role in resolving this two-pronged problem: lack of basic moral values and lack of harmony among religions in a non-religious world? For those who have understood what Vipassana is and who have been practising it as a way of life, the answer is definitely "yes."

To understand why, we must understand what Vipassana is. Briefly, it is a technique of purifying the mind, deconditioning the mind of its defilements by self-observation and introspection. It is an effort to change the habit pattern of the mind which always reacts blindly either with craving or aversion. The effort is experiential, and this is the unique feature of this technique. We must make the effort for ourselves, walk the path ourselves. Someone else cannot do it for us, nor can we achieve it through intellectualization.

The great sage of India, Gotama Buddha, discovered, or rather rediscovered, this technique through his deep meditation. He attained enlightenment and was liberated from all defilements of the mind. Then with great compassion and love he distributed it to the suffering mankind. He did not establish any "ism" or cult. He taught Vipassana, the way to purify the mind.

Vipassana is taught in ten-day residential courses. It is a very demanding course requiring the student to observe noble silence and follow strict rules throughout the duration of the course. There are ten hours of meditation daily, with instructions given periodically, and with a discourse in the evening explaining and clarifying the technique, given by the teacher, S.N. Goenka.

There are three steps to the training given in a meditation course. The first is a code of morality. One undertakes not to kill, not to steal, not to tell lies, not to conduct sexual misconduct and not to use intoxicants. One cannot work to liberate oneself from defilements if at the same time one continues to harm others or perform deeds of body and speech which only multiply these defilements. Hence, the code of morality is essential.

The next step is to achieve some mastery over our unruly minds by focusing the attention on the natural, normal breath (not controlled and regulated breath as in *prāṇāyāma*). This practice calms the mind and promotes concentration which enables one to take the next step: purifying the mind of defilements by developing insight into one's own nature. Vipassana is experiencing one's own reality by the systematic and dispassionate observation of the ever-changing sensations within oneself. It is a process of self-purification through self-observation and introspection.

> Everyone faces the problem of mental impurities. The problem is not sectarian, therefore the remedy cannot be sectarian. It must be universal.

The ten-day course gives only an outline of the technique. One doesn't become a seasoned practitioner by taking just one course. It should be followed by practice in daily life and by taking these ten-day courses periodically as boosters to get established in the practice and to reap lasting benefits. It is only then that one realizes the full power of this technique. The mind gradually gets free of its negativities of craving and aversion, and their offspring: jealousy, hatred, selfishness, greed, tension, etc. One becomes peaceful and harmonious and then distributes this peace and harmony to others.

Man is a social being. The basis of any healthy harmonious society is always the healthy harmonious individual. Only if each individual has a pure peaceful mind can we expect peace and harmony in society. Vipassana is a unique way of obtaining peace and harmony at the individual and experiential level; hence it is the best way to attain peace and harmony in society.

Vipassana does not teach any dogmas or creeds which build barriers and divisions between communities. Our beliefs and convictions colour and distort our vision. In the name of religion we have shackled ourselves in golden chains of meaningless rites and rituals. The essence of pure religion is performing acts of body, speech and mind with a pure heart full of love and compassion. Then it doesn't matter what clothes we wear, what rites and rituals we perform, or what beliefs we hold or do not hold. Today our minds are so full of the defilements of anger, hatred, greed and delusion that we have lost the essence of true religion and cling to empty husks: these religious practices. To make matters worse, we quarrel and argue over them! Religion has degenerated into sectarianism. This prevents us from self-examination, introspection into the impurities of our minds and from making efforts to eradicate these impurities.

As Goenkaji rightly points out, the problem is not sectarian, therefore the remedy cannot be sectarian. It must be universal. Everyone faces the problem of mental impurities. It is not Hindu anger and greed, Christian anger and greed, or Buddhist anger and greed. The malady is universal. The remedy must also be universal.

Vipassana is such a remedy. No one will object to practising morality, developing discipline of the mind and developing insight into one's own reality by which it is possible to free the mind of negativities. No one is asked to convert from one organized religion to another. If at all there is conversion it is from misery to happiness, from defilement to purity, from bondage to liberation, from ignorance to enlightenment; it is conversion to a better person.

So Vipassana with its universal approach rises above all sectarian religions of the world and promotes secularism—national and emotional integration in the true sense of the word. This takes place not by some cosmetic surgery on the surface but deep at the roots of the problem: in the mind and heart of each individual. The spread of Vipassana and the practice of Vipassana in all levels of society will liberate each one of us to the best of our abilities and capacities and to that extent will promote the good and happiness of humanity.

Parenthood in Dhamma

by Sachiko Weeden

Dhamma helps us in our life in every way, and certainly in parenthood. Being a parent is a noble task and is probably one of the most difficult and delicate jobs in our society.

It requires infinite patience. To be a truly good parent you must have infinite love with total detachment. Aren't these the qualities Dhamma teaches us? The arrival of your child is a God-sent (Dhamma-sent) test for whether you have really cultivated these qualities in yourself through your meditation.

First come those sleepless nights after your baby's birth. When my daughter was born, for weeks I used to sleep three hours and sit two hours a day. Then come the tantrums, not to talk of the constant demands and total deprivation of any kind of freedom whatsoever. But worst of all is the attachment, the strong attachment you develop for your child.

Goenkaji talks about *nekkhamma pāramī*, the quality of renunciation. When you are a mother or father, you must work hard on this quality. It is torture to leave your small child even for ten days. It requires strong determination and devotion to Dhamma.

Don't take this "mother's love" for granted either. It can be a total love of one-way traffic, but it can also be tainted with so much ego and self-centeredness. You must watch yourself very carefully. See how many parents spoil or even destroy their children with their strong ego and attachment: "My child should be like this, like that."

As in Goenkaji's story about the man who hires a private secretary to tell him when anger has arisen, your child can help you be aware of your own mental state. As soon as your mind becomes unbalanced, a sensitive child will let you know by his or her own distress.

Striving to become a better mother or father is nothing but trying to become a better meditator.

My Experience

by Venerable Sanghabodhi

Before I came in contact with Goenkaji and pure Dhamma, I suffered from immeasurable dukkha (misery), swimming helplessly in the ocean of saṃsāra (rounds of suffering). I had much sadness and depression because I had lost my wife and four youngest children, who were killed like animals by the Communists in Cambodia. Over one million of my countrymen were killed, including many friends and relatives. I had lost my country as well.

I tried many ways to get rid of this suffering: by serving others, by volunteer social activities, by donations, staying in Buddhist temples learning Dhamma, reading the *Tipiṭaka* (Buddhist scriptures), serving monks, etc. All these helped me only at the superficial level.

In 1980, I took my first course with Goenkaji in California, due to the help of an American *sāmaṇera* (novice monk) named P. Santa. I will never forget this *sāmaṇera* for the rest of my life. I will always share my merits with him for guiding me to this wonderful path, which is the best way to come out of misery.

In mid-1980 I took two courses. I then came to Dhammagiri in 1981 and stayed for two months, also going on a pilgrimage with Goenkaji for fifteen days.

In May 1982, on the full moon day of Vesākha, I ordained as a *sāmaṇera* under the Bodhi tree in Bodh Gaya and later became a *bhikkhu* (monk).

Up to now I have taken forty-two courses, including three long courses. With the permission of Goenkaji, and with the help of other Cambodians, I translated the Vipassana instructions and discourses from English into Cambodian. This work has not only helped me to gain a deeper understanding of Dhamma, so that I can practise Vipassana more seriously and properly, but it has also helped hundreds of Cambodians in Europe, America, Canada and Thailand to come out of misery and gain peace and harmony.

In general, a big change has come in my life. I personally feel relieved from *dukkha*. I feel peaceful, harmonious and, I feel, I am becoming gradually liberated. When I experience *dukkha,* I try to accept it, and thus free myself from it. I am very fortunate and happy to have found this pure Dhamma, which has helped me so much. Through this practice, I have gained much more mental and physical health than I could have expected. My capacity to work has increased considerably. My mind is more balanced and I can face easily the vicissitudes of life.

The relationships with my family and relatives has become very good. I enjoy helping others without expecting anything in return. I am happier than if I had become ruler of the world.

I want to express my very deep gratitude to Goenkaji, who helped me to rid myself of *dukkha.* And the best way to pay back this debt of gratitude to Goenkaji is to get this Dhamma seed planted in Cambodia, when my country becomes independent and peaceful.

The Ven. Sanghabodhi conducts Vipassana courses using Goenkaji's instruction and discourse tapes.

The Wounded Healer

by Dr. Paul Fleischman

The following article is an excerpt from an article entitled "Vipassana Meditation: Healing the Healer." Dr. Fleischman has supervised post-doctoral fellows in psychiatry in the School of Medicine, Yale University, and has also taught psychiatry and religion at Yale.

In my professional work as a supervisor of psychiatrists-in-training and as a psychiatrist to other psychiatrists, psychologists, social workers, physicians and health professionals, I have become acquainted with a syndrome that could be called "the wounded healer." The wounded healer functions as a high-quality professional. He or she is typically well-trained, diligent, self-educating, and reliably kind and knowledgeable in dealing with patients. But, inside, known only to themselves, and carefully concealed from others, the wounded healer feels alone, frightened, anxious, depressed. His or her professional attainments are genuine, and form excellent compensations for experiences of deprivation earlier in life. The wounded healer is typically an avoidant, proper, lonely person, who gives generously professionally in order to get the human contact he or she feels otherwise deprived of. He or she is apt to hide deep feelings of hurt even from his or her spouse. The wounded healer permits him or herself to become a patient only cautiously, sometimes waiting decades for the right healer to come along. As professionals themselves, they judge carefully. Their progress in psychotherapy is slow, because rather than having a single issue or focus, what they seek is the nurturing and sustained attention of therapy itself. They want cure less than they want participation, membership, an adoptive parent to heal and hold them as their original parents, for any one of various reasons, could not.

Originally, when I was first sought out by one or two established psychiatrists to be their psychiatrist, I was flattered by their estimation of me and I considered their problems in a purely individual light. Over the years, as the treatment of the wounded professional has become my major activity, I have come to understand that the problem is not only individual. The wounded healer, I now believe, represents something essential at the core of healing.

Freud and Jung insisted that analysts be analyzed. All people need healing, most particularly healers. The wounded healer will have his or her own unique constellation of individual and personal problems, but he or she also experiences the pain of pain. The very vulnerability and compassion that sets the healer on that lifelong journey, coupled to the constant exposure to human suffering, requires a treatment of its own. I have come to understand that the wounded healer is so cautious, circumspect and careful in selecting his or her own healer not merely out of pride, shame, professional scruples or trained judgment but also because he or she seeks personal healing that respects the previous truth of his or her own suffering. In the words of the Argentine potter and poet Antonio Porchia: "He who has seen everything empty itself is close to knowing what everything is filled with." A wounded healer's pain is not only a problem, but a valuable source of empathy and insights. It is the magnet that draws healers towards the fate of healing. The wounded healer brings to his or her healer not merely blind pain, but the kernel of noble suffering.

Noble suffering is human misery that drives towards insight, determination, release. It is the knowledge that suffering is existential. The deep note of noble suffering is what differentiates true healing from superficial patch-ups and fraudulent elixirs. The wounded healer is a person suffering from a deep, human, personal pain, who is able to perceive in his or her own plight the kernels of the universal truth about all pain and all plights, and who is accordingly sensitized to, and activated by, a lifelong calling to heal.

When I came to understand myself as a variant of the wounded healer, I appreciated Vipassana more deeply. Its age-old tradition of friendship and comradeship rings the most fundamental note of the human scale. Many contemporary psychotherapies and healings seem to me to be blindly organized around success, happiness, bourgeois attainment: two cars, two children, two houses, two wives. In Vipassana I had located a healing where my life wasn't organized around the opulence of my vacations or the applause and acclaim I received. The path begins with the attitude that suffering can have a noble, enlightening function.

In Vipassana, my birth and death on the shore of the mysterious ocean of the universe is a common bond to all beings. Vipassana is an ideal healing for healers, I believe, because it validates and affirms the direction given to life by conscious confrontation with the dismay that accompanies birth and death. Vipassana does not aim to palliate pain with comfort. Its goal is not health. Every person becomes sick and dies. The goal of Vipassana is the realization that the self is an illusory prison which leads to birth, death, suffering. The sense of a self is an illusion based upon the conditioning exerted by somatic sensations upon the mind. Vipassana meditation brings into the open the existential link

between sensations, self-concepts, and suffering, and permits a reawakening to the world beyond one's self. It operates at the common root where individual, isolated anguish opens out into the stream of undivided, selfless love. It heals by activating virtues that transcend self-success, self-pleasure, self-life. The meditator steps out into that which exists beyond the transient boundaries of body and mind.

> **V**ipassana does not aim to palliate pain with comfort. Its goal is not health. Every person becomes sick and dies. Vipassana heals by activating virtues that transcend self-success, self-pleasure, self-life.

Do I refer all my patients to Vipassana then? How, why, can I value and practise psychiatry? Vipassana meditation courses are open to anyone, but not everyone will take them. There can be no conversion, exhortation, arm-twisting or imposition on this respectful and non-harmful path. The ten-day course is hard work. A lifetime on the path is rarer, harder work. It requires no exceptional intelligence, no athletic skill, no particular cultural background, but it does require character strength and a call.

Vipassana meditators who continue to walk the path for their lifetime come from all walks of life; of course, the vast majority are not themselves healers. Some are illiterate, some poor, some old, some crippled, some physically ill. Indian peasant farmers, German sociologists, Australian carpenters and French psychotherapists practise this way of life. Like the image of Noah's ark, every kind is represented. But there are some requirements, though they tend to be intangible. Meditators must "have the seed." Like the life of any seed, the seed of meditation eludes the microscope of words: is it basic good faith; or a sense of determination; or enough miseries and losses to *have* to keep going; or an unfathomable curiosity about their own true nature; or an intuition of values that transcend immediate life; or a yearning for peace; or a recognition of the limitations of mundane routines? It was said by the Buddha that at the heart of the path lies *ahiṃsā,* non-harmfulness. Is it an inkling of the infinite curative value that this most treasured and elusive cumulative virtue provides, that constitutes the seed? In any case, a life of meditation is a path for those who hear the call, seek it out, and sit down to observe. Some may not seek it, some may not value it, some may not tolerate it, some may have other valuable paths to take.

The French psychoanalyst, Jacques Lacan, wrote, "Psychoanalysis may accompany the patient to the ecstatic limit of the 'thou art that,' in which is revealed to him the cipher of his mortal destiny, but it is not in our mere power as practitioners to bring him to that point where the real journey begins." Vipassana meditation is based on one thing: "This is suffering; this is the way out of suffering." It is the path where the real journey begins. It is a healing by observation of and participation in the laws of nature. Even the stars are born and die, but beyond the transiency of the world there is an eternal that each of us can comprehend. Vipassana heals by focusing onto particular pain the invisible spectrum of the universal.

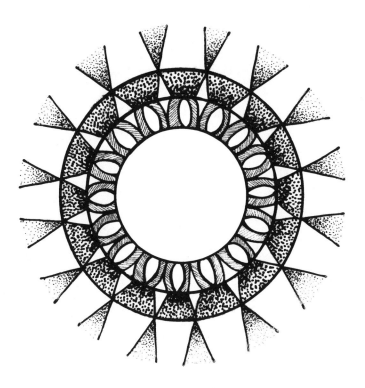

Vipassana: Going to the Root of Addiction

by Dr. Raman Khosla

Drug addiction is a very complex disorder, being neither a medical disorder alone, nor a psychological problem, nor a social disturbance, but a biopsychosocial disorder. Complex in its causation, effects and treatment, the addict demonstrates the "revolving door" phenomenon characterized by initiation, continuation, abuse, cessation and relapse.

In recent psychiatric diagnosis and understanding, tremendous importance has been given to the concept of craving, understood in substance abuse language as "one drink, another drink." In the World Health Organization (WHO) International Classification of Diseases ICD-10 draft (1988), as many as four out of seven concepts in the diagnosis of substance abuse are related to the phenomenon of "craving."

The available treatment modalities in alcohol and drug abuse are divided into three major groups: chemical treatment, psychotherapeutic approaches and behavioural therapies. Chemical treatment includes acute detoxification (usually using benzodiazepines or clonidine), and chronic maintenance treatment (using disulfiram, naltrexone or methadone). Psychotherapies include self-help groups like Alcoholics Anonymous or Narcotics Anonymous; family therapies; and individual psychotherapies—supportive, cognitive or analytic-reconstructive. Behaviour therapies comprise a wide variety of procedures, such as relaxation procedures, like Jacobson's progressive muscle relaxation, or biofeedback procedures. They also include aversion therapies, systemic desensitization, covert sensitization, social skills and assertiveness training.

There are many disadvantages to these treatment modalities:

1. None of them helps *on its own*. One to two year studies show not more than one third of all drug addicts to be totally free of drugs, even with optimal treatment combination.

2. The problem of matching an addict to treatment—i.e., which addict will benefit from which treatment—has not been solved, despite many attempts to do so.

3. The creation of an iatrogenic (health professional created) substitute dependence of the addict on lesser evils: substitute chemicals, external instruments or other humans (such as therapists).

4. None of them tackles craving, the most powerful cause of relapse. Craving is a psychological drive or desire, having the three important components of cognition, conation and mood. Most therapies tackle only the secondary biopsychosocial consequences of the drug.

5. Finally, the most significant element is that the personality is dominated by its unconscious aspects. We attempt to change it analytically or cognitively using the conscious mind, thereby affecting only the tip of the iceberg. Intellectual insight alone does not help drug abusers. Drives, mood states, motivation, and other personality components are very difficult to handle with psychotherapeutic procedures. The hallmarks of a drug addict's personality—i.e., emotional immaturity, emptiness, need for immediate gratification, attitudes that are escapist, manipulative and irrational—are extremely resistant to change by intellectual means.

Meditation offers a different approach. Meditation is defined as a family of techniques which have in common a conscious attempt to focus attention or awareness in a non-analytical way, and an attempt not to dwell on the discursive, ruminative content of thought. All forms of meditation help drug addicts, who show short-term improvement. However, with most forms of meditation this is due to a non-specific physiological relaxation response. Only the meditation technique of Vipassana addresses the mental defilements of craving and its obverse (aversion), at the deepest roots of the mind.

Vipassana meditation is a way of living. Although Vipassana is not a specific treatment modality for drug addiction or for any other mental or physical illness, many psychosomatic diseases do show improvement as a by-product of the process of purifying the mind.

As opposed to most meditation methods, which aim at concentration or relaxation of the mind, the aim of Vipassana goes beyond that. The goal is purification of the mind by removing all its negativities and hence uncovering all the positive qualities that are inherent in the nature of every human mind. The ultimate goal is a totally pure or deconditioned mind. A creative self-aware mind with positive emotions replaces the routine reactive mind, which constantly obeys the stimulus-response principle, with no self-awareness. As a consequence, mental equanimity or balance of mind increases in every life situation.

The basis of mental purification in Vipassana is that it tackles mental impurities at their roots, that is, at the level of physical bodily sensations. Awareness of the sensations on the body is the basic proven function of the unconscious mind. The importance of the mind has been repeatedly emphasized by Gotama the Buddha, the master psychologist beyond comparison, who rediscovered Vipassana. The Buddha said: "Mind precedes all phenomena. Mind matters most, because everything is mind-made. Mind can become one's worst enemy or one's best friend."

Psychoanalysts, behaviourists and cognitive psychologists all accept emotion, but only its psychological component. They completely ignore its physical component of sensation. Every sensation is a reality, the product of an underlying biochemical reaction. And every emotion is accompanied by a sensation. In this way the emotions can be explored through the concrete medium of body sensations. Therefore the emphasis in Vipassana is on *vedanā*, the feeling of bodily sensations. *Vedanā* is the third of the four parts of the mind described by the Buddha. In modern terms these four parts of the mind are best described as consciousness, perception, sensation and reaction. Although a Vipassana meditator will observe body (*kāya*), sensations (*vedanā*), mind (*citta*) and mental contents (*dhamma*), the focus for the meditator is very clearly on the observation of sensations (*vedanānupassanā*).

Hence the advantage of Vipassana is that it works at the level of both mind and matter. The exploration of matter is done using the instrument of mind; the exploration of mind is done using the unique and wonderful instrument of matter. Herein lies the basic difference between Vipassana and other psychologies, which approach mind at the level of the intellect alone.

In Vipassana, there is no dependence on any instrument, chemical or human being (therapist, teacher or guru) or group of beings. In the words of the Buddha: "You are your own master and you make your own future."

The basic practical difference between Vipassana and all other meditation techniques is that it does not involve verbalization or visualization or any external object as used in other types of meditation. Insight or wisdom in Vipassana is not received or intellectual knowledge, but experiential insight, at the level of feeling of body sensations. Walking on the path of truth (Dhamma), personal realization of truth automatically changes the habit pattern of the mind, which subsequently lives according to the truth alone. The truth is the natural law of mind and body. All laws of physics are observed by any Vipassana meditator to be the same inside as well as outside the individual. Hence Vipassana is not just a scientific art of living, but the true science of the mind, the true psychology.

As regards drug abuse, the basis of all addiction has been found to be craving (taṇhā). Literally "thirst," taṇhā or craving is the mental habit of insatiable longing for what is not, which implies an equal and irremediable dissatisfaction with what is.

The root of all craving is vedanā (sensation). All human behaviour is the result of reactions to inner body sensations, be they mental, vocal or physical reactions. All reactions are either in the group of "I want/like" (craving) or "I don't want/like" (aversion), which are two sides of the same coin. This leads to clinging (upādāna), which leads only to unhappiness. In the teaching of the Buddha: "All suffering which arises has reaction as its cause. If all reactions cease to be, there is no more suffering."

In craving there is a marked attachment to the habit of seeking sensual gratification. Addicts take a drug because they wish to experience the pleasurable sensation it produces in them, even though they know that by taking it, they reinforce their addiction. Deeper than this is the addiction to the condition of craving. The object of craving is secondary, best seen in those persons who are addicted to multiple drugs. More fundamentally, addicts seek to continually maintain the state of craving itself, because it produces a pleasurable sensation within them, which they wish to prolong. Hence, the basis of all addictions is an addiction to one's own inner bodily sensations—liking and craving for the pleasant sensations and disliking and aversion for the unpleasant ones. Craving then becomes a habit which they cannot break. Just as an addict gradually develops tolerance towards the addictive drug and requires larger doses to achieve the desired effect, this addiction to craving becomes steadily stronger, the more people seek to satisfy it. The greater the craving, the more it leads to unhappiness because it prevents

> Although Vipassana is not specifically a treatment for drug addiction or for any other mental or physical illness, many psychosomatic diseases do show improvement as a by-product of the process of purifying the mind.

people from seeing the reality of every moment. They see instead only the distorted truth, as if through a dark glass.

Vipassana has helped and will continue to help alcohol and drug addicts because it tackles the root of all addiction, which is craving. Though we have substantial anecdotal evidence, there is a need for long-term scientific studies demonstrating the tremendous efficacy of Vipassana in helping alcohol and drug abusers.

To conclude with the ever-inspiring words of the Buddha: "If the roots remain untouched and firm in the ground, a felled tree still puts forth new shoots. If the underlying habit of craving and aversion is not uprooted, suffering arises anew over and over again."

A Hindu who learns Vipassana may continue to call himself a Hindu;
a Muslim a Muslim, and so on for a Jain, a
Christian, a Buddhist.

The important point is to become a good
person, living a happy and harmonious life.
Dhamma helps everyone to become a good
human being.

—S.N. Goenka

The Role of Vipassana in Psychiatric Practice

by Dr. R.M.Chokhani

The following was presented as a paper at the Vipassana Seminar held at Dhamma Giri in 1986; it has been duly revised and updated.

One of the more widespread examples of modern adaptations of traditional consciousness-training practices is the Vipassana meditation technique, which has recently become popular among both the lay public and workers in the mental health field.

Vipassana is a Pāli word meaning "insight." It is a system of self-transformation by self-observation; the object is to eventually reach a state of calmness and balance of mind (Thray Sithu Sayagyi U Ba Khin, 1963) and live a life of altruism, beneficial for one and all (Goenka S.N., 1990).

Meditation as a practice of self-liberation was developed in different cultures by and for members of religious groups in the context of their cosmology. The teachings of Gotama the Buddha embody a psychological system as well as a cosmology (Kutz I., Borysenko J.J. & Benson H., 1985). Known as *Abhidhamma,* this is the most systematic and intricately laid out psychology— presenting a set of concepts for understanding mental activity and methods for healing mental disorders, which differ markedly from the outlook of contemporary psychotherapies (Goleman D., 1977).

The *Abhidhamma* Model of Mind

This model of mental activity is an "object relation" theory in the broadest sense: its basic dynamic is the ongoing relationship of mental states to sensory objects. "Sense objects" include percepts in the five main sensory modalities, plus thought or cognitive activity (which in this system is seen as a "sixth sense"). "Mental states" are in continuous change and flux: in this analysis, the rate of change of the smallest unit of mental states—a mind moment which is a moment of awareness—is incredibly fast, described as arising at the rate of millions in the time of a flash of lightning.

Each successive mental state is composed of a set of properties or mental factors which gives it its distinctive characteristics: there are fifty-two basic perceptual, cognitive and affective categories of these properties (Narada Thera, 1968). The basic dichotomy in this analysis of mental factors is that between pure, wholesome or healthy and impure, unwholesome or unhealthy mental properties. Just as in systemic desensitization, where tension is supplanted by its physiologic opposite, relaxation, healthy states are antagonistic to unhealthy ones, inhibiting them. Vipassana meditation aims to eradicate these unhealthy properties from the mind; the operational definition of mental health is their complete absence, as in the case of an arahant (saint) (Goleman D. 1977).

Mechanism and Psychological Effects

"Everything that arises in the mind is accompanied by physical sensation", said the Buddha; this interrelationship of mind and body is the key to the practice of Vipassana meditation. Vipassana trains the concentrated attention to follow the mechanics of mental processing with the base of physical sensations, in a detached fashion. This perspective of an observer allows the controlled release of mental contents like craving and aversion, past and future in a seemingly endless stream of memories, wishes, thoughts, conversations, scenes, desires, dreads, lusts. Thousands upon thousands of emotionally-driven pictures of every kind rise to the surface of the mind and pass away without provoking a reaction, while simultaneously anchoring one in concrete, contemporary reality (Fleischman P.R., 1986).

The mind is deconditioned with meditation altering the process of conditioning *per se,* so that it is no longer a prime determinant of future acts (Goleman D.,1977). A refinement of awareness occurs and one responds consciously to life situations thereby becoming free from limitations which were forged by mere reactions to them. One's life becomes characterized by increased awareness, reality-orientation, non-delusion, self-control and peace (Fleischman P.R.,1986). Such a person is able to make quick decisions, correct and sound judgment and concerted effort—mental capabilities which definitely contribute to success in contemporary life.

Vipassana, Health and Healers: A Research Review

Considerable data is available, documenting the various biopsychosocial benefits that accrue from the practice of Vipassana meditation; it indicates the vast therapeutic potential that Vipassana has. For instance, many case report studies have been recorded, on the positive effects of Vipassana in different psychosomatic disorders, such as chronic pain, headaches, bronchial asthma, hypertension, peptic ulcer, psoriasis etc. and so also in different mental disorders including alcoholism and drug addiction. Beneficial effects of Vipassana have also been studied in special population groups

such as students, prisoners, police personnel and individuals suffering from chronic pain and various other mental disorders.

However, healing—not the cure of disease, but the essential healing of human suffering—is the purpose of Vipassana. Suffering springs from ignorance of one's own true nature. Insight, truth—experiential truth—alone frees one (Fleischman P.R.,1991). "Know thyself," all wise persons have advised. Vipassana is a practical way to examine the reality of one's own mind and body, to uncover and solve whatever problems that lie hidden there, to develop unused potential and to channel it for one's own good and the good of others.

All people need healing, most particularly healers. "Physician heal thyself," is a well-known phrase. Freud and Jung insisted that analysts be analysed. The very vulnerability and compassion that sets the healer on a life-long journey to heal, coupled with the constant exposure to human suffering, requires a treatment of its own. Vipassana is acceptable and relevant to healers of diverse disciplines because it is free of dogma, experientially based and focused on human suffering and relief. With its practice, healers are able to deepen their autonomy and self-knowledge, at the same time augmenting their ability to be a professional anchor to others in the tumult of their lives. Vipassana is verily the path of all healing, including self-healing and other-healing (Fleischman P.R., 1991).

We find that most of the empirical research has been concerned with looking at the physiological and/or behavioural measures related to the use of Vipassana meditation as a self-regulation strategy. Attention also needs to be paid to the classical perspective of Vipassana—phenomenological aspects of meditation-induced altered states of consciousness.

Model for Clinical Application

The clinical utility of Vipassana meditation is more likely to be in terms of providing a general psychological pattern of positive mental states rather than a response to any particular presenting problem. Generally, the conventional psychotherapies are generated as treatments for the latter. All the same, the author has been using a cognitive therapeutic technique, derived from the system of Vipassana meditation, as a supplementary treatment and has found it to be effective for stress management and reduction of fears and phobias.

It should be noted that the therapist must be well-conversant with the technique of Vipassana meditation and a mature meditator himself. Speaking in Vipassana parlance, the patient observes his respiration (Anapana meditation), while the therapist practises *mettā* (loving-kindness meditation).

Before commencing the formal therapy, the therapist explains to the patient its potential benefits, particularly relaxation. This helps reduce the latter's apprehension and enables him to cooperate and participate actively in the treatment. In addition, it is necessary to ensure that the physical environment is one that will facilitate relaxation; the room should be quiet and free from interruptions, and the patient's couch should be reasonably comfortable.

The patient is asked to lie comfortably on the couch, close his eyes and observe the flow of respiration by concentrating on the area of the upper lip just below the nostrils—whether in-breath or out-breath, deep or shallow, fast or slow; natural breath, bare breath and only breath. When his mind wanders, the patient is instructed to passively disregard the intrusion and repeatedly focus his attention on his breath, without getting upset or disturbed about the drift of his mind.

Two things happen. One—his mind gets concentrated on the flow of respiration. Two—he becomes aware of the relationship between his mental states and the flow of respiration: that whenever there is agitation in the mind—anger, hatred, fear, passion, etc.—the natural flow of respiration gets affected and disturbed. He thus learns to simply observe and remain alert, vigilant and equanimous.

The patient is advised to continue practising the technique on his own, twice daily, in the morning and in the evening, each session lasting for about thirty minutes. The therapist reviews the progress of his patient from time to time, simultaneously counselling and motivating him to undertake a regular ten-day Vipassana meditation course. The patient is thus encouraged to continue to strive for his personal autonomy, that is, to take personal responsibility in his own health and well-being.

Conclusion

It is my contention that this technique shortens the total duration of treatment and helps the patient cope better in the community by providing a general pattern of stress-responsivity less likely to trigger specific over-learned maladaptive responses, whether psychological or somatic. Moreover, there is a change in the patient's internal state, whereby his attention is focused, his perceptual and motor systems function optimally and his anxiety is minimized. This happens in spite of, and while meeting, a great variation in the external environmental demand by virtue of self-regulating and developing one's internal capacities with Vipassana meditation.

Multicentered controlled clinical trials of this technique with sophisticated experimental designs would help us to study its value and limitations in the prevention and treatment of various psychiatric disorders. Also, it needs to be clarified as to which patient with what clinical problem will benefit from Vipassana meditation as the treatment of choice vis-a-vis other self-regulation strategies, viz., biofeedback, hypnosis, progressive relaxation, etc.

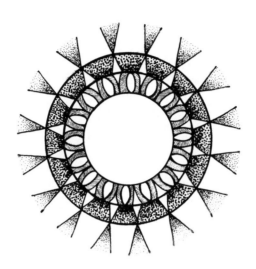

References

Fleischman P.R. (1986), *The Therapeutic Action of Vipassana* and *Why I Sit,* Buddhist Publication Society, Kandy, Sri Lanka.

Goleman D. (1977), *Meditation and Consciousness: An Asian Approach to Mental Health,* Am. J.Psychother.30:41–54.

Kutz I., Borysenko J.J. & Benson H. (1985), *Meditation and Psychotherapy,* Am.J.Psychiatry, Vol.142, No. 1:1–8.

Narada Thera (1986), *A Manual of Abhidhamma,* Buddhist Publication Society, Kandy, Sri Lanka.

Surya N.C. (1979), *Personal Autonomy and Instrumental Accuracy,* in *"Psychotherapeutic Processes,"* editors: M. Kapur, V.N. Murthy, K. Satyavathi and R.L. Kapur, N.I.M.H.A.N.S., Bangalore, India:1–19.

Thray Sithu Sayagyi U Ba Khin (1963), "The Essentials of Buddha Dhamma in Meditative Practice," this Journal 31–35.

Wolpe J. (1958), *Psychotherapy by Reciprocal Inhibition,* Stanford University Press, Palo Alto, California, USA.

The Fruits of Dhamma

by John Beary

This article was first published in 1982 when the Dhamma community in Japan was embryonic. For developments since then please see Centres: Japan Vipassana Centre.

The Buddha gave us certain criteria to enable us to distinguish Dhamma from non-Dhamma. These criteria are in the form of the qualities of Dhamma and are six in number:

> *Svākkhāto bhagavatā dhammo*
> *sandiṭṭhiko, akāliko,*
> *ehi-passiko, opaneyyiko*
> *paccattam veditabbo viññuhī'ti.*

Clearly expounded is the teaching of the exalted one; to be seen for oneself, giving results here and now, inviting one to come and see, leading straight to the goal, capable of being realized for himself by any average intelligent person.

Of these qualities, let's take a closer look at the features of *ehi-passiko* ("inviting one to come and see") and see how this quality of Dhamma is currently affecting the spread of Dhamma.

Around the world today we are witnessing a great surge of enthusiasm for Dhamma as more and more people come in contact with it via Vipassana meditation. Centres are arising and more and more courses are being conducted, as old students who have grown in Dhamma and have experienced its benefits wish to share it with others. It is significant to note that this movement continues to spread, much as it must have in the Buddha's time, by word of mouth from individual to individual and not through any public relations campaign.

What is it that continues to attract people on a personal level to the Dhamma and the practice of Vipassana? What accounts for today's surge of interest in meditation in ever-increasing numbers of people around the world?

Of the many answers to these questions, one springs forth from the above mentioned qualities of Dhamma: that is *ehi-passiko*, whereby once having tasted pure Dhamma a meditator feels an irresistible urge to tell friends and family how good it is, how much it has helped him. This usually takes the form of urging them, for their own good, not to come and believe, but to come and see for themselves the beneficial results of Dhamma.

Another perhaps more powerful aspect of *ehi-passiko* appears to be at work in the world now, and it is this feature which, I think, accounts for the present snowballing spread of Dhamma via Vipassana meditation. This feature resides in each student's behaviour and the quality of his or her interaction with other people in society. As meditators have become more and more established in *sīla, samādhi* and *paññā* (moral conduct, control of the mind, and wisdom), a concomitant change in their attitudes and values has certainly taken place. All reasonable people place much more importance on how a person acts rather than on what one says or espouses. Today as more and more meditators settle down into the business of raising families and assuming responsible roles in society, those behavioural changes fashioned by their experience and growth in Dhamma will surely be the beacons which attract others to come out of darkness.

> **V**ipassana meditation continues to spread, much as it must have in the Buddha's time, by word of mouth from individual to individual and not through any public relations campaign.

Now this is not to say that all meditators are automatically shining examples of Dhamma; but if they are practising properly then another two qualities of Dhamma will also be operating. One is *opaneyyiko,* i.e., that the Dhamma is a straight path on which no effort, no step is wasted as each step brings one closer and closer to the goal. Another quality is *akāliko,* whereby the fruits of Dhamma are experienced here and now at each stage along the path. This being so, the Dhamma is then beneficial in the beginning, beneficial in the middle and beneficial in the end. We all know what a struggle it is to maintain *sīla,* and to keep our *samādhi;* what it is to maintain the delicate balance of mind in a world blinded by ignorance and addicted to greed and hatred. What can it be that keeps us pressing on, other than the continuous reinforcement inherent in the Dhamma as each effort bears fruit here and now? We've seen these fruits ripen in time and become manifest in ways that, while setting us apart from the many unwholesome aspects of the world, grant us the inner strength and peace of mind to be different.

These fruits of Dhamma are nowhere more vividly displayed than in the development of our own perfections. These ennobling qualities of generosity, virtue, patience, self-sacrifice, industriousness, truthfulness, determination, compassion, equanimity and wisdom each become strengthened by continued practice, and each by its very nature becomes an observable phenomenon in our daily lives for all to see. It is in these fruits of Dhamma (which are good, concrete, vivid, personal, here and now, observable to others as well as to the meditator) that the most powerful aspect of *ehipassiko* resides. They say to all: "Here is something good, something for our welfare, something for us to aspire to." Sometimes as old students we lose sight of just how much we've changed, and we take these fruits for granted. But each of us has only to reflect on our own lives before coming to the Dhamma and the direction we were headed in at that time, to know what a great change has taken place for the better.

It is these changes then, these fruits of Dhamma, which say to others, in the strongest language possible: "You too, come and see." Now that a large number of meditators have been ten to twelve years in Dhamma the fruits of those struggle-filled years attract others to the path.

Here in Japan the Dhamma community is a case in point. When a few Western meditators began arriving here in the mid seventies, they were a transient few, new to Japan and new to Dhamma. But over the years some of them became more established residents here and grew more established in Dhamma. As they developed in Dhamma, they soon realized that they were having a noticeable impact on the Japanese society as well as the foreign community here. As people had a chance to observe the behaviour of meditators over the years, they became more and more interested in them and in the Dhamma as well—so much so that the spread of Dhamma here is beginning to pick up quite a bit of momentum. The recent courses organized for Goenkaji have been huge successes. The expressed interest in future courses, group sittings and self-courses has resulted in the arising of a

Dhamma house in Kyoto, to serve as a physical centre around which the various Dhamma activities revolve, as well as the formation of the Japan Vipassana Association (J.V.A.) to administer and organize the various activities.

In a land where language barriers and cultural barriers might throw up many obstacles to the spread of Vipassana, we are finding that *ehi-passiko* continues unimpeded on the strength of its strongest feature: the observable fruits of Dhamma.

This very aspect of *ehi-passiko* sets our Dhamma work apart from that of the stereotyped missionary. We have no need to advertise ourselves or the fruits of Dhamma. We have no need to preach morality or to proselytize about the benefits of Dhamma, for these very benefits become visible in our actions in daily life and need no commercial amplification.

Our job then, if we are really interested in the spread of Dhamma, is to get ourselves established in Dhamma, to nurture the seed our Dhamma father Goenkaji has given us to grow and bear fruit. These fruits will then perform our missionary work for us as they have for the Dhamma for 2,500 years. Our zeal for the spread of Dhamma should never lose sight of the fact that whatever good we hope to do by providing Dhamma service is only effective if our own practice receives priority. We can help no one without first having helped ourselves.

By this process then, of one torch lighting another, may the darkness of ignorance and suffering be dispelled throughout the world.

May all beings be happy.

Jaba jaba antara jagata meṅ,
jāge citta vikāra.
Maiṅ bhī vyākula ho uthūṅ,
vikala karūṅ sansāra.

Maiṅ bhī vyākula nā banūṅ,
jagata vikala nā hoya.
Jīvana jīne kī kalā,
śuddha Dharama hai soya.

Whenever in the inner world
mental defilements arise,
I become agitated
and make the outer world agitated.

May I and may the world
be free from agitation.
This is the art of living,
this is the pure Dhamma.

—*Hindi dohas of S. N. Goenka*

Personal Experiences

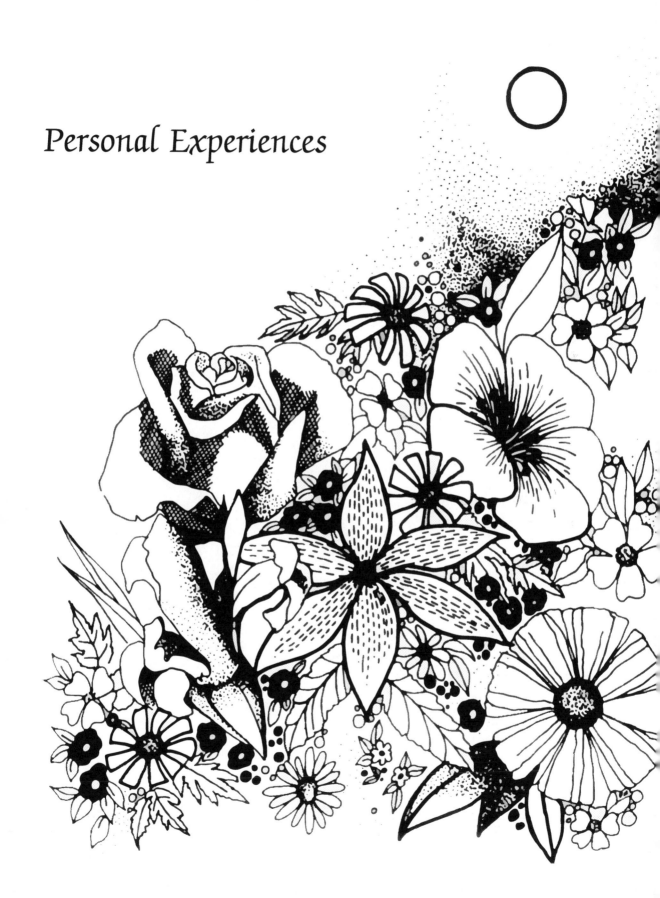

Letter from Venerable Ashin Arseinna

The following is an abridged translation of a letter from Ven. Ashin Arseinna sent to Goenkaji after his visit to Dhamma Giri in March 1990.

Sayagyi S.N. Goenka,

On the evening of last eleventh of March, we parted company with you at Dhammagiri, and arrived back in Myanmar on the twenty-ninth of March...

The Dhamma experiences encountered during our trip are very precious, especially, because the technique you taught... is a technique whereby the arising and passing away phenomenon which is actually taking place in the body is noted with much patience so that it is experienced as it actually is. I am truly happy that I actually experienced it and even now at this moment, am experiencing it.

This technique is the technique that we have understood, accepted and practised. It makes me so happy and pleased to learn that your Dhamma work of dispersion of the *sāsana* [the Buddha's dispensation of the teaching] by this technique is spreading all over the world from India. I am earnestly wishing and sending *mettā* to you for further progress in your work. I also have faith that it will definitely progress and spread...

There is another fact that I am happy about. In ancient days, because of the Dhamma work done by Emperor Siridhamma Asoka, the Dhamma was dispersed in the nine regions: Thera Sona and Thera Uttara arrived at Suvaṇṇabhūmi (Myanmar). Then the Buddha's Dhamma spread throughout the country, and it continues to be beneficial to all. Similarly, even today, because of your diligence, the Buddha's Dhamma has reached the whole world and is benefiting many people. That is why I would like to say that you, Sayagyi, are a modern day Siridhamma Asoka...

I have read and known about your Dhamma work even before I visited you, and have been sending *mettā* to you. In the future too, I will be forever sending *mettā* because we are both travellers to *nibbāna* on the path of Dhamma...

I am sending my *mettā*. May you be healthy and happy both in body and mind and may your endeavour in the Dhamma work increase manyfold.

Ashin Arseinna (Ayasma Ācinna)
Karen Pariyatti Monastery, Oaklan,
Bahan, Rangoon, Myanmar.
30 June 1990

Durlabha jīvana manuja kā,
durlabha Dharama milāpa.
Dhanyabhāga donoṅ mile,
dūra kareṅ bhava tāpa.

Rare is a human life,
rare to encounter the Dhamma.
We are fortunate to have both;
let us work to banish suffering.

—*Hindi dohas of S.N. Goenka*

Letter from Venerable Bhaddanta Jotipala

The following letter, written in the spring of 1990, is from Aggamahāpaṇḍita (foremost great scholar) Bhaddanta Jotipala.

The Great Dhamma Teacher, Guruji S. N. Goenka, has the following exceptional qualities:

Teaching the True Dhamma.

Forming good relationships and dealings with others, regardless of race, religion, nationality, social status and financial standing in such a way as to make them accept the Dhamma.

Is fully endowed with the characteristics and virtues of noble persons—such as *saddhā* [faith], *cetana* [wholesome mental volitions], *mettā* [loving-kindness], *karuṇā* [compassion], *nivāta* [humility] and *nimmāna* [lack of conceit].

Keeping *khanti* [patience] in hand in distributing the Dhamma gems to places all over the world. Because of this the Dhamma has taken root, progressed and prospered in Dhamma centres throughout the world.

Not being satisfied with such success in the spread of Dhamma, still endeavouring for much more outstanding success in the dispersion of the Dhamma.

Because of the above-mentioned five primary virtues, I formed the opinion that the great meditation master, S.N. Goenka is fully endowed with the above qualities and is very worthy of the honour and appellation of:

World Dispenser of the *Sāsana*—*Dhamma Magguddesaka*

Great Lay Devotee—*Mahā Upāsaka*

Bodhisatta King Janaka, reflecting and finding satisfaction in the success attained after his diligent endeavour[1] thought:

> *Vāyametheva puriso.*
> *Na nibbindeyya paṇḍito;*
> *Passāmi vohamattānaṃ*
> *Udakā thalamubbhataṃ.*

A man of courage should indeed
strive earnestly,
A man of wisdom should never turn away
from the endeavour;
I see you and myself,
Pulled out of the flood (of *saṃsāra*), and
safe on the shore.

(Mahājanak Jātakaṃ, verse 136)

from Bhaddanta Jotipala
State Central Executive of the Sangha,
Kya Khut Waing Sayadaw,
Kya Khut Waing Monastery, Bagu, Myanmar

---

1 In this Jātaka story King Janaka nearly drowned in a shipwreck, but due to his valiant effort he saved himself and his companions.

Letter to a Student

by Father Anthony de Mello

Extracts from a letter to a Vipassana student in America written on 1 April 1985.

It was indeed interesting to learn that Vipassana is being practised in the United States…

Some people are more helped by Vipassana, others less. That is only natural, for no two persons are alike and some people are helped by some methods, others by others.

What is beyond question, however, is that Vipassana is perfectly compatible with the Catholic religion. There is absolutely no opposition between the two; on the contrary, Vipassana would help one to become a better Christian and a better Catholic. And your own experience has proved this to you.

I certainly wish you well in your spiritual quest.

Yours sincerely,
Anthony de Mello, S.J.

(The late Father de Mello was a well-known author on spirituality and had attended courses at Dhamma Giri. He was the founder of the Sādhāna Institute in Pune, India.)

Vipassana—the Non-Sectarian Way

by Sadhvi Vinodinibai

What is sectarianism? "My sect is the best; only people of my sect are religious and can be noble and truthful." This is the kind of thinking that goes into sectarianism.

People do not understand the difference between sectarianism and true religion. Sectarianism has a foundation of three or four basic concepts:

1) People of different sects have faith in their own respective deities or founders.

2) Each sect has its own ideas concerning the proper kind of clothes to wear. Only those people who wear these clothes are considered religious by them; others are considered irreligious.

3) Those who perform the rites and rituals approved by the sect are the only ones considered religious by them; others are not.

4) Each sect has its own philosophy and theory. Only those who believe in it are considered to be religious; the rest are considered non-believers.

In the practice of Vipassana there is no importance given to these concepts. Pure religion is universal.

Nature has its eternal laws. Understanding these laws, living one's life in accordance with them and liberating the mind of its impurities and defilements is the goal of Vipassana meditation. Every human being becomes agitated as a result of these defilements, and by becoming liberated from them one can enjoy peace and harmony.

> By practising this meditation technique a deeper understanding of one's own religious philosophy and theory is gained.

The Buddha gave three steps in this meditation— *sīla, samādhi and paññā. Sīla* means not harming anyone by actions of body and speech. Who in this world, belonging to any sect, can have any objection to this? By leading a good life each individual can bring about peace and harmony in his or her own family, society, country, and thus the whole world.

The second step is *samādhi,* concentration of the mind. But it must be concentration without craving or aversion as its object. It is the development of concentration by observing the natural and normal breath which is universal. It is not an external, imaginary object. No sect can have any objection to this.

The third and most important step is *paññā— bhāvana-mayā-paññā* [experiential wisdom]. It is by observing the sensations on the body objectively and understanding their impermanent nature, and thus developing equanimity, that one gains liberation from impurities.

The unconscious mind generates craving and aversion every moment by identifying with pleasant and unpleasant sensations. This can be experienced only through Vipassana meditation.

Which sect would object to a scientific method of liberating oneself from one's defilements without using an external object of concentration, and through insight meditation?

No sect can have any special authority on this scientific technique. Any individual who follows the technique and makes effort can succeed.

In this meditation practice there is no external object for meditation; no external chains. In fact, by practising this meditation technique a deeper understanding of one's own religious philosophy and theory is gained. Whoever practises this Jewel of Dhamma begins to experience the benefits of it. Total liberation from one's impurities is not possible by any other practice.

I happened to come to a Vipassana course accidentally and I express my infinite gratitude to Goenkaji for establishing me in pure Dhamma with great love and compassion. It is a very long path. But the very fact of having found this path is itself a matter of great merit.

May everyone enjoy peace and happiness.

The world is facing serious problems. It is just the right time for everyone to take to Vipassana meditation and learn how to find a deep pool of quiet in the midst of all that is happening today.

—Sayagyi U Ba Khin

A Journey into Vipassana Meditation

by Jyoti (Jayashakti) Asher

My memories revert back to my very first Vipassana course in June 1988 at Dhamma Giri. I was completely unaware of the depth of Vipassana meditation and where the path would lead me, but this was the turning point that brought a complete change in my life.

I was initiated in the traditional Hindu *Sanyas* (the path of renunciation) in the year 1969 and was plodding on in the usual way on the so-called spiritual path with rituals, ceremonies, mantra, meditation, hatha yoga, reading and recitation of the holy scriptures, attending *Kumbha Melas*, etc., thinking this was the be-all and end-all of truly following the sublime path of renunciation.

Within the span of twenty years of the so-called path of renunciation neither my lurking fears of darkness, being alone, spirits, ghosts, dead bodies, etc., were reduced nor did all the spiritual practices eradicate the anger, hatred, greed and the ego.

As head of the Yoga Ashram at Calcutta, one day I came across ten Vipassana discourse cassettes. After hearing the discourses I felt that every word that was spoken was meant for me. The lectures appealed very much to my rational mind. After hearing the ten-day discourses

> I was completely unaware of the depth of Vipassana meditation and where the path would lead me, but this was the turning point that brought a complete change in my life.

my mind started working on those lines and thoughts. Truly my mind was not under my control. Somehow I had generated anger and was desperately trying to control it. I tried being in silence for two days meditating and watching my thoughts. But that did not help at all.

Then I remembered that I used to receive information and circulars about the Vipassana meditation courses held at the Jain House in Calcutta. During those years I was not the least interested in any other sort of meditation. But after hearing about the pure Dhamma from these tapes, I decided within a period of three months to take a few Vipassana courses. Then it also occurred to me that a devotee in Calcutta had presented me with a Vipassana Journal and I started reading the articles which seemed quite appealing and enlightening.

Finally I arrived at Dhamma Giri to take my very first course in Vipassana. I went through a hectic period just trying to concentrate my flickering mind below the nostrils and above the upper lip. To my utter amazement I found that concentration, i.e., Anapana on the given spot, even for ten seconds, was so difficult. My mind went all haywire, brooding about the past, planning for the future. I would think of anything but being in the present, i.e., concentrating on respiration. I was feeling miserable and was trying to fight my own battle.

The course on the whole was a nightmare as far as I was concerned. I experienced severe constipation, loss of appetite, stomach-aches, slight heat in the head, and physical discomfort. I was unable to sit for the one hour *adhiṭṭhāna* (strong determination) sitting. Half an hour would be the most I could manage.

And I remember clearly a dream that I had during that course in which an unknown person was after me and I woke up startled feeling quite relieved at the thought that it was only a dream. After waking up after midnight another sort of fear caught hold of me. The trees and the bushes outside my window of the residential quarter were casting moving and dancing shadows on the opposite wall of my room. Due to the fright I spontaneously started repeating a mantra calling out for help to the Divine Mother. (I always thought that there was an unknown entity, a power, a force, a Lord-God-Almighty who was always hearing the call of distress, and who was ever-ready to give a helping hand.) Hardly had I repeated it three times, when I collected myself and commanded my mind to stop chanting mentally since this technique did not allow any sort of verbalization. I wanted to be true to myself and desired to stick to the discipline that was required from a student. It worked and I stopped chanting the mantra at once. Still, after this turmoil I found it quite difficult to stir out of my bed that night to go to the toilet although the room had an attached bathroom, because the fear was so great. However, in spite of all the different kinds of difficulties, I carried on with my meditation practice very sincerely, seriously, continuously, and completed the course.

This was followed immediately by my first *Satipaṭṭhāna* course. I remember feeling rather irritated with a construction worker who was constantly banging and drilling holes in the walls of the cells. The echo was resounding in the pagoda and I was really disturbed. I approached the man concerned and mentioned to him to be more considerate towards the meditators and that I had not come all the way from Calcutta to hear the harsh sounds of drilling. But then,

by afternoon, I realized that I was not the only one disturbed and besides, he was only doing his assigned duty. Later, whenever we met, he used to give me a smile. On the whole, the course felt better than the previous two; maybe because I was able to concentrate at least for half a minute.

Then after a gap of ten days, I took another course in August which was my fourth course. During this course I was able to sit for the one hour *adhiṭṭhāna* without moving my body. I was able to concentrate for at least one minute. Also, I realized that the blank areas in my back and chest opened up and at times I would feel a flow of subtle sensations.

In September I attended a twenty-day course and was able to successfully complete it with increased confidence and gratitude. After the twenty-day course I went back to the Yoga Ashram and Mission in Calcutta only to hand over my entire charge and responsibility, and resign from the Trusteeship as well. That former path, I realized, could not lead me to liberation. All those practices that I had undertaken had not improved my nature nor eradicated my impurities of craving, aversion and ignorance. Now I felt that I had the seed of enlightenment, and with the practice of Vipassana the seed was beginning to sprout. Otherwise how could I have left all that I had; how could I have given up such an important position. Everything was just natural and spontaneous.

Returning to Dhamma Giri very soon I took another five courses. I had now sat ten courses in eight months. It was time to learn through serving.

Gradually I understood that serving during the courses is applied Vipassana. I was trying to put into practical use this wonderful, simple and unique technique whilst working. I found it rather difficult and most of the time I was reacting to the unwanted situations. Now I understand that it was nothing outside me. I was reacting to the unpleasant sensations in my body. But I'm sure that with the constant practice of being with the bodily sensations I will gradually come out of these reacting impulses and my equanimity will increase.

I remember an incident that occurred about one and a half months back. A very close member of my family expired. Earlier I would have been afraid to even stand beside the dead body. But here I was near the corpse and all I could do was send her *mettā* (loving-kindness). Even before she died I visited her daily in the hospital to be with her during her ailment and also to meditate the Vipassana way, being aware of sensations and giving her *mettā*. My best wishes and welfare flowed to her constantly for her peaceful exit from this earthly plane. I felt that this was the best and the only effective prayer that I could offer her. Partings due to death are difficult and I think about how emotional I would have been prior to my practice of Vipassana meditation. And although the actual incident of her death created an emotional disturbance in me for some time, I was able to be with the sensations and I found at once the emotion calmed down.

Another change that has taken place is that earlier I would accept personal donations as a *Sanyasini*. But now I just can't do it. Sometimes I wonder whether it is the same me. I really don't need anything from anybody. I am happy the way I am. I remember the words of my father who is no more on this earthly plane advising me never to be at the receiving end but always to be on the giving end. Dhamma works! It looks after you, takes care of you. One doesn't feel stranded in the presence of Dhamma. ***Dhammo have rakkhatu dhammacāri***. Indeed, the Dhamma protects one who walks on the path of Dhamma.

As I started to grow more in Dhamma I found I was coming out of the outer appearances which are so deceptive. If the mind is not pure, what is the use of wearing the ochre robes and acting like a renunciate? I was not being true to myself, with the ego, anger, hatred, attachment and ignorance weighing heavy on me. It is not the clothes that matter, it is not the ceremonies, the mantras, the visualizations, the readings of holy scriptures, the rituals. These things don't make a difference. The *real* difference comes when true renunciation springs from the mind, and one works with *sampajañña* (the thorough understanding of impermanence). So I discarded my orange garb. Now I already feel a difference in my mental state and attitude. There is a change from within as I am constantly reminded of *anicca* (impermanence).

To sum up, I feel that this technique is so simple, easy and effective in all respects, and worth practising for the rest of my life. And why did I not come across this kind of Vipassana meditation twenty years ago! Anyway, I shouldn't dwell on the past. It is better late than never!

I have embarked on a very, very long journey. The task is tremendous but the path is clear. With a feeling of gratitude towards Buddha, Dhamma and the Sangha and Goenkaji who has been my constant source of great inspiration, I pledge to stand by and tread on the true and pure path of Dhamma. My head bows low at the altar of Dhamma.

My First Course

by Sarah Bridgland

This talk was given at the International Seminar on the Importance of Vedanā and Sampajañña held at Dhamma Giri in March 1990.

My name is Sarah and I'm ten years old. This is my first time doing a ten-day course and I'm here to tell you my experience doing this ten-day course.

I loved the idea of being able to come to India, but having to do the course was a different story. I do want to, I don't want to, I do, I don't. It was like that for a few weeks, but one day my mother told me to meet Ram Singh and his wife Jagdish. So that morning I walked over with some flowers. Me and my mother sat down on the floor, but Ram Singh said we could not sit on a lower level than him and so we sat on chairs.

I gave him the flowers and said hello, and my mother introduced me and then herself and then told Ram Singh about how my elder brother, David, went to India last year. You could say that my brief visit to Ram Singh was *sukha* (pleasant)— *sukha, sukha,* not an iota of *dukkha* (unsatisfactoriness). "I'm going to India!" I said, and that was definite.

A few weeks later we arrived in India at about two o'clock in the morning Indian time. The next day we set off to Igatpuri (Dhamma Giri). Once we had settled in we went and got ready for an hour's group sit and introduction to meditation and Goenkaji.

Next day after breakfast I got ready for eight o'clock group sit and then went to the hall. A very big amount of females went in and I went along with them. I went to my place near the front, sat down and got comfortable then closed my eyes, but after about ten seconds opened

them again and looked around, and after five minutes everyone was in and a strange talking started. All the time I had my eyes open, but the strange talking said "close your eyes," so I did.

I started concentrating on the area under the nostrils and above the upper lip. Hot, cold, fast, slow, left, right, prickly, smooth, hard, soft— these were all my sensations. But suddenly they all went, they all left me. Where had they all gone? Then soon I realized my mind had wandered, wandered to school, so off I went to find my mind, to find it and bring it back to the area of the lower nostril and upper lip. But when I found it I got pulled into the thoughts of school and my fellow classmates, and this is what happened in all my other hours, half hours, minutes and seconds of all my meditation hours.

Until along came the wonderful technique of Vipassana. Along came day four and we were to learn Vipassana after morning group sit. Vipassana was to be taught and I closed my eyes and got comfortable. This morning, I thought, I couldn't possibly sit through two hours even if it was Vipassana, and I even expressed my feelings to my mother and two friends by the name of Debbie and Uwana who helped me get through the ten days.

But now in the hall I was eager to learn Vipassana and I totally neglected my first thoughts. At last Goenkaji, Mataji and Vimala, the assistant teacher for females, and the male assistant teacher came in and at last I was to learn Vipassana. I paid little attention to Goenka's first minor speech but finally I was taught Vipassana. "Feeling sensations all over the body" and I did. Again I got prickly, smooth, soft, hard, fast, slow and all other sensations over my body. But again my mind wandered, but this time I brought it back and started again.

I was also taught the minor technique of *mettā-bhāvanā.*

To finish of my rather long speech I would like to tell you about a rather important day that probably happens to most people on their courses. This day was around day five and this was probably the best day of the course. That day I was full of anger, meanness, unkindness and wouldn't do anything I didn't want to do, and showed it all immensely. But late that same night I realized that that day was the day that all my *saṅkhāras* didn't like me anymore and decided to go to someone else, and then I suddenly felt happy.

When the course was over I couldn't believe how somebody could ever be so happy as I was that day and practically vowed to myself to come back next year, maybe with my younger brother.

I'm *sukha, sukha, sukha,* not an iota of *dukkha,* a thousand times over.

Thank you.

Anicca is inside of everybody. It is within reach of everybody. Just a look into oneself and there it is—anicca to be experienced...

anicca is, for householders, the gem of life which they will treasure to create a reservoir of calm and balanced energy for their own well-being and for the welfare of society.

—*Sayagyi U Ba Khin*

He Taught Us the Way to Control the Mind

by Kalyani G.

"The most rewarding experience of my life. Life can never be the same again!" were the first words uttered by an American student at the end of ten days of silent meditation. His experience was shared by over 180 Sri Lankans and foreigners who participated in a course of meditation conducted by that great teacher from India, S.N. Goenka, recently in Sri Lanka.

Goenkaji and this course in meditation has subsequently become the subject of much discussion in Buddhist and non-Buddhist circles in Colombo. It may therefore be of interest to readers to recall and recount the experience for the benefit of those who were unable to participate.

The message of Goenkaji was an exposition of the Dhamma by a Master. It was not a message which came in the way of any organized religion. No part of it was in conflict with the preachings or teachings of the great religions. It was, nevertheless, a refreshing breath of fresh air which was exhilarating in every sense of the word.

Goenkaji's message was a simple one. He reminded us that every word, every action has the mind as its forerunner. The mind is supreme. Everything starts in the mind. There is nothing which happens to a person which has not first been conceived in the mind. Emotional states—sadness, anger, joy—harsh words, words of love, murderous thoughts and actions, or physical acts of kindness—all have been conceived and arisen in and from the mind of man.

This mind of ours has always been accepted as being wayward, wandering, shifting like quicksilver, and restless. It is also well-known that it is easier to tame a wild elephant or a horse than to tame and control the mind. If only this could

be done, then all our thoughts, emotions, words, and actions could be controlled. Such control is the key to peace, tranquillity and happiness. Control of the mind comes through the observation of the mind. How does one observe the mind, cultivate a state of self-awareness, and engage in self-observation?

The mind keeps wandering—reliving the past, a past which has gone forever, a past which can never be obtained again; or living in the future, indulging in fantasies—dreaming away, wasting precious psychic energy.

So the first step is to bring the roaming mind back into our bodies and to become aware of our physical bodies. In the so-called "normal" state of being, we get no sense impressions from our bodies unless we are in pain. How do we come back from our wandering to observe ourselves? The simplest way to come within ourselves and to remain in a state of self-awareness, is to be aware of our breath. This is the time-tested and most certain method, and Goenkaji introduced the students of meditation to this. With eyes closed, and seated comfortably, we concentrated on our breath. We observed our breath as we inhaled and exhaled. "Just observe" was his expression, "as if a sentry were standing at the nostrils, observing those who went in and came out."

How simple it sounds—but how difficult it actually was! So long as the breath is hard, heavy or pronounced, one could observe it and be aware of it; but as it gets subtler, it not only becomes harder to observe, but the problem is compounded by the quicksilver mind, slipping away quietly to the past or the future.

Once "discovered" (as we progress, the periods of wandering become shorter), we bring it back—bring our minds back—by breathing more consciously, and feeling the hard breath once again. This is the practice of *Sammā Samādhi* or Right Concentration.

> Almost every thinking man, whatever may be his faith or religion, accepts at an intellectual or philosophical level that all things are transient. We have only to look at an old photograph of ourselves to realize how much we have changed.

The next question that poses itself is whether this is an end in itself. The practice of Right Concentration is important, for it is through such practice that we are able to avoid dissipating our psychic energies (there is no purpose in thinking of the past—it is gone; there is no purpose in dreaming of the future: we must be the masters of the moment). Right Concentration is the vehicle that helps us to attain a higher level of consciousness, a level of awareness that makes it possible to have a "first hand experience" of the true nature of things. This is universal truth; that all things are transient and subject to decay; that we, as well as the world around us, are subject to a state of flux.

Almost every thinking man, whatever may be his faith or religion, accepts at an intellectual or philosophical level that all things are transient. We have only to look at an old photograph of ourselves to realize how much we have changed. I have changed both physically and psychologically. I am not even the person I was last month. Every cell of my body has changed, changed, and changed again. A living body experiences changes every moment. As long as there is

life, there is continuous change. However, only when we are alive can we perceive, feel or experience this tremendous river rolling, rippling and flowing along. Just as we cannot bathe in the same river twice, so with our own lives, but the change is so fast that we can't observe it.

Goenkaji compared it to the electricity in a bulb: though it seems all the while that it is the same electric current that is passing through, there is change occurring within the bulb all the time.

The observance of this change that is going on within us is scientifically possible—and possible in the most simple way. As stated before, in the ordinary state of being we get vague or no sense impressions in our bodies. But if we develop our powers of concentration, then we can penetrate that thin partition between ordinary consciousness and a higher level which enables us to observe the changes taking place within us. Now, we in our conscious state become aware of the changes taking place.

After four days of intense practice in the art of concentration, we were now on the threshold to being introduced into a new experience in consciousness. The concentration which we had developed we now applied to our bodies. Without a revulsion for the unpleasant sensations, or a craving for the pleasant sensations, we learned to just observe the sensations. In the course of such observations, what becomes most apparent to one is that all these sensations arise only to pass away.

The quiet mind, deep in meditation, observes the continuous changes occurring in us, both on the surface and even within. Here we witness—not at an intellectual level or a philosophical level, or even at an emotional or devotional level, but at an actual level—the Truth that all things are transitory, are continuously changing, and will ultimately decay and pass away. We just observe these changes occurring, without aversion to the pains which arise (particularly through long hours of sitting), and without craving for the pleasant sensations we experience whilst meditating. We just observe with equanimity—*upekkhā*. We do not react, we just observe, for both the painful and the pleasant sensations pass away. We thereby train ourselves to be even-tempered. This is the essence of the Middle Path—awareness and equanimity!

Awareness and equanimity are the two principal pillars of the superstructure which is essentially three-tiered. The first tier is *sīla* or morality, the second: *sammā samādhi* (right concentration), and the top tier is *paññā* or wisdom, achieved through *bhāvanā* or meditation. This is the essence of Buddha's teachings.

It is not possible in a short article such as this to relate and recapture the magnitude of the experience—an experience which transported us abruptly into another level of consciousness, a level of consciousness which all of us could experience if only we observed *sīla* and practised *samādhi*. The experience enabled us to realize that what was true of us within (the changing nature of ourselves) was also true of the world outside us. Our relationship to external phenomena changes. In our daily lives we invariably blame the instability of the outer world when anything goes wrong with our lives—never the instability within us. We almost always want to change the world outside us, not the world within us...

The introspection, the self-observation, made us alive to the illusion that is "I," alive to the realization that there is no permanent and unchangeable "I." Each time we think or say "I," this "I" is different. Some "I"s are of course stronger than others. Religion, caste, traditions, even education, could create very strong "I"s which dominate the weaker "I"s.

Many were the realizations—some almost commonplace, some truly astounding. Yes, the experiences were many. To all of us who had the good fortune to participate in this meditation course conducted by Goenkaji, it certainly was an experience without parallel—an experience for which we shall be eternally grateful to Goenkaji and those others who made this possible.

It was undoubtedly unforgettable.

A Catholic Priest on Vipassana

by Father Peter Lourdes

The following reflection was written by Father Peter Lourdes, consulting psychologist and programme director of the National Vocation Service Centre in Pune, India.

In February 1986, I attended a ten-day course in Vipassana offered by S.N. Goenka at the Vipassana International Academy (V.I.A.) at Igatpuri. With me was a group of four Catholic priests, two brothers and twenty-eight sisters. A priest and two sisters from my staff also joined me. I programme and direct a six-month course for Formators (church personnel in charge of the training of future brothers, sisters and priests). The Unit on Spirituality calls for an experience of other forms of spirituality respected in this part of the world. All of us were participating in this experience.

I am a priest with a degree in psychology from Rome and a Ph.D. from Loyola University of Chicago. My doctoral thesis was "The implications of the Transcendental Meditation (TM) Program for Counselling Psychology." In a course in Comparative Mysticism at Loyola, I was asked to present TM to the class. My background in psychotherapy, comparative mysticism, TM and my personal life in a religious order were tremendous assets during my Vipassana days at V.I.A., and I seem to have touched something I was looking for over the years. I returned to Pune and continued Vipassana together with a group of sisters and priests of whom I am Spiritual Director.

People who know I am a priest sometimes wonder what a Catholic priest is doing in a Buddhist centre! Roger Coreless of Duke University reports that Thomas Merton remarked he felt more in tune with D.T. Suzuki (a Zen Buddhist) than with the average Catholic mass-goer. I am no Merton, but I felt the same in Igatpuri and often feel so in my ministry. Spirituality has been a lifelong quest for me. I have dared to search for it in waters outside the Bark of Peter.

How does that square with my Catholic affiliation? I think Vipassana is one way of reaching the goals of the mystical spirituality of my Catholic tradition.

My Catholic tradition also has a theological side to it. That is the side which is usually transmitted to us from conventional catechisms, church-going, family upbringing, preaching and so on. The theory (or theology if you will) of the Vipassana technique does not generally fit my Catholic theological world view. But I do not think that is important.

The reason why I do not think it is important is this: I consider my Christian theology just one way of interpreting and talking about transcendent experience. I think the experience is more important than talking about it. In the experience, I feel closer to the mystics of our Christian tradition, and to those of our Hindu, Muslim and Buddhist traditions, than to our theologians and mass-goers.

In my Christian tradition, I think, "theological spirituality" is more dominant than the mystical one. I seem to find that in Goenka's variety of spirituality, the mystical is all. It reaches out so heart-warmingly to the really Real and will not settle for anything less.

Does not the Christian tradition have the same thrust? I believe it does, but it does not seem to have a simple and clear-cut method like Vipassana. Whatever methods it had may have died with the monasteries.

Where I am at present in my spiritual journey, I feel hungry for the ineffable God of our humanity rather than the talked-about God of our theology and Sunday school.

Although I do not wish to be messianic, I often feel sad that I cannot interest all my fellow Christians in the mystical dimensions of our common human thirst for the Beyond.

I invite all of you to join me and all human beings in an attempt to hear and march to a different drum right within the rank and file of our own religious groups, or outside.

A Western Christian Looks East

by Fr. Daniel J. O'Hanlon S.J.

This article appeared in "Studies in the Spirituality of Jesuits," Vol. XVI May 1984, No. 3.

When I was in my early fifties, after well over thirty years as a Jesuit, I began to be interested in enriching my prayer and meditation, indeed my whole process of human and spiritual growth, through contact with traditional Asian psycho-spiritual paths. Here is a description of what that experience has been like for me...

In December 1973, after I had been in India several months, I did a ten-day Vipassana meditation course with a remarkable man by the name of Goenka, a lay teacher from Burma. About twelve hours a day were devoted to sitting meditation practice, at times gathered together with him in the meditation hall and at times in our own space. I say space and not room, since because of the large number of participants, the majority of them young Westerners, the physical accommodations were very primitive. Along with a couple of others I had a few square feet of space on the solid stone floor of a small curtained-off area of the Benares Burmese Buddhist Temple. And that December in Benares was a wintry one. The practice which we worked at hour after hour, day after day, was simply awareness of sensation in our bodies, just attending to these sensations without either clinging to them or pushing them away. That was the basic practice.

Although I had never been taught this kind of practice before, I did not, even at that time, feel it to be in any way out of tune with my previous experience of meditation and prayer. Somewhat later—I don't remember exactly how much later—when I read *The Cloud of Unknowing* for the first time and reread the writings of St. John of the Cross, I found descriptions in a Christian framework of a kind of awareness much like that which was part of the Vipassana practice taught by Goenka. Of course, I had learned along the way many other methods of stilling the "monkey mind" and allowing the

When I read *The Cloud of Unknowing* for the first time, and reread the writings of St. John of the Cross, I found descriptions in a Christian framework of a kind of awareness much like that which was part of the Vipassana practice taught by Goenka.

awareness of inner reality deeper than words or concepts to come alive. But I mention Goenka explicitly because I think those ten days in the cold and drafty Benares Buddhist temple were especially powerful. I gained a better sense of what Buddhism is all about from those ten days of practice than from all the books and lectures I had previously been through. I had begun this sabbatical year with the conviction that direct experience of these religious traditions was the best way to really get to know them, and these ten days confirmed that conviction in me.

Let me illustrate one of the ways in which just that one ten-day experience changed me. When the ten days were over, I got on a crowded third-class train for Bodh Gaya, an overnight journey eastward from Benares. As frequently happens, there was no place to sleep but on the floor in one of the crowded compartments, and I was lucky to find even that instead of having to sit or stand. Several young Bengali lads on their way back to Calcutta saw me there and began to poke fun at this "old Western hippie." Now one might expect that under the circumstances, trying to sleep on the floor of a moving train after a week and a half of strenuous days sitting in silent meditation, I would find it hard not to answer in kind, or at least be pretty annoyed. What actually happened was that I too found the situation amusing, laughed and joked about it with them and they ended up sharing their food with me.

But to come back to the connection between my earlier patterns of spiritual practice and things I learned from the East: I think that the principal new thing for me was the discovery of very simple and effective ways of stilling the agitation of mind and body in order to allow a deeper, wordless kind of awareness to come alive…

I made two new discoveries through contact with Asian practice. First, I found that one can move toward the goal of prayer, beyond just words and concepts, without necessarily *beginning* with words and concepts. I discovered that by such simple things as watching my breath, observing sensations in my body, practicing hatha yoga with emphasis on simple immediate awareness, and chanting or silently repeating a mantra with no attention paid to analysis of the words, it was possible to move into the later stages of the process Guigo described (as contemplation). My first discovery, then: one does not *need* to begin with words or ideas.

My second discovery was that it is possible to allow love to simply emerge out of awareness, without making its cultivation the first object of concern. Note what I am saying here: not that love is unimportant, not that its direct cultivation is a poorer path to follow, but that there are other ways to go as well. In the East great attention is paid to awareness, free of clinging to what is there or trying to get rid of it. More attention is given to this simple awareness, this bare immediate attention, than to the direct cultivation or excitation of feelings and desires. This practice seems to spring out of the conviction that love and compassion are the natural movement of our true self. When the surface mind and disordered desires are still, the true self awakens without need of any further assistance from us. Indeed, our clumsy efforts to poke at it and deliberately rouse it often have the same effect as poking at a sea anemone. It simply closes up tight. But give it stillness, leave it undisturbed, and it opens wide like a water lily in full bloom...

As I continued to enrich my life of prayer and meditation with Eastern resources, I found that there were many effective ways of entering into it without beginning with words, and that the direct practice of simple immediate awareness released in me without further effort such "affective" fruits as compassion, love, patience, and empathy.

Vipassana: My Spiritual Pilgrimage

by Mohammed Arif Joiya

In 1976 I went to Arogya Mandir, a nature cure institute at Gorakhpur, and benefited greatly from my stay there. In those days I also read many spiritual books and entered into religious discussions with various colleagues. All this awakened me but did not quench my thirst. On the contrary, it made me more agitated and spurred me on to a further search. I was looking for a teacher who would really make me experience the truth. I wanted to realize within myself the esoteric expressions in the form of living peace and energy. Not being satisfied with entertaining discourses, I wanted to realize and experience the truth for myself.

Temples, mosques, pagodas, and *gurudwaras* [Sikh temples] along with all the scriptures could not hold my mind. I was still overwhelmed by an empty, unsatisfied life. In such a wounded state, I opened myself and expressed my spiritual aspirations before Dr. Vithaldas Modi, founder of Arogya Mandir, and demanded a way out. He advised me to attend a Vipassana meditation course and sent me a small pamphlet and application form for Vipassana. I read and understood it, but was frightened: "Oh! This is the religion of Buddhists, atheists. These Buddhists don't believe in Soul and God. What can they teach? I am a Muslim. I cannot commit this crime." But my heart within again said that the advice of Dr. Modi should be obeyed. "Why should he wish ill of me? Whatever he advises is certainly for my benefit and welfare. Let me try and see." So I went to the Vipassana International Meditation Centre near Hyderabad in February 1978 to attend a Vipassana course.

I arrived late but was pleased to find the place very quiet and peaceful. Mr. Bachubhai Shah, who was an organizer, received me with great love and hospitality. He said, " Arifbhai, you have missed a day but I am sure that Goenkaji will accept you on the course. Don't worry. You may take a bath and have breakfast while I go and speak to him about you." I was pleased with this pure, affectionate reception and reassurance from Mr. Bachubhai.

While I was waiting I started looking around at the students observing Noble Silence. And I was experiencing a slight fever which I had been feeling from the moment I had stepped onto this holy land. This was the fever of some unknown fear. I felt that my ego was going to be sacrificed, and I was ready for it.

Goenkaji sent for me. I went, bowed down and smiled. He and his wife were seated on chairs. He appeared to be a scientist, a doctor, or a literary person.

"Come and sit down."
I sat on the border of the carpet and smiled.
"What is the nature of your work?"
"I am a physical training teacher in Udasar, Sir."
"Hmmm... What is the problem?"
"Stammering speech, Sir. A little difficulty."
"Okay. It will be alright. There will be instructions in the evening. Until then observe your breath and remain aware of it."
"Very good, Sir."
"Then go," he said smilingly.
I bowed down, paid respects, and smilingly came out of the hall.

I started thinking, "What sort of Guru have I got? He is a worldly person. Could there be a Guru like this? Married! Householder! No beard, no moustache, clean shaven? No marks on the forehead? No long hair? No ochre robes? He had on a terylene half-sleeved shirt, and colourful checked *lungi*. At least he should have been wearing *khādi* (home-spun) cloth. Absolutely modern, very ordinary. How can he teach meditation? Never mind, I have come, so let me try and see."

After a short while when I, along with hundreds of meditators, started following the instructions of Goenkaji of observing and remaining aware of the breath and feeling its touch, a silent voice within me arose and whispered, "Oh! This is exactly what I was looking for. I've got it. I must work hard. I'm already one day late so I should not waste a single moment." I started meditating with great enthusiasm.

In the evening the instructions were given. Goenkaji said, "Repeat what I say in Pāli." I repeated that for the duration of the meditation course I would abstain from killing, theft, sexual misconduct, speaking lies and taking intoxicants. I liked the five precepts. But along with them I had to repeat, "I take refuge in Buddha. I take refuge in Dhamma. I take refuge in Sangha." At that moment I refrained, but later there was a little discontentment in the mind. "Look, Modiji trapped me. He put me in a whole new position as if a snake has swallowed a rat. Oh! Khan Saheb, these people have sunk your ship. Now go in your society as a Buddhist."

At any rate I recovered and started to observe the breath. Again the same train of thought came. But when the awareness of breath steadied a little, this problem automatically and gradually resolved itself. Now I didn't want to think of these problems. I started progressing. During the rest period, even after finishing lunch, etc., I continued meditation. The fact that I was a day late and other meditators must be farther advanced inspired me more. I continued meditation without any other thought.

A television screen started shining before my closed eyes. I very clearly perceived the shaping of dormant impurities of the mind starting to arise and pass away. It was like the dirtiest, wildest film I had ever seen. Such obnoxious prejudices appeared which made me feel like vomiting. But I understood at the same time that it was doing me good. Impurities were coming out. It was a good thing.

On the fourth day Vipassana was given. A new voice arose within my heart. "I have practised this technique some time in the past. It is very simple and familiar!" I continued to progress from the gross to the subtle.

By day seven I realized that this technique of meditation is so simple that any child or even an illiterate person can learn and effectively practise it. Just to observe the natural breath with closed eyes and continued awareness that it is coming in, going out, and it is touching somewhere. Continuing to observe the breath, the witnessing faculty of the mind establishes automatically. And then one has to observe objectively the sensations throughout the body from head to toe in a particular order. Sensations may be pleasant or painful. Both have to be observed with equanimity. By repeating the same process over and over again, quiet concentration of the mind and equanimity gradually increase.

As I slept that night, a terrible thing happened. It was almost midnight. I saw that a very ferocious demon had seized my neck with both hands and had started shaking my head around and around and said, "Oh evil soul! You have brought me here in this ashram! Just wait, I will show you." And with enormous force he threw my body on the ground. Along with it the very sweet voice of Goenkaji came to my ears, "Son, do not worry. Come near me. Come, do not be frightened." I awoke fearful and frightened, looked around with open eyes and saw the foreign meditators who were my roommates fast asleep. Immediately I understood that it was a nightmare. It was a play of my mind. It was a trick to force me to leave the course by any means. Impurities were being eradicated. All the torture was due to that. I came out of the room; saw the lights on and the trees standing with their branches and leaves swinging and singing, as if some quiet festival was being celebrated. I started listening and then realized, "Oh! This is a conspiracy of the unconscious mind. I now understand. I am not leaving without completing the course." I relaxed, smilingly returned to bed,

and meditating while lying down, eventually went to sleep.

> I would like to tell my young educated Muslims that they should really try Vipassana. Vipassana is the only solution to all the problems of mankind, because it is universal and it gives such positive fruits.

Dawn broke. There was meditation in the hall. After lunch I was overwhelmed with another experience. I felt that my head and hands were swinging as though they belonged to someone else. I was in a very tranquil, detached, equanimous witnessing state. "Oh Gotama Buddha! How did you discover this unique meditation technique? You kept on teaching people this sacred art. And once again this art has become available for people's welfare. Salutations to you, my Lord. Again and again I prostrate before your compassionate feet. Endless prostrations." I now understood the meaning of "I take refuge in Buddha" as refuge in one's own *bodhi* or enlightenment, not the personality of Siddhārtha Gotama. The meaning of "I take refuge in Dhamma" is that one has to be established in one's own true nature, not in any sectarian religion. The meaning of "I take refuge in Sangha" is to take refuge in those noble ones who have become well-established in Dhamma, whatever their race, colour or nationality. From this sacred moment onwards, the word death, full of theories and tears, just melted from the book of my life and flowed away like melted snow. Oh, no! No being dies. Death is impossible. Everyone keeps on moving on the journey according to one's own actions. And the final destination of the journey is *nirvana*. Now I understood what one's own religion is and what the religion of others is. Without purifying the mind of impurities by Vipassana and realizing our own nature, life is lived in the religion of others. Living in one's own nature is **Svadharma,** the true Dhamma.

On the ninth day a new meditation technique was taught—the technique of *mettā bhāvanā* whereby one shares one's own merits with beings all around. This meditation filled me with love and compassion and made me cry.

When I came out of the course I felt that I had no enemies. All were my relatives. My mind was filled with love, compassion and sympathetic joy towards everyone. I thought that I must have performed some good action in a past life, and as a consequence of that I was born in the lap of the affectionate and compassionate Mother-India: salutations to you, Mother-India. Now I really understood why India is designated as the "world teacher." A sort of pride arose in me to be an Indian. I felt one with all created beings of the earth.

Now the only religion for me is to help miserable people to be free of their miseries: may all beings walk on the path of pure Dhamma; may all be religious in the true sense of the term. By adopting the practice of Vipassana I have found

the right direction in life and this has made life worthwhile. The path is long but it becomes straight and easy.

Vipassana has naturally helped me to come out of bad habits. It has given me the strength to smile in desperate situations. It has also given me the strength to discharge my responsibilities. I feel less nervous. Day by day I am gaining strength to address bigger and bigger audiences. My life was incomplete without Vipassana.

I would like to tell my young educated Muslims that they should really try Vipassana and see the results. It is a necessity today that people of all different walks of life unite. By escaping from harmful sectarianism they can help establish a really strong national unity. Vipassana is the only solution to all the problems of mankind, because it is universal and it gives such positive fruits.

I bow my head down to my teacher Sri Satya Narayan Goenka and assistant teacher Dr. Vithaldas Modi.

Salutations to Buddha!

Salutations to Dhamma!

Salutations to Sangha!

Appreciations

I have realized that meditation is a unique course which could show me a new life. Being of Iranian nationality and Muslim religion, I heartily advise not only all my Muslim brothers to participate in this wonderful technique, but also all human beings of different religions and to all humanists. So far I have attended four courses, and the more I come to the camps, the more I gain something new which is really beneficial in my life. Being more faithful to the masses, and realizing the nature of myself and the others, I had gone through many psychological books; but I found that while psychology is the foundation of the life, this meditation technique is the base of psychology itself.

May all human beings develop their wisdom, purify themselves to reach an absolute humanity through Buddha's thought: *sīla, samādhi, paññā.*

— *Khusrow Dehdasht Heidari*
Hyderabad
December 1976

I am so much impressed by the course that I can not resist expressing my appreciation, but on the other hand, the fear of underestimating the real merit and the beauty of it do not permit me to dare make any comment but to suggest that the proper way to comprehend and appreciate the Vipassana meditation course will be to experience it personally.

— *His Excellency Mohammed Mehrdel*
Bombay

The basis of any healthy harmonious society is always the
healthy and harmonious individuals who populate it.
Only if each individual has a pure, peaceful mind
can we expect peace in society.

—*S.N. Goenka*

I Have Found My Path

by Dr. Chandrakala

I heard of Vipassana ten or twelve years ago, but my first encounter with it came at Dhamma-thali, Jaipur in July 1987.

For the first three days of the course the practice of Anapana was followed continuously. The technique appeared acceptable and easily tangible as well, but to practise it was hard. We tried to control our mind with the help of our natural breath. Until then I was aware only of external, imaginary means of taming the mind, so in Anapana it was amazing to find self-reliance in the object of focusing the mind.

We were taught Vipassana on the fourth day and with that my course started as well. The required hard labour of the practice together with the daily one hour sittings of *adhiṭṭhāna* (sitting without moving) threatened to be beyond me. On the fifth day the intense heat produced in the body totally disheartened me, and my enthusiasm started ebbing. To top everything, at times I could not even grasp the technique of Vipassana properly.

I had great apprehension in my mind regarding sensations which we were told was the foundation for the practice of Vipassana. When I could not work any further I put off working with sensation, and spent time working on Anapana. I made a firm resolve to keep the practice going with full allegiance and devotion.

After *mettā* (loving-kindness meditation) on day ten I had an unprecedented experience. I felt a happy change in and out of my body. It felt light and weightless and full of rapture; the mind too was highly delighted, inundated with happiness. Cheerfulness appeared to be scattered all over me. At the conclusion of the course I decided to take another course right then and there.

Having wandered for long in the quest for the ultimate, stumbling at every door, being frustrated in every way, from every place, thoroughly disappointed, dejected, weary and exhausted I arrived at the gate of the Vipassana Centre and the refreshing touch of soothing vibrations granted me great relief. It appeared as though I had arrived at my destination. In my heart there was devotion for Lord Buddha; therefore it was easy and natural to have faith in the path shown by him. Very soon the coloured curtains started shifting from the eyes, the heavy coatings of paint and varnish started peeling off the intellect and all illusions and delusions were removed. I was relieved of the beliefs, empty rites and rituals, and baseless blind faith. A great load appeared to have lifted off my mind and intellect.

The true path of Dhamma was revealed and understood. As soon as I found Vipassana all my hustle and bustle came to an end. Now there is absolutely no need to run and wander about. All quintessence is confined within this three and a half cubit long body. Herein lies the attainment and also the means to attain it. Herein lies our bondage and also our freedom. This is our suffering and is also the way out of that suffering. Inside also lies the mostly-only-talked-about ultimate truth.

Some wise person has said, "Blessed are those who have found their work." I am really fortunate that I have found my path. My quest is accomplished.

Breath of Freedom: Anapana in Prison

by Michael Lane

Prison inmates lie at the bottom of the social ladder. They are despised by some, who regard them as no better than subhumans or animals. Inmates must live with this humiliating knowledge and are likely to project it onto themselves: "If I am an animal, I will act like one." The truth is that we all suffer from the same dual ailment of attachment and aversion. These self-made complexities generate frustration and may erupt in verbal or physical violence. Those of us who have so far managed to escape incarceration (whether by habit, brains, or luck) have no reason to feel proud as long as we are still sick.

The medicine for this sickness of complexity is simplicity, according to assistant teacher Dr. Sneh Jindal. In her twelve years in the Psychology Department at the Ohio Department of Rehabilitation and Correction, she left a legacy of "Anapana" (breath meditation) that continues to work changes in the lives of inmates and ex-inmates. The practice she gave them was simple—focus on the breath coming in, going out, coming in, going out and then focus on sensation on the upper lip and nostrils, where the breath passes. That's all—so simple that no one can do it and remain tangled in complexities.

Inmates' and ex-inmates' own words in letters to Dr. Jindal and others, testify to the condition they had faced. Stressful lives had led to their crime and incarceration in the first place. On top of that, the hardships of prison life and the cynical indifference or contempt of prison officials made their lives perpetually stressful. Ten inmates, in a joint letter to the editor of the prison newsletter, wrote, "We... were confused in life and faced a variety of charges and vari-ous crimes. We were very secure in our ways of thinking and sure that all others, plus the whole world, were wrong. We assured ourselves that our actions were right and that society had no right to put us in prison. This very idea created anger, dissatisfaction, and a very strong desire for revenge."

One inmate wrote, "My feelings were of a person that didn't care about life itself. I had a bad outlook on life and didn't really care what really was in the future for me. All I did was live day by day, and tomorrow didn't matter... I didn't go along with none of their programs... I didn't bother with too many people, for I was a loner and wanted it to stay that way. Most of the time I found myself fighting and landing right back in the hole." Others reported similar experiences: "I approached [everything] with indifference, defiance, hostility"—"I was depressed most of the time, and my mind seemed to be running all the time. My way of thinking was always on the negative side of things. It was hard for me to concentrate on any one thing for very long"—"The prison system does something to us. A lot of us build in our system an extreme amount of anger."

Inmates attended meditation sessions with Dr. Jindal for two hours a week and were urged to practise on their own daily in the morning and in the evening. One reported, "After a couple of weeks I seemed to be able to relax more, and I was less depressed. I became less short-tempered with my fellow inmates... After... about three to four weeks I was able to totally block out the noises and confusion around me." A self-described "six-time loser" (working on his sixth sentence) wrote, "I soon learned through practice and a sincere desire to change that I could prevent anger from welling up within me simply by reminding myself that only I could make me angry... Meditation has taught me how to relax completely. It puts me in a frame of mind that allows me to deal with the ordinary stress and strain that will creep up on a person as he goes about his daily life. Even being locked away in a prison doesn't bother me the way it used to." Another found, "In becoming aware, one learns that he himself is solely responsible for the way he feels, thinks, and acts." Letter after letter tells the same story: "She is showing us how to get rid of this anger"—"I stay poised, serene, balanced, and calm"—"By being able to go within myself, I have learned how to make the necessary change in my attitude, thinking and behavior"—"Your training has helped me so much"—"She helped me find myself"—"I feel better inside and about

> **W**e now realize nearly all the difficulties that we have had to face were due to our own projections. Meditation has paved the path for us to live and grow spiritually, physically, mentally, and morally both within and outside the walls of confinement.

things around me since I started this therapy"—"I have found the right way to deal with the pressures of life-stress, something I thought I would always be a slave to"—"You taught me and others how to meditate, how to relax, how to get rid of anger"—"You've shown me a magic ingredient." The ten authors of the joint letter wrote, "This meditation technique... is very simple and understanding. It is... a positive and sure approach towards self-awareness, inner development...

We now realize that nearly all of the difficulties that we have had to face throughout our past were due to our own projections... The practice of meditation... has paved the path for us to live and grow spiritually, physically, mentally, and morally both within and outside of the walls of confinement." The same letter expresses the conviction that meditation did not challenge, but rather enhanced, their various religious faiths.

The following experience is unusually complete, interesting, and well-told and gives a hint of Dr. Jindal's good-humored perseverance that won the hearts of the men: "My first unusual [meditation] experience was frightening and left me feeling that I'd entered into something that I could neither understand or cope with. I wanted no part of something that had frightened me and which I could not explain...Dr. Jindal, despite my telling her not to send me any more passes, continued to send passes for me." The writer goes on, "It's difficult to say when the transformation took place... At any rate, I decided to really give it my sincere efforts for a few days. As the days passed, I found myself drawn deeper and deeper into the joys of meditation and the peace I found in, or as a result of, meditation. It's difficult to explain how it is that in learning to expect nothing—no particular experience, that is—you begin to receive so much. Meditation instills in you a kind of unselfishness, a nonpossessiveness, that seems to provide you with everything."

Although Dr. Jindal, whom inmates came to love "as a mother," is no longer in the Psychology Department, Anapana is there to stay: "I meditate every night... Meditation is a way of life for me now"—"I meditate two times a day, never less than an hour and a half"—"Meditation will be a part of my life"—"Meditation is my way of life… and I shall have it with me for every step of the remainder."

These are powerful lessons in self-discovery and hope from a group of men for whom one might think there was little hope. The simple technique of Anapana turned around the lives of men who were considered to be, and considered themselves to be, failures. They tried it, and it proved its solid worth in their own practical experience. Let's take this lesson to heart and, if we have not already done so, take a first step—even if it has to be a baby step— toward breaking down the invisible, and therefore more effective, walls that imprison us.

The above excerpts are from numerous letters written by students of Anapana at the Chillicothe Correctional Institute, Chillicothe, Ohio, U.S.A.

What is happiness? For all that science has achieved in the field of materialism, are the peoples of the world happy? They may find sensual pleasures off and on, but in their heart of hearts, they are not happy when they realize what has happened, what is happening and what may happen next. Why? This is because, while man has mastery over matter, he is still lacking in mastery over his mind.

—*Sayagyi U Ba Khin*

How Vipassana Helped Free Me from Drugs

by Praveen Ramakrishnan

My introduction into Vipassana was by sheer fate. Even today, it amazes me that such a fickle-minded person as me could change and develop a strong sense of willpower.

I was led into the world of narcotics at the age of fifteen, upon my admission into college in 1978. First, mild intoxicants and then—since one finds dissatisfaction in milder forms of pleasure—I moved on to the use of heroin, and its derivatives. This habit of mine started initially just for the thrill of it, but I began to realize that I could do nothing without the assistance of the drug. I tried many times to reason with myself, but since I lacked willpower, I could never face the fact that I was a drug addict. Soon the matter came to be known by my near and dear ones. I lost face in society, and even after trying to quit the habit, I was drawn to the drug because of an emptiness which no amount of reasoning could help.

Soon the hospital trips started. I was detoxified many times but the effect would last for a maximum period of one month. Then there would be a relapse. The counselling from the doctors, who were purely commercially motivated, had stopped having the mild impact it had once made on me. My studies started faltering. The peace at home was destroyed. Soon even my own family members were against me. Fortunately, they had not given up on me entirely. My life became intolerable.

One day, out of the blue, one of my father's close friends, who had taken a ten-day course of Vipassana, convinced my father that a course or two would help me, and that even if it failed, I had nothing to lose. So, in March 1983, I made a trip to the hospital and was detoxified for the last time. Then my journey to Dhammagiri started.

I was brought to Dhammagiri against my wishes, and my first impression of the place was of an open jail with closed boundaries.

The camp was conducted by an assistant teacher, and on entry into the place, I was taken to be introduced to him. A Dhamma worker was then assigned for my welfare, and I checked in. Now the journey began.

The course began as usual with Anapana. Since my mind was not used to even the mildest forms of concentration without any external help, I found it extremely difficult. I thought about running away on the first day, but I knew that without any money, I would not get very far. Therefore I decided to stay, with a little compulsion from the Dhamma worker. The love shown by him was one of the turning points. Though he was only a year or two older than me, the maturity and the wisdom he possessed were far beyond my comprehension. I tried to make him angry, but he would not change his outlook towards me. This further encouraged me, and then Vipassana was taught on the fourth day. Initially I would not adhere to the rule of *adhiṭṭhāna* (strong determination) but on the ninth day I decided to give it a try. I managed to sit through the torture of a whole hour without changing my posture, and that somehow opened my outlook. I decided that if this pain could be tolerated for an hour, then in the same manner, I would be able to give up drugs, though the task was not an easy one.

Some rules of the camp were amended for my convenience. The rules of noble silence and seriousness were waived. Also, I was served dinner, which was to my benefit, since I was physically quite weak.

After I got out of the camp, my first thought was to go to Bombay, and to have a mild dose of the drug. But on my arrival, I found that my craving was reduced. I decided to put it off for a day. The day turned into two, and then day by day I found out that I could do without the drug. I have been free of drugs for the last six years, and the craving for the drug is no longer there.

I returned to Dhammagiri in 1986, and served and sat courses for nine months, which helped me to further strengthen my foundation in life, and to improve my practice.

In conclusion, the pains which were brought on during every withdrawal process, which made me succumb to the drug, were finally eliminated with the help of Vipassana. Now, I feel that I am a socially useful and normal human being.

The Vipassana Research Institute

The Vipassana Research Institute

An Introduction

The Vipassana Research Institute (V.R.I.) was established in 1985 for the purpose of conducting research into the sources and applications of the Vipassana technique. V.R.I. is adjacent to the Vipassana International Academy (V.I.A.), known as Dhamma Giri ("hill of Dhamma"), located in the small town of Igatpuri in the state of Maharashtra, India. This small town is 136 kms (c. eighty-five miles) northeast of Bombay in the Western Ghat mountains. V.I.A. is one of the world's largest centres for the practice of Vipassana, offering on-going meditation courses for up to 500 people per course, throughout the year.

Goenkaji realized the importance of establishing a research institute when, eight years ago, he began to teach courses on the *Satipaṭṭhāna Sutta*, the main discourse in which the Buddha systematically explains the technique of Vipassana. Goenkaji noticed that students attending the Satipaṭṭhāna courses, who are studying the words of the Buddha while at the same time applying them in their meditation practice, feel inspired and filled with gratitude. They experience the positive quality of confidence that comes when they compare their own experience with the Buddha's words. Naturally, some of them feel inspired to undertake further study; and, to provide this opportunity, the Vipassana Research Institute was established.

The Institute's research work focuses on two main areas: translation and publication of the Pāli texts, and research into the application of Vipassana in daily life.

Pāli was the *lingua franca* of northern India twenty-five centuries ago, the dialect in which the Buddha taught. Just as Sanskrit is the canonical language of Hinduism, and Latin the canonical language of Catholicism, Pāli is the classical language in which the teachings of the Buddha have been preserved. The Pāli sources are the *Tipiṭaka* (the Pāli canon); the commentaries, called the *Aṭṭhakathā*; the sub-commentaries, called *Ṭīkā* and other sub-subcommentaries such as *Anu-ṭīkā, Madhu-ṭīkā,* etc.

While it is lesser-known than other classical languages, Pāli has its own august tradition. Within three months after the Buddha passed into **parinibbāna** (the final extinction of a fully liberated being), a special council of five hundred **arahants** (enlightened ones) was convened. Their express purpose was to collect and arrange the voluminous teachings of the Buddha, whose ministry had spanned forty-five years. They organized the Buddha's teaching into what is now commonly known as the *Tipiṭaka* (which means literally "three baskets"). The *Tipiṭaka* consists of three collections: the *Vinaya-piṭaka* (collection of monastic discipline); the *Sutta-piṭaka* (collection of popular discourses); and the *Abhidhamma-piṭaka* (collection of profound teachings).

The collected teachings of the Buddha were maintained in an oral tradition until several centuries after the conclusion of the first Great Council. The *Tipiṭaka* is a vast record, in forty-one volumes, containing 82,000 discourses given by the Buddha, and 2,000 discourses given by his chief disciples. The commentarial literature is also extensive, exceeding the *Tipiṭaka* in length.

Since the first Great Council, five other councils of monks and scholars have been held to review and purify the Pāli canon, the most recent council having been held in Burma in 1954–56. This demonstrates the concerted effort, consistent in different languages and countries through 2,500 years, to maintain the purity of the teaching by keeping the recorded words of the Buddha as close as possible to the original.

While the *Tipiṭaka* and commentarial literature are available in the languages and scripts of the different Theravada Buddhist countries, they are, unfortunately, out of print in Devanāgarī (the script of Hindi, Sanskrit and many other Indian languages). Therefore, the words of the Buddha are not readily available to those who speak the languages of the country in which the Buddha's teachings originated.

V.R.I. has entered the entire Pāli canon, its *Aṭṭhakathā*, and *Ṭīkā* on computer in Devanāgarī and is preparing to publish simultaneously the *Tipiṭaka, Aṭṭhakathā* and *Ṭīkā*, not only for its own research purposes, but for the use of various educational and research institutions in India and abroad. In this series the first set of eleven volumes of Dīghanikāya with its commentaries and sub-commentaries is now available. Eleven volumes of Majjhima-nikāya, the second set, are under print. Each volume will contain a critical introduction highlighting the relevance of the various *suttas* (discourses) to Vipassana meditation. Translation into Hindi will follow the publication of the Pāli texts. The Institute is also publishing the Pāli texts in Roman script. At present, only those texts which have not been published by the Pāli Text Society, London, are being published.

V.R.I. has also produced a CD-ROM in 1997, which contains the entire *Tipiṭaka, Aṭṭhakathās, Ṭīkās* and *Anuṭīkās*, as authenticated by the Sixth Council (*Chaṭṭha Saṅgāyana*). This is available in Devanāgarī, Burmese and Roman scripts, and offers an easy-to-use search and navigation facility through the voluminous text, serving as a valuable tool for those researching the teaching of the Buddha

Work has started on a new version of the CD ROM which will contain more *Aṭṭhakathās, Ṭīkās,* books on grammar, a Pāli-English dictionary in Roman script, and Ashokan inscriptions in Devanāgarī script. It will also include two more scripts: Thai and Sinhalese.

In addition to researching the Pāli texts, the Institute conducts research into the personal and interpersonal effects of Vipassana meditation. This work includes studying the effects of controlling and purifying the mind, and improved moral conduct and harmonious personality development, which is the result of practising Vipassana. The application of Vipassana in the areas of health, education and social development is also being studied This research will enable a comparison with the results that are mentioned in the Pāli texts and the commentaries.

From time to time, V.R.I. sponsors international seminars on various aspects of the research work as it applies to the actual experience of Vipassana. Their special feature is the opportunity for the participants to practise Vipassana in a ten-day course prior to the presentation of the seminar papers. The experiential aspect of these conferences has proven to be popular, as well as beneficial. In a very tangible way, the practice of meditation throws light on the research presented in the papers.

Over the centuries, some of the terms used in the Pāli texts have lost their original meanings, and have not been clearly interpreted in the currently-available translations. This fact becomes evident to a serious student of Vipassana, when, through practice, one grasps the deeper significance of these terms. When we consider the relevance of the technique in transforming individuals and, through them, social groups, we can appreciate the importance of thorough study of the precise meanings of terms used in the Pāli sources. Right understanding aids in right practice.

Clearly, the research work is best done by those with direct experience of the Buddha's teaching. V.R.I. offers an annual year-long residential Vipassana and Pāli Studies Programme. Those who participate, both students and teachers, are regular meditators. Since its inception in 1986, more than one hundred students have completed the programme, some of whom are currently assisting in the research work. The programme provides a foundation in both the theory and practice of Vipassana. Periods of academic study are alternated with participation in the V.I.A. meditation programme. Daily meditation practice, intensive retreats, and service at the Academy are integral parts of the curriculum: they give depth to the academic experience, and this in turn deepens the experience of meditation and service. This combination of scholarly and meditative approaches makes the Pāli programme unique. V.R.I. is one of the few places in the world where Dhamma students can integrate both *pariyatti* (theory) and *paṭipatti* (what Goenkaji calls "the gem set in gold") in one setting.

The Institute also publishes works of historical research and interest to Vipassana meditators, such as this journal.

Presented here are a few short papers which were prepared for some of the earlier seminars.

From time to time, V.R.I. sponsors international seminars on various aspects of the research work as it applies to the actual experience of Vipassana.

The Gem Set in Gold: *Pariyatti* with *Paṭipatti*

by S.N. Goenka

The following article by Goenkaji, inaugurating the Vipassana Research Institute, appeared in the Hindi language Vipashyanā Patrikā, January–February 1985. It has been translated and slightly adapted.

On 19 January 1971, my dear teacher Sayagyi U Ba Khin, to whom I am ever grateful, passed away. It was always the deep wish of Sayagyi to help repay Burma's debt to the Buddha and to the land of the Buddha, India, by re-establishing the Dhamma there in the country of its birth. He hoped that the Ganges of Dhamma, which long ago flowed from India to Burma, could now be channelled back to the land of its source in order to slake the thirst of millions of suffering people. A seedling from the tree of Dhamma which gives fruit in every season had been transplanted centuries ago in Burma from India. The mother tree had withered, but the seedling had flourished and grown. Now a cutting must be taken from it and planted in the fertile soil of India, to give sweet fruit and cool, pleasant shade. And this invaluable jewel of the Indian heritage should also be shared with every land throughout the world.

To realize this holy wish of Sayagyi, only a small step had been taken in his lifetime. In the fifteen years since he breathed his last, many more steps have been achieved, and if the progress at times was slow, it has been sure and steady. Now, with the gathering momentum of all these years of work, the time has come for the Dhamma to spread at a greater pace. Up until now, centres have arisen in various places in India and abroad, and nearly fifty assistant teachers have started conducting courses for the good and happiness of many. Now still more courses must be offered in many more areas by more assistant teachers. Not only that, but

meditators must be helped to experience the teaching at deeper levels.

I remember well my own experiences on the path. After I first learned the technique while living in Burma, I kept up a regular daily practice but had to devote much more of my time to my business and family responsibilities. Suddenly, however, there came a change in fortune: in 1964, the government took over all businesses and industries. This action, unfortunate for me in the eyes of others, was actually my good fortune, since a heavy burden was now lifted from my shoulders.

The following five years were the golden age of my life. I had always longed to study and absorb the words of the Buddha relating to Vipassana, but in the hurly-burly of active life how to find the time? Now here I was with unlimited time and with my teacher close at hand. The result was that my practice took wing. In meditation I could go more deeply than ever before, and when I read the words of the Buddha I would feel a thrill of delight throughout my body. I felt sometimes as if the Buddha was speaking directly to me, as if every word was aimed specifically at me. At home, I would read a *sutta* and then go to my teacher, who would take up certain points from it and expound deeply upon them. This was a veritable shower of nectar, the nectar of Dhamma.

Sayagyi, that incarnation of compassion, was always ready to discuss Dhamma with me. Even while sick in bed and badly needing rest, if he came to know that his Dhamma son was waiting to see him, compassion and joy arose in him and he would speak with me, explaining in depth a Dhamma text. As someone might card cotton or wool, combing out snarls and tangles, Sayagyi would remove all confusions, all ambiguities.

> **W**hen students participate in courses on the *Satipaṭṭhāna Sutta*, studying the words of the Buddha while at the same time applying them in meditation, they feel as if the technique is revealed to them for the first time in all its brilliant clarity.

The translations gave only grammatical explanations. But the explanation of this Vipassana yogi, this king of yogis, was of a different order altogether. He explained according to the experience of meditation, and in this way he could penetrate to the most profound meaning of the text.

His words always filled me with joy and inspiration. And then, after explaining Dhamma to me, he would tell me to go and meditate. At such times I was able to penetrate deeply at the experiential level as well. Layer after layer of illusions and delusions would pass away, leaving the truth crystal clear. By the time I rose from meditating I would feel freed of all knots, liberated from all confusion.

From these experiences boundless gratitude would arise in me, first to the Buddha and then to his Dhamma sons, the chain of teachers and pupils extending link by link from the Buddha to Sayagyi U Ba Khin. To all of them I felt deep gratitude for preserving this technique in its original purity without any admixture whatsoever. At the same time gratitude would arise in me towards all those who had preserved the words

of the Buddha free from any corruptions, so that today it is still possible to read them and be inspired by them. *Pariyatti* and *paṭipatti*—study accompanied by practice—these two seemed to me like a gem, the beauty of which is enhanced by its golden setting.

How greatly I benefited from these experiences, yet how little are such experiences accessible to meditators today! Although the *Tipiṭaka* (Pāli canon) has appeared in Devanāgarī script in India, for many years these books have been out of print. Further, whatever portion of the Tipiṭaka was translated into Hindi decades ago is also unavailable now, while little if anything has been translated into other Indian languages. Meditators in India are, therefore, cut off from the words of the Buddha.

In the West, it would seem that students are more fortunate, since the entire *Tipiṭaka* has appeared in Roman script and has been translated into English. But, in fact, the passages of it relating directly to meditation have presented unusual difficulties to most scholars. These passages have been translated in a way that sometimes creates confusion in the minds of meditators who read them.

When students participate in courses on the *Satipaṭṭhāna Sutta*, studying the words of the Buddha while at the same time applying them in meditation, they are inspired and filled with gratitude. They feel as if the technique is revealed to them for the first time in all its brilliant clarity. Naturally they would like to study even more. How happy they would be if they could study in their own language, not only the *Tipiṭaka*, but also the voluminous literature of the commentaries!

It is not expected or necessary that all should be motivated to study the texts, but certainly there are many who are able and eager to do so, who could easily plunge into the ocean of the *Tipiṭaka*. For them the opportunity must be provided.

Not only the Pāli texts, but also those in Sanskrit and Prākrit contain references to Vipassana. If a meditator undertakes the necessary research, this technique will be revealed as the essence of the entire Indian spiritual tradition. It is a large task, no doubt, but the time has come to make a beginning, no matter how small.

Doing so, however, must never be at the expense of meditation practice. Otherwise, Vipassana centres might degenerate into places where people merely read, write or talk about the Dhamma, and the real purpose might be lost. Our aim is always to experience the Dhamma within ourselves in order to emerge from all suffering. The means to do so is the practice of Vipassana meditation. Reading, writing and study are merely to find guidance and inspiration in order to go more deeply in the practice, and thus to come closer to the goal of liberation.

Without sacrificing this object, opportunities should be created near all the centres for *pariyatti*, study of Dhamma. It must begin at the main centre, Dhamma Giri. At the foot of the hill, on the approach to the Academy, is a suitable place to establish facilities for the study of Pāli and for research on the original texts. All who participate, not only students but also teachers, must be regular meditators, and meditation must be an important part of the curriculum. If this is the case, their study will enable the participants to meditate more deeply and experience Dhamma more profoundly within themselves.

The Dhamma can stand the test of those who are anxious to do so. They can know for themselves what the benefits are.

—*Sayagyi U Ba Khin*

Vedanā and the Four Noble Truths

Vipassana Research Institute

The Four Noble Truths are the essence of the Buddha's teaching. In the *Aṅguttara-nikāya* the Buddha said:

> *Vediyamānassa kho panāhaṃ, bhikkhave, idaṃ dukkhaṃ ti paññāpemi ayaṃ dukkha-samudayo ti paññāpemi ayaṃ dukkha-nirodho ti paññāpemi ayaṃ dukkha-nirodha-gāminī-paṭipadā ti paññāpemi.[1]*

To one who experiences sensations, meditators, I teach the truth of suffering, I teach the truth of the arising of suffering, I teach the truth of the cessation of suffering and I teach the truth of the path leading to the cessation of suffering.

In this passage the Buddha states unequivocally that the Four Noble Truths can be understood, realized and practised only through the experience of *vedanā* (sensation).

He further analysed the Noble Truths in the light of *vedanā* by saying:

> *Yaṃ kiñci vedayitaṃ, taṃ pi dukkhasmiṃ.[2]*

Whatever sensations one experiences, all are suffering.

Not only is *dukkha vedanā* (unpleasant sensation) suffering, but *sukha vedanā* (pleasant sensation) and *adukkhamasukha vedanā* (neutral sensation) are also suffering, because of their impermanent nature. Arising and passing away, *anicca* (impermanence), is the characteristic of *vedanā*. Every pleasant sensation has a seed of *dukkha* in it because it is bound to pass away. We are so bound by ignorance that when a pleasant sensation arises, without knowing its real nature of impermanence, we react to it by developing craving and clinging towards it. This leads to suffering: *taṇhā dukkhassa sambhavaṃ* —craving is the origin of suffering.[3]

In fact, craving is not only the origin of suffering but suffering itself. As craving arises, suffering arises. The Buddha elucidated the second of the Four Noble Truths not as *taṇhā-paccayā dukkha* but instead as *dukkha-samudaya*. In other words, craving is not merely the precondition of suffering; it is itself inseparable from suffering. The same emphasis is apparent in the statement *taṇhā dukkhassa sambhavaṃ*. Verily *taṇhā* and *dukkha* are sahajāta (co-nascent). As soon as *taṇhā* arises, one loses the balance of the mind, becoming agitated and tense. In other words, one experiences *dukkha*.

Similarly, when *vedanā* arises and results in *taṇhā*, it is *dukkha*. Thus whenever the term *vedanā* is used in relation to the practice of Dhamma, it conveys the sense of *dukkha*. Even a neutral sensation is *dukkha* if its impermanent nature is ignored. Therefore, not only for *dukkha vedanā* but for *sukha vedanā* and *adukkhamasukha vedanā* as well, the Buddha correctly used the word *vedanā* as a synonym for *dukkha*.

Emphasizing this fact again in relation to the Four Noble Truths, the Buddha said in the *Dvayatānupassanā-sutta* of the *Suttanipāta*:

> *Yaṃ kiñci dukkhaṃ sambhoti sabbaṃ vedanāpaccayā ti- ayamekānupassanā.*
> *Vedanānaṃ tveva asesavirāga-nirodhā natthi dukkhasssa sambhavo ti- ayaṃ dutiyānupassanā.[4]*

Whatever suffering arises, it is because of sensation—this is the first *anupassanā* (constant observation). With the complete cessation of sensation there is no further arising of suffering—this is the second *anupassanā*.

The first *anupassanā* is the constant observation of vedanā as dukkha. The second anupassanā consists of the reality which is beyond the field of vedanā as well as beyond the field of phassa (contact) and of *saḷāyatana* (the six sense doors). This is the stage of *nirodha-samāpatti* of an *arahant* (fully liberated one), the experience of the state of *nibbāna*. By this second anupassanā, the meditator realizes the truth that in the field of *nirodha-samāpatti* there is no dukkha, because there is no vedanā. It is the field beyond the sphere of vedanā.

The Buddha continues in the same sutta:

> *Sukhaṃ vā yadi vā dukkhaṃ,*
> *adukkhamasukhaṃ saha*
> *ajjhattaṃ ca bahiddhā ca,*
> *yaṃ kiñci atthi veditaṃ.*
> *Etaṃ dukkhaṃ ti ñatvāna*
> *mosadhammaṃ palokinaṃ*
> *phussa phussa vayaṃ passaṃ,*
> *evaṃ tattha virajjati*
> *Vedanānaṃ khayā bhikkhu,*
> *nicchāto parinibbuto.*[5]

Whatever sensations one experiences in the body, pleasant, unpleasant or neutral, inside or outside, all are suffering, all are illusory, all are ephemeral. A meditator observes that wherever there is a contact in the body, sensations pass away (as soon as they arise). Realizing this truth with the extinction of sensation, the meditator is freed from craving, fully liberated.

A person well-established in this truth becomes liberated from the habit of craving and

clinging towards sensation and reaches the state where there is no more *vedanā* (*vedanā-khaya*). (This is the stage of *nibbāna* reached in the second *anupassanā*.) A meditator who has experienced this state of *arahata-phala* becomes

> **W**hatever sensations one experiences in the body, pleasant, unpleasant or neutral, inside or outside, all are suffering, all are illusory, all are ephemeral.

nicchāto (freed from all desires). Such a person becomes *parinibbuta* (totally liberated).

Therefore, to experience and understand *dukkha-sacca* (suffering), *samudaya-sacca* (its arising), *nirodha-sacca* (its cessation) and *dukkha-nirodha-gāminī-paṭipada-sacca* (the path leading to the cessation of suffering), one has to work with sensations and realize the truth of *vedanā* (vedanā-sacca), the arising of vedanā (*vedanā-samudaya-sacca*), the cessation of vedanā (*vedanā-nirodha-sacca*) and the path leading to the cessation of vedanā (*vedanā-nirodha-gāminī-paṭipadā-sacca*).

This process is clearly described in the Samādhi-sutta of the Vedanā-saṃyutta:

> *Samāhito sampajāno, sato Buddhassa sāvako*
> *Vedanā ca pajānāti, vedanānaṃ ca*
> *sambhavaṃ.*
> *Yattha cetā nirujjhanti, maggaṃ ca*
> *khayagāminaṃ.*
> *Vedanānaṃ khayā, bhikkhu nicchāto*
> *parinibbuto ti.*[6]

A follower of the Buddha, with concentration, awareness and constant thorough understanding of impermanence, knows with wisdom the sensations, their arising, their cessation and the path leading to their end. A meditator who has reached the end of sensations is freed from craving, fully liberated.

The Buddha further says very emphatically that the practice of the *ariyo aṭṭhaṅgiko maggo* (the Noble Eightfold Path) has the purpose of understanding *vedanā* and reaching the state of *vedanā-nirodha* (cessation of sensations):

> *Tisso imā, bhikkhave, vedanā. Katamā tisso? Sukhā vedanā, dukkhā vedanā, adukkamasukhā vedanā. Imā kho, bhikkhave, tisso vedanā. Imāsaṃ kho, bhikkhave, tissannaṃ vedanānaṃ abhiññāya pariññāya parikkhayāya pahānāya...ayaṃ ariyo aṭṭhaṅgiko maggo bhāvetabbo...*[7]

There are these three types of bodily sensations. What are the three? Pleasant sensation, unpleasant sensation and sensation which is neutral. Meditators, the Noble Eightfold Path should be practised for the complete knowledge, the full realization, the gradual eradication and the abandonment of these three bodily sensations.

Sensations (*vedanā*) are the tools by which we can practise the Four Noble Truths and the Noble Eightfold Path; and by realizing the characteristic of anicca (impermanence) we free ourselves from the bonds of *avijjā* and *taṇhā* and penetrate to the ultimate truth: *nibbāna*, freedom from suffering, a state which is beyond the field of *vedanā*, beyond the field of *nāma-rūpa* (mind and matter).

1. *Aṅguttara-nikāya* I, Nal. 163, PTS 176.
2. *Majjhima-nikāya* III, Nal. 288, PTS 208.
3. *Suttanipāta*, Nal. 383, PTS 140.
4. Ibid., Nal. 383, PTS 139.
5. Loc. cit.
6. *Saṃyutta-nikāya* IV, Nal. 183, PTS 204.
7. Ibid. V, Nal. 56, PTS 57.

Sampajañña—the Constant Thorough Understanding of Impermanence

Vipassana Research Institute

In this paper, we will discuss how *sampajañña* (or *sampajāno*) is explained by the Buddha in the suttas and how the term can be correctly translated into English.

Whenever the Buddha was asked to describe *sati* (mindfulness or awareness), his explanation invariably included the term sampajañña.

> *Katamā ca, bhikkhave, sammā-sati? Idha, bhikkhave, bhikkhu kāye kāyānupassī viharati ātāpī sampajāno satimā, vineyya loke abhijjhā-domanassaṃ.[1]*

And what, meditators, is right awareness? Here, a meditator dwells ardently, with constant thorough understanding and right awareness, observing the body in the body, having removed craving and aversion towards this world (of mind and matter).

From this it becomes evident that according to the Buddha, whenever there is *sammā-sati* or *satipaṭṭhāna*, it is always with *sampajañña*. That means it is with *paññā* (wisdom). Otherwise it is mere *sati*, which is mere remembrance or awareness.

In the *Sutta* Piṭaka, the Buddha gave two explanations of the term *sampajañña*. In the *Saṃyutta-nikāya* the Buddha defines *sampajāno* as follows:

> *Kathañca, bhikkhave, bhikkhu sampajāno hoti? Idha, bhikkhave, bhikkhuno viditā vedanā uppajjanti, viditā upaṭṭhahanti, viditā abbhatthaṃ gacchanti; viditā saññā uppajjanti, viditā upaṭṭhahanti, viditā abbhatthaṃ gacchanti; viditā vitakkā uppajjanti, viditā upaṭṭhahanti, viditā*

> *abbhatthaṃ gacchanti. Evaṃ kho, bhikkhave, bhikkhu sampajāno hoti.[2]*

And how, meditators, does a meditator understand thoroughly? Herein, meditators, a meditator knows sensations arising in him, knows their persisting, and knows their vanishing; he knows perceptions arising in him, knows their persisting, and knows their vanishing; he knows each initial application (of the mind on an object) arising in him, knows its persisting, and knows its vanishing. This, meditators, is how a meditator understands thoroughly.

In the above statement, it becomes clear that one is *sampajāno* only when one realizes the characteristic of impermanence, and that too on the basis of experience of sensation (*viditā vedanā*). If this is not realized through *vedanā*, then it is merely an intellectualization, as our fundamental contact with the world is based on sensation. It is through sensation that direct experience occurs. The statement further indicates that *sampajāno* lies in experiencing the impermanence of *vedanā*, *vitakkā* (the initial application of the mind on an object) and *saññā* (perception). Here we should note that impermanence of *vedanā* is to be realized first because according to the Buddha:

> *Vedanā-samosaraṇā sabbe dhammā.[3]*

Everything that arises in the mind is accompanied by sensation.

The second explanation given by the Buddha of *sampajañña* emphasizes that it must be continuous. He states:

Kathañca, bhikkhave, bhikkhu sampajāno hoti? Idha, bhikkhave, bhikkhu abhikkante paṭikkante sampajānakārī hoti. Ālokite vilokite sampajānakārī hoti. Samiñjite pasārite sampajānakārī hoti. Saṅghāṭi-patta-cīvara-dhāraṇe sampajānakārī hoti. Asite pīte khāyite sāyite sampajānakārī hoti. Uccāra-passāva-kamme sampajānakārī hoti. Gate ṭhite nisinne sutte jāgarite bhāsite tuṇhī-bhāve sampajānakārī hoti.[4]

And how, meditators, does a meditator understand thoroughly? Again, meditators, a meditator in going forwards and backwards understands impermanence thoroughly, in looking straight ahead and sideways understands impermanence thoroughly, in bending and stretching understands impermanence thoroughly, in wearing the robes and carrying the bowl understands impermanence thoroughly, in chewing and drinking, eating and savouring understands impermanence thoroughly, in attending to the calls of nature understands impermanence thoroughly, in walking, standing, sitting, sleeping and waking, speaking and remaining silent understands impermanence thoroughly.

The same passage has been repeated in other suttas, including the section on *sampajañña* under *Kāyānupassanā* in the *Mahāsatipaṭṭhāna-sutta.*

The emphasis on the continuity of *sampajañña* is very clear. One should develop constant thorough understanding of impermanence in whatever one does: in walking forward and backward, in looking straight and sideways, in bending and stretching, in wearing robes and so on. In sitting, in standing and even in sleeping one has to experience constant thorough understanding of impermanence. This is *sampajañña.*

With proper understanding of the teaching of the Buddha, it becomes clear that if this continuous *sampajañña* consists only of the thorough understanding of the processes of walking, eating and other activities of the body, then it is merely *sati.* If, however, the constant thorough understanding includes the characteristic of arising and passing away of *vedanā* while the meditator is performing these activities, then this is *paññā.* This is what the Buddha wanted people to practise.

The Buddha describes this more specifically in a passage from the *Aṅguttara-nikāya*, using language that is bound to bring to mind the *sampajāna-pabba* of the *Mahāsatipaṭṭhāna-sutta:*

> *Yataṃ care yataṃ tiṭṭhe, yataṃ acche yataṃ saye, yataṃ samiñjaye bhikkhu, yatamenaṃ pasāraye, uddhaṃ tiriyaṃ apacinaṃ, yāvatā jagato gati, samavekkhitā ca dhammānaṃ khandānaṃ udayabbayaṃ.*[5]

Whether the meditator walks or stands or sits or lies, whether he bends or stretches, above, across, backwards, whatever his course in the world, he observes the arising and passing away of the aggregates.

Thus the emphasis is on the continuity of awareness of anicca (impermanence) with the base of body sensation. The Buddha frequently stressed that the meditator should not lose the thorough understanding of impermanence even for a moment: *sampajaññaṃ na riñcati.*[6] For a meditator who follows his advice on

> It becomes clear that the Buddha's teaching is not for intellectual entertainment but for direct experience, because this alone can free one from the ingrained habit pattern of reacting with craving and aversion.

the proper practice of Vipassana, being *sampajāno* without any interruption, the Buddha gives the following assurance: either the meditator will attain the highest stage (*arahata*) or the penultimate stage (*anāgāmitā*).[7]

Every language, however rich it may be, has its limitations and we cannot expect even the richest of languages to be capable of giving precise equivalents to the technical Pāli words used by the Buddha. If the term *sampajañña* is translated too concisely into English its meaning can be lost. It has usually been translated as "clear comprehension," "bare comprehension," etc.

Superficially these translations appear to be correct. Some have taken this to mean that one must merely have clear comprehension of bodily activities. The limitations of this translation may have had the effect of misleading some meditators on the path of Dhamma. The Buddha clearly emphasized the thorough understanding of *anicca* in all bodily and mental activities. Therefore, to understand the term *sampajañña*, we have translated it as: "The constant thorough understanding of impermanence." It is felt that this translation conveys more fully the precise meaning of the term used by the Buddha.

---

1. *Dīgha-nikāya* II, Nal. 234, PTS 314.

2. *Saṃyutta-nikāya* V, Nal. 155–6, PTS 180–1.

3. *Aṅguttara-nikāya*, Nal. IV. 184, PTS V. 107.

4. *Dīgha-nikāya* II, Nal. 76, PTS 95.

5. *Aṅguttara-nikāya* II, Nal. 16, PTS 14.

6. *Saṃyutta-nikāya* IV, Nal. 194, PTS 218.

7. *Dīgha-nikāya* II, Nal. 235, PTS 251.

Vedanā in Paṭiccasamuppāda

Vipassana Research Institute

Paṭiccasamuppāda (the Law of Dependent Origination) is fundamental to the teaching of the Buddha. Emphasizing its importance, the Buddha said:

Yo paṭiccasamuppādaṃ passati,
so dhammaṃ passati.
Yo dhammaṃ passati,
so paṭiccasamuppādaṃ passati.[1]

One who sees *paṭiccasamuppāda*
sees the Dhamma.
One who sees the Dhamma
sees *paṭiccasamuppāda.*

Paṭiccasamuppāda explains that *saṃsāra*, the process of repeated existences, is perpetuated by a chain of interconnected links of cause and effect; it also reveals the method of breaking this chain and putting an end to the process.

The Buddha said:

Taṇhādutiyo puriso,
dīghamaddhāna saṃsāraṃ
Itthabhāvaññathābhāvaṃ,
saṃsāraṃ nātivattati.[2]

The man with craving as his companion has been flowing in the stream of repeated existences from time immemorial. He comes into being, experiences various types of miseries, dies again and again, and does not put an end to this unbroken process of becoming.

This is *saṃsāra*, the world of suffering, as explained by the Buddha. He further said:

Etamādīnavaṃ ñatvā,
taṇhaṃ dukkhassa sambhavaṃ
Vītataṇho anādāno,
sato bhikkhu paribbaje.[3]

Rightly understanding the perils of this process, realizing fully craving as its cause, becoming free from craving and attachment, one should mindfully lead the life of detachment.

Such an approach, he said, will have great benefit:

Nandī-saṃyojano loko,
vitakkassa vicāranaṃ
Taṇhāya vippahānena,
nibbānaṃ iti vuccati.[4]

Pleasure is the binding force in the world. Rolling thought processes are its ever-changing base.
With the complete eradication of craving, The state called *nibbāna* is attained.

These statements made by the Buddha describe the nature of *saṃsāra*, the state of suffering, and the nature of *nibbāna*, the state of final emancipation. But how can detachment be developed, and craving eradicated?

This is the practical aspect of Dhamma discovered by Siddhattha Gotama, the realization that made him a Buddha (enlightened one), and that he in turn revealed to the world by the doctrine of Paṭiccasamuppāda.

According to this doctrine, twelve links form the wheel of becoming (*bhava-cakka*). They are:

1. *avijjā*   (ignorance)
2. *saṅkhāra*   (volitional activities)
3. *viññāṇa*   (consciousness)
4. *nāma-rūpa* (mind and matter)
5. *saḷāyatana* (six sense doors)

6. *phassa*   (contact)

7. *vedanā*   (sensation)

8. *taṇhā*   (craving)

9. *upādāna*   (clinging)

10. *bhava*   (becoming)

11. *jāti*   (birth)

12. *jarā-maraṇa*   (decay and death)

Dependent on *avijjā* there arises *saṅkhāra*;

dependent on *saṅkhāra* there arises *viññāṇa*;

dependent on *viññāṇa* there arises *nāma-rūpa*;

dependent on *nāma-rūpa* there arises *saḷāyatana*;

dependent on *saḷāyatana* there arises *phassa*;

dependent on *phassa* there arises *vedanā*;

dependent on *vedanā* there arises *taṇhā*;

dependent on *taṇhā* there arises *upādāna*.

Thus this vicious circle of misery rotates on and on.

In other words, the origin of each link depends upon the preceding one. As long as this chain of twelve causal relations operates, the wheel of becoming (*bhava-cakka*) keeps turning, bringing nothing but suffering. This process of cause and effect is called *anuloma-paṭiccasamuppāda* (the Law of Dependent Origination in forward order). Every link of *anuloma* results in misery (*dukkha*), as a result of *avijjā* which is at the base of every link. Thus the process of *anuloma* clarifies the first two Noble Truths, *dukkha-sacca* (suffering), and *samudaya-sacca* (its origination and multiplication).

Our task is to emerge from this *bhava-cakka* of *dukkha*. Explaining how to do so, the Buddha said that when any one of the links of the chain is broken, the wheel of becoming comes to an end, resulting in the cessation of suffering. This is called *paṭiloma-paṭiccasamuppāda* (the Law of Dependent Origination in reverse order) which clarifies the third and fourth Noble Truths, *nirodha-sacca* (the cessation of suffering), and *nirodha-gāminī-paṭipadā-sacca* (the path that leads to the cessation of suffering). How can that be achieved? Which link of the chain can be broken?

Through deep insight, the Buddha discovered that the crucial link is *vedanā*. In the *anuloma-paṭiccasamuppāda*, he says "*vedanā-paccayā taṇhā*" (with the base of sensation, craving and aversion arise). *Vedanā* is the cause of *taṇhā*, which gives rise to *dukkha*. In order to remove the cause of *dukkha* or *taṇhā*, therefore, one must not allow *vedanā* to connect with *taṇhā*; in other words, one must practise Vipassana meditation at this juncture so that *avijjā* becomes *vijjā*, or *paññā* (wisdom). One has to observe *vedanā*, to experience and to comprehend the truth of its arising and passing away, i.e., *anicca*.

Through Vipassana meditation, as one experiences *vedanā* properly, one comes out of the delusion of *nicca-saññā* (perception of permanence) by the development of *anicca-bodha* or *anicca-vijjā* (the wisdom of impermanence) towards *vedanā*. This is practised by observing with equanimity the arising and passing away of *vedanā*. With *anicca-bodha*, the habit pattern of the mind changes. Instead of the earlier pattern of *vedanā-paccayā taṇhā*, through *anicca-vijjā* it becomes *vedanā-paccayā paññā* (with the base of sensation wisdom arises). As *paññā* becomes stronger and stronger, naturally the *saññā*, and with it *taṇhā*, becomes weaker and weaker. The process of the multiplication of suffering with the base of *avijjā* then becomes the process of the cessation of suffering, with *vijjā* as the base. As this process continues, a time comes where there is the complete cessation of *vedanā* as well as *taṇhā*: "*vedanā-nirodhā, taṇhā-nirodho*" (with the cessation of sensation, craving and aversion cease).

This state of emancipation is a state beyond mind and matter, where both *vedanā* and *saññā* cease. One can experience this for a few seconds, minutes, hours, or days when, according to one's own capacity, one becomes established in *nirodha-samāpatti* by practising Vipassana. After the period of *nirodha-samāpatti* (the attainment of cessation), when one comes back to the sensual field of mind and matter, one again experiences *vedanā*. But now the whole habit pattern of the mind has been changed, and continued practice leads to the stage where one does not generate aversion or craving at all because the *anusaya kilesa* and the *āsava* (the deep-rooted mental impurities) are eradicated. In this way by the breaking of one link, *vedanā*, the whole process is shattered and the wheel of repeated existence is broken completely.

If we want to advance on the path of liberation, we have to work at the level of *vedanā* because it is here that the rotation of the wheel of misery can be arrested. With *vedanā* starts the turning of the *bhava-cakka* (wheel of becoming), leading (because of *avijjā*) to *vedanā-paccayā taṇhā*, which causes suffering. This is the path which ignorant persons (*puthujjana*) follow, since they react to *vedanā* and generate *taṇhā*. And from here also the *Dhamma-cakka*, (wheel of Dhamma) or the wheel of cessation of suffering (*dukkha-nirodha-gāminī-paṭipadā*) can start to rotate, leading to *vedanā-nirodhā, taṇhā-nirodho*: the end of craving, as a result of *anicca-vijjā* or *paññā*, leading to the cessation of suffering. This is the path which wise persons (*sapaññā*) follow by not reacting to *vedanā*, because they have developed *anicca-bodha* by the practice of Vipassana.

Many of the contemporaries of the Buddha held the view that craving causes suffering and that to remove suffering one has to abstain from the objects of craving. In order to develop detachment, the Buddha tackled the problem in a different way. Having learned to examine the depths of his own mind, he realized that between the external object and the mental reflex of craving is a missing link: *vedanā* (sensation). Whenever we encounter an object through the five physical senses or the mind, a sensation arises; and based on the sensation, *taṇhā* arises. If the sensation is pleasant we crave to prolong it, and if it is unpleasant we crave to be rid of it. It is in the chain of Dependent Origination that the Buddha expressed his profound discovery.

Phassa-paccayā vedanā
Vedanā-paccayā taṇhā.[5]

Dependent on contact, sensation arises
Dependent on sensation, craving arises

The immediate cause for the arising of craving and of suffering is, therefore, not something outside of us but rather the sensations that occur within us. To free ourselves from craving and suffering we must deal with this inner reality of sensations. Doing so is the practical way to emerge from suffering. By developing *anicca-vijjā* (the wisdom of impermanence) we learn to cut the knots of our misery and witness the true nature of Dhamma. *Vedanā* then is the cause of our bondage when not properly observed, as well as the means of our liberation when properly observed by understanding the Dhamma, the law of *paṭiccasamuppāda*.

---

1. *Majjhima-nikāya* I, Nal. 241, PTS 191.
2. *Suttanipāta*, verse 339, Nal. 383, PTS 139.
3. Ibid., verse 340, Nal. 383, PTS 140.
4. *Saṃyutta-nikāya* I, Nal. 37, PTS 39; *Suttanipāta* verse 134, Nal. 436, PTS 202.
5. *Vinaya, Mahāvagga*, Nal. 3, PTS 2.

Vedanā in the Practice of Satipaṭṭhāna

Vipassana Research Institute

The practice of the four-fold *satipaṭṭhāna*, the establishing of awareness, was highly praised by the Buddha in the suttas (discourses). Mentioning its importance in the *Mahāsatipaṭṭhāna-sutta*, the Buddha called it *ekāyano maggo* — "the only way for the purification of beings, for overcoming sorrow, for the extinguishing of suffering, for entering the path of truth and experiencing *nibbāna* (liberation)."[1]

In this sutta, the Buddha presented a practical method for developing self-knowledge by means of *kāyānupassanā* (constant observation of the body), *vedanānupassanā* (constant observation of sensation), *cittānupassanā* (constant observation of the mind), and *dhammānupassanā* (constant observation of the contents of the mind).[2]

To explore the truth about ourselves, we must examine what we are: body and mind. We must learn to directly observe these within ourselves. Accordingly, we must keep three points in mind: 1) The reality of the body may be imagined by contemplation, but to experience it directly one must work with *vedanā* (bodily sensation) arising within it. 2) Similarly, the actual experience of the mind is attained by working with the contents of the mind. Therefore, as body and sensation cannot be experienced separately, the mind cannot be observed apart from the contents of the mind. 3) Mind and matter are so closely interrelated that the contents of the mind always manifest themselves as sensation in the body. For this reason the Buddha said:

Vedanā-samosaraṇā sabbe dhammā.[3]

Whatever arises in the mind is accompanied by sensation.

Therefore, observation of sensation offers a means, indeed the only means, to examine the totality of our being, physical as well as mental.

There are four dimensions to our nature: the body and its sensations, and the mind and its contents. These provide four avenues for the establishing of awareness in *satipaṭṭhāna*. In order that the observation be complete, every facet must be experienced, as it can by means of *vedanā*. This exploration of truth will remove the delusions we have about ourselves. Likewise, to come out of the delusion about the world outside, the truth about the contact of the outside world with our own mind-and-matter phenomenon must be explored.

The outside world comes in contact with the individual only at the six sense doors: the eye, ear, nose, tongue, body and mind. As all these sense doors are contained in the body, every contact of the outside world is at the body level. According to the law of nature, with every contact there is bound to be sensation. Every time there is a contact with any of the six sense objects, a sensation will arise on the body. Therefore, just as the understanding of *vedanā* is absolutely essential to understand the interaction between mind and matter within ourselves, the same understanding of *vedanā* is essential to understand the interaction of the outside world with the individual.

If this exploration of truth were to be attempted by contemplation or intellectualization, we could have easily ignored the importance of *vedanā*. However the crux of the Buddha's teaching is the necessity of understanding the truth not merely at the intellectual level, but by direct experience. For this reason *vedanā* is defined as follows:

> *Yā vedetī ti vedanā, sā vedayati lakkhaṇā, anubhavanarasā...*[4]

That which feels the object is vedanā; its characteristic is to experience, its function is to realize the object...

However, merely to feel the sensations within is not enough to remove our delusions. Instead, it is essential to understand the *ti-lakkhaṇa* (three characteristics) of all phenomena. We must directly experience *anicca* (impermanence), *dukkha* (suffering), and *anattā* (substancelessness) within ourselves. Of these three the Buddha always gave importance to *anicca* because the realization of the other two will easily follow when we have experienced deeply the characteristic of impermanence. In the *Meghiya-sutta* of the *Udāna* he said:

> *Aniccasaññino hi, Meghiya,*
> *anattasaññā saṇṭhāti, anattasaññī*
> *asmimānasamugghātaṃ papuṇāti diṭṭheva*
> *dhamme nibbānaṃ.*[5]

In him, Meghiya, who is conscious of impermanence the consciousness of what is substanceless is established. He who is conscious of what is substanceless wins the uprooting of the pride of egotism in this very life, namely, he realizes *nibbāna*.

Therefore, in the practice of *satipaṭṭhāna*, the experience of *anicca*, arising and passing away, plays a crucial role.

The *Mahāsatipaṭṭhāna sutta* begins with the observation of the body. Here several different starting points are explained: observing respiration, giving attention to bodily movements, etc. It is from these points that we progressively can develop *vedanānupassanā*, *cittānupassanā* and *dhammānupassanā*. However, no matter where the journey starts, there come stations through which everyone must pass on the way to

the final goal. These are described in important sentences repeated not only at the end of each section of *kāyānupassanā* but also at the end of *vedanānupassanā*, *cittānupassanā* and each section of *dhammānupassanā*. They are:

1. Samudaya-dhammānupassī vā viharati
2. Vaya-dhammānupassī vā viharati
3. Samudaya-vaya-dhammānupassī vā viharati.[6]

1. One dwells observing the phenomenon of arising.

2. One dwells observing the phenomenon of passing away.

3. One dwells observing the phenomenon of arising and passing away.

These sentences reveal the essence of the practice of *satipaṭṭhāna*. Unless these three levels of *anicca* are practised, we will not have wisdom. Therefore, in order to practise any of the fourfold *satipaṭṭhāna* one has to develop the constant thorough understanding of impermanence known as *sampajañña* in Pāli. In other words, one must meditate on the arising and passing away of phenomena (*anicca-bodha*), objectively observing mind and matter without reaction. The realization of *samudaya-vaya-dhamma* (impermanence) should not be merely a contemplation, or process of thinking, or imagination or even believing; it should be performed with *paccanubhoti* (direct experience). Here the observation of *vedanā* plays its vital role, because with *vedanā* a meditator very clearly and tangibly realizes *samudaya-vaya* (arising and passing away).[7] *Sampajañña* in fact is knowing the arising and passing away of *vedanā* and thereby all four facets of our being.

It is for this reason that in each of the four *satipaṭṭhāna*, being *sampajāno*, as well as being *ātāpī* (ardent) and *satimā* (aware) are essential qualities and the three are invariably repeated for each of the *satipaṭṭhāna*. And as the Buddha explained, *sampajañña* is observing the arising and passing away of *vedanā*.[8] Hence the part played by *vedanā* in the practice of *satipaṭṭhāna* should not be ignored, or this practice of *satipaṭṭhāna* will not be complete.

In the words of the Buddha:

> *Tisso imā, bhikkhave, vedanā. Katamā tisso? Sukhā vedanā, dukkhā vedanā, adukkhamasukhā vedanā-imā kho, bhikkhave, tisso vedanā. Imāsaṃ kho, bhikkhave, tissannaṃ vedanānaṃ pariññāya cattāro satipaṭṭhānā bhāvetabbā.[9]*

Meditators, there are three types of bodily sensations. What are the three? Pleasant sensations, unpleasant sensations and neutral sensations. Practise, meditators, the four-fold *satipaṭṭhāna* for the complete understanding of these three sensations.

The practice of *satipaṭṭhāna* is complete only when one directly experiences impermanence. Bodily sensation provides the nexus where the entire mind and body are tangibly revealed as an impermanent phenomenon leading to liberation.

---

1. *Dīgha-nikāya* II, Nal. 217, PTS 290.

2. Loc. cit.

3. *Aṅguttara-nikāya*, Nal. IV, 184; PTS V, 107.

4. *Abhidhammattha-saṅgaho*, Hindi translation and commentary by Ven. Dr. U. Rewata Dhamma, Varanaseya Sanskrit Vishva Vidyalaya, Varanasi, Vol. I p. 101.

5. *Udāna*, Nal. 105, PTS 37.

6. *Dīgha-nikāya* II, Nal. 218–234, PTS 292–314.

7. See footnote 5.

8. *Saṃyutta-nikāya* V, Nal. 155, PTS 180.

9. Ibid. V, Nal. 163, PTS 180.

Vipassana Meditation Courses Conducted by S.N. Goenka

KEY:

APC = Anapana Course
CC = Children's Course
OLC = Old Student Long Course
OSC = Old Student Short Course

STP = Satipaṭṭhāna Sutta Course
TSC = Teacher's Self Course
*   = Student number not available

Course No.	Location	Course Dates		Students Old	New
1	Panchayatiwadi, Bombay	3-7-69	13-7-69	0	14
2	Agarwal Bhavan, Madras	24-7-69	3-8-69	1	14
3	Nemaniwadi, Bombay	14-8-69	24-8-69	7	11
4	Birla Dharamshala, Sarnath	11-9-69	21-9-69	0	20
5	Birla Mandir, New Delhi	25-9-69	5-10-69	0	11
6	Tibdevala Dharamshala, Calcutta	9-10-69	19-10-69	2	30
7	Primary School, Tadepalligudam	23-10-69	2-11-69	6	14
8	Maha Bodhi Society, Egmore, Madras	4-12-69	14-12-69	7	8
9	Panchayatiwadi, Bombay	27-12-69	6-1-70	7	12
10	Geeta Bhuvan Dharamshala, Delhi	15-1-70	25-1-70	4	17
11	Buddha Temple, Madhoganj, U.P.	29-1-70	8-2-70	5	20
12	Yadav Dharamshala, Pushkar, Ajmer	19-2-70	29-2-70	2	2
13	Sugarmill Bungalow, Barachakia	12-3-70	22-3-70	8	40
14	Samanvaya Ashram, Bodh Gaya	9-4-70	19-4-70	2	23
15	Shivner Building, Bombay	14-5-70	24-5-70	11	28
16	Private Bungalow, Baroda	4-6-70	14-6-70	8	13
17	Rama's Temple, Sadra, Ahmedabad	23-7-70	2-8-70	0	28
18	Dalmia Building, Varanasi	13-8-70	23-8-70	8	11
19	Hindu Dharamshala, Barachakia	31-8-70	10-9-70	21	16
20	Shanti Kutir, Dalhousie	4-10-70	14-10-70	0	11
21	Ladakh Buddhist Vihara, Delhi	18-10-70	28-10-70	11	9
22	Shivner Building, Bombay	5-11-70	15-11-70	19	37

Course No.	Location	Course Dates		Students Old	New
23	Samanvaya Vidyapith, Bagha (for children)	2-12-70	12-12-70	1	37
24	Burmese Vihara, Bodh Gaya	13-12-70	23-12-70	16	43
25	Samanvaya Ashram, Bodh Gaya	24-12-70	3-1-71	8	23
26	Burmese Vihara, Bodh Gaya	4-1-71	14-1-71	56	41
27	Burmese Vihara, Bodh Gaya	17-1-71	27-1-71	70	22
28	Nemaniwadi, Bombay	1-3-71	11-3-71	24	35
29	Nemaniwadi, Bombay	14-3-71	24-3-71	36	42
30	Nemaniwadi, Bombay	31-3-71	10-4-71	36	46
31	Narayanwadi, Bombay	11-4-71	21-4-71	38	28
32	Diksha Bhumi, Buddhist Vihara, Nagpur	25-4-71	5-5-71	3	34
33	Shreyas School, Ahmedabad	23-5-71	2-6-71	22	20
34	Nemaniwadi, Bombay	8-7-71	18-7-71	20	40
35	Samanvaya Ashram, Bodh Gaya	29-7-71	8-8-71	21	36
36	Nemaniwadi, Bombay	12-8-71	22-8-71	24	33
37	Bamanwadi, Jain Temple, Sirohi	26-8-71	5-9-71	20	29
38	Nemaniwadi, Bombay	9-9-71	19-9-71	28	27
39	Burmese Buddhist Temple, Kushinagar	22-9-71	2-10-71	17	55
40	Grand View Hotel, Dalhousie	6-10-71	16-10-71	42	75
41	Mohatta House, Bikaner	22-10-71	2-11-71	41	43
42	Panchayatiwadi, Bombay	5-11-71	15-11-71	32	28
43	Panchayatiwadi, Bombay	2-12-71	12-12-71	28	79
44	Loya Temple, Dharamsala, Alandi, Poona	23-12-71	2-1-72	59	90
45	Burmese Vihara, Bodh Gaya	19-1-72	29-1-72	74	116
46	Burmese Vihara, Bodh Gaya	30-1-72	9-2-72	118	43
47	Hindu Dharamshala, Barachakia	11-2-72	21-2-72	32	20
48	Buddhist Vihara, Pratapgarh	23-2-72	4-3-72	11	29
49	Nemaniwadi, Bombay	12-3-72	22-3-72	28	58
50	Mahatma Gandhi Ashram, Sevagram	27-3-72	6-4-72	13	25
51	Nemaniwadi, Bombay	13-4-72	23-4-72	34	41
52	Hindi Vidya Bhavan Hostel, Bombay	28-4-72	8-5-72	55	60
53	City Hotel, Poona	20-5-72	30-5-72	26	46
54	Jain Boarding, Ahmedabad	3-6-72	13-6-72	22	66
55	Green View Hotel, Nasik	2-7-72	12-7-72	47	97

Course No.	Location	Course Dates		Students Old	New
OSC-1	Green View Hotel, Nasik	13-7-72	17-7-72	36	—
56	Hindu Dharamshala, Jalna	3-8-72	13-8-72	23	121
57	Prince Hotel, Raxaul	2-9-72	12-9-72	18	44
58	Grand View Hotel, Dalhousie	29-9-72	9-10-72	50	55
59	Grand View Hotel, Dalhousie	10-10-72	20-10-72	92	45
60	Grand View Hotel, Dalhousie	21-10-72	31-10-72	108	36
61	Nemaniwadi, Bombay	9-11-72	19-11-72	27	43
62	Burmese Vihara, Varanasi	1-12-72	11-12-72	80	103
OLC-1	Burmese Vihara, Varanasi (20-day)	1-12-72	21-12-72	12	—
OLC-2	Burmese Vihara, Varanasi (30-day)	1-12-72	1-1-73	9	—
63	Burmese Vihara, Varanasi	11-12-72	21-12-72	110	61
64	Burmese Vihara, Varanasi	22-12-72	1-1-73	87	40
TSC-1	Burmese Vihara, Bodh Gaya	3-1-73	17-1-73	*	—
65	Burmese Vihara, Bodh Gaya	20-1-73	30-1-73	83	117
66	Sundari Bhavani Temple, Morvi	13-2-73	23-2-73	16	42
67	Panchayatiwadi, Bombay	1-3-73	11-3-73	84	112
OLC-3	Panchayatiwadi, Bombay (20-day)	1-3-73	21-3-73	5	—
OLC-4	Panchayatiwadi, Bombay (30-day)	1-3-73	31-3-73	7	—
68	Panchayatiwadi, Bombay	11-3-73	21-3-73	108	27
69	Panchayatiwadi, Bombay	21-3-73	31-3-73	120	15
70	Shri Rama Kalyan Mandapam, Madras	12-4-73	22-4-73	45	85
71	Seva Kendra, Baroda	28-4-73	8-5-73	28	57
72	Nisargopachar Ashram, Urlikanchan	20-5-73	30-5-73	8	36
73	Maheshwari School Hostel, Poona	30-5-73	9-6-73	39	49
74	I.I.T., Bombay	1-7-73	11-7-73	51	64
75	Kusum Industries, Hyderabad	13-7-73	23-7-73	15	59
76	Grand View Hotel, Dalhousie	1-8-73	11-8-73	85	158
77	L.J. Sanatorium, Darjeeling	16-8-73	26-8-73	28	12
78	L.J. Sanatorium, Darjeeling	26-8-73	5-9-73	32	58
79	Navnalanda Mahavihara, Nalanda	20-9-73	30-9-73	7	25
80	Shri Rama Kalyan Mandapam, Madras	13-10-73	23-10-73	67	73
OLC-5	Shri Rama Kalyan Mandapam, Madras (25-day)	13-10-73	7-11-73	38	—
81	Shri Rama Kalyan Mandapam, Madras	28-10-73	7-11-73	35	17

Course No.	Location	Course Dates		Students Old	New
82	Jain Mandir, Bhadreshwar (Bhuj)	21-11-73	31-11-73	28	86
83	Bhatia Sanatorium, Devlali	6-12-73	16-12-73	25	63
84	Burmese Vihara, Varanasi	22-12-73	1-1-74	33	62
85	Burmese Vihara, Rajgiri	3-1-74	13-1-74	65	62
TSC-2	Burmese Vihara, Bodh Gaya	14-1-74	25-1-74	*	—
86	Balvidya Ranjitpura, Pratapgarh	25-1-74	4-2-74	59	100
87	Saint Mary's Church, Khandala	3-3-74	13-3-74	26	96
88	Jain Adhyatma Sadhna Kendra, NDelhi	28-4-74	8-5-74	1	54
89	K.J. Somaiya College, Bombay	11-5-74	21-5-74	65	90
90	K.J. Somaiya College, Bombay	21-5-74	31-5-74	69	89
91	Kacchi Bhavan Dharamshala, Hyderabad	13-7-74	23-7-74	27	53
92	Grand View Hotel, Dalhousie	1-8-74	11-8-74	55	120
93	Grand View Hotel, Dalhousie	11-8-74	21-8-74	110	44
94	Tibetan Library, Dharamshala	22-8-74	1-9-74	10	73
95	Mahatma Gandhi Ashram, Sabarmati	9-9-74	19-9-74	25	39
96	Dadawadi Jain Temple, Ajmer	20-9-74	30-9-74	26	46
97	Jain A. Sadhana Kendra, New Delhi	1-10-74	11-10-74	52	55
98	Udyan Karyalaya, Poona	13-10-74	23-10-74	42	44
99	Hindi Vidyabhavan Hostel, Bombay	28-10-74	7-11-74	65	76
100	Shri Rama Krishna Dharamshala, Indore	20-11-74	30-11-74	25	27
101	Burmese Vihara, Varanasi	3-12-74	13-12-74	63	95
102	Burmese Vihara, Varanasi	13-12-74	23-12-74	55	83
103	Nirayatan, Rajgiri	24-12-74	4-1-75	82	42
104	Burmese Vihara, Bodh Gaya	4-1-75	14-1-75	148	72
TSC-3	Burmese Vihara, Bodh Gaya	19-1-75	30-1-75	*	—
105	Muslim Dargah Mosque, Ningal (Bhuj)	15-2-75	25-2-75	35	104
106	Muslim Dargah Mosque, Ningal (Bhuj)	25-2-75	7-3-75	42	68
107	Jain-Vishwa Bharati, Ladnu	9-3-75	19-3-75	36	126
108	Jain-Vishnu Bharati, Ladnu	19-3-75	29-3-75	22	34
109	Sawai Mansingh Stadium, Jaipur	30-3-75	9-4-75	137	105
110	Nav-sarjan High School, Nargol	1-5-75	11-5-75	53	65
OLC-6	Nav-sarjan High School, Nargol (20-day)	1-5-75	21-5-75	6	—
OLC-7	Nav-sarjan High School, Nargol (30-day)	1-5-75	31-5-75	28	—

Course No.	Location	Course Dates		Students Old	New
111	Nav-sarjan High School, Nargol	11-5-75	21-5-75	33	43
112	Nav-sarjan High School, Nargol	21-5-75	31-5-75	32	25
113	Kusum Industries, Hyderabad	3-7-75	13-7-75	38	53
114	New Amdar Nivas, Nagpur	9-8-75	19-8-75	36	125
115	Shri Rama Kalyan Mandapam, Madras	21-8-75	31-8-75	45	43
116	Grand View Hotel, Dalhousie	14-9-75	24-9-75	40	69
117	Central Jail, Jaipur	27-9-75	7-10-75	0	120
118	Kasturba University Hostel, Jaipur	7-10-75	17-10-75	55	80
119	Bharati Seva Sadan, Raxaul	18-11-75	28-11-75	26	29
120	Vandana Apts., Calcutta	29-11-75	9-12-75	30	111
121	Burmese Vihara, Bodh Gaya	10-12-75	20-12-75	73	80
122	Navnalanda Maha Vihara, Nalanda	20-12-75	30-12-75	52	37
TSC-4	Burmese Vihara, Bodh Gaya	9-1-76	19-1-76	*	—
123	Rajasthan Police Academy, Jaipur	27-1-76	6-2-76	0	93
124	Dhamma Khetta, Hyderabad	4-9-76	14-9-76	51	71
125	Dhamma Khetta, Hyderabad	16-9-76	27-9-76	49	45
126	Dhamma Giri, Igatpuri	27-10-76	7-11-76	38	51
127	Dhamma Giri, Igatpuri	6-11-76	17-11-76	25	42
128	Dhamma Giri, Igatpuri	20-11-76	1-12-76	33	5
129	Dhamma Giri, Igatpuri (30-day)	2-12-76	13-12-76	22	55
OLC-8	Dhamma Giri, Igatpuri	2-12-76	1-1-77	35	—
130	Dhamma Giri, Igatpuri	20-12-76	31-12-76	47	42
131	Central Jail, Jaipur	4-1-77	15-1-77	35	108
132	Burmese Vihara, Bodh Gaya	19-1-77	30-1-77	36	93
TSC-5	Burmese Vihara, Bodh Gaya	30-1-77	10-2-77	15	—
133	Dhamma Giri, Igatpuri	11-2-77	22-2-77	44	45
134	Dhamma Giri, Igatpuri	3-3-77	14-3-77	61	69
135	Dhamma Giri, Igatpuri	31-3-77	11-4-77	51	27
136	Dhamma Giri, Igatpuri	21-4-77	1-5-77	43	51
137	Dhamma Giri, Igatpuri	22-5-77	2-6-77	63	72
138	Dhamma Giri, Igatpuri	2-6-77	13-6-77	63	91
139	Dhamma Khetta, Hyderabad	15-7-77	26-7-77	53	68
140	Dhamma Khetta, Hyderabad	22-8-77	2-9-77	59	89

Course No.	Location	Course Dates		Students Old	New
141	Well-View Hotel, Darjeeling	20-9-77	30-9-77	26	53
142	Blind & Deaf College Hostel, NDelhi	10-10-77	20-10-77	63	61
143	Dhamma Giri, Igatpuri	16-11-77	27-11-77	50	95
144	Dhamma Giri, Igatpuri	10-12-77	21-12-77	65	75
TSC-6	Dhamma Giri, Igatpuri	19-1-78	30-1-78	*	—
145	Dhamma Khetta, Hyderabad	4-2-78	14-2-78	77	88
146	Dhamma Giri, Igatpuri	11-3-78	22-3-78	97	127
147	Dhamma Giri, Igatpuri	5-4-78	16-4-78	58	75
148	Dhamma Giri, Igatpuri	10-5-78	21-5-78	37	57
149	Dhamma Giri, Igatpuri	31-5-78	11-6-78	62	104
150	Dhamma Khetta, Hyderabad	12-7-78	22-7-78	43	57
151	Dhamma Khetta, Hyderabad	4-8-78	15-8-78	54	68
152	Dhamma Thali, Jaipur	20-9-78	1-10-78	56	86
153	Dhamma Giri, Igatpuri	18-10-78	29-10-78	57	95
154	Dhamma Giri, Igatpuri	18-11-78	29-11-78	55	115
155	Dhamma Giri, Igatpuri	14-12-78	25-12-78	107	61
156	Dhamma Giri, Igatpuri	4-1-79	15-1-79	113	92
TSC-7	Dhamma Giri, Igatpuri	19-1-79	31-1-79	*	—
157	Dhamma Khetta, Hyderabad	8-2-79	19-2-79	91	63
158	Dhamma Giri, Igatpuri	12-3-79	23-3-79	115	94
159	Dhamma Thali, Jaipur	31-3-79	10-4-79	42	40
160	Dhamma Giri, Igatpuri	12-4-79	23-4-79	50	87
161	Dhamma Giri, Igatpuri	10-5-79	21-5-79	81	104
162	Youth Hostel, Gaillon, France	1-7-79	11-7-79	12	60
163	Buddhist Temple, Plaige, France	14-7-79	24-7-79	14	62
164	College Français, Montreal, Canada	26-7-79	6-8-79	62	124
165	Priors Field School, Godalming, Surrey, U.K.	9-8-79	20-8-79	68	77
166	Priors Field School, Godalming, Surrey, U.K.	21-8-79	1-9-79	101	63
OSC-2	Dhamma Giri, Igatpuri	4-10-79	7-10-79	58	—
167	Dhamma Thali, Jaipur	27-10-79	7-11-79	75	74
168	Dhamma Giri, Igatpuri	14-11-79	25-11-79	66	98
169	Dhamma Giri, Igatpuri	4-12-79	14-12-79	70	83
170	Dhamma Giri, Igatpuri	21-12-79	1-1-80	73	73

Course No.	Location	Course Dates		Students Old	New
171	Dhamma Khetta, Hyderabad	4-1-80	14-1-80	59	57
TSC-8	Dhamma Giri, Igatpuri	19-1-80	30-1-80	*	—
172	Dhamma Giri, Igatpuri	1-2-80	12-2-80	91	129
173	Dhamma Giri, Igatpuri	29-2-80	11-3-80	58	85
174	Dhamma Giri, Igatpuri	15-3-80	26-3-80	74	50
175	University of Ceylon, Peradeniya Campus, Kandy, Sri Lanka	1-4-80	12-4-80	26	112
176	Ananda College Hostel, Colombo, Sri Lanka	17-4-80	28-4-80	21	84
OSC-3	Dhamma Giri, Igatpuri	30-4-80	4-5-80	89	—
177	Dhamma Giri, Igatpuri	13-5-80	24-5-80	61	194
178	Dhamma Khetta, Hyderabad	8-6-80	18-6-80	42	54
OSC-4	Dhamma Khetta, Hyderabad	18-6-80	24-6-80	34	—
179	Dhamma Khetta, Hyderabad	24-6-80	5-7-80	45	68
180	Hoch-Ybrig, Switzerland	18-7-80	28-7-80	40	81
181	College Francais, Montreal, Canada	31-7-80	10-8-80	70	52
182	Christian Church, Chicago, IL, U.S.A.	13-8-80	23-8-80	34	33
183	Philo (Mendocino), CA, U.S.A.	26-8-80	5-9-80	92	128
184	Boy Scout Camp, Sydney, Australia	14-9-80	26-9-80	48	71
185	Youth Hostel, Perth, Australia	28-9-80	9-10-80	17	59
186	Dhamma Thalī, Jaipur	11-11-80	22-11-80	40	42
OSC-5	Dhamma Thalī, Jaipur	22-11-80	26-11-80	95	—
187	Dhamma Thalī, Jaipur	26-11-80	7-12-80	26	54
188	Dhamma Giri, Igatpuri	10-12-80	21-12-80	65	125
189	Dhamma Giri, Igatpuri	21-12-80	31-12-80	74	58
OSC-6	Dhamma Giri, Igatpuri	1-1-81	4-1-81	74	—
190	Dhamma Giri, Igatpuri	7-1-81	18-1-81	87	88
TSC-9	Dhamma Giri, Igatpuri	18-1-81	30-1-81	22	—
191	Dhamma Khetta, Hyderabad	2-2-81	13-2-81	47	53
192	Dhamma Giri, Igatpuri	15-2-81	26-2-81	102	202
193	Anand Kuti Vihar, Swayambhu, Nepal	25-3-81	5-4-81	50	193
194	Dhamma Giri, Igatpuri	10-5-81	21-5-81	69	183
195	Dhamma Thalī, Jaipur	25-5-81	5-6-81	58	76
196	Goshen, Massachusetts, U.S.A.	14-6-81	25-6-81	45	129

Course No.	Location	Course Dates		Students Old	New
197	I.M.C., Splatts House, U.K.	3-7-81	14-7-81	89	79
198	Dhamma Khetta, Hyderabad	21-7-81	1-8-81	88	128
199	Youth Hostel, Kyoto, Japan	13-8-81	24-8-81	28	57
200	Boys' Camp, Willetts, CA, U.S.A..	1-9-81	12-9-81	106	185
201	Boy Scout Camp, Sydney, Australia	27-9-81	7-10-81	50	114
202	Youth Hostel, Perth, Australia	8-10-81	18-10-81	10	70
OSC-7	Dhamma Giri, Igatpuri	1-11-81	8-11-81	67	—
203	Dhamma Thali, Jaipur	21-11-81	1-12-81	53	60
204	Dhamma Giri, Igatpuri	5-12-81	16-12-81	104	165
SPS-1	Dhamma Giri, Igatpuri	16-12-81	22-12-81	86	—
OLC-9	Dhamma Giri, Igatpuri (30-day)	23-12-81	22-1-82	25	—
205	Dhamma Giri, Igatpuri	23-12-81	31-1-82	136	131
TSC-10	Dhamma Giri, Igatpuri	5-1-82	20-1-82	47	—
206	Dhamma Giri, Igatpuri	20-1-82	31-1-82	104	165
207	Dhamma Giri, Igatpuri	31-1-82	11-2-82	106	154
208	Shiva Temple, Mamiragachhi, Calcutta	26-2-82	9-3-82	74	162
209	Dhamma Khetta, Hyderabad	18-3-82	29-3-82	88	92
210	University of Ceylon, Peradeniya Campus, Kandy, Sri Lanka	31-3-82	11-4-82	61	100
OSC-8	Dhamma Giri, Igatpuri	13-4-82	18-4-82	105	—
211	Dhamma Giri, Igatpuri	25-4-82	6-5-82	116	197
212	Convent School, Buddhanilkanth, Kathmandu, Nepal	9-5-82	20-5-82	120	219
213	Boys' Camp, Willetts, CA, U.S.A.	28-5-82	8-6-82	102	86
214	Sandwich, MA, U.S.A..	9-6-82	20-6-82	82	50
215	Nice, France	28-6-82	10-7-82	107	130
216	Dhamma Khetta, Hyderabad	14-7-82	25-7-82	77	113
217	Dhamma Thali, Jaipur	4-8-82	15-8-82	85	149
218	Youth Hostel, Ise, Japan	18-8-82	28-8-82	35	65
219	Sorel, Quebec, Canada	1-9-82	12-9-82	72	62
220	Boys' Camp, Willetts, CA, U.S.A..	13-9-82	24-9-82	155	160
221	Sydney, Australia	29-9-82	10-10-82	78	130
222	Y.M.C.A., Auckland, New Zealand	11-10-82	22-10-82	32	90

Course No.	Location	Course Dates		Students Old	New
223	Dhamma Thalī, Jaipur	18-11-82	29-11-82	89	85
OLC-10	Dhamma Giri, Igatpuri (30-day)	30-11-82	30-12-82	38	—
224	Dhamma Giri, Igatpuri	10-12-82	20-12-82	126	101
225	Dhamma Giri, Igatpuri	1-1-83	12-1-83	149	155
OLC-11	Dhamma Giri, Igatpuri (30-day)	1-1-83	1-2-83	*	—
TSC-11	Dhamma Giri, Igatpuri	19-1-83	1-2-83	120	—
226	Dhamma Khetta, Hyderabad	3-2-83	14-3-83	165	108
STP-2	Dhamma Khetta, Hyderabad	15-2-83	23-2-83	*	—
227	Dhamma Giri, Igatpuri	12-3-83	22-3-83	151	146
228	University of Ceylon, Peradeniya Campus, Kandy, Sri Lanka	30-3-83	10-4-83	66	61
229	Dhamma Giri, Igatpuri	12-4-83	23-4-83	93	136
230	Dhamma Giri, Igatpuri	6-5-83	17-5-83	81	117
231	Kathmandu, Nepal	18-6-83	29-6-83	135	145
232	Dhamma Thalī, Jaipur	30-6-83	10-7-83	70	96
233	Dhamma Khetta, Hyderabad	13-7-83	23-7-83	71	106
234	Langley School, Norfolk, U.K.	29-7-83	7-8-83	52	56
235	Dhamma Dharā, Shelburne Falls, MA, U.S.A..	12-8-83	23-8-83	65	75
236	Santa Cruz, CA, U.S.A.	1-9-83	11-9-83	146	139
237	Amanohashidate, Japan	14-9-83	25-9-83	54	50
238	Dhamma Thalī, Jaipur	22-10-83	2-11-83	91	101
239	Dhamma Bhūmi, Blackheath, Australia	12-11-83	22-11-83	73	36
240	Dhamma Bhūmi, Blackheath, Australia	23-11-83	3-12-83	53	35
241	Dhamma Giri, Igatpuri	10-12-83	21-12-83	110	166
OLC-12	Dhamma Giri, Igatpuri (30-day)	10-12-83	9-1-84	*	—
TSC-12	Dhamma Giri, Igatpuri	14-1-84	27-1-84	*	—
242	Dhamma Thalī, Jaipur	1-2-84	11-2-84	64	107
SPS-3	Dhamma Thalī, Jaipur	11-2-84	22-2-84	176	—
243	Dhamma Khetta, Hyderabad	11-3-84	22-3-84	72	106
244	R.K. Mandapam, Madras	22-3-84	2-4-84	61	54
245	Palace Hotel, Chail	17-4-84	27-4-84	19	131
246	Dhamma Giri, Igatpuri	20-5-84	31-5-84	105	150
247	Dhamma Khetta, Hyderabad	6-7-84	17-7-84	93	61

Course No.	Location	Course Dates		Students Old	New
248	Dhamma Dhārā, Shelburne Falls, MA, U.S.A.	30-7-84	10-8-84	65	51
OLC-13	Dhamma Dhārā, Shelburne Falls, MA, U.S.A.	30-7-84	21-8-84	25	—
249	Dhamma Dhārā, Shelburne Falls, MA, U.S.A.	11-8-84	21-8-84	75	52
250	Langley School, Norfolk, U.K.	22-8-84	2-9-84	185	144
251	Dhamma Thalī, Jaipur	23-9-84	4-10-84	132	94
252	Dharmashriṅga, Kathmandu, Nepal	7-10-84	18-10-84	126	158
253	Dhamma Bhūmi, Blackheath, Australia	30-10-84	10-11-84	44	31
254	Dhamma Bhūmi, Blackheath, Australia	10-11-84	20-11-84	74	49
255	Dhamma Giri, Igatpuri	30-11-84	11-12-84	174	165
OLC-14	Dhamma Giri, Igatpuri (30-day)	11-12-84	9-1-85	127	—
STP-4	Dhamma Giri, Igatpuri	9-1-85	18-1-85	181	—
TSC-13	Dhamma Giri, Igatpuri	19-1-85	31-1-85	115	—
256	Jain Bhavan, Calcutta	10-2-85	20-2-85	52	136
257	Dhamma Thalī, Jaipur	21-2-85	2-3-85	34	73
258	Dhamma Khetta, Hyderabad	10-3-85	20-3-85	80	91
APC-1	Dhamma Giri, Igatpuri	11-4-85	15-4-85	0	53
259	Dhamma Giri, Igatpuri	9-5-85	20-5-85	132	169
260	Dhamma Giri, Igatpuri	24-5-85	4-5-85	121	165
261	Dhamma Thalī, Jaipur	6-7-85	17-7-85	69	96
262	Dhamma Dhārā, Shelburne Falls, MA, U.S.A.	29-7-85	8-8-85	98	75
263	Dhamma Dhārā, Shelburne Falls, MA, U.S.A.	9-8-85	20-8-85	109	70
264	Norwich, Norfolk, U.K.	27-8-85	7-9-85	78	130
265	Dhamma Khetta, Hyderabad	18-9-85	28-9-85	88	104
266	Jain Bhavan, Calcutta	17-10-85	26-10-85	65	104
267	Anandkuti Vidyapath, Nepal	27-10-85	8-11-85	61	161
268	Dhamma Giri, Igatpuri	7-12-85	18-12-85	150	135
APC-2	Dhamma Giri, Igatpuri	19-12-85	22-11-85	93	43
SPS-5	Dhamma Giri, Igatpuri	24-12-85	2-1-86	173	—
TSC-14	Dhamma Giri, Igatpuri	5-1-86	21-1-86	99	—
OLC-15	Dhamma Giri, Igatpuri (30-day)	24-1-86	22-2-86	193	—
269	Dhamma Giri, Igatpuri	28-1-86	8-2-86	88	118
270	Dhamma Giri, Igatpuri	9-2-86	20-2-86	80	99
CC-1	Jamnabai Narsee School, Bombay	17-4-86	21-4-86	0	77

Course No.	Location	Course Dates		Students Old	New
271	Dhamma Giri, Igatpuri	1-5-86	12-5-86	42	80
272	Dhamma Giri, Igatpuri	13-5-86	24-5-86	49	62
273	Dhamma Giri, Igatpuri	25-5-86	5-6-86	46	75
274	Langley School, Norfolk, U.K.	13-8-86	24-8-86	156	130
275	Dhamma Bhūmi, Blackheath, Australia	12-9-86	22-9-86	80	53
SPS-6	Dhamma Bhūmi, Blackheath, Australia	22-9-86	30-9-86	91	—
276	Dhamma Giri, Igatpuri	16-10-86	26-10-86	97	108
277	Dhamma Thalī, Jaipur	5-11-86	16-11-86	114	95
278	Dhamma Khetta, Hyderabad	19-11-86	30-11-86	56	47
SPS-7	Dhamma Giri, Igatpuri	9-12-86	18-12-86	211	—
279	Dhamma Giri, Igatpuri (Pāli Seminar)	20-12-86	30-12-86	173	94
TSC-15	Dhamma Giri, Igatpuri	4-1-87	19-1-87	118	—
OLC-16	Dhamma Giri, Igatpuri (30-day)	21-1-87	20-2-87	126	—
OLC-17	Dhamma Giri, Igatpuri (40-day)	21-1-87	29-2-87	41	—
280	Dhamma Giri, Igatpuri	21-1-87	1-2-87	96	104
281	Dhamma Giri, Igatpuri	4-2-87	15-2-87	89	71
282	Dhamma Giri, Igatpuri	18-2-87	1-3-87	112	151
283	Dhamma Thalī, Jaipur	19-3-87	30-3-87	85	84
OSC-9	Dhamma Giri, Igatpuri	11-4-87	15-4-87	66	—
284	Dhamma Giri, Igatpuri	16-4-87	27-4-87	93	142
OSC-10	Dhamma Giri, Igatpuri	10-5-87	13-5-87	90	—
285	Dhamma Giri, Igatpuri (Education Seminar)	14-5-87	25-5-87	71	129
SPS-8	Dhamma Giri, Igatpuri	25-5-87	3-6-87	153	—
286	Dhamma Khetta, Hyderabad	27-6-87	8-7-87	71	84
287	Dhamma Dharā, Shelburne Falls, MA, U.S.A.	29-7-87	9-8-87	94	62
288	Dhamma Dharā, Shelburne Falls, MA, U.S.A.	11-8-87	22-8-87	63	57
289	California Vipassana House, U.S.A.	18-8-87	29-8-87	49	50
OSC-11	California Vipassana House, U.S.A.	31-8-87	4-9-87	108	—
290	Dhamma Giri, Igatpuri	8-10-87	19-10-87	98	97
291	Jain Bhavan, Calcutta	25-10-87	5-11-87	97	100
292	Dharmashriṅga, Nepal	29-10-87	9-11-87	100	124
293	Dharmashriṅga, Nepal	9-11-87	20-11-87	61	72
294	Dhamma Thalī, Jaipur	12-11-87	23-11-87	74	65

Course No.	Location	Course Dates		Students Old	New
295	Dhamma Giri, Igatpuri	17-11-87	28-11-87	95	143
STP-9	Dhamma Giri, Igatpuri	29-11-87	8-12-87	170	—
296	I.I.T., Delhi (Health Seminar)	15-12-87	25-12-87	48	114
297	Dhamma Giri, Igatpuri	21-12-87	31-12-87	121	124
TSC-16	Dhamma Giri, Igatpuri	4-1-88	19-1-88	108	—
298	Dhamma Giri, Igatpuri	21-1-88	1-2-88	82	95
OLC-18	Dhamma Giri, Igatpuri (30-day)	22-1-88	18-2-88	140	—
OLC-19	Dhamma Giri, Igatpuri (40-day)	22-1-88	28-2-88	40	—
299	Dhamma Giri, Igatpuri	4-2-88	15-2-88	93	112
300	Dhamma Giri, Igatpuri	18-2-88	29-2-88	148	132
301	Dhamma Thalī, Jaipur	19-3-88	29-3-88	54	47
302	Dhamma Thalī, Jaipur	30-3-88	10-4-88	33	45
OSC-12	Dhamma Giri, Igatpuri	14-4-88	18-4-88	135	—
OSC-13	Dhamma Giri, Igatpuri	19-4-88	22-4-88	50	—
303	Dhamma Giri, Igatpuri	25-4-88	6-5-88	80	262
304	Dhamma Giri, Igatpuri (Special 10-day)	7-5-88	17-5-88	195	—
305	Dhamma Giri, Igatpuri	8-8-88	19-8-88	101	77
306	Dhamma Khetta, Hyderabad	10-7-88	21-7-88	65	91
307	Dhamma Khetta, Hyderabad	21-7-88	1-8-88	39	46
308	Dhamma Mahī, France	8-8-88	19-5-88	101	77
309	Dhamma Mahī, France	20-8-88	31-8-88	84	93
310	Dharmashrińga, Nepal	29-9-88	11-11-88	91	76
311	Dhamma Thalī, Jaipur	13-10-88	24-10-88	70	65
312	Dhamma Giri, Igatpuri	24-10-88	4-11-88	47	72
313	Dhamma Giri, Igatpuri (Special 10-day)	24-10-88	4-11-88	34	—
314	Dhamma Bhūmi, Blackheath, Australia	16-11-88	27-11-88	74	43
315	Dhamma Medinī, New Zealand	21-11-88	2-12-88	33	16
316	Dhamma Bhūmi, Blackheath, Australia	27-11-88	8-12-88	67	62
TSC-17	Dhamma Giri, Igatpuri	14-12-88	29-12-88	109	—
317	Dhamma Giri, Igatpuri	1-1-89	1-12-89	102	131
318	Dhamma Giri, Igatpuri (Special 10-day)	1-1-89	1-12-89	42	—
OLC-20	Dhamma Giri, Igatpuri (30-day)	14-1-89	13-2-89	137	—
OLC-21	Dhamma Giri, Igatpuri (45-day)	14-1-89	28-2-89	48	—

Course No.	Location	Course Dates		Students Old	New
319	Dhamma Giri, Igatpuri	17-1-89	28-1-89	104	96
320	Dhamma Giri, Igatpuri	31-1-89	11-2-89	97	105
321	Dhamma Giri, Igatpuri	15-2-89	26-2-89	196	175
322	Dhamma Giri, Igatpuri	1-4-89	12-4-89	91	172
323	Dhamma Giri, Igatpuri	13-4-89	24-4-89	109	147
STP-10	Dhamma Giri, Igatpuri	13-4-89	21-4-89	158	—
324	Dhamma Giri, Igatpuri (Special 10-day)	24-4-89	6-5-89	30	—
325	Dhamma Giri, Igatpuri	24-4-89	6-5-89	101	189
OSC-14	Dhamma Giri, Igatpuri	7-5-89	11-5-89	75	—
OLC-22	Dhamma Giri, Igatpuri (20-day)	18-5-89	8-6-89	27	—
326	Dhamma Giri, Igatpuri	18-5-89	29-5-89	96	192
327	Dhamma Giri, Igatpuri	30-5-89	10-6-89	110	262
328	Dhamma Khetta, Hyderabad	30-6-89	11-7-89	8	90
STP-11	Dhamma Khetta, Hyderabad	11-7-89	19-7-89	33	—
329	Dhamma Mahī, France	30-7-89	9-8-89	88	93
330	Dhamma Dharā, Shelburne Falls, MA, U.S.A.	11-8-89	22-8-89	80	75
OSC-15	California Vipassana Center, Occidental, CA, U.S.A.	26-8-89	30-8-89	57	—
OSC-16	Dhamma Bhānu, Japan	1-9-89	5-9-89	31	—
331	Dhamma Thalī, Jaipur	27-9-89	8-10-89	85	59
332	Dharmashriṅga, Kathmandu, Nepal	13-10-89	23-10-89	91	86
333	Dhamma Giri, Igatpuri	28-11-89	9-12-89	75	140
OSC-17	Dhamma Giri, Igatpuri	9-12-89	12-12-89	76	—
TSC-18	Dhamma Giri, Igatpuri	14-12-89	29-12-89	128	—
334	Dhamma Giri, Igatpuri	1-1-90	12-1-90	101	284
STP-12	Dhamma Giri, Igatpuri	3-1-90	12-1-90	111	—
OLC-23	Dhamma Giri, Igatpuri (30-day)	14-1-90	14-2-90	143	—
OLC-24	Dhamma Giri, Igatpuri (40-day)	14-1-90	28-2-90	60	—
335	Dhamma Giri, Igatpuri	17-1-90	28-1-90	96	112
336	Dhamma Giri, Igatpuri	31-1-90	11-2-90	88	138
337	Dhamma Giri, Igatpuri (Pāli Seminar)	17-2-90	28-2-90	169	82
338	Dhamma Giri, Igatpuri	8-3-90	19-3-90	164	258
339	Bangkok, Thailand	21-3-90	31-3-90	20	81

Course No.	Location	Course Dates		Students Old	New
340	Dhamma Giri, Igatpuri	25-4-90	6-5-90	122	242
341	Dhamma Giri, Igatpuri (Special 10-day)	25-4-90	6-5-90	45	—
342	Dhamma Giri, Igatpuri	7-5-90	18-5-90	103	209
CC-2	Dhamma Giri, Igatpuri (Teenagers')	7-5-90	18-5-90	27	149
343	Dhamma Giri, Igatpuri	1-6-90	12-6-90	124	251
OLC-25	Dhamma Giri, Igatpuri (30-day)	1-6-90	1-7-90	31	—
344	Dhamma Mahī, France	4-7-90	15-7-90	90	50
345	Dhamma Mahī, France	16-7-90	27-7-90	85	65
346	Dhamma Khetta, Hyderabad	1-8-90	12-8-90	61	77
347	Dhamma Thalī, Jaipur	13-9-90	24-9-90	68	69
348	Dharmashriṅga, Kathmandu, Nepal	3-10-90	13-10-90	69	80
349	Dhamma Bhūmi, Blackheath, Australia	29-10-90	9-11-90	54	68
OSC-18	Dhamma Rasmi, Queensland, Australia	3-11-90	7-11-90	31	—
STP-13	Dhamma Bhūmi, Blackheath, Australia	9-11-90	17-11-90	81	—
TSC-19	Dhamma Giri, Igatpuri	15-12-90	5-1-91	166	—
OLC-26	Dhamma Giri, Igatpuri (30-day)	17-1-91	15-2-91	215	—
OLC-27	Dhamma Giri, Igatpuri (45-day)	17-1-91	3-3-91	92	—
350	Dhamma Giri, Igatpuri	19-1-91	30-1-91	127	103
351	Dhamma Giri, Igatpuri	19-2-91	2-3-91	102	111
352	Dhamma Giri, Igatpuri	19-2-91	2-3-91	133	116
STP-14	Dhamma Giri, Igatpuri	20-3-91	28-3-91	100	—
353	Bentota, Sri Lanka	10-5-91	21-5-91	30	200
354	Mahabodhi Society, Madras	30-5-91	9-6-91	49	60
355	Dhamma Khetta, Hyderabad	4-6-91	15-6-91	80	91
356	Dhamma Dharā, Shelburne Falls, MA, U.S.A.	22-7-91	2-8-91	100	98
OLC-28	Dhamma Dharā, Shelburne Falls, MA, U.S.A.	22-7-91	2-8-91	30	—
357	Dhamma Sirī, Kaufman, TX, U.S.A.	5-8-91	16-8-91	15	20
358	Dhamma Mahāvana, North Fork, CA, U.S.A.	10-8-91	21-8-91	61	42
359	Dhamma Bhānu, Japan	29-8-91	8-9-91	27	17
360	Daw Dhammethi Nunnery, Rangoon	8-9-91	19-9-91	0	170
361	Daw Dhammethi Nunnery, Rangoon	20-9-91	1-10-91	0	130
362	Dhamma Giri, Igatpuri	14-11-91	25-11-91	143	175
TSC-20	Dhamma Giri, Igatpuri	12-12-91	9-1-92	156	—

Course No.	Location	Course Dates		Students Old	New
OLC-28	Dhamma Giri, Igatpuri (30-day)	21-1-92	21-2-92	182	—
OLC-29	Dhamma Giri, Igatpuri (45-day)	21-1-92	6-3-92	74	—
363	Dhamma Giri, Igatpuri	23-1-92	3-2-92	116	106
364	Dhamma Giri, Igatpuri	6-2-92	17-2-92	110	128
365	Dhamma Giri, Igatpuri	25-2-92	7-3-92	119	147
366	Dhamma Giri, Igatpuri	4-4-92	15-4-92	140	243
367	Dhamma Giri, Igatpuri (Special 10-day)	4-4-92	15-4-92	43	—
368	Dhamma Giri, Igatpuri	17-4-92	28-4-92	152	277
OSC-19	Dhamma Giri, Igatpuri	1-5-92	5-5-92	131	—
369	Dharmashriṅga, Kathmandu, Nepal	22-5-92	1-6-92	97	94
370	Dharmashriṅga, Kathmandu, Nepal	2-6-92	13-6-92	71	116
371	Dhamma Thalī, Jaipur	1-8-92	12-8-92	61	49
372	Dhamma Thalī, Jaipur	14-8-92	25-8-92	81	64
373	Dhamma Thalī, Jaipur	26-8-92	6-9-92	54	64
374	Dhamma Giri, Igatpuri	7-11-92	18-11-92	136	126
TSC-21	Dhamma Thalī, Jaipur	1-12-92	1-1-93	100	—
OLC-30	Dhamma Thalī, Jaipur (30-day)	20-1-93	19-2-93	178	—
OLC-31	Dhamma Thalī, Jaipur (45-day)	20-1-93	6-3-93	34	—
375	Dhamma Thalī, Jaipur	22-2-93	5-3-93	104	75
376	Dhamma Giri, Igatpuri	13-3-93	24-3-93	133	190
377	Dhamma Giri, Igatpuri	31-3-93	11-4-93	96	188
378	Dhamma Giri, Igatpuri	16-5-93	27-5-93	120	272
379	Dhamma Giri, Igatpuri	29-5-93	9-6-93	102	267
380	Dhamma Giri, Igatpuri	16-6-93	27-6-93	61	233
STP-15	Dhamma Giri, Igatpuri	16-6-93	25-6-93	85	—
381	Dhamma Giri, Igatpuri	29-6-93	10-7-93	76	183
382	Dhamma Khetta, Hyderabad	17-7-93	28-7-93	53	57
383	Dhamma Kamala, Thailand	24-9-93	5-10-93	49	22
384	Dhamma Joti, Myanmar	8-10-93	19-10-93	52	93
385	Dhamma Joti, Myanmar	19-10-93	30-10-93	33	93
386	Dhamma Joti, Myanmar	30-10-93	10-11-93	47	117
387	Dhamma Giri, Igatpuri	19-11-93	30-11-93	142	262
TSC-22	Dhamma Giri, Igatpuri	10-12-93	9-1-94	139	—

Course No.	Location	Course Dates		Students Old	New
OLC-32	Dhamma Giri, Igatpuri (30-day)	25-1-94	25-2-94	170	—
OLC-33	Dhamma Giri, Igatpuri (45-day)	25-1-94	12-3-94	60	—
388	Dhamma Giri, Igatpuri	27-1-94	7-2-94	121	155
389	Dhamma Giri, Igatpuri	10-2-94	21-2-94	117	104
390	Dhamma Giri, Igatpuri	26-2-94	9-3-94	146	158
391	Dhamma Giri, Igatpuri	13-3-94	24-3-94	112	158
392	Tihar Jail, Delhi	4-4-94	15-4-94	122	930
393	Dhamma Kūṭa, Sri Lanka	25-4-94	6-5-94	64	75
394	Dharmashriṅga, Nepal	1-6-94	12-6-94	59	95
395	Dharmashriṅga, Nepal	14-6-94	25-6-94	154	119
396	Dharmashriṅga, Nepal	1-7-94	12-7-94	39	113
397	Dhamma Giri, Igatpuri	6-11-94	16-11-94	213	255
398	Dhamma Giri, Igatpuri	16-11-94	27-11-94	204	272
TSC-23	Dhamma Giri, Igatpuri	10-12-94	10-1-95	149	----
LC-34	Dhamma Giri, Igatpuri (30-day)	25-1-95	24-2-95	166	----
399	Dhamma Giri, Igatpuri	26-1-95	6-2-95	117	147
400	Dhamma Giri, Igatpuri	9-2-95	20-2-95	142	121
LC-35	Dhamma Giri, Igatpuri (45-day)	25-1-95	8-3-96	49	----
401	Dhamma Giri, Igatpuri	26-2-95	8-3-95	149	241
STP-16	Dhamma Giri, Igatpuri	28-3-95	5-4-95	167	----
402	Dhamma Giri, Igatpuri	12-4-95	23-4-95	129	336
403	Dhamma Giri, Igatpuri	24-4-95	4-5-95	110	216
404	Dhamma Joti, Myanmar	15-5-95	26-5-95	56	71
405	Dhamma Joti, Myanmar	26-5-95	6-6-95	49	65
406	Dhamma Kamala, Thailand	17-6-95	28-6-95	49	36
407	Dhamma Joti, Myanmar	12-7-95	23-7-95	28	66
408	Dhamma Joti, Myanmar	26-7-95	6-8-95	12	38
409	Dhamma Joti, Myanmar	9-8-95	20-8-95	19	42
410	Kolhapur (Hatkangale)	31-10-95	11-11-95	39	64
411	Dhamma Giri, Igatpuri	8-11-95	19-11-95	171	288
TSC-24	Dhamma Giri, Igatpuri	10-12-95	10-1-96	197	----
LC-36	Dhamma Giri, Igatpuri (30-day)	23-1-96	23-2-96	96	----
LC-37	Dhamma Giri, Igatpuri (45-day)	23-1-96	6-3-96	46	----

Course No.	Location	Course Dates		Students Old	New
412	Dhamma Giri, Igatpuri	24-1-96	4-2-96	120	154
413	Dhamma Giri, Igatpuri	7-2-96	18-2-96	125	143
414	Dhamma Giri, Igatpuri	28-2-96	10-3-96	204	263
415	Dhamma Giri, Igatpuri	28-10-96	8-11-96	165	341
TSC-25	Dhamma Giri, Igatpuri	1-12-96	31-12-96	158	----
LC-38	Dhamma Giri, Igatpuri (30-day)	16-1-97	16-2-97	132	----
LC-39	Dhamma Giri, Igatpuri (45-day)	16-1-97	2-3-97	79	----
416	Dhamma Giri, Igatpuri	17-1-97	28-1-97	144	174
417	Dhamma Giri, Igatpuri	30-1-97	10-2-97	102	151
418	Dhamma Giri, Igatpuri	12-2-97	23-2-97	126	135
419	Dhamma Giri, Igatpuri	26-2-97	9-3-97	192	210
420	Dhamma Giri, Igatpuri (Special 10-day)	12-3-97	23-3-97	41	----
421	Dhamma Giri, Igatpuri	12-3-97	23-3-97	129	324
CC	Jamnabai Narsee High School, Mumbai	26-4-97	---	10	40
CC	Kirtan Kendra	27-4-97	---	15	45
422	Dhamma Giri, Igatpuri	26-3-97	6-4-97	118	285
LC-40	Dhamma Giri, Igatpuri (20-day)	25-3-97	15-4-97	54	----
423	Ackworth Leprosy Hospital, Mumbai	15-5-97	26-5-97	---	42
424	Kamla Mehta Blind School, Mumbai	4-9-97	15-9-97	---	46
425	Dhamma Giri, Igatpuri	28-10-97	8-11-97	201	212
426	Dhamma Giri, Igatpuri	16-11-97	27-11-97	218	351
TSC-26	Dhamma Giri, Igatpuri	1-12-97	1-1-98	239	----
LC-41	Dhamma Giri, Igatpuri	13-1-98	13-2-98	115	----
LC-42	Dhamma Giri, Igatpuri	13-1-98	28-2-98	87	----
427	Dhamma Giri, Igatpuri	17-1-98	28-1-98	156	210
428	Dhamma Giri, Igatpuri	31-1-98	11-2-98	130	205
429	Dhamma Giri, Igatpuri	14-2-98	25-2-98	203	309

Mere arjita puṇya meṅ
bhāga sabhī kā hoya.
Isa maṅgala-maya Dharma kā
lābha sabhī ko hoya.

May the merits I have acquired
be shared by one and all.
May this munificent Dhamma
benefit one and all.

—*Hindi dohas of S. N. Goenka*

Glossary of Pāli Terms

Included in this list are Pāli terms that appear in the text as well as some other terms of importance in the teaching of the Buddha.

Abhidhamma   see *Tipiṭaka*.

adhiṭṭhāna   strong determination. One of the ten *pāramī*.

akāliko   a quality of Dhamma meaning 'to be experienced here and now.'

akusala   unwholesome, harmful. Opposite *kusala*.

anāgāmī   non-returner; a person who has reached the third stage of enlightenment characterized by the eradication of the fourth and fifth fetters: ill will and passion. This person will attain the arahant stage either during this lifetime or in a subsequent rebirth in a *rūpa-brahmā loka*. See *ariya*.

Ānanda   bliss, delight.

Ānāpāna   respiration. *Ānāpāna-sati*: awareness of respiration.

anattā   non-self, ego-less, without essence, without substance. One of the three basic characteristics. See *lakkhaṇa*.

anusaya-kilesa   see *kilesa*.

Arahant/arahat   Fully liberated being; a person who has reached the fourth and final stage of enlightenment, characterized by the eradication of the last five fetters: craving for existence in the material world, craving for existence in the immaterial world, conceit, restlessness and ignorance. See *Buddha*, *ariya*.

ariya   noble; saintly person. One who has purified his mind to the point that he has experienced the ultimate reality (*nibbāna*). There are four levels of *ariya*: *sotāpanna* ('stream-enterer'): *sakadāgāmi* ('once-returner'); *anāgāmi* ('non-returner'); and *arahat* (who will undergo no further rebirth after his present existence).

ariya aṭṭhaṅgika magga   the Noble Eightfold Path. See *magga*.

ariya sacca   Noble Truth. See *sacca*.

arūpa-brahmā loka   immaterial celestial plane reached by the attainment of formless *jhānas* (absorption *samādhi*). See *loka*.

asaṅkheyya   literally, 'incalculable,' a number equal to 10140.

asubha   impure, repellent, not beautiful. Opposite *subha*, pure, beautiful.

Assutavā/assutavant   uninstructed; one who has never even heard the truth, who lacks even *suta-mayā paññā*, and therefore cannot take any steps towards his liberation. Opposite *sutavā*.

aṭṭhakathā   commentary of Pāli Canon texts.

avijjā   ignorance, illusion. The first link in the chain of Conditioned Arising (*paṭicca samuppāda*). Together with *rāga* and *dosa*, one of the three principal mental defilements. These three are the root causes of all other mental impurities and hence of suffering. Synonym of *moha*.

āyatana   sphere, region, especially the six spheres of perception (*saḷāyatana*), i.e., the five physical senses plus the mind, and their corresponding objects, namely:

eye (*cakkhu*) and visual objects (*rūpa*),

ear (*sota*) and sound (*sadda*),

nose (*ghāna*) and odour (*gandha*),

tongue (*jivhā*) and taste (*rasa*),

body (*kāya*) and touch (*phoṭṭhabba*),

mind (*mano*) and objects of mind,
   i.e., thoughts of all kinds (*dhamma*).

These are also called the six faculties. See *indriya*.

bala   strength, power. The five mental strengths are faith (*saddhā*), effort (*viriya*), awareness (*sati*), concentration (*samādhi*), wisdom (*paññā*). When they are in a less developed form, these are called the five faculties. See *indriya*.

bhaṅga   dissolution. An important stage in the practice of Vipassana, the experience of the dissolution of the apparent solidity of the body into subtle vibrations which are constantly arising and passing away.

Bhante/bhante   literally, 'venerable sir'; term used to address monks.

bhava   (the process of) becoming. *Bhava-cakka*: the wheel of continuing existence. See *cakka*.

bhava saṅkhāra   see *saṅkhāra*.

bhāvanā   mental development, meditation. The two divisions of *bhāvanā* are the development of calm (*samatha-bhāvanā*), corresponding to concentration of mind (*samādhi*), and the development of insight (*vipassanā-bhāvana*), corresponding to wisdom (*paññā*). Development of *samatha* will lead to the states of *jhāna*; development of *vipassanā* will lead to liberation. See *jhāna, paññā, samādhi, vipassanā*.

bhāvanā-mayā paññā   wisdom developing from personal, direct experience. See *paññā*.

bhavaṅga   seat of birth-producing *kamma*.

Bhavatu sabba maṅgalaṃ   "May all beings be happy." A traditional phrase by which one expresses one's goodwill towards others. (Literally, "May there be every happiness.")

Bhikkhu/bhikkhu   (Buddhist) monk; meditator. Feminine form *bhikkhunī*: nun.

bhūmi   land.

bodhi   enlightenment.

Bodhisatta   literally, 'enlightenment-being.' One who is working to become a Buddha. Used to designate Siddhattha Gotama in the time before he achieved full enlightenment. Sanskrit: *bodhisattva*.

bojjhaṅga   factor of enlightenment, i.e., quality that helps one to attain enlightenment. The seven such factors are awarenesss (*sati*), penetrating investigation of Dhamma (*Dhamma-vicaya*), effort (*viriya*), bliss (*pīti*), tranquillity (*passaddhi*), concentration (*samādhi*), equanimity (*upekkhā*).

Brahmā   inhabitant of the higher heavens; the term used in traditional Indian cosmology to designate the highest being in the order of beings, traditionally considered to be an almighty Creator-God, but described by the Buddha as subject, like all beings, to decay and death.

brahma-vihāra   the nature of a *brahmā*, hence sublime or divine state of mind, in which four pure qualities are present: selfless love (*mettā*), compassion (*karuṇā*), joy at the good fortune of others (*muditā*), equanimity towards all that one encounters (*upekkhā*); the systematic cultivation of these four qualities by a meditation practice.

brahmācariya   celibacy; a pure, saintly life.

brāhmaṇa   literally, a pure person. Traditionally used to designate a member of the priestly caste in India. Such a person relies on a deity (*brahmā*) to 'save' or liberate him; in this respect he differs from the *samaṇa*. The Buddha described the true *brāhmaṇa* as one who has purified his mind, i.e., an *arahat*.

Buddha   enlightened person; one who has discovered the way to liberation, has practised it, and has reached the goal by his own efforts.

There are two types of Buddha:
1) *pacceka-buddha*, 'solitary' or 'silent' Buddha, who is unable to teach the way he has found to others;

2) *sammā-sambuddha*, 'full' or 'perfect' Buddha, who is able to teach others.

cakka   wheel. *Bhava-cakka*, wheel of continuing existence (i.e., process of suffering), equivalent to *saṃsāra*. *Dhamma-cakka*, the wheel of Dhamma (i.e., the teaching or process of liberation). *Bhava-cakka* corresponds to the Chain of Conditioned Arising in its forward order. *Dhamma-cakka* corresponds to the chain in reverse order, leading not to the multiplication but to the eradication of suffering.

cetiya   pagoda.

Chaṭṭha Saṅgāyana   Sixth Recitation. The six major councils in which the entire Pāli canon was recited, edited and purified are known as *Saṅgāyana*. The most recent one (*Chaṭṭha Saṅgāyana*) was held in Rangoon, Burma in 1954–56.

cintā-mayā paññā   wisdom gained by intellectual analysis. See *paññā*.

citta   mind. *Cittānupassanā*, observation of the mind. See *satipaṭṭhāna*.

dāna   charity, generosity, donation. One of the ten *pāramī*.

deva   deity.

Dhamma   phenomenon; object of mind; nature; natural law; law of liberation, i.e., teaching of an enlightened person. *Dhammānupassanā*, observation of the contents of the mind. See *satipaṭṭhāna*. (Sanskrit: *dharma*.)

Dhammapada   'verses on *Dhamma*' contained in *Sutta-piṭaka* of *Tipiṭaka*.

dhātu   element (see *mahā-bhūtāni*); natural condition, property.

dohā   rhyming couplet (Hindi).

dosa   aversion. Together with *rāga* and *moha*, one of the three principal mental defilements.

dukkha   suffering, unsatisfactoriness. One of the three basic characteristics (see *lakkhaṇa*). The first Noble Truth (see *sacca*).

ehi-passiko   a quality of Dhamma meaning 'inviting one to come and see.'

gāthā   verse of poetry.

Gotama   family name of the historical Buddha.   (Sanskrit: *Gautama*.)

indriya   faculty. Used in this work to refer to the six spheres of perception (see *āyatana*) and the five mental strengths; see also *bala*.

jāti   birth, existence.

jhāna   state of mental absorption or trance. There are eight such states which may be attained by the practice of *samādhi*, or *samatha-bhāvanā* (see *bhāvanā*). Cultivation of them brings tranquillity and bliss, but does not eradicate the deepest-rooted mental defilements.

kalāpa/aṭṭha-kalāpa   smallest indivisible unit of matter, composed of the four elements and their characteristics. See *mahā-bhūtāni*.

kalyāṇa-mitta   literally, 'friend to one's welfare,' hence one who guides a person towards liberation, i.e., spiritual guide.

kamma   action, specifically an action performed by oneself that will have an effect on one's future. See *saṅkhāra*. (Sanskrit: *karma*.)

kāya   body. *Kāyānupassanā*, observation of body. See *satipaṭṭhāna*.

khandha   mass, group, aggregate. A human being is composed of five aggregates: matter (*rūpa*), consciousness (*viññāṇa*), perception (*saññā*), feeling/sensation (*vedanā*), reaction (*saṅkhāra*).

khaṇika samādhi   concentration lasting for a moment; concentration sustained from moment to moment. See *samādhi*.

kappa   an aeon, the duration of one world cycle. *Bhadda-kappa*, the current aeon, one in which five *Buddhas* will arise. Gotama Buddha was the fourth.

kilesa   mental defilement, negativity, mental impurity. *Anusaya kilesa*, latent defilement, impurity lying dormant in the unconscious.

kusala   wholesome, beneficial. Opposite *akusala*.

lakkhaṇa   sign, distinguishing mark, characteristic. The three characteristics (*ti-lakkhaṇa*) are anicca, dukkha, anattā. The first two are common to all conditioned phenomena. The third is common to all phenomena, conditioned and unconditioned.

lobha   craving. Synonym of *rāga*.

loka   1. the macrocosm, i.e., universe, world, plane of existence, divided into three major divisions: *Arūpa loka*, an immaterial world of brahmās; *Rūpa loka*, a fine material world of brahmās; and *Kāma loka*, a sensual world of devas, humans and lower beings. 2. the microcosm, i.e., the mental-physical structure. *Loka-dhammā*, worldly vicissitudes, the ups and downs of life that all must encounter, that is, gain or loss, victory or defeat, praise or blame, pleasure or pain.

magga   path. *Ariya aṭṭhaṅgika magga*, the Noble Eightfold Path leading to liberation from suffering. It is divided into three stages or trainings:

I. *sīla*, morality, purity of vocal and physical actions:

   i. *sammā-vācā*, right speech;

   ii. *sammā-kammanta*, right actions;

   iii. sammā-ājīva, right livelihood;

II. *samādhi*, concentration, control of one's own mind:

   iv. *sammā-vāyāma*, right effort;

   v. *sammā-sati*, right awareness;

   vi. *sammā-samādhi*, right concentration;

III. *paññā*, wisdom, insight which totally purifies the mind:

   vi. *sammā-saṅkappa*, right thought;

   vii. *sammā-diṭṭhi*, right understanding.

magga   the fourth of the Four Noble Truths. See *sacca*.

mahā-bhūtāni   the four elements, of which matter is composed:

   paṭhavī-dhātu—earth element (weight);

   āpo-dhātu—water element (cohesion);

   tejo-dhātu—fire element (temperature);

   vāyo-dhātu—air element (motion).

maṅgala   welfare, blessing, happiness.

Māra   death; negative force, evil one.

mettā   selfless love and good will. One of the qualities of a pure mind (see *brahma-vihāra*); one of the *pāramī*. *Mettā-bhāvanā*, the systematic cultivation of mettā by a technique of meditation.

micchā-diṭṭhi   wrong view.

moha   ignorance, delusion. Synonym of *avijjā*. Together with *rāga* and *dosa*, one of the three principal mental defilements.

muni   sage.

nāma   mind. *Nāma-rūpa*, mind and matter, the mental-physical continūm. *Nāma-rūpa-viccheda*, the separation of mind and matter occurring at death or in the experience of *nibbāna*.

ñāṇa   wisdom, knowledge. When it is 'knowledge' in the sense of 'experiential knowledge' it is analogous to *paññā*. See *yathā-bhūta*.

nibbāna   extinction; freedom from suffering; the ultimate reality; the unconditioned. *Parinibbāna*, death of an enlightened person. (Sanskrit: *nirvana*.)

nirodha   cessation, eradication. Often used as a synonym of *nibbāna*. *Nirodha-sacca*, the truth of the cessation of suffering, third of the Four Noble Truths. See *sacca*.

nivaraṇa   obstacle, hindrance. The five hindrances to mental development are craving (*kāmachanda*), aversion (*vyāpāda*), mental or physical sluggishness (*thina-middha*), agitation (*uddhacca-kukkucca*), doubt (*vicikicchā*).

oḷārika   gross, coarse. Opposite *sukhuma*.

opaneyyiko   also *opanayiko*, a quality of *Dhamma* meaning 'no step is wasted.'

Pāli   line; text; the texts recording the teaching of the Buddha; hence language of these texts. Historical, linguistic, and archaeological evidence indicates that this was a language actually spoken in northern India at or near the time of the Buddha. At a later date the texts were translated into Sanskrit, which was exclusively a literary language.

pañca sīla   see *sīla*.

paññā   wisdom. The third of the three trainings by which the Noble Eightfold Path is practised (see *magga*). There are three kinds of wisdom: received wisdom (*suta-mayā paññā*), intellectual wisdom (*cintā-mayā paññā*), and experiential wisdom (*bhāvanā-mayā paññā*). Of these, only the last can totally purify the mind; it is cultivated by the practice of *vipassanā-bhāvanā*. Wisdom is one of the five mental strengths (see *bala*), the seven factors of enlightenment (see *bojjhaṅga*), and the ten *pāramī*.

pāramī/pāramitā   perfection, virtue; wholesome mental quality that helps to dissolve egoism and thus leads one to liberation. The ten *pāramī* are: charity (*dāna*), morality (*sīla*), renunciation (*nekkhamma*), wisdom (*paññā*), effort (*viriya*), tolerance (*khanti*), truthfulness (*sacca*), strong determination (*adhiṭṭhāna*), selfless love (*mettā*), equanimity (*upekkhā*).

parinibbāna   see *nibbāna*.

pariyatti   theory of meditation.

Paṭicca samuppāda   the Chain of Conditioned Arising; causal genesis. The process, beginning in ignorance, by which one keeps making life after life of suffering for oneself.

paṭipatti   practice of meditation.

paṭisandhi   moment of taking up next birth; conception.

paṭivedha   penetration towards the final goal.

phassa   contact.

pīti   rapture, joy.

pragya   wisdom (Hindi). See *paññā*.

pūjā   honour, worship, religious ritual or ceremony. The Buddha instructed that the only proper *pūjā* to honour him is the actual practice of his teachings, from the first step to the final goal.

puñña virtue; meritorious action, by performing which one attains happiness now and in future. For a lay person, *puñña* consists in giving charity (*dāna*), living a moral life (*sīla*), and practising meditation (*bhāvanā*).

rāga craving. Together with *dosa* and *moha*, one of the three principal mental defilements. Synonym of *lobha*.

rūpa-brahma loka celestial plane of fine material existence, attained by the first four *jhānas*.

sacca truth. The Four Noble Truths (*ariya-sacca*) are:

1. the truth of suffering (*dukkha-sacca*);
2. the truth of the origin of suffering (*samu-daya-sacca*);
3. the truth of the cessation of suffering (*nirodha-sacca*);
4. the truth of the path leading to the cessation of suffering (*magga-sacca*).

sādhu well done; well said. An expression of agreement or approval.

sakadāgāmi 'once returner'; one who has reached the second stage of enlightenment characterized by weakening of the fourth and fifth fetters: ill will and passion. This person will return to the material world for a maximum of one more lifetime. See *ariya*.

Sākya clan in which Siddhattha Gotama was born.

saḷāyatana six sense doors.

samādhi concentration, control of one's own mind. The second of the three trainings by which the Noble Eightfold Path is practised (see *magga*). When cultivated as an end in itself, it leads to the attainment of the mental absorption (*jhāna*), but not to total liberation of the mind. Three types of *samādhi* are:

1. *khaṇika samādhi*, momentary concentration, concentration sustained from moment to moment;

2. *upacāra samādhi*, 'neighbourhood' concentration, of a level approaching a state of absorption;

3. *appanā samādhi*, attainment concentration, a state of mental absorption (*jhāna*).

Of these, *khaṇika samādhi* is sufficient preparation in order to be able to begin the practice of Vipassana.

samaṇa recluse, wanderer, mendicant. One who has left the life of a householder. While a *Brāhmaṇa* relies on a deity to 'save' or liberate him, a *samaṇa* seeks liberation by his own efforts. Hence the term can be applied to the Buddha and to his followers who have adopted the monastic life, but it also includes recluses who are not followers of the Buddha. *Samaṇa* Gotama ('Gotama the recluse') was the common form of address used for the Buddha by those who were not his followers.

sāmaṇera novice monk.

samāpatti attainment; the eight *samāpattis* refer to the attainments of the eight *jhānas*. *Nirodha samāpatti*, the attainment of cessation, also known as the ninth *jhāna*, was the result of Buddha's having included the understanding of *anicca* in the practice of *jhāna*.

samatha calm, tranquillity. *Samatha-bhāvanā*, the development of calm; synonymous with *samādhi*. See *bhāvanā*.

sampajāna having *sampajañña*. See following.

sampajañña understanding of the totality of the mind-matter phenomenon, i.e., insight into its impermanent nature at the level of sensation.

saṃsāra cycle of rebirth; conditioned world; world of suffering.

samudaya arising, origin. *Samudaya-sacca*, the truth of the origin of suffering, second of the four Noble Truths.

sandiṭṭhiko   quality of Dhamma meaning 'to be realized within this life.'

saṅgha   congregation, community of *ariya*, i.e., those who have experienced *nibbāna*; community of Buddhist monks or nuns; a member of the *ariya-saṅgha*, *bhikkhu-saṅgha*, or *bhikkhunī-saṅgha*.

saṅkhāra   (mental) formation; volitional activity; mental reaction; mental conditioning. One of the five aggregates (*khandā*), as well as the second link in the Chain of Conditioned Arising (*paṭicca samuppāda*). *Saṅkhāra* is the *kamma*, the action that gives future results and that is actually responsible for shaping one's future life. *Bhava-saṅkhāra*, a *saṅkhāra* which is responsible for rebirth. (Sanskrit: *saṃskāra*.)

saṅkhārupekkhā   literally, equanimity towards *saṅkhāra*. A stage in the practice of Vipassana, subsequent to the experience of *bhaṅga*, in which old impurities lying dormant in the unconscious rise to the surface level of the mind and manifest as physical sensations. By maintaining equanimity (*upekkhā*) towards these sensations, the meditator creates no new *saṅkhāra*, and allows the old ones to pass away. Thus the process leads gradually to the eradication of all *saṅkhāras*.

saññā   (from *samyutta-ñāṇa* conditioned knowledge) perception, recognition. One of the five aggregates (*khandhā*). It is ordinarily conditioned by one's past *saṅkhāra*, and therefore conveys a coloured image of reality. In the practice of Vipassana, *saññā* is changed into *paññā*, the understanding of reality as it is. It becomes *anicca-saññā*, *dukkha-saññā*, *anatta-saññā*, *asubha-saññā*—that is, the perception of impermanence, suffering, egolessness, and of the illusory nature of physical beauty.

sanyāsi   wanderer, ascetic, monk (Hindi).

saraṇa   shelter, refuge, protection. *Ti-saraṇa*: Triple Refuge, i.e., refuge in Buddha, Dhamma, and Sangha.

sāsana   dispensation of the Buddha; period of time of the dispensation.

satthā   teacher, master.

sati   awareness. A constituent of the Noble Eightfold Path (see *magga*), as well as one of the five mental strengths (see *bala*) and the seven factors of enlightenment (see *bojjhaṅga*). *Ānāpāna-sati*, awareness of respiration.

satipaṭṭhāna   the establishing of awareness. There are four interconnected aspects of *satipaṭṭhāna*:

1. observation of body (*kāyānupassanā*);

2. observation of sensations arising within the body (*vedanānupassanā*);

3. observation of mind (*cittānupassanā*);

4. observation of the contents of the mind (*dhammānupassanā*).

All four are included in the observation of sensations, since sensations are directly related to the body as well as to mind. The *Mahā-Satipaṭṭhāna Suttaṃ* (*Dīgha Nikāya*, 22) is the main primary source in which the theoretical basis for the practice of *vipassanā-bhāvanā* is explained.

sato   aware. *Sato sampajāno*: aware with understanding of the impermanent nature of the mental-physical structure in its totality, by means of observation of sensations.

Siddhattha   literally, 'one who has accomplished his task.' The personal name of the historical Buddha. (Sanskrit: *Siddhārtha*.)

sīla   morality; abstaining from physical and vocal actions that cause harm to oneself and others. The first of the three trainings by which the Noble Eightfold Path is practised (see *magga*). For a lay person, *sīla* is practised in daily life by following the Five Precepts (*pañca sīla*).

sotāpanna   stream-enterer; one who has reached the first stage of enlightenment characterized by eradication of the first three fetters: personality belief, doubt, and attachment to rites and rituals. This person cannot be reborn in lower realms and will attain full liberation in a maximum of seven lifetimes. See *ariya*.

sugata   literally, well-gone, faring well. A frequent epithet of the Buddha.

sukha   pleasure, happiness. Opposite *dukkha*.

sukhuma   subtle, fine. Opposite *oḷārika*.

suta-mayā paññā   literally, wisdom gained from listening to others. Received wisdom. See *paññā*.

sutavā/sutavant   instructed; one who has heard the truth, who has *suta-mayā paññā*. Opposite *assutavā*.

sutta   discourse of the Buddha or one of his leading disciples. (Sanskrit: *sutra*).

taṇhā   literally, 'thirst.' Includes both craving and its reverse image of aversion. The Buddha identified *taṇhā* as the cause of suffering (*samudaya-sacca*) in his first sermon, the "Discourse Setting in Motion the Wheel of Dhamma" (*Dhamma-cakkappavattana Sutta*). In the Chain of Conditioned Arising (*paṭicca samuppāda*) he explained that *taṇhā* originates as a reaction to bodily sensations.

tathāgata   literally, 'thus-gone' or 'thus-come.' One who by walking on the path of reality has reached ultimate reality, i.e., an enlightened person. The term by which the Buddha commonly referred to himself.

Theravāda   literally, 'teaching of the elders.' The teachings of the Buddha, in the form in which they have been preserved in the countries of south and south-east Asia (Myanmar, Sri Lanka, Thailand, Laos, Cambodia). Generally recognized as the oldest form of the teachings.

Ṭīkā   sub-commentary of Pāli Canon.

ti-lakkhaṇa   see *lakkhaṇa*.

Tipiṭaka   literally, 'three baskets.' The three collections of the teachings of the Buddha, namely:

1. *Vinaya-piṭaka*, the collection of monastic discipline;

2. *Sutta-piṭaka*, the collection of discourses;

3. *Abhidhamma-piṭaka*, the collection of the higher teaching, i.e., systematic philosophical exegesis of the Dhamma. (Sanskrit: *Tripiṭaka*.)

udaya   arising. *Udaya-vaya*, arising and passing away, i.e., impermanence (also *udayabbaya*). Experiential understanding of this reality is achieved by observation of the constantly changing sensations within oneself.

upādāna   attachment, clinging.

upekkhā   equanimity; the state of mind free from craving, aversion, ignorance. One of the four pure states of mind (see *brahma-vihāra*), the seven factors of enlightenment (see *bojjhaṅga*), and the ten *pāramī*.

uposatha   sabbath day; fast day; occurring four times in the month.

uppāda   appearance, arising. *Uppāda-vaya*, arising and passing away. *Uppāda-vaya-dhammino*, having the nature of arising and passing away.

vaya/vyaya   passing away, decay. *Vaya-dhamma*, the phenomenon of passing away.

vedanā   feeling/sensation. One of the five aggregates (*khandhā*). Described by the Buddha as having both mental and physical aspects; therefore *vedanā* offers a means to examine the totality of the mental-physical phenomenon. In the Chain of Conditioned Arising (*paṭicca samuppāda*), the Buddha explained that *taṇhā*, the cause of suffering, arises as a reaction to *vedanā*. By learning to observe *vedanā* objectively one can avoid any new reactions, and can experience directly within oneself the reality of impermanence (*anicca*). This experience is essential for the development of detachment, leading to liberation of the mind.

vedanānupassanā   observation of sensations within the body. See *satipaṭṭhāna*.

vihāra   monastery.

viññāṇa   consciousness, cognition. One of the five aggregates (*khandā*).

Vipassana   literally, 'to see in a special way'; introspection, insight which purifies the mind; specifically insight into the impermanent, suffering, and egoless nature of the mental-physical structure. *Vipassanā-bhāvanā*, the systematic development of insight through the meditation technique of observing the reality of oneself by observing sensations within the body.

viveka   detachment; discriminatory intelligence.

yathā-bhūta   literally, 'as it is.' The existing reality. *Yathā-bhūta-ñāṇa-dassana*, experiential knowledge of truth as it is.

Vipassana Meditation Centers

Courses of Vipassana meditation in the tradition of Sayagyi U Ba Khin as taught by S.N. Goenka are held regularly in many countries around the world.

Information, worldwide schedules, and application forms are available from the Vipassana website: *www.dhamma.org*.

About Pariyatti

Pariyatti is dedicated to providing affordable access to authentic teachings of the Buddha about the Dhamma theory (*pariyatti*) and practice (*paṭipatti*) of Vipassana meditation. A 501(c)(3) non-profit charitable organization since 2002, Pariyatti is sustained by contributions from individuals who appreciate and want to share the incalculable value of the Dhamma teachings. We invite you to visit *www.pariyatti.org* to learn about our programs, services, and ways to support publishing and other undertakings.

Pariyatti Publishing Imprints

Vipassana Research Publications (focus on Vipassana as taught by S.N. Goenka in the tradition of Sayagyi U Ba Khin)

BPS Pariyatti Editions (selected titles from the Buddhist Publication Society, co-published by Pariyatti in the Americas)

Pariyatti Digital Editions (audio and video titles, including discourses)

Pariyatti Press (classic titles returned to print and inspirational writing by contemporary authors)

Pariyatti enriches the world by

- disseminating the words of the Buddha,
- providing sustenance for the seeker's journey,
- illuminating the meditator's path.